Lecture Notes in Computer Science 4909

Commenced Publication in 1973
Founding and Former Series Editors:
Gerhard Goos, Juris Hartmanis, and Jan van Leeuwen

T0240501

Irene Eusgeld Felix C. Freiling
Ralf Reussner (Eds.)

Dependability
Metrics

Advanced Lectures

 Springer

Volume Editors

Irene Eusgeld
ETH Zürich, Institut für Energietechnik
ML J 14, Sonneggstr. 3, 8092 Zürich, Switzerland
E-mail: eusgeld@mavt.ethz.ch

Felix C. Freiling
University of Mannheim, Laboratory for Dependable Distributed Systems
68159 Mannheim, Germany
E-mail: freiling@informatik.uni-mannheim.de

Ralf Reussner
Universität Karlsruhe (TH), Faculty of Informatics
Am Fasanengarten 5, 76131, Karlsruhe, Germany
E-mail: reussner@ipd.uka.de

Library of Congress Control Number: 2008927605

CR Subject Classification (1998): D.2.8, D.2, D.4.8, D.4

LNCS Sublibrary: SL 2 – Programming and Software Engineering

ISSN   0302-9743
ISBN-10   3-540-68946-X Springer Berlin Heidelberg New York
ISBN-13   978-3-540-68946-1 Springer Berlin Heidelberg New York

Springer is a part of Springer Science+Business Media

springer.com

© Springer-Verlag Berlin Heidelberg 2008

Typesetting: Camera-ready by author, data conversion by Scientific Publishing Services, Chennai, India
Printed on acid-free paper   SPIN: 12279678   06/3180   5 4 3 2 1 0

Preface

With the growing ubiquity of computing systems it is essential that we can place reliance on the services they deliver. This is particularly obvious and important in areas like aircraft avionics, global financial transaction processing, or nuclear power plant control where human lives or large financial values are at stake. But also the worldwide daily nuisances of computer viruses or data corruptions caused by crashing operating systems collectively impose high costs on society, which are beginning to become economically relevant.

Within computer science, the term *dependability* has been introduced as a general term to cover all critical quality aspects of computing systems. Following the terminology of Laprie [26, 293], a system is dependable if trust can justifiably be placed in the service it delivers (we will define dependability and related terms more precisely later in this book). In the early days of computer science, researchers thought that *program correctness* was the key to dependability meaning that a program always terminates and satisfies its postcondition if it is started in a state where its precondition holds. Today we know that many other factors influence the well-functioning of a computer system. Examples of these factors are:

- Hardware reliability: The occurrence of hardware faults, which cannot be neglected in critical systems.
- Non-functional properties: The growing importance of properties which cannot be expressed so easily as pre- and postconditions. As an example, consider the performance requirement that the average response time should be below some value.
- Usability: The fact that a computer system is used by human operators who can accidentaly misuse the system.

Consequently, the area of system dependability has established itself as a central research area in computer science.

Justifying reliance in computer systems is based on some form of evidence about such systems. This in turn implies the existence of scientific techniques to derive such evidence from given systems or predict such evidence of systems. In a general sense, these techniques imply a form of measurement. This book is about measuring dependability. It is the foundation of the *dependability metrics project* that aims at increasing the state of the art of dependable systems by improving the way in which we measure them. The focus of this book is to give an *overview over the current state of the art* in measuring the different aspects of dependability. It thus complements other foundational work in subdisciplines of dependability like work by Birolini [58] in the area of hardware reliability.

The main impulse for this project resulted from a research seminar which was held October 30 – November 1, 2005, at Schloss Dagstuhl in Wadern, Germany. The seminar is part of a series of such events which are sponsored by the German

Computer Science Society (Gesellschaft für Informatik). The aim of this series is to bring together young researchers to work on interesting new foundational aspects of computer science and lay the setting for further development.

We are grateful to the Gesellschaft für Informatik for supporting this event. We also wish to thank the staff at Schloss Dagstuhl for giving us a wonderfully productive time during the seminar. Thanks also go to the computer science departments of RWTH Aachen University and University of Mannheim for hosting the dmetrics CSCW server and mailing list. Finally, we wish to thank Springer for offering to publish this volume as part of *Lecture Notes in Computer Science* and Michael Kuperberg and Melanie Pietruska for their effort during the final phase of publication.

August 2007   Irene Eusgeld
Felix C. Freiling
Ralf Reussner

Organization

The Dagstuhl seminar on Dependability Metrics is part of a series of seminars organized with support by the German Computer Science Society (*Gesellschaft für Informatik*, GI). It was held during October 30 – November 1, 2005 at Schloss Dagstuhl, Germany, as event number 05442.

Organizers

Irene Eusgeld	Swiss Federal Institute of Technology (ETH), Zurich, Switzerland
Felix Freiling	University of Mannheim, Germany
Ralf Reussner	University of Karlsruhe (TH), Germany

Participants

Steffen Becker	Falk Fraikin	Matthias Rohr
Zinaida Benenson	Jens Happe	Antonino Sabetta
Rainer Böhme	Thorsten Holz	Felix Salfner
Kenneth Chan	Heiko Koziolek	Max Walter
Maximillian Dornseif	Philipp Limbourg	Ute Wappler
Irene Eusgeld	Martin Mink	Steffen Weiss
Bernhard Fechner	Thomas Nowey	Lijun Zhang
Viktoria Firus	Iman Poernomo	

Table of Contents

IV   Performance Metrics

V   Overlapping Metrics

Appendix

1 Introduction to Dependability Metrics

Irene Eusgeld[1] and Felix C. Freiling[2]

[1] Swiss Federal Institute of Technology (ETH), Zurich, Switzerland
[2] University of Mannheim, Germany

The goal of this book is to give a wide overview about the metrics that exist for different aspects of dependability, namely reliability, security, and performance. The following chapter attempts to define the term dependability and give an overview of this book.

1.1 Definition of Dependability

There are multiple meanings and connotations implied by the term "to depend on something". It is a mixture of trust and reliance that can be positive or negative. In society there are many relations that imply some form of dependence. In this book we are mainly concerned with the dependence on technical systems. This is motivated from the fact that in our modern world we almost constantly depend on such systems — when we work, when we travel, when we communicate. Since some time, these systems consist to a large extent of digital electronics. Consequently, academia and industry have for a long time been interested in improving the degree up to which we may depend on such systems. Briefly spoken, if we may depend on a system, this system is called *dependable*.

The term *dependability* has been assigned many different precise meanings in the literature. A 1988 survey of several definitions of computer-based system dependability [389] resulted in the following summary:

> *Dependability* of a computer system may be defined as justifiable confidence that it will perform specified actions or deliver specified results in a trustworthy and timely manner.

The definition today has not substantially changed. Some details however are noteworthy.

In 2004, Avižienis et al. [26] attempt to summarize and clarify the discussion of terms. They identify two alternative definitions that stress different aspects of the term. The first and "original" [26, p. 13] definition stresses the need for justification of trust in a system:

> [...] *dependability* is the ability to deliver service that can justifiably be trusted.

The second definition provides a criterion for deciding if the service is dependable:

> [...] *dependability* of a system is the ability to avoid service failures that are more frequent and more severe than is acceptable.

I. Eusgeld, F.C. Freiling, and R. Reussner (Eds.): Dependability Metrics, LNCS 4909, pp. 1–4, 2008.

The above definitions build upon continued discussions on terms and definitions, which were documented 1992 in a book edited by Laprie [293]. That book contains a 34-page English text together with translations in German, French, Italian and Japanese as well as a substantial glossary and cross-index. The main step forward made in the article of Avizienis *et al.* is the integration of security as a natural part of dependability. In Laprie's book [293], security was one of four main attributes of dependability but was treated rather like an "add on" that was mentioned only briefly on half a page. Security itself encompassed a notion of availability which was not contrasted to the "first class" notion of availability. This has changed. In the 2004 paper, Avižienis et al. [26] lift security to stand almost next to dependability (note that the title of the paper now mentions the word "security" next to "dependability").

1.2   Attributes of Dependability

Our book builds upon the work by Avižienis et al. [26] but considers a slightly broader view on dependability. Dependability has many facets and there are many different attributes of a system that make it dependable. In the literature, there are many opinions about the number of attributes dependability reaching from a very narrow point of view like "dependability is availability" [218] to a very broad view like "reliability, availability, performance, integrity, robustness, serviceability, resilience, maintainability, testability, safety, security" [389]. Avizienis *et al.* [26] enumerate the following attributes of dependability and security:

- Availability: readiness for correct service.
- Reliability: continuity of correct service.
- Safety: absence of catastrophic consequences on the user(s) and the environment.
- Integrity: absence of improper system alterations.
- Maintainability: ability to undergo modifications and repair.
- Confidentiality: absence of unauthorized disclosure of information.

Inclusion of *performance* into a general definition of dependability goes back to an ISO standard [6] in which, according to Avizienis *at al.* [26], can be traced back to a definition from the telephony area with its emphasis on availablity and service continuity.

1.3   Selected Attributes

In order to keep this book concise, we decided to focus on three very different but equally important attributes of dependable systems:

- Reliability.
- Security.
- Performance.

The attributes and their respective research areas differ in many ways, especially since they have roots in different research communities. For example, security and reliability evolved from different historical motivations. On the one hand, reliability was mainly concerned with quantifying the trust we can put in a system that can have random hardware faults, as is natural given the non-negligible failure rates of old computing equipment. On the other hand, security was concerned with keeping data secret in computing systems, mostly by controlling access to such data. Later in the development of dependable computing people noticed that it is difficult to distinguish random and unintentional hardware faults from intentional and malicious faults and ignorance of the latter is therefore difficult to justify. Similarly, the security community realized the importance of integrity and availability, which have for a long time been studied by the dependability community.

The attribute of performance has been neglected as an aspect of dependability for a long time. It has several historical roots that lie in the fields of process optimization on the one hand and software engineering on the other.

One important classical attribute of dependability, namely *safety*, is not subject of this book. Readers interested in safety can find some helpful information in Part II of this book on reliability metrics, because many methods and models, such as e.g. Markov chains, fault (hazard) tree analysis and others are similar for both fields.

1.4   Outlook on the Book

Dependability is the ability of a system to deliver service that can justifiably be trusted. Justification of trust implies ways to measure attributes of dependability, i.e., a set of dependability metrics which are the topic of this book. The focus is to survey the state of the art of metrics for chosen attributes of dependability. The term metric is used in a very broad sense ranging from coarse qualitative metrics to rigourous quantitative metrics.

In this book we survey the state of the art for measuring three attributes of dependability: reliability, security and performance. We cover every attribute in a separate part of this book. Since it appears to be the oldest and most developed of the chosen attributes, we start with discussing reliability metrics first followed by security and performance metrics. The book opens with an additional part on foundations of dependability metrics where we discuss general questions and methods used throughout the book.

As an outlook, we briefly enumerate some of the discussed metrics to give the reader a better feeling for the scope of the different parts of the book.

Reliability related metrics have been traditionally quantified. Metrics such as mean time to failure, point availability, and failure rate are commonly accepted and widely used. They are discussed in the Part II on reliability metrics. Continuous integration of hardware and the disappearance of the border between hard- and software have lead to increased system complexity and difficulty in testing for initial system verification. This corresponds to an increased effort in the area of software testing and is discussed in the context of *software reliability* (see Chapter 10).

Security metrics have evolved from early attempts to compare cryptographic protocols (e.g., the length of cryptographic keys) to modern approaches that try to evaluate and compare the security of entire organizations. The problem with security metrics is the difficulty to make predictions. This has opened the path for very sceptical prophecies for this area [344]. Indirect metrics based on market mechanisms are a possible approach towards prediction of security. They are surveyed and discussed together with other security metrics in Part III.

The aspects of performance measurement of computer-based systems are surveyed in Part IV. This includes *workload characterisation* (number and type of service demands) and *characterisations of system configuration* (number of operational processors, maximum number of threads, available memory, bandwidth of networks, etc.) and resulting *performance metrics* like *response time* and *throughput*.

It is increasingly obvious that several dependability aspects interact in complex computer systems that can hence not be considered independently. As an example consider the problem of ensuring *secure fault-tolerance*, i.e., improved reliability (by fault-tolerance) and a preserved security policy at the same time. It is well-known [312, 417] that fault-tolerance mechanisms can undermine the security of a system. The area of combined dependability metrics is an area of active research and is surveyed for the two aspects performance and reliability ("performability") and reliability and security in Part V of this book. This final part shows that only a combined consideration of important dependability attributes will lead to our design objective: a development of systems, on which we can really trust.

Part I

Foundations

2 On Metrics and Measurements

Rainer Böhme[1] and Felix C. Freiling[2]

[1] Technische Universität Dresden, Germany
[2] University of Mannheim, Germany

The following chapter attempts to define the notions of metric and measurement which underlie this book. It further elaborates on general properties of metrics and introduces useful terms and concepts from measurement theory, without being overly formal.

2.1 On Measurement

In many cases, *to measure* means to attach a number to an object, i.e., to represent some aspect of the object in a quantitative way. For example, scientists can measure the temperature and the humidity of a location at a certain time by coding observations (temperature, humidity) related to the object (location) with numbers. More generally, a measurement function assigns an element of a set to an object, where the specific element is chosen depending on an observation. The set must not necessarily comprise numbers but can also consist of unordered symbols. For example, classifying the weather today as "rainy", "dry", "foggy" etc. is also regarded as measurement. However, not every assignment of numbers to objects is considered as measurement. For example, the matriculation number of a student is not a measurement because the number is chosen regardless of the student's attributes (here we ignore that higher matriculation numbers may be an indicator of later admission).

In the setting of this book we usually want to measure *attributes* of systems or parts thereof, such as methods or processes. As system can be complex, there are many different measurable attributes. Any form of measurement is an *abstraction*: it reduces the complexity of one or several attributes of the original system to a single symbol. The main purposes of this form of abstraction are to *classify* and *compare* systems.

It is important to stress the difference between an attribute and its measurement. For example, the complexity of a software system is an attribute which can be measured in many different ways. However, the difference between an attribute and its measurement sometimes blurs because measurements are also taken to *define* the attributes.

Measurement is closely connected to the notion of a metric. In the course of this book we will use the term *metric* for a precisely defined method which is used to associate an element of an (ordered) set V to a system S. This definition is used in the area of software quality. In other areas, the term metric only refers to the set V, which contains *indicator values* that answer certain questions asked about a system. As we will see later, our understanding neither corresponds to the strict mathematical definition of a metric (where it is a generalisation of the notion of a distance).

In general, a metric can be formalised as a function M that takes a particular system from the set of systems S and maps it to an element of V:

$$M : S \mapsto V$$

I. Eusgeld, F.C. Freiling, and R. Reussner (Eds.): Dependability Metrics, LNCS 4909, pp. 7–13, 2008.

For example, M may be the assignment of a distance between two measurement points of a system. Then V is the set of real numbers, a totally ordered set. The set V can also be a discrete set like the set of natural numbers in the "lines of code" metric for software. The set V must also not necessarily be totally ordered; it can also be a partially ordered set or an unordered set like in the classification example above where V consists of the elements $\{foggy, rainy, dry\}$ etc.

Attributes can have certain properties which should be reflected in their metrics. For example, the complexity of a software package can be categorised as "low" or "high". Some attributes are meaningful in the context of composed systems. For example, the attribute "size of a program" can be measured in lines of code. Given two programs x and y we can define their composition z as the concatenation of x and y. The metric "lines of code" reflects additivity in the following sense: the sizes of program x and program y together sum up to the size of their composition z. Similarly, some attributes allow to state relations between systems. Taking the "size" metric lines of code again, it is possible to say that some program is twice as large as another program.

Determining a suitable metric for an attribute of a system is not always easy. A good metric should reflect the relevant properties of the attribute in a homomorphic way. This means that certain statements which can be made for a certain attribute of systems should be reflected in the measurements of that attribute. In particular, two properties should hold:

- Any sensible *relation* between systems regarding a particular attribute should be reflected by a corresponding relation between the measurements of this attribute. For example, a system x which is more complex than a system y should be ordered appropriately if some complexity metric c is used, i.e., $c(x) > c(y)$ should hold.
- Any meaningful *operation* on attributes of a system should have a corresponding operation on the measurements of that attribute. Assume there exists an addition operation ("plus") for the "size" of programs. If the size of program x "plus" the size of program y equals the size of program z, then this should be reflected in the appropriate metric for size. For example, lines of code is an appropriate metric if the "plus" operator refers to concatenation of source code.

Any relations or operations on measurements which do not have a corresponding relation or operation on attributes must not be used to process the measurements.

2.2   On Scales

The result of measurements is data, which is further processed or analysed to answer questions of interest to the researcher or practitioner. A useful approach to classify types of data is given in the notion of *scales*. The term scale refers to the range V of a metric, and the relation between elements within V. The most commonly used typology of scales goes back to Stevens [459], who defined a hierarchy of four different types of scales based on the invariance of their meaning under different classes of transformation. He further proposed to derive permissible procedures for data analysis and statistical inference depending on the scale level.

Nominal Scale

The simplest type of scale is the *nominal scale* (also known as *categorial scale*). With a nominal scale, V is an unordered discrete set. Classifications usually employ the nominal scale, for example when classifying computers according to their operation system ($V = \{\text{Windows}, \text{Unix}, \text{OS}/2\}$). Measurements on a nominal scale can be compared for identity or distinction and a number of measurements can be aggregated by counting the frequencies in each class (or combination of classes if data from more than one scale are analysed at a time).

Nominal scales can be transformed into other nominal scales by applying a bijective mapping, i.e., a $1 : 1$ correspondence between the elements of both scales V_1 and V_2. If more than one category in V_1 is mapped to a single element in V_2 then the transformation loses information and thus is irreversible. It might still be useful to apply such a transformation to aggregate data and increase the number of observations in each (combined) category.

The special case where V consists of two elements only is called *dichotomic scale* (examples: "yes"/"no", "0"/"1'", "male"/"female").

Ordinal Scale

The *ordinal scale* differs from the nominal scale in that V is a discrete *ordered* set. Examples for ordinal scales include severity measures for earthquakes or grades given to students in examinations. In contrast to the nominal scale, two measurements on the same ordinal scale can be compared with operators "less than" or "greater than". This allows the data analyst to create ranks and compute rank correlations. Ordinal scales also allow for simple models of measurement error and they can be included as dependent variables in regression models (ordinal logit or probit models).

Two ordinal scales can be transformed into each other by applying a bijective mapping f which preserves the ordering relation (monotonic mapping), i.e., if $a < b$ on one scale then $f(a) < f(b)$ on the other scale. As ordinal scales are one step higher in the hierarchy than nominal scales, a downgrading (with information loss) to the nominal level is always possible.

Interval Scale

The *interval scale* is an extension of the ordinal scale where the distance between adjacent elements in V is both meaningful and constant (equidistance). Interval scales therefore support the difference operator, so that the difference between two points on the same scale can be compared to the difference between two other points.

Interval scale A can be transformed into interval scale B by linear transformations (adding/subtracing a constant, multiplying/dividing by a constant) since the relative distance between any two scale points is not changed.

The standard example for an interval scale is the measurement of temperature. For example, let scale A be the scale of measurement in degrees Fahrenheit and scale B be the measurement in degrees Celsius. To transform a measurement in scale A into scale B we can then use the formula:

$$f(x) = \frac{5}{9}(x - 32)$$

Other applications for the interval scale include multi-point rating scales in questionnaires when the scale points are labeled with increasing numbers or are not annotated at all. If more detailed annotations are given then the semantic difference between any two scale points may vary and thus the resulting data should be treated as ordinal rather than interval.

A number of measurements can be summarised with statistics of location (mean), scale (variance) and higher moments. Moreover, interval scales allow for continuos distribution error models, such as Gaussian measurement errors. This implies that the entire class of parametric statistics can be applied to data on interval scales. Again, interval scales can be converted to ordinal (and nominal) scales by cutting the scale at some breakpoints and assigning the observations to the categories between.

Ratio Scale

The *ratio scale* is an extension of the interval scale where the origin (value of 0) is defined in a natural way. Examples for ratio scales are length, mass, pressure, time duration or monetary value. Additional possible operations for analysis are multiplication of a measurement with a constant factors, taking logs and finding roots (among others). Therefore statistical measures such as the geometric mean and the coefficient of variation are defined for ratio scales only. Transformations between different ratio scales can be achieved by simply multiplying measurements with a scaling factor. For example, converting a length metric in metres into a length in imperial feet is done by using a scaling factor of 3.2808.

Interval and ratio scales are sometimes subsumed to *cardinal scales*.

Summary

Table 1 shows an overview of the different scale types discussed so far. Nominal and ordinal scale are usually referred to as *qualitative scales*, whereas interval and ratio scale are called *quantitative scales*. From a measurement point of view it is recommended to collect data at the highest possible scale level. In particular metrics with at least a quantitative scale are useful because they enable parametric statistics, which are more powerful than non-parametric methods. The term *parametric* refers to a distribution assumption where inference can be made on the parameters of the distribution rather than on individual data points. For example, a comparison of means from two sequences of measurements is a parametric method because the mean is a parameter of the distribution of the data.

As a final remark: although very popular, Steven's typology of scale levels has been criticised for not being comprehensive (it is easy to find pathological examples that do not fit well in one of the four categories) and for imposing unnecessary restrictions to data analysis by adhering to strict mathematical standards, which are difficult to meet

Table 1. The hierarchy of scale levels

Scale level	Examples	Operators	Possible analyses
Quantitative scales			
Ratio	size, time, cost	$*, /, \log, \sqrt{\ }$	geometric mean, coefficient of variation
Interval	temperature, marks, judgement expressed on rating scales	$+, -$	mean, variance, correlation, linear regression, analysis of variance (ANOVA), ...
Qualitative scales			
Ordinal	complexity classes	$<, >$	median, rank correlation, ordinal regression
Nominal	feature availability	$=, \neq$	frequencies, mode, contingency tables

with real data [484]. Nevertheless, even the critics acknowledge that the typology provides simple guidance and protects naive data analysts from errors in applying statistics. Therefore we deem it useful to keep in mind when designing and discussing dependability metrics.

2.3 On Mathematical Metrics and Norms

In mathematics, a metric is a precisely defined term. It is the abstraction of a *distance*. Formally, a metric d on a set X is a function which assings a "distance" value (a real number) to pairs of elements from X:

$$d : X \times X \mapsto R$$

The function d must satisfy several conditions to be a mathematical metric, i.e., for all $x, y, z \in X$ must hold:

- every distance is non-negative, i.e., $d(x, y) \geq 0$,
- the distance is zero for identical inputs, i.e., $d(x, x) = 0$,
- the distance is symmetric, i.e., $d(x, y) = d(y, x)$, and
- the triangle inequality holds, i.e., $d(x, z) \leq d(x, y) + d(y, z)$.

For example, consider the (two-dimensional) Euclidian distance where X is the set of coordinates in a two-dimensional space, i.e., $X = R \times R$. The Euclidian distance d_E calculates the distance of two points in X. Given two elements (x_1, y_1) and (x_2, y_2) of X, d_E is defined as

$$d_E = \sqrt{(x_2 - x_1)^2 + (y_2 - y_1)^2}$$

It is easy to see that the conditions above hold for the Euclidian distance.

Somewhat closer to the notion of metric defined in section 2.1 is the mathematical notion of a *norm*. In mathematics, a norm is an abstraction of a positive length or size. A norm is a function p that maps an element of a set X to the real numbers:

$$p : X \mapsto R$$

The set X is usually a multi-dimensional vector space. To be called a norm, p must satisfy the following conditions for all $x, y \in X$:

- the norm is always be positive, i.e., $p(x) \geq 0$,
- the norm is scalable, i.e., $p(ax) = |a| p(x)$ for some scalar a,
- the triangle inequality holds, i.e., $p(x + y) \leq p(x) + p(y)$,
- the norm is zero for the zero vector only, i.e., $p(x) = 0$ if and only if x is the zero vector.

Standard examples are the (two-dimensional) Euclidian norm p_E which assigns a length to a (two-dimensional) vector. More precisely, $X = R \times R$ and for any $(x, y) \in X$ p_E is defined as follows:

$$p_E = \sqrt{|x|^2 + |y|^2}$$

Another notation for $p_E(x)$ is $||x||_2$.

Another well-known norm is is the Taxicab (or Manhatten) norm, which assigns to a vector the "length" if you would take a taxi in a rectangular street grid from the origin point to the point described by the vector. Here, $X = N \times N$ (where N denotes the set of natural numbers) and for any element $(x, y) \in X$ the Manhatten norm is defined as $x + y$.

There is a close relationship between norms and metrics in the sense that every norm implicitly defines a metric and special types of metrics implicitly define a norm. For example, given a norm p on a set X, the construction $d : X \times X \mapsto R$ with $d(x, y) = p(x - y)$ satisfies all the properties of a metric in the mathematical sense.

It is obvious that the mathematical definition of a metric requires the properties of a ratio scale in Steven's terminology. Since by far not every measurable aspect satisfies these conditions, we will use the term metric in a less rigourous way throughout this book.

2.4   Classification of Metrics

This volume presents a large number of metrics for measuring the dependability of systems. Metrics can be classified by a number of aspects, most importantly by the way they are constructed and the attributes of systems they represent. However, there are also some possibilities to classify metrics according to their abstract properties, such as:

- *Scale level*, and hence the granularity of V, as discussed in section 2.2.
- *Construction:* a metric can be derived in different ways, which results in the difference between *analytical* vs. *empirical* metrics. An analytical metric measures the system by analysing its structure or its properties using *models* of the system. An empirical metric measures by observing the real behavior of the system.
- *Directness:* it is possible to distinguish *direct* vs. *indirect* metrics. A direct metric measures the system itself, whereas an indirect metric measures the effects of the system onto another system. For example, the stock market price of the share of company X is an indirect metric of the expected performance of company X. Analytical metrics can also be regarded as indirect metrics.

- *Obtrusiveness:* metrics that require a modification of the system for the purpose of being measured are called *obtrusive* metrics, as opposed to *unobtrusive* ones, which can be taken without touching (i.e. influencing) the system.

2.5 On the Quality of Metrics

It is easy to define metrics, but much harder to find meaningful ones. An important quality of a metric is whether it reflects the attributes in question in a homomorphic way (see section 2.1). This can be regarded as a notion of *validity* of a metric. Closely related is the question of the *granularity* of a metric, i.e., does it allow to distinguish all systems that differ in their respective attributes?

There are also practical considerations when defining a metric: its *availability* and its *cost*. Is it always possible to compute the metric for a given system? An empirical performance metric of a production system is obviously much harder to collect than an analytical one, because the production system will not always be available for benchmarking or the costs to conduct the measurement are much higher.

Finally, a very desirable quality of a metric is its *stability*: different people measuring the attribute in question should roughly get the same results. This property is sometimes called *scale reliability* which should not be confused with the attribute of dependability called *reliability*.

3 Validation of Predictions with Measurements

Rainer Böhme[1] and Ralf Reussner[2]

[1] Technische Universität Dresden, Germany
[2] University of Karlsruhe (TH), Germany

This chapter discusses ways to validate metrics and raises awareness for possible caveats if metrics are used in a social environment.

3.1 What Does Validation Mean for Analytical Metrics?

The definition of an analytical metric is rather simple. For example, it is quite easy to define

$$\text{maintainability} := \text{lines of code}/\text{number of methods}$$

Besides the facts that this metric "lines of code" needs further specification (e.g., whether comments or blank lines are counted) and that no unit is defined, the main problem is whether this analytical metric really tells us useful information about the actual maintainability. To answer this question, a metric has to be validated. As analytical metrics are used to make a prediction on a quality property of a system, validating an analytical metric means comparing its predictions with independent measurements of actual outcomes. This pretty much resembles the situation in physics, where a theory (which corresponds to analytical metrics in our terminology) is used to make predictions on the real world. The theory itself has to be validated with experiments. As a very simple example, Newton's theorems on mechanics allow to predict the speed of objects in free fall (depending on time, $v(t) = g \cdot t$). This simple analytical metric for speed (or prediction model) can be validated by comparing the predicted values with measurements on real objects. In our example, this comparison would reveal that the influence of aerodynamic resistance on falling objects is not negligible and that the simple formula given above is only accurate for objects falling in vacuum.

As a consequence, analytical metrics always require validation with one or more empirical metrics that measure the same concept as predicted by the analytical metric, or a closely related phenomenon.

Against this backdrop, a common problem of metrics for many internal quality attributes, such as extensibility, maintainability, and readability, becomes evident. While many analytical metric are easy to define, it is sometimes hard and costly to validate them with measurements. The designer of metrics often faces the following dilemma: either s/he *defines* a directly measurable attribute as metric, which renders validation trivial but might result in little expressiveness in the application of metrics. Alternatively, a more meaningful and abstract definition may be preferred, which in turn makes it more difficult to *find* good and observable indicators to compute and validate the metric. Defining maintainability as the fraction of lines of code and number of methods corresponds to the first option. However, maintainability could also be defined in many different ways (e.g., as the amount of time spent to apply a specific change to the code).

I. Eusgeld, F.C. Freiling, and R. Reussner (Eds.): Dependability Metrics, LNCS 4909, pp. 14–18, 2008.
© Springer-Verlag Berlin Heidelberg 2008

But then it is hard both to demonstrate that the fraction of lines of code and number of methods by measurements is a good indicator as well as to measure the time needed for the specific change (because it depends on various other factors, such as experience, technology, etc).

Note that the difficulty to validate metrics may vary between the different aspects of dependability. For example, validation of performance metrics is relatively easy, as time or throughput are already quantitative criteria that can be measured empirically, if the way of measurement is defined in sufficient detail to rule out ambiguities. By contrast, accurate measurement of reliability metrics is much harder in practice, mainly because the object of study involves events that happen very rarely. Hence, a remarkably high number of tests has to be conducted to allow statistical inference for high reliability scores.

3.2 Different Types of Validation for Prediction Models

The validation of entire prediction models includes the validation of the underlying analytical metrics, but requires further steps of validation on top of that.

We distinguish three levels of validation for prediction models.

Level I (metric validation): This level is concerned with the above described validation of the metrics, i.e., the comparison of predictions and measurements. Note that this requires an implementation of the analytical metric to perform the predictions. Since this is as obvious as the requirement that an analytical metric should be computable, we do not introduce an extra "Level 0" for implementation validity.

Level II (applicability validation): This kind of validity is concerned with the applicability of the prediction approach and the analytical metrics included. This means, it is checked whether the input data can be acquired reliably and whether the results of the metric can be interpreted meaningfully. If input data is obtained by humans rather than by automated measurements, a level II validation can be conducted as an experiment or a case study with human participants in the sense of empirical software engineering (e.g., Tichy [470]). One of many examples for such studies has been published recently by Koziolek and Firus [282].

Level III (benefit validation): If the analytical metric and the prediction approach is part of a software or system development method (e.g., for the systematic selection of design alternatives), then the overall approach has to demonstrate its benefits over other competing approaches, again by empirical validation. For example, if an approach is motivated by lowering development costs and time, this can be validated by a comparison between two development projects. However, such a comparison requires high effort. Firstly, it is expensive to develop the same product twice. As it is unlikely to convince a company to do so, this is mainly the domain of non-profit research with dedicated funding. Secondly, differences in the course of the projects may not only be caused by the different development methods taken, but also by additional factors, such as human experience, etc. To control the influences of such third variables, experiments have to be repeated, which increases costs even further.

3.3   Reactivity: Limits for Metrics and Quantification

To conclude the chapter on validation, we want to draw the reader's attention to some limitations of metrics when employed in a social environment. As this popular fallacy is not of measurement-theoretical nature but occurs in real-world applications, we think it is best suited in a validation context.

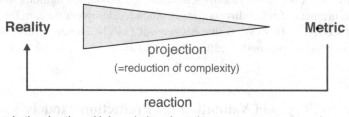

Fig. 1. Feedback mechanism when measurements have real consequences

The origin of the problem is a feedback mechanism between the result of a measurement and the reaction of people who face consequences from the outcome of the measurement. The purpose of metrics is to make justified statements about reality, which is not measurable in its entirety. Therefore, since every metric has a much lower dimensionality than reality, it is a simplification or—in mathematical terms—a projection. People, however, who might be affected by the measurement outcome, may have means to react by changing the measured objects in reality (see Fig. 1). In many cases, metrics are deliberately employed with the intention to stimulate this feedback, for example when employers measure the performance of their employees and directly link whatever metrics' outcome to a compensation scheme.

Now consider the choice of strategic individuals who have knowledge about the measurement process and in particular about those dimensions which are neglected by the metric's implicit projection. If they have an incentive to improve the outcome of a measurement in a period between t_0 and t_1, then it is rational to choose, among the alternative actions of constant costs, the one with maximum impact on the metric's projection plane. In other words, people adapt their behavior to the anticipated measurement process if they see a chance in achieving a more favourable outcome for themselves. As illustrated in Fig. 2, this kind of reaction is not necessarily in line with the assumed relationship between those (unmeasurable) properties of reality that were intended to be measured and the observable indicators employed to construct the metric.[1] Hence, the interaction of strategic individuals subject to consequences of measurement outcomes may thwart well-meant principles for designing good metrics.

---

[1] Note that the figure is fair in a sense that the action radius is modeled as a circle. In many cases the situation might even turn worse, such as an ellipsoid with focal points orthogonal to the assumed relationship.

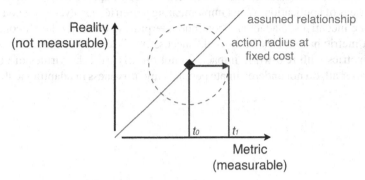

Fig. 2. Rational decision makers foster favourable measurement result

As a consequence, since rational decision-makers are very inventive to achieve a favourable measurement, metrics are prone to loose their power in providing objective pictures of reality. If the adaptation proceeds gradually over time, for instance because the exact circumstances of measurement and the implications of its outcome is not communicated ex ante, then one can observe a "wear-out" of metrics.

There are numerous examples for wear-outs, such as unemployment figures or structural development indicators on the macro level (where governments act strategically), or processor and graphic card benchmarks (where manufacturers tune their hardware precisely on the benchmark operations), just to name a few.

Finally we will discuss some principles for possible counter-measures to mitigate the adverse effects. The best solution would be to ensure that the aspect of reality to be measured corresponds well to the actual indicators. When this alignment is difficult or impossible, then the choice of indicators should reflect the cost of reactions orthogonal to the projection. In other words, one can try to reshape the action radius in Fig. 2 to an ellipsoid with focal points on the assumed relationship. This makes deviations, if not preventable, at least costly. As a result, strategic individuals would rethink their optimal reaction and a wear-out of metrics becomes less likely. Note that this countermeasure corresponds to the economic principle of "incentive compatibility". Using more than one metric as decision criteria is another option to make it difficult for strategic individuals to adapt their reaction to all metrics at the same time (which is obviously most effective for orthogonal metrics). This approach is equivalent with limiting the information loss at the projection step.

All these countermeasures can be combined in an endeavor to reduce the danger of strategic reactions and wear-out, but they are unlikely to solve the problem ultimately. Therefore a general awareness of the problem is probably the most useful recommendation, both for design and application of metrics. When designing a metric, possible contexts for its application are largely obscure. Hence, good proposals for new metrics should state the original objective of measurement,[2] discuss possible limitation due to

---

[2] See also the discussion of goal-oriented measurement below in Chap. 3.6.

adaption, and use telling names and a clear terminology to prevent over-interpreation in different areas of application. When implementing a metric, however, one should clearly evaluate the incentives to adapt and continue interpreting carefully the outcomes, especially if a metric has already been used "successfully" for a long time. In brief, when defining metrics with real-world impact, do not blindly trust the virtues of quantification and, after all, do not underestimate people's inventiveness in adapting to the metrics in use.

4 Consistent Metric Usage: From Design to Deployment

Kenneth Chan and Iman Poernomo

King's College London, U.K.

This chapter provides an overview of how the semantics of software metrics should be consistently treated across design, implementation, deployment and management phases of the software development lifecycle.

4.1 Introduction

The use of software metrics has become increasingly common in software design. Recent research has focused on ways of improving systems through prediction and analysis of metric values. For instance, the designer can now employ a range of scalable approaches to performance analysis over models of system behaviour. However, metrics are ultimately about an implemented and deployed system and, consequently, must have an evaluative semantics that cannot be purely abstract and based in design.

This chapter provides an overview of how the semantics of software metrics should be consistently treated across design, implementation, deployment and management phases of the software development lifecycle. Consistent treatment is difficult to achieve, and leads us to consider two issues.

The first issue concerns the necessity of an empirical component to metric semantics. While metric based predictions are often made at the design stage, it is only through instrumentation and monitoring of actual implemented systems that we can know the effectiveness of the predictions. Metrics must be defined in such a way to permit empirical validation. There is no point in specifying and predicting required response times for software at design time unless response time can actually be validated over implementations. Furthermore, while validation of prediction is particularly important during system testing, it is increasingly important to continue to apply validation after system deployment, as part of continual management. This can be seen in the growth of QoS policy-driven management systems, in which Service Level Agreements (SLAs), often involving QoS metric-based requirements, are monitored and maintained.

Therefore, the validation of a metric must be possible in principle, as described in Sect. 3.1. In addition, methods of validation must be practical and sufficiently efficient to enable effective application at testing and/or management phases: the management and administration of a SLA involving response time constraints will not be impeded if the algorithm for computing response time is inefficient.

The second issue concerns maintaining the consistency of metric semantics between phases of the software lifecycle. From design to maintenance, the same metric will be used in different ways within a range of different languages. For example, a metric constraint might be written in QML at a design, but monitored using Windows Management Instrumentation at implementation, and managed via some vendor-specific SLA

I. Eusgeld, F.C. Freiling, and R. Reussner (Eds.): Dependability Metrics, LNCS 4909, pp. 19–36, 2008.

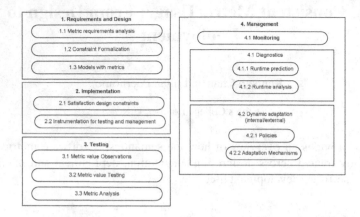

Fig. 1. Treatment of metrics within the software development lifecycle

language. Even with a medium sized system, the consistent treatment of metrics through each of these languages becomes a problem.

It is desirable to achieve greater levels of automation and increased trustworthiness that goes beyond current industry practices with respect to consistency and validation. This chapter deals with how current research is progressing toward these objectives. Our literature review draws upon several topics of research: in particular, runtime service management and model driven architecture.

This chapter provides an overview of the state of the art in empirical validation of metric-based requirements. We proceed as follows:

- We discuss how metrics are employed across the development lifecycle and identify the problem of consistency and validation in Section 4.2.
- Section 4.3 discusses some relevant notions from the theory of science.
- Section 4.4 provides a review of related work in empirical validation of metric-based prediction.
- We summarize how current research addresses the problem of consistency in section 4.5.
- Concluding remarks are given in section 4.6.

4.2   From Design to Deployment

It is increasingly understood that much benefit can be gained from a model-based prediction and assessment of metric constraint conformance prior to implementation. Much recent research has advocated a range of compositional behavioural models that facilitate the estimation of performance and reliability characteristics. There exist a range of performance-oriented software development processes that are suitable for industrial contexts: for example, in the SPE method [451], quality of service constraints are integrated within a system design and evaluated over a model of system execution, with the goal of improving the performance of the final implementation.

The increasing recognition on the importance of software quality of service has resulted in various techniques for integrating QoS within the phases of software development.

The Software Development Lifecycle

Fig. 1 illustrates how current research treats metrics within the software development lifecycle.

Design. At design and analysis of a system, metrics are typically involve the following issues:

1.1. Metric based constraints are specified alongside the system initial design.
1.2. Metric-based constraints are usually specified in some informal way that is easy to understand by people without the technical knowledge. To impose these informal constraints over the actual system design may prove difficult without first formalising them, as there will be no guarantee that informal elements will have a well understood semantics when employed at later stages of development.
1.3. An increasingly important part of system design is the modelling of the system under development. Most developers now employ UML as the toolset for modelling component based systems, but the metamodel of UML and most other modelling tools do not have dependability parameters built in. Implementation of a range of dependability attributes have been proposed in, for example, the UML Profile for QoS, but it remains a question as to how these attributes may be correctly attached to a system design model.

Implementation. Once the system design is ready for implementation, the developers will entirely be responsible for ensuring that the desired dependability attributes will materialise, as well as making sure there will be some means of proving to the client that they are getting what they asked for. This prompt for extra measures during implementation alongside the functional aspects of the system. Components during runtime will appear largely as black boxes to the runtime environment, exposing only services that it is designated to provide. This makes it difficult to evaluate metric values readily. For example, many dependability attributes of a component often require some means of probing the insides of a component. Components therefore need to be carefully developed in such that it may explicitly provide the extra information required to determine their associated metric constraints. Components which are explicitly implemented to cater for QoS properties alongside their functional properties are called metric measurable components.

Testing. Testing is the primary means to prove satisfaction of metric-based constraints.

3.1. For implementation of a metric-measurable system, it is possible to make direct observations over many of important attributes. If the semantics of the metrics and mechanisms are preserved throughout the previous phases, the values obtained by observation can be checked against those required in the corresponding design specification. This is provided that the evaluative mechanisms used in testing are consistent with the metric semantics employed at design.

3.2. Not all metric values can be observed directly, some may require prolonged observation. A good example will be the *reliability* of a component, which requires continuous monitoring over a period of time. This requires extra infrastructure, either a standard or a custom one, to run alongside the software-under-test in order to draw concluding results from such observations.

3.3. The analysis of the system can indeed happen throughout the pre- deployment stage of a software development. Much of this volume will be dedicated to various dependability analysis methodologies at the design level. In fact, when dependability properties are taken into account within a development it is often a good practice to conduct analysis at various stages and levels in the process.

Deployment and Management. While metric values are checked for conformance to constraints, medium and large scale software often demands further, ongoing monitoring even after deployment of the software, as part of general system management.

4.1 Apart from static analysis of QoS attributes based on assumptions over various factors, with the information obtained by monitoring it is possible to do dynamic analysis during runtime of a system, as well as making dynamic predictions on the QoS aspects of the system. Runtime analysis and predictions distinguish themselves from the various methodologies in the pre-deployment phase as they rely on a live feed of information, provided by a monitoring infrastructure such that the input data inherit guaranteed credibility.

4.2 QoS policies are used for supporting activities such as QoS negotiation and runtime adaptations, dictating the type and magnitude of adaptations that may occur. The metrics used in these policies should be similar to those used in the design phase as these policies usually form part of the system's design.

4.3 Adaptation can be made during runtime to ensure robustness of a system in execution by means of runtime reconfiguration strategies that operate when QoS constraints are violated. A QoS-aware component may have adaptation mechanisms built in: such mechanisms are called the *internal adaptations*. Mechanisms that invoke adaptations outside the software itself are called *external adaptations*. Depending on the QoS policy, adaptations may be *reactive* if they are passively invoked on violation of constraints contained in the policy, or they may be *proactive* if the system actively predicts the occurrences of a violation and invoke adaptations preventing it from happening at all.

When defining a metric for any particular dependability property, it should preferably be able to support all the activities stated, making it possible that its semantic consistency to be carried all the way through from design to the actual lifetime of the software. Otherwise if the consistency breaks down somewhere down the process, it will be notoriously difficult to repair, causing more problems than the benefits obtained from defining the metrics.

Consistency and Validation

System metrics are concerned with some aspect of an implemented system. Even though metrics should be employed within the design phase to build models, a metric's evaluative semantics cannot be purely abstract and must be given with respect to implementation. This is in contrast to mathematical metrics, whose semantics is given over an abstract, platonic domain, without reference to physical reality: throughput ultimately concerns the amount of work performed by an actual system over a period of time, while the Minkowski metric defines a model of distance over hyperbolic space.[1]

This empirical aspect leads to difficulties in the usage of metrics across the development lifecycle. The moment one begins to make employ metrics to make statements at the design stage, one runs into consistency and validation problems.

– *Consistency.* Consider a metric for module coupling. We can define a method for measuring the degree of coupling between components in a UML2 superstructure components-and-connectors diagram. This will provide a prediction of the degree of coupling in the final implementation. Assume our implementation is then in a combination of SML and C# code running in the .NET environment. Because we have defined the coupling metric over two different languages – the UML2 metamodel and the .NET languages – how do we know that coupling as we have defined it for the UML2 model is an accurate representation of the notion of coupling in our implementation? How do we know that the definitions are semantically equivalent?

– *Validation.* Even if the semantics of metrics across design and implementation is consistent, a related problem concerns the accuracy of predictions made at the design stage. Consider a M/1/1 queuing model of a system that is used to estimate response time. How do we guarantee that this estimation is accurate? Do we provide some formal guarantee that the system completely implements the model, and that any prediction over the model is therefore accurate for the model? While desirable, this is expensive and potentially infeasible if the model involves a probabilistic behavioural aspect (as would be the case for reliability and performance models). Alternatively, do we manually instrument the system and independently calculate response time of the actual system? This will do the job, but detailed manual instrumentation can also be expensive for complex systems. It can also be done incorrectly (the wrong things might be instrumented for a given metric).

Empirical and Analytical Metrics

Not all metrics lead to a consistency and validation problem. Let us consider the problem following the definitions of Section 2.4.

Recall that empirical metrics can only make an empirically measurable observation over some aspect of the system and offer no recourse to model-based prediction. In software engineering, the most obvious empirical metrics are syntactic measures over an implementation: for example, a code documentation measure. There are also metrics that specifically concern the design – such as conformance to a standard, or the degree of completeness of specification. These metrics also do not result in a validation problem, obviously, as they are never predicted and are useful only when we can immediately measure them.

In contrast, the semantics of an analytical metric involves a function over some property of a system that has an abstract representation in a design-stage model. For

---

[1] Although, of course, hyperbolic space can also be used to provide a useful model of physical reality.

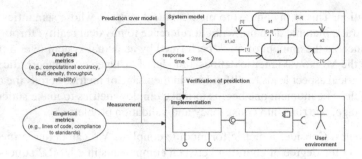

Fig. 2. Usage relationships between empirical and analytical metrics from design to implementation

example, response time of a method for a class is an analytical metric because we can define a timed, state-based model of class object execution that will represent the time it takes for methods to finish a computation. In this way, analytical metrics can be *predicted* prior to measurement: they are predicted with respect to a model we build of the system. Analytical metrics are the larger subset of metrics. Even many syntactic measures are analytical. For example, depth of inheritance could be predicted over a UML class hierarchy diagram – but this will still be a prediction of inheritance with respect to an implementation of the diagram – perhaps the final implementation may not strictly preserve the inheritance relations of the original design, either by intention or mistake.

Fig. 2 represents the relationships between empirical and analytical metrics and system models and implementations.

What is the best way to treat consistency and validation?

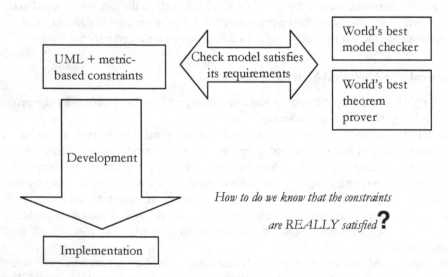

Fig. 3. The abstraction gap between prediction of system properties and an empirical guarantee that properties are satisfied

Consistency is, in practice, handled by careful manual development from model to implementation. Metric-based requirements of a system are tested during the testing and maintenance phases of the software lifecycle model. Some inconsistencies may still remain, and further time-intensive effort is often demanded of developers and testers to check for and eliminate consistency discrepencies between specification and implementation. While feasible for smaller systems, manually developed test cases are inadequate for large scale enterprise systems, due to regular modifications and extensions, a reconfigurable deployment environment and regular subsystem overhauls. Small changes in both hardware and software contexts of a deployed systems violates testing results which are usually obtained under the assumption of a constant executional environment.

If the metric-based requirements are predictions, then the testing and maintenance phases serve to validate them. The validation of a metric presupposes that the metric is testable. This is an obvious statement, but opens metric-based prediction up to the same problems that scientific theories face with respect to empirical validation. We can draw some insight on testing from the philosophy of science, with its concerns regarding the nature of what makes a good scientific theory and how empirical validation figures in science. Karl Popper's notion of *falsifiability* is particularly useful.

4.3   The Falsifiability Criterion

A state of the art metric-oriented model will involve a structural and behavioural system specification together with a set of metric constraints. An example would be a UML model with quality of service annotations provided in QML. Using the techniques surveyed in other chapters of this book, it is possible to apply a range of analysis techniques that will provide predictions about what the values of metrics will be for a system that implements the model.

Design-stage analysis is very valuable. However, there remains the problem of addressing the abstraction gap[2] between predictions over a model and ensuring that predictions are actually met in the implementation. Fig. 3 illustrates this.

We obtain metric values with respect to an implemented system. It follows that the semantics of a software metric must, in some way, prescribe how this evaluation can be achieved.

Falsifiability

In the book *Logic of Scientific Discovery* [399], the philosopher Karl Popper attempted to identify what distinguishes a scientific theory.

Prior to Popper, philosophers supposed that a scientific theory is a view of the world developed through repeated empirical observation and inductive logic. For example, the speed of light has been measured by attaching a mirror to a rock on the moon. A laser on the earth is fired at the mirror, which then reflects the laser back to earth. This way the time of the laser pulse can be measured and the speed of light can be calculated.

---

[2] Kurt Wallnau identified this as a central problem at the Second Workshop on Predictable Assembly held in Manchester, March 2006.

According to traditional philosophy of science, we have a scientific theory that the speed of light is constant because we repeat the experiment many times and always get the same result. By induction, we infer that the speed of light is constant.

Popper was not satisfied with this explanation of a scientific theory, as it admits theories he believed to be unscientific. For example, the theory of Marxism has thousands of empirical examples to show that capitalist societies inevitably lead to the rebellion of the working class. Similarly, a Freudian might claim that certain psychological problems stem from the Oedipus complex and have many case studies to prove this.

In the place of empiricism and induction, Popper proposed the concept of falsifiability as the distinguishing feature of a scientific theory:

> scientific theory = set of claims + method of falsifiability

Falsifiability is essentially a property of a theory that enables us to prove it to be false. If a theory can be empirically shown to be false, then it is falsifiable. For example, our theory of the speed of light is falsifiable, as the experiment permits the possibility of a counter-instance that will show the theory to be false. We accept the theory as true, not because of a large number of positive outcomes of the experiment, but because the theory has yet to be falsified.

In contrast, a range of undesirable theories are no longer scientific under this criterion. For example, the Marxist idea that capitalist societies inevitably lead to the rebellion of the working class can never be falsified – a counter-example of a particularly successful capitalist society does not entail the overall idea is false. Similarly, a Freudian might claim that all psychological problems stem from the Oedipus complex and have many case studies to prove this – but there is no potential way of falsifying the theory.

An Epistemological View of Metrics

We explicitly define our understanding of how an analytical metric's semantics informs its empirical validation.

A metric definition, to used across the development lifecycle, requires three things

- Some system property that can be measured
- A semantics for the property – that explains when a metric measurement is good or bad for a particular system
- A means of predicting or measuring the metric.

Predictions of metric values over a model essentially form a small scientific theory. They are abstract (model-based) predictions about reality (the actual system implementation). Following Popper, the definition of any analytical metric must also include falsification criteria: that is, it must indicate how to show that a predicted metric value is not accurate for an actual implementation. Even if we do not accept Popper's doctrine for the theory of science, we can still adapt his arguments to our context. Without a means of falsification, metric value predictions are as trustworthy as an astrological prediction: perhaps a prediction might be true, but we have no way of showing it to be false.

Our discussion might be summarized with the following slogan:

metric = measurable system property + semantics + method of falsification

What Is a Good Metric?

Another interesting aspect of Popper's philosophy that has some baring on our discussion is that of epistemological understanding of simplicity [399][136–145]. Here he argues that the simplest, most elegant theories are the ones that are most readily falsifiable. For example, a scientific law written as a first order function is more easily falsifiable than one written as a second order function (although the latter is still falsifiable), and so on. In this sense he associates degree of strictness of a theory – the degree in which a theory imposes the rigour of law upon nature – with its degree of falsifiability. "Simple statements, if knowledge is our object, are to be prized more highly than less simple ones *because they tell us more; because their empirical content is greater; and because they are better testable.*"

This observation is salient to the considerations of this book and leads us to impose a hierarchy of usefulness for metrics. Predictable metrics that lead to statements with a high degree of falsifiability should be prized more highly than those that do not lead to such statements. What is a good metric? It is, ideally, *simple* in Popper's sense. The slogan here is

good metric = simple metric

Predictable Assembly

By defining a metric's semantics to include some means of falsification, we are, at least implicitly, prescribing how empirical validation should be done. Using the Software Engineering Institute's (SEI's) terminology [497], falsifyable metrics permit *predictable assembly*.

Predicable assembly is a process of designing and predicting system behaviour and then certifying that the implemented system does, in fact, live up to the predictions. The commitment to empirical measurement need not be absolute instrumentation of the metric itself. It could take the form of a validation that the system abstraction accurately reflects the nature of the system it is abstracting. An example validation would be that the probabilistic transitions in a Markov chain model do in fact represent the usage profile of the modelled system. In this case we would need a guarantee (by means of some theory or empirical study for instance) that the Markov chain model is an accurate reflection of the system.

Wallnau's SEI report [497] outlines the SEI's Predictable Assembly from Certifiable Components (PACC) initiative. The aim of PACC is to develop compositional engineering methods and tools necessary to reliably predict the behaviour of assemblies of components so that they can be certified with trust. The main relevant notion to our discussion is the Prediction-enabled Component Technology (PECT) framework. This is conscious design of component technology incorporating automated and trustworthy analysis and prediction of system behaviour.

Models are viewed as constraints imposed over the implementation of software components. These constraints are divided into two categories: constructive and analytical constraints. The satisfaction of constructive constraints implies that a component is successfully implemented as specified by the model. Analytical constraints are aspects correlating to architecture styles and patterns, or assertions made during the construction of the component model.

The important principle here is that components should only be trusted if it is possible to predict their satisfaction of both types of constraints. The PECT realise this concept by means of two key ingredients: a construction framework and a set of one or more reasoning frameworks. The construction framework supports all component construction activities for the particular component technology, while each reasoning framework supports the property prediction activities of component based software based on a certain computational theory. Each of these reasoning frameworks is linked up with the construction framework by means of some formally defined interpretations, bridging the semantic gap between the construction domain and the analysis domain.

4.4 Validation

As noted in Section 2, validation of metric-based predictions occurs both at the testing and deployment and management phases of the development lifecycle.

Direct and Indirect Validation

The manner in which metric value validation is performed depends in part on the simplicity of the metric and the aspect of the system architecture being measured.

Complex predictions may be difficult or costly to validate through direct instrumentation. For example, it might not be feasible to assess the fault-tolerance of every component in a widely distributed, web-service based implementation, where many third party components might be unavailable for instrumentation. If a number of complex properties can be predicted based on a more simple, more readily testable or instrumentable properties, then it should be possible to exploit predictions during the testing phases to make indirect validation of complex properties. This can occur only if the prediction is based on a model that is consistently preserved by the implementation.

For the purposes of our discussion, we can classify metric validation into two kinds:

- Strong guarantee. This involves empirical measurement for a metric that has simple falsification criteria. Immediate metrics are suited to this: for example, lines of code or class cohesion. Predictable metrics associated with coarse grain system components also often provide strong guarantees: for example, the response time of a web server.
- Weak guarantee. This is more common for analytical metrics that are associated with an architecture of finer grained components. We determine a metric's value only through measuring other properties that it depends on, and often need to utilize aspects of the prediction model in order to calculate the metric itself. This usage of the model blurs the boundary between prediction and validation. validation is "weaker" in the sense that there is still a predictive aspect and assumption

of model correctness. For example, we can calculate the stability of a system queue by measuring the rate of request arrivals and the average service time. However, this calculation uses a prediction model of how the queue works (that will include, amongst other things, the service discipline) that is presupposed to hold over the implementation. The model is used for both design and runtime prediction.

The best metrics are simple and yield strong guarantees. However, in practice, many interesting metrics are not subject to immediate measurement and so weak guarantees are the best we can hope for.

Testing

Testing is a means of identifying and rectifying constraint violations prior to deployment. Several researchers on validation of metric constraints have focused on the testing phase. We now highlight some key research.

The PerfTTCN language [428] is a means of describing test relating performance properties of a software implementation. It has been suggested that using a standardised test language has the benefits of making described tests more understandable, unambiguous and reusable, as well as making test results comparable. Medium scale case studies on the use of PerfTTCN have shown its usefulness in a range of contexts.

Bryant's group at the University of Alabama have developed a formal method, designed to operate within their UniFrame framework, for specifying QoS metric constraints and constraint conformance testing [515].

The method's procedure begins with a requirements analysis phase, involving the creation of a catalogue for the required QoS constraints, consisting of a range of acceptable parameters. A formal specification of the QoS constraints is then defined, using Two-Level Grammars (TLG) are used. (Since TLG can be transformed into OCL-augmented UML models as well as executable codes, the method is potentially consistent with OMG's Model Driven Architecture (MDA) concept.)

The framework then exploits the TLG formalism to provide generate detailed contracts to *guarantee* the required constraints both at component levels and at the overall architectural level. The usefulness of the TLG formalism is that its specifications can be transformed into OCL-augmented UML models *and* executable code, both of which preserve the semantics of the TLG specification in a clear way. Importantly, instrumenting code can also be synthesized from the TLG QoS constraints, used for static and dynamic contract-based checks. The contracts are employed during testing to make sure the constructed system meets the QoS requirements With this method, every QoS parameter need to be formally specified using TLG.

Post-deployment Validation

Various metric values of deterministic software, in particular QoS metrics, are analyzable from a static point of view during a pre-deployment testing phase. However, there also exist systems which operate in highly variable environments and therefore have metric values that cannot be known a priori. In these dynamic systems it may not be possible to pre-determine the QoS metric values the system may exhibit.

In the service-oriented context, metrics are the primary entities involved in the specification of Service Level Agreements (SLAs). A SLA is a formal written agreement between two parties: the service provider and the service recipient. In the terms of a software development, it usually consists of a set of clauses describing a service to be provided by the software product and any extrinsic properties that the service is expected to meet. These properties are usually constraints over Quality of Service (QoS) metrics, with the focus on dependability characteristics such as performance, reliability and security.

Clauses contained in a SLA are considered as constraints imposed over the implementation of the delivered software product, such that the development team will have to provide proof of satisfaction for all of the clauses specified. In that sense, SLA clauses should only specify observable software properties that they will be possible to be validated over an implementation. Such characteristics should inherit the following elements:

- A *metric*: the unit of for a scalable range of values representing all possible instances for the particular type of QoS attribute.
- A *target*: the desired value, specified in terms of the metric, that the SLA requires from an implementation.
- A *benchmark*: the mechanism for producing the metric values reflecting the particular QoS attribute exhibited by an implementation.

An agreement must be reached between the two parties over the benchmarks, targets and metrics used in a SLA, which will form part of the design specification of a system. The development team will then be responsible for maintaining the consistency of the metrics used throughout the development to ensure that the resulting software properties legitimately satisfy those targets stated in a SLA. This implies that the semantics of the metrics and mechanisms have to be carried through from the development cycle all the way down to testing and deployment.

The bulk of research in empirical validation of metric constraints deals with the specification and enforcement SLAs within complex enterprise systems.

SLA management systems generally work through some kind of monitoring infrastructure, to instrument and observe relevant system's behaviour and generate the data needed for interpreting the system's current conditions at a higher level. By relating them to the system's architecture it is then possible to deduce whether the system's behaviour is without acceptable bounds.

Runtime validation and monitoring work in Chen and Rosu [93] focused on specification based monitoring and on predictive analysis of systems, specific to Java. Based on annotations, Monitoring Oriented Programming (MoP) tried to combine together the system specification and the implementation by extending programming languages with specifications taken from, for instance, extended regular expressions and Linear Temporal Logic. That work couples the code with nonfunctional constraints so changing required constraints entails opening code.

David Garlan et al [180] propose a generic 3-layer view for such a monitoring and adaptation framework, consisting of performance monitoring, architecture modelling, detection of constraint violations and automated architectural repair and Task management layers. Garlan's group has done extensive work on the architecture layer and its mapping to the monitoring level. An important idea is the concept of Probes and Gauges for bridging the abstraction gap between monitoring and architectural level.

In essence Probes are software implementation elements that are embedded into the system-under-observation, exporting information that reflects the runtime behaviour of the system. The Gauges are then responsible for semantically mapping this information to the corresponding elements in the system's architecture. This allows checking for violation against constraints specified at the architecture level, and provides the data required for runtime adaptation mechanisms.

Garlan also describes how a definition of Gauges can be attached to ACME based architectural description. Infrastructure implementations of such Gauges have also been included for illustration purposes.

Wang's group at Boeing [501] have attempted to capture all aspects of a runtime management system for Quality of Service (QoS). While it contains a range of related services, the core services of such a system are: monitoring, diagnostic and adaptation.

The notion of monitoring depicts the explicit observation of runtime behaviour of software systems. Two types of monitoring approaches have been distinguished - active reporting and passive polling. In the former approach the monitored software actively produce information which it then reports to the monitoring interface. In the latter the application provides an interface for the monitoring system to poll for information.

QoS Diagnostics service analyses the information obtained by the monitoring service, and using the policies store in its repository, it deduces where any action needs to be taken to remedy any QoS related problems. When appropriate, it decides the kind of adaptations the software system may need and passes on the request to an adaptation manager, which would in turn carry out appropriate operations to provide a compromising solution to the arisen QoS problem.

The significance of such a system is that we can introduce policies which can dictate the overall behaviour of a software system with regards to QoS. With the current information obtained by a monitoring service we can more accurately determine the state of the system, allowing us to pre-emptively tackle QoS related issues.

Dinda defines an interesting framework for not simply monitoring QoS properties, but predicting their future values. In Dinda [121], ARIMA forecasting techniques are employed host load prediction of CORBA based systems and the performance prediction methods of Balsamo et al. [38] and Fortier and E.Michel [165]. This is a promising approach that should be applicable to a wider range of metric values.

Huh et al. [147] suggest using runtime prediction and adaptation for the handling of resource related problem of dynamic systems. It presents a resource management approach for dynamic allocation to handle execution times represented using a time-variant stochastic model. Resource managers are responsible for actively monitoring the software system, making estimations on resource demands of the software based on interpolation and extrapolation of its hardware/software usage profile. The software may then be prevented from starvation of resources. A case study has also been provided to show feasibility of this approach.

A SLA has to encapsulate all the information required to describe the constraints that a service is expected to adhere to. The types of constraint found in SLAs differ from service to service, hence a structured language will be needed to effectively understand

and communicate the implications of various constraints. Skene et al.[450] define a structured language, SLAng, for describing the QoS SLAs. A QoS catalogue for SLAng has been defined based on the OMG UML Profile for QoS, which allows SLAng to be used directly in conjunction with UML, enabling the construction of QoS-enabled UML models. Different SLAs, usually referring to different services, may be composed. The concept of conformance, defined in relation to QML, may be employed for checking compatibility between SLAs. Mechanisms compatibility checks are provided that can be used within a monitoring system for managment of SLAng constraints.

Grunske and Neumann [199] illustrate how QoS properties may be integrated in software architecture specification for embedded systems. Several architecture notations (ROOM, CCM and HRT-HOOD) were been evaluated for their level of support in specifying QoS properties. A metamodel called RT-COOL is then proposed and defined for the purpose of QoS-enabled modelling, which supports for hardware-level specification alongside the embedded software. Also suggested in the article are the architectural evaluation techniques optimised for the RT-COOL model, along with examples. Nevertheless this is an article aimed towards embedded systems; hence the methodologies and techniques it detailed may not be applicable to software in other domains.

Botella et al.[70] have defined a QoS specification language NoFun, based largely on the quality attributes set out in the ISO 9126 standard. The various QoS characteristics are classified in ways similar to of which has been done in the standard. The article then defines the domains that NoFun may be used in, the metamodel that integrates NoFun as part of its component models and the types of quality attributes in NoFun. Attempts have also been made to map the NoFun language onto UML modelling, utilising OCL as its counterpart in the UML metamodel. An example of such modelling has also been included in the article.

Adaptation

A related issue of validation at the management stage concerns what is done when a metric-based constraint is falsified and shown to be violated? In the testing phase, the action is clearer: some reengineering may be attempted. However, this is often not a possibility in post-deployment phases. An increasingly common solution is to employ some form of runtime software adaptation, in which a system is dynamically reconfigured in an attempt to conform to constraint requirements.

There are many systems that permit dynamic adaptation of architectures based on real time QoS information.

We have already mentioned that Wang's group at Boeing integrates adaptation into its SLA management system [501].

In Zeng et al. [524], UDDI is used to provide adaptation based on monitored QoS properties to assemble web service architectures of optimal performance. Al-Ali et al. [14] defines a language of QoS policies for grid services that are enforced by means of adaptation mechanisms. A different approach to QoS adaptation is considered in Sharma et al. [438] for the case of embedded systems. These systems do not involve forecasting of values as part of their adaptation strategies. The ARIMA methods need not only be applied to compute QoS queue characteristics. These strategies have the potential to be combined with such (non-queued) QoS-based runtime adaptation technologies.

Valetto and Kaiser [480] have investigated how adaptation may be feasible for dynamic software. The infrastructure used in the case was similar to that of Garlan's probes and gauges approach, such that minimalist probes are injected into the software to provide gauges with sufficient information to deduce a specific QoS property of the system. The computed value for a property is then sent back to the architectural-level analysis module which determines whether any adaptation should be in place. A detailed case study has been included in the article, of which the above infrastructure is applied to a mass-market messaging service. It was found to be effective and efficient to have such automatic handling of QoS in place, as it may replace some otherwise error-prone manual tasks.

4.5   Consistency of Metric Semantics

It is important metrics are handled *consistently* across the software development life-cycle. The major obstacle to automating consistency of requirements is that abstract representations of QoS employed at analysis and design phases are usually semantically different from, or, at best, have orthogonal purposes to, component properties that should be tested or instrumented in a runtime implementation. For example, it is common with such specification to contain references to contextual properties which are difficult to capture without explicit support from the operating platform. QoS monitoring and instrumentation during testing and maintenance phases also requires components to be made QoS-aware, imposing a direct impact on their implementations.

This problem is very much an open one. The most important and interesting work in achieving consistency of metric semantics is done within the Model Driven Architecture context.

Model Driven Architecture (MDA) is often proposed as a solution to help improve functional and architectural consistency between design and implementation (for example, in making sure that all interfaces of an abstract UML class are transformed into appropriate operations in a corresponding web service based implementation). However, in and of itself, MDA does not solve the problem of QoS consistency across levels and the need to monitor. Conformance to QoS constraints, even though validated at a certain level of abstraction, will not be automatically preserved by model transformations to a lower level.

A theoretic ideal would be to prove QoS requirement satisfaction for an abstract model of system execution (using, for example, probabilistic model checking) and then apply provably consistent transformations over this model to an implementation. QoS satisfaction would then be formally guaranteed by the transformation. However, in practice, this would require heavy use of formal methods and is too costly to be feasible.

This paper advocates a pragmatic remedy: transform architectures into implementations together with instrumentation for monitoring and management. Instead of proving QoS properties hold over the transformed code, we simply instrument the system for runtime checks on conformance to design-level QoS requirements. While not proving a formal proof that requirements are met, the approach provides a level of trust by automatically supplying the means to validated whether QoS requirements are being met in the deployed system.

The most interesting metamodelling-based approaches to nonfunctional conformance checking currently come from Model Driven Architecture research. Solberg et al. [453] present a good argument for the capturing and handling of QoS-requirements as an essential part of the MDA approach. Merilinna [350] defines a range of horizontal MDA transformations (transformations involving the same abstract modelling language) that systematically construct QoS-oriented system designs from basic specifications.

A central concept of MDA is the automatic generation of component software via transformations over the abstract model of a system. The biggest challenge for the inclusion of QoS into a development process is the integration of QoS contracts into a system model, and carrying these abstract interpretations of QoS down through the transformations. The article by Jezequel et al. [260] provides a mechanism for tackling the above.

It has suggested that a QoS contracts may be attached to the provided interfaces of a component given the QoS contracts on its required interfaces. A QoS contract metamodel, namely QoS Constraint Language(QoSCL) has been introduced to allow QoS contracts and their dependencies to be modelled in a UML2 modelling environment, and by mapping the metamodels it is then made possible to attach QoSCL contracts to components modelled in UML2.

The article also employed the idea of contract-aware component, such that components not only behave as required but also explicitly implemented to allow validation of its behaviour. It is suggested that validation techniques are generally classified into two families - testing and formal reasoning. The article the turn its focus to the testing of extra functional behaviour.

The testing strategy used in Jezequel's approach is similar to that of Garlan's probes and gauges paradigm. For relating it to MDA probing codes are weaved into components. Monitoring components are then used for observation the behaviour of components, checking for any violations of contracts. An example has been provided to illustrate how that can be done.

Examples have also been included for illustrating we can make use of the attached provided and required QoS contracts to assert predictions on component QoS. An example has also been shown on how contracts expressed in OCL can be transformed to a specific CLP-compliant language using model transformation.

Grunske et al. [198] address the QoS refinement process at software architecture level using horizontal transformations (transformations between models of the same metamodel). In the light that the functional aspects of software may be specified in software architecture as interface specifications, a framework for defining functional behaviour preserving transformations has been presented. QoS refinement may be achieved with the application and subsequent analysis with different architectural patterns and styles. A proof algorithm is also introduced for verifying behaviour equivalence of such architectural transformations. This article serves as a fine example of how horizontal transformations may be practically employed as part of a performance engineering process.

Solberg et al. [453] point out the shortcomings of MDA in relation to Quality of Service in software, with the reason being a lack of precise relations between different models, as well as between models and implementations with respect to QoS. It was suggested that the capturing and handling of QoS-requirements has to be an essential part of the MDA approach in order to gain successful system development of real time and embedded systems. The article describes some significant aspects of a QoS-aware MDA approach for system development and execution. In particular it has been stressed that QoS specifications should become an inherent part of the transformations, PIM and PSM models in MDA. Examples and pointers have been given as to how QoS may be incorporated in a MDA process. Nevertheless the article is critical on the importance of integrating QoS in every stage of the MDA process for the successful treatment of QoS in a MDA-based development.

While quality of service enabled metamodels are being developed readily (e.g. QML), the focus is usually over the construction of QoS-enabled models from specification to system design. The thesis of Merilinna [350] suggests a compliment using horizontal transformation, that is, model transformation which retains abstraction level while refining or enriching a model. The main objective was to enable transformations between different design styles and patterns. For example, as a refinement process a non QoS- enabled platform independent model may be enriched through a transformation to include quality metric parameters, while retaining its abstraction at the platform independent level. A model can also be transformed into designs using different styles and patterns and then compared for various properties. The thesis also addresses the issue of traceability of transformation, via inclusion of transformation record as a product of transformation. By virtue transformations are performed based on rules of element mapping between metamodels. A transformation record includes the mapping used in the transformation as well as the transformation being made. Using this information we are able to trace or reverse any transformations of models between metamodels.

4.6   Conclusions

As our survey shows, there has been progress towards solving the problem of consistency and validation. However, there is still much work to be done.

Better support of metric validation at the testing phase is needed. A promising potential means of achieving this would be to apply the kind of MDA techniques described above to test case generation.

There is a subtle issue that remains with respect to implementation of falsification. In the state of the art, the evaluative semantics of a metric is implemented through monitoring and instrumentation code, generated by some model driven process. But what guarantee do we have that this generated code *really does* provide the means of falsifying a metric constraint? For example, an measurement of something like reliability requires us to instrumentation of code and depends on us the instrumentation really does provide a reliability value.

Formal methods has the potential to play a greater role. The problem of consistency and validation have been long discussed within the context of *functional* properties of a system. While formal methods approaches such as refinment calculus or the B methodology have been effective in developing code that is consistent with its model and providing a guarantee that design properties are correctly implemented, they have been less effective in practice of most industrial software engineering projects, particularly in the enterprise domain. Simply because a metric-oriented property is less complicated than a functional property, and nonfunctional predictions may be made over less complicated behavioural models than those required for functional predictions, intuition leads us to believe the application of some formal methods techniques to the consistency and validation of metric-oriented properties is more practical and scalable than for functional properties. We believe this is a key open problem in the field.

5 Basic and Dependent Metrics

Ralf Reussner and Viktoria Firus

University of Karlsruhe (TH), Germany

Besides the distinction between empirical and analytical metrics, metrics can also be distinguished whether they are *basic* or *dependent*.

5.1 Defining Basic and Dependent Metrics

The concept of basic and dependent metrics is not established in literature, much more, it is introduced firstly in this volume. The rationale behind this distinction is a clarification of metrics like scalability, efficiency, and others which themselves are defined in terms of other metrics. Unfortunately, their presentation in literature is inhomogeneous and most often oriented towards a specific application domain (e.g., scalability might be defined differently in terms of users, threads, resources, etc, and can mean response time, throughput or other metrics). Hence, the following is motivated by the lack of a general treatment of such metrics.

A *basic metric* can be any analytical or empirical metric, where its dependencies on other variables is not made explicit (i.e., where influencing variables are assumed to be constant). For example, the throughput (as measured at a specific data connection within a system) can be considered as a basic metric, if influencing variables (e.g., the message length, the number of processes utilising the connection concurrently, etc) is considered to be constant.

A *dependent metric* is an analytic or empirical metric where its influencing variables are made explicit. An example is the scalability of the throughput in terms of the number of clients accessing a data connection. Here, a metric (the throughput) is given in dependency of another variable (the number of clients). Accordingly, a dependent metric is given by a set of tuples (metric, variable(s)). In case of a empirical metric as a metric of a dependent metric, these tuples can be a finite set of pairs of measured values and values for variables (e.g., throughput in dependency of threads: {(1 MB/sec, 1), (500 KB/sec, 2), (320 KB/sec, 3)}). In case of an analytical metric as a metric of a dependent metric, the dependency is most likely given as an analytical formula, e.g., *throughput* $\in O(1/\text{number of threads})$.

5.2 Examples

For practical reasons of performance and parallelisation evaluation, a set of dependent metrics has evolved (see for example Kumar et al. [288, pp. 118]), in particular in the domain of high performance computing, which also has found its application in other domains.

Scalability: Change of metric A in dependency of change of a variable B. E.g., "Change of response time when increasing the number of users."

I. Eusgeld, F.C. Freiling, and R. Reussner (Eds.): Dependability Metrics, LNCS 4909, pp. 37–38, 2008.

Speedup (S): Change of metric A in dependency of change of a variable B describing the amount of a resource. E.g., "Change of response time when increasing the number of servers."

Efficiency (E): The *efficiency* is the gain (speedup) related to the amount of resources to be spend to achieve this gain. Hence, $E = S/B$.

Costs: The *costs* are the results of metric A times the amount of resources to be used to get these results. Hence, costs are the product $A * B$.

Note that the term *efficiency* is defined here as a dependent attribute and not, as in the ISO 9126 as a set of performance-related metrics. Similarly, the definition of the term *costs* differs from its use in complexity theory (where it usually relates to time of memory consumption) or in the business domain (where it relates to expenditures of any kind).

The main result of this discussion is, that a dependent metric, (e.g., scalability) is not tied to a specific metric (e.g., throughput). It can also be defined for reaction-time or response-time. Although dependent metrics are often defined using such a performance metric, the concept of dependent metrics is not limited to this group of metrics. For example, it also makes sense, to define a reliability-scalability metric, e.g., the MTTF in dependency of the number of users.

6 Goal, Question, Metric

Heiko Koziolek

University of Oldenburg, Germany

This chapter gives an overview over the Goal-Question-Metric (GQM) approach, a way to derive and select metrics for a particular task in a top-down and goal-oriented fashion.

6.1 Motivation

Defining metrics for a measurement or prediction approach in a *bottom-up* manner is generally considered problematic. Without inclusion of the context and the goal of measuring or prediction, it is usually unclear which metrics shall be selected and how the selected metrics can be interpreted. If lots of data has been measured without a predefined plan for the evaluation, it will usually be very difficult to select the relevant data and to draw proper conclusions from the measurements.

Therefore, embedding metrics into a goal-oriented framework is widely regarded as a good practice. The Goal-Question-Metric (GQM) approach presents such a framework. It was developed by Basili and Weiss during the 1980s [42] and later extended by Rombach [41]. Opposed to the bottom-up approach, metrics are defined *top-down* in GQM. First, specific goals are stated, then questions are asked, whose answers will help attaining the goals. The metrics are defined in a third step to provide a scheme for measuring.

By applying GQM, goals and metrics are tailored for a specific measurement setting. Stating goals in advance leads to a selection of only those metrics that are relevant for achieving these goals. This reduces the effort for data collection, because only necessary data needs to be recorded, nothing more, nothing less. The interpretation of the metrics after measurement is rather effortless, because GQM creates an explicit link between the measured data and the goals of measuring before data collection. This way, misinterpretations of data can be avoided.

Although the GQM approach was originally used to improve software products and development processes, the underlying concepts are generic and applicable in any measurement setting.

The next section describes the process of applying the GQM-paradigm in detail. Another section explains how goals, questions, and metrics should be defined.

6.2 Goal-Oriented Measurement

The method of applying the GQM paradigm consists of four phases [481]: planning, definition, data collection, interpretation (see Fig. 1).

For the initial *planning* phase, first a GQM-team is established and the desired improvement area (e.g., reliability, performance, security, etc.) is identified. Afterwards, the team selects and characterises the product or process to be studied. The result of this

I. Eusgeld, F.C. Freiling, and R. Reussner (Eds.): Dependability Metrics, LNCS 4909, pp. 39–42, 2008.
© Springer-Verlag Berlin Heidelberg 2008

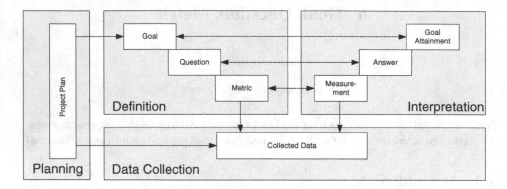

Fig. 1. The 4 phases of the GQM-method [481]

phase is a project plan that outlines the characterisation of the product or process, the schedule of measuring, the organisational structure, and necessary training and promotion activities for people involved in measurements.

During the *definition* phase, measurement goals are defined. A template for goal definition will follow in the next section. For the purpose of defining goals, GQM interviews may be conducted with people involved in the process or product under study. Based on the goals, questions are stated, asking for specific quality attributes and making certain aspects of the goals more concrete. For each question a hypothesis with an expected answer should be defined. Afterwards, metrics are defined for each question and checked on consistency and completeness. Results of this phase are a GQM plan, a measurement plan, and an analysis plan.

The actual measurement takes place in the *data collection* phase. Data collection may be performed manually or electronically and may involve automated data collection tools. A measurement support system consisting of spreadsheets, statistical tools, database applications and presentation tools should be established for this phase.

In the *interpretation* phase, the collected data is processed according to the metrics defined before to gain measurement results. The measurements can then be used to answer the questions, and with the answers it can be evaluated if the initial goals have been attained.

6.3   GQM Paradigm

A GQM plan consists of goals, questions, and metrics in a hierarchical structure (see figure 2). Before measuring, the elements are defined in a top-down manner. After measuring, the plan can be used bottom-up to interpret the results.

Goals are defined on a conceptual level and later made operational by questions. For clearness, each GQM plan should contain one goal. Goals can be derived by studying the policy and the strategy of the organisation that applies GQM. Interviewing relevant people and checking available process or product descriptions may also help in defining goals. If goals are still unclear, first modelling the organisation might be necessary to derive them.

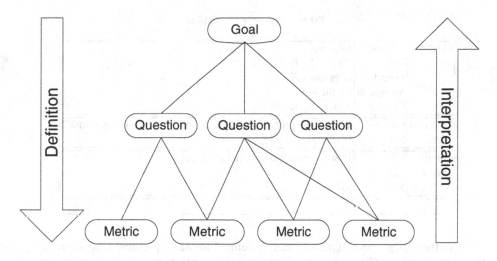

Fig. 2. The GQM-paradigm [481]

Goals must be documented in a structured way, preferably using the following template. Goals are defined for a purpose (e.g. understanding, improving, controlling), for the object under study (e.g. process, product), for a specific issue or quality attribute (e.g. reliability, security, performance), from a perspective (e.g. user, developer), and within certain context characteristics (e.g. involved persons, environment, resources, organisations). For example, a goal could be:

"Improve (=purpose) the reliability (=issue) of product X (=object) from the viewpoint of the user (=perspective) within organisation Y (=context)."

Several *questions* are usually asked to achieve each goal. While goals are on a more abstract and conceptional level, questions shall refine goals and make them operational. By answering the stated questions, it should be possible to conclude if a goal has been reached. Questions should be defined on an intermediate level between goals and metrics. They should neither be too abstract, in which case it would be difficult to reveal the relationship to the collected data, nor should they be too detailed, so that an interpretation of the answers towards the goal would be difficult. If questions are stated in a quantitative way, data can be collected by measurements. If questions are stated in a qualitative way, questionnaires are necessary to answer them. Expected answers to the questions are formulated as hypotheses. Hypotheses increase the learning effect from measurements, because they allow comparing knowledge before and after measurements. For example, a question could be:

"What is the probability of failure on demand for function Z in product X?"

A matching hypothesis would be:

"The probability of failure on demand for function Z in product X is below 0.0001 percent."

Table 1. Example GQM plan

Goal	Purpose	Improve
	Issue	the reliability
	Object	of product X
	Viewpoint	for the user
	Context	within organisation Y
Question	Q1	What is the probability of failure on demand for function Z?
Metric	M1	POFOD
Question	Q2	How erroneous does function Z behave?
Metric	M2	MTTF
Metric	M3	MTTR
...	...	...

After these steps, several *metrics* can be defined for each question. One metric may be used to answer different questions under the same goal. Metrics are on a quantitative level making it possible to assign numbers to a quality attribute. Metrics are means to map reality into comparable values. They must be defined to answer the asked questions and be able to approve or disprove the stated hypotheses. Already existing data can be used to define metrics. A metric may be objective, so that different people measuring the metric would gain the same results (e.g. the number of jobs completed during a time span). Instead, subjective metrics may produce different results depending on the persons measuring (e.g. the readability of a text). Objective metrics are suitable for more mature objects, while subjective metrics can be used for more unstable or unclear objects.

A simple GQM plan can be found in Tab. 1. Any GQM plan needs permanent evaluation and improvement. Imprecise goals need to be corrected and no more matching metrics need to be updated.

7 Quality of Service Modeling Language

Steffen Becker

University of Karlsruhe (TH), Germany

This chapter gives an overview over the the Quality of Service Modeling Language (QML), a language which can be used to describe QoS offerings or needs of specified services.

7.1 Motivation

A specification of the quality of a service is an important prerequisite for building dependable systems. During the requirements phase it can be used to gather the quality needs of the end user of a software system. During the design phase it helps in making design decisions and in early, architecture based quality evaluations. During runtime and testing it can be checked by monitoring tools to find insufficient quality characteristics of the running system. Further on, Quality of Service (QoS) negotiations, graceful QoS degration or self-healing systems rely on specifications of the desired QoS levels.

In order to support the specification of QoS, the Quality of Service Modeling Language (QML) has been developed at HP Software Technology Laboratory by [170]. It is a language which can be used to describe QoS offerings or needs of specified services. A short overview of the most important concepts of the QML is given in the following and further detailed by utilizing a running example.

7.2 Main QML Concepts

QML introduces several concepts to model quality characteristics of services. *Dimensions* characterize a measurable value and several dimensions are bundled into *contract types*. For specific contract types multiple *contracts* using the dimensions of the type can be specified. Finally, *profiles* bind contracts to interface methods.

Dimensions

QML can be used to model *any* type of quality characteristic, e.g, it has no explicit quality model. Hence, it allows the specification of any generic quality attribute. Nevertheless, the specification has to introduce the type of the utilized attributes. This is done by using quality dimensions.

A dimension can be seen as the declaration of a domain of a variable. It tells the range of possible values of instances of the declared type. To give an example consider the quality characteristic performance. A typical attribute for performance is the timing related parameter delay. The delay describes the time which passes between the issue of a call and its return to the caller. Hence, it is a non-negative float point number having some kind of unit like seconds or microseconds associated to it. Additionally, in QML

I. Eusgeld, F.C. Freiling, and R. Reussner (Eds.): Dependability Metrics, LNCS 4909, pp. 43–47, 2008.
© Springer-Verlag Berlin Heidelberg 2008

allows to specify a *direction* of the dimension, e.g., a specification of an ordering of the actual values. This allows to say, whether small or large values are better. For the example of delay small numbers are better as they indicate faster response times. Using QML, the delay dimension would look like code fragment 1.

```
delay : decreasing numeric msec;
```

Code fragment 1: A QML dimension

The first parameter (decreasing or increasing) describes whether smaller or larger values are better. The second determines the type of the dimension. Here we use a numeric type allowing float point values. Additional types available in QML are enumerated domains and set domains. Enumerations contain a list of names and a value can have exactly one of the names as content. A set domain is also a set of names, but the values are any possible subset of the set of names. Additionally, in both cases, it is possible to define an order on the set of names to introduce again a goodness relationship. An example for each concept can be found in code fragment 2.

As detailed in Sect. 7.2, the specification of the direction can be used to check the interoperability of interfaces. For decreasing types like response times, a provided *smaller* response time than the required response time is conform. For increasing type like network throughput, a provided *larger* throughput is conform to a required smaller throughput.

```
cypher_algorithm : enum { RSA, DSA };
cypher_strenght : increasing enum { 1024, 2048, 4192 }
                  with order { 1024 < 2048, 2048 < 4192 } bits;
login_mechanisms : set { password, smartcard, fingerprint };
```

Code fragment 2: QML enumeration and set domains

Finally, every dimension can have an optional unit specification, like `bits` or `msec` in the examples above.

Contract Types

After introducing the dimensions and their associated specification of a partial order the following shows how to further abstract and bundle the dimensions into *contract types*. A contract type is closely related to a quality characteristic as introduced by [246]. Typical characteristics are performance, reliability or security. Note again, that QML does not define any dimension or contract type. This has to be done by the users of QML.

Hence, contract types bundle related dimensions and subsume them using a common characteristic. To give an example, we introduce a performance contract type. Performance can be determined by several dimensions. In this case the specification uses the delay and the throughput of services to describe their performance. The complete contract type can be found in code fragment 3.

```
type Performance = contract {
   delay : decreasing numeric msec;
   throughput : increasing numeric business_transactions / sec;
};
```

Code fragment 3: An example QML performance contract type

Contracts

Based on a contract type there can be several contracts. A contract is used to constrain each dimension in the contract type. The domain of each dimension is divided into a set of values which are valid and another set of invalid values. If the dimension supports an ordering the use of comparison operators (greater than, less than) is also allowed in a contract.

For example, we need to specify that a service has an upper bound concerning its delay and a lower bound of its throughput. This is a situation likely to happen in a banking application. A transaction has to be finished in time so that there are no delays in the overall business process. Also a certain amount of fund transfers has to be done per second as otherwise the system would collapse.

Using QML, this situation can be described using a contract as depicted in code fragment 4 which is based on the contract type taken from code fragment 3.

```
FundTransferContract = Performance contract {
        delay < 100ms;
        throughput > 10.000 business_transactions / sec;
};
```

Code fragment 4: An example QML contract

Aspects

Several of the dimension values cannot be measured exactly using a single figure. For example, the delay caused by a service call varies over time. Hence, the delay can only be characterized using statistical means. QML supports four different types of stochastical information. Mean and variance are characteristic attributes of probability density functions. Percentiles and frequencies describe probability distribution functions in more detail. An explanation of these basic statistical concepts can be found in basic statistic literature and is omitted here. An example is depicted in code fragment 5 (units are omitted).

Profiles

After the definition of contracts including the introduced constraints, one has to decide which constraints should be applied to which services. This binding between interface methods and constraints is done using *profiles* in QML. A profile maps contracts to single methods or all methods of an interface respectively. This is done by stating either for

```
FundTransferContract = Performance contract {
        delay {
                mean < 100;
                variance < 10;
        };
        throughput {
                percentile 0    < 9.000;
                percentile 50   < 10.000;
                percentile 80   < 12.000;
        };
};
```

Code fragment 5: Example QML aspect specification

a whole interface or for single methods which contracts they have to fulfil. Additionally it is possible to introduce new contracts or strengthen existing ones inline.

Take a look at code fragment 6.

```
interface BankSystem {
        void TransferMoney (Account a, Account b);
        [...]
}

transferMoneyProfile for BankSystem = profile {
        require FundTransferContract;
        from TransferMoney require Performance contract = {
                        delay < 80ms;
                };
};
```

Code fragment 6: Example QML profile

The first statement of the profile applies the defined `FundTransferContract` to each service of interface `BankSystem`. The second statement applies an inlined performance contract additionally to the already applied one. This contract defines an upper limit for the delay of the `TransferMoney` service of 80ms. Note, that the other constrains concerning the mean and the variance and the constrains for the minimum throughput also apply to service `TransferMoney`.

Contract Refinement

Besides the possibility of using inlined contracts, QML has also explicit support for contract refinement, which allows the specification of contracts based on existing ones. This is especially useful for programming languages supporting subtyping as the contract of a subtype should be a refinement of the contract of its supertype. The refined contract has to be conformant to the original one (see Sect. 7.2 for further details).

Assume we want to define the inlined contract of example 6 explicitly, for example to reuse it. The result can be found in code fragment 7.

```
SpecialFundTransferContract = FundTransferContract refined by {
                        delay < 80ms;
};
```

Code fragment 7: Example QML contract refinement

Conformance

The pure specification of QoS offerings or requirements helps when doing monitoring during runtime. Using the collected data it is possible to determine whether the client or the server of a service is responsible for an insufficient quality. Nevertheless, the checking of the quality specifications already at design time is desired if systems should be built which do prevent interoperability mismatches by design.

To support the task of the developer to check for interoperability problems when binding a client requesting a certain service with specific quality requirements to a server offering that service with a specified quality profile QML introduces a *conformance relation*. This relation has to be built from the basic dimensions and contract types. Additionally, it has to include a concept how to deal with statistical information given in aspects.

For elementary, ordered dimensions the conformance relation is reduced to the order given by the used data type. For decreasing values smaller values are conforming to larger ones. For example, an upper bound for the delay of 80ms is conform to an upper bound of 100ms. For increasing values it is the other way round. The concepts is applied in the same way for user defined orders of enumerated or set domains.

Taking aspects into account is a bit more complicated as it is not intuitively clear how to define the conformance relationship in this case. QML uses the definitions shown in Tab. 1.

For percentiles and frequencies QML uses a very strict definition of conformance which on the other side is the only mathematical exact one. Nevertheless, it implies that you need the same set of percentiles on the server side than you have on the client side. In practice this might be a restriction which renders the conformance checks impractical.

Table 1. QML conformance rules for aspects (taken from Frølund and Koistinen [170])

aspect	conformance rule
frequency	For every constraint of type frequency $R = P$ in D there must be a constraint with the same aspect signature in S that is stronger or equally strong with respect to the value P.
percentile	For every constraint of type percentile $P = V$ in D there must be a constraint with the same aspect signature in S that is stronger or equally strong with respect to the value V.
mean	If D has an mean constraint, the mean constraint for S must be stronger or equal to the one in D.
variance	If D has a variance constraint, the variance constraint of S must be smaller or equal to the variance of D.

D = Demand
S = Service

8 Markov Models

Michael Kuperberg

University of Karlsruhe (TH), Germany

This chapter gives a brief overview over Markov models, a useful formalism to analyse stochastic systems.

8.1 Introduction to Markov Models

To estimate the dependability metrics of a system, knowledge about its behaviour is necessary. This behaviour can be measured during the operation of the system, resulting in a behaviour model (possibly without knowledge of the system's interna). Alternatively, a model of the system can be created at design time to predict its behaviour, so that the internal structure of the system is reflected by the model.

The constructed system will execute in an environment where it will be subject to indeterministic influences (for example, the availability of services the system depends on might exhibit random behaviour). This means that the model must reflect the random/stochastic behaviour of the entire system and that the mathematical parameters must be determined at design time or identified at runtime.

In both scenarios, *Markov models* prove useful, since they are accompanied by algorithms that allow to compute relevant figures (metrics) or random distributions of those figures. For example, the behaviour of a software component with the identified states "working" (S_w) and "broken" (S_b) can be expressed by the Markov model shown in figure 1. Transitions denote possible state changes and are annotated with probabilities. With this Markov model, metrics such as *Mean Time To Failure* (MTTF) (see Sect. 9.3) and others can be computed.

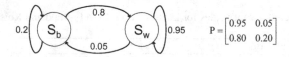

Fig. 1. Graph and transition probabilities matrix P for the Markov model of a simple software component

The concepts and formulas that Markov models are built on will be introduced in the next sections in detail, accompanied by examples and the characteristics that can be obtained from the models. In figure 1, the Markov model is accompanied by the matrix P that specifies its transition probabilities. For example, the probability to change from "working" state to "broken" state is 0.05.

The Markov model shown here is a so-called discrete-time Markov chain. It is assumed that the system's state only changes after a fixed time interval. For example,

I. Eusgeld, F.C. Freiling, and R. Reussner (Eds.): Dependability Metrics, LNCS 4909, pp. 48–55, 2008.

if the component state is determined every second and the component is definitely in working condition when started up ($t = 0$), the initial state probability vector $\mathbf{p_0}$ (here, $\mathbf{p_0} = \begin{pmatrix} 1 & 0 \end{pmatrix}$) can be used to start the second-after-second chain of states. By multiplying $\mathbf{p_0}$ with the matrix P, $\mathbf{p_1}$ is obtained, which corresponds to the component's state probabilities at time $t = 1$: $\mathbf{p_1} = \begin{pmatrix} 0.95 & 0.05 \end{pmatrix}$.

The above example has an important property, the *Markov property* which describes the situation where the probability to be in a particular state of a model at time $t + 1$ depends only on the state in which the model was at time t, as well as on the state transition probabilities (matrix P) associated with the model. This independence of past states (at time $t - 1, t - 2$ etc.) is sometimes referred to as *memorylessness* of a Markov model and has a large impact on the applicability of the model. The formal definition of the Markov property (not only for discrete time values as in the above example, but also for continuous time Markov models) will be given in the next sections.

A *Markov chain* consists of a set of discrete *states* and is in exactly one of these states at any point of time[1]. Markov chains are widely used, for example in queuing theory (cf. Sect. 9.2). The notion of a *chain* was chosen because the Markov chain is a stochastic process that "walks" from one state to *exactly* one state at transition time, allowing for a sorted representation of the chain's condition.

The transition probabilities characterise the Markov chain and allow for meaningful classification of both Markov chains and their single states. In some cases, the structure of the Markov model is unknown and must be reconstructed from data that has been collected empirically, for example in *Hidden Markov Models* (HMMs, see [323]).

We will start with the discussion of discrete-time Markov chains (DTMCs) in Sect. 8.2 and then generalise to continuous-time Markov chains (CTMCs) in Sect. 8.3, before presenting applications of Markov models for dependability analysis in Sect. 8.4. Markov Reward Models (MRMs) are treated separately in Sect 24.2 of Chap. 24.2.

8.2   Discrete-Time Markov Chains - DTMC

Overview

Formally, a discrete-time Markov chain (DTMC) is defined as a stochastic process with the *discrete* parameter space $T := \{0, 1, 2, \ldots\}$. The (discrete) state space I of a DTMC consists of random variables X_t with $t \in T$ ($X_0 = s_0$ is the starting state) and permits to state the Markov property for DTMCs as

$$P(X_n = s_n | X_0 = s_0, X_1 = s_1, \ldots, X_{n-1} = s_{n-1}) = P(X_n = s_n | X_{n-1} = s_{n-1})$$

From now on, a shorter notation for probability mass functions will be used:

$$p_{ij}(m, n) := P(X_n = j | X_m = i) \quad \text{and} \quad p_i(n) := P(X_n = i)$$

We will limit ourselves to *homogeneous* Markov chains: for them, the transition probability from state j at time m to state k at time n only depends on the "distance" $n - m$ between both states and is independent of actual values of m or n.

---

[1] The more general notion of *Markov processes* is not limited to discrete states but will not be considered here.

Formally, for homogeneous DTMCs, $p_{ij}(d) := p_{i,j}(t, t+d) \ \forall t \in T, d \geq 0$.
The above software component example is a homogeneous discrete time Markov chain, since the transition probabilities are independent of the time.

Using the homogeneous one-step transition probabilities $p_{ij}(1)$, it is straightforward to compute the probability of the chain $s_0, s_1, \ldots, s_n$: its probability is

$$p_{s_0} \cdot p_{s_0 s_1}(1) \cdot p_{s_1 s_2}(1) \cdot \ldots \cdot p_{s_{n-1} s_n}(1)$$

(where p_{s_0} is the probability to be in initial state s_0). The one-step transition probabilities are collected in the *transition probability matrix* $P := [p_{ij}(1)]$ for which $0 \leq p_{ij}(1) \leq 1$ and $\sum_{k \in I} p_{ij}(1) = 1$ hold, $\forall j \in I$. The graph in figure 1 is called the *state transition diagram*.

To obtain the n-step transition probabilities $p_{ij}(n)$ for any n other than 1, we define $p_{ij}(0)$ to be 1 if $i = j$ and 0 otherwise. Then, using known $p_{ij}(1)$, we can generalise to any n through the *Chapman-Kolmogorov equation* if the length n of a transition is split into two parts (of length l and m) and all possible states reached after l transitions are considered.

$p_{ij}(n)$ is then seen as the sum of probabilities of "ways" that pass through all possible states j after l transitions: with $l + m = n$, $l > 1$, $m > 1$,

$$p_{ik}(l + m) = \sum_{j} p_{ij}(l) p_{jk}(m)$$

It can be proved that the calculation of n-step transition probabilities can equivalently be done by obtaining the n-step stochastic matrix $P(n)$ from the one-step matrix P with the formula $P(n) = P^n = P \cdot P(n-1)$. If the probabilities for states $0, 1, \ldots$ at time t are collected into a vector $\mathbf{p}(t) := [p_0(t), p_1(t), \ldots]$, the formula to compute $\mathbf{p}(n)$ using the matrix P is

$$\mathbf{p}(n) = \mathbf{p}(0) \cdot P(n) = \mathbf{p}(0) \cdot P^n$$

For the software component example (which had $P = \begin{pmatrix} 0.95 & 0.05 \\ 0.80 & 0.20 \end{pmatrix}$

and $\mathbf{p}(0) = \begin{bmatrix} 1 & 0 \end{bmatrix}$), the computation of $\mathbf{p}(2)$ yields

$$\mathbf{p}(2) = \begin{bmatrix} 1 & 0 \end{bmatrix} \cdot \begin{pmatrix} 0.95 & 0.05 \\ 0.80 & 0.20 \end{pmatrix}^2 = \begin{bmatrix} 1 & 0 \end{bmatrix} \cdot \begin{pmatrix} 0.9425 & 0.0575 \\ 0.9200 & 0.0800 \end{pmatrix} = \begin{bmatrix} 0.9425 & 0.0575 \end{bmatrix}$$

State Classification

States are classified according to the number of visits to detect tendencies and specifics of a model. To illustrate the state classification with an appropriate example, we will extend our previous example with additional states, as shown in figure 2.

It is obvious that for the state S_i (where the component is initialised), the Markov process will not return to it, since no transitions to S_i exist. Such states of a DTMC are called *transient* or, equivalently, *nonrecurrent*. A state that cannot be left once a Markov process has entered it is called *absorbing* and can be recognised by $p_{ii}(1) = 1$ (there is no such state in figure 2).

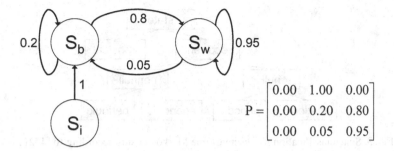

$$P = \begin{bmatrix} 0.00 & 1.00 & 0.00 \\ 0.00 & 0.20 & 0.80 \\ 0.00 & 0.05 & 0.95 \end{bmatrix}$$

Fig. 2. Graph and transition probabilities matrix P for an extended Markov model of a software component

States S_b ("broken") and S_w ("working") are *recurrent* since the process will eventually return to them with probability 1 after some unspecified time t. These two states *communicate* since there are directed paths from S_b to S_w and vice versa (in contrast, S_i and S_w do *not* communicate).

For recurrent states, one interesting measure is the mean recurrence time, which can be used for the *mean time to failure* (MTTF) metric. With $f_{ii}(n)$ as the probability that the process will return to state i after exactly n steps for the *first* time, the mean recurrence time μ_i for state i can be computed to be

$$\mu_i = \sum_{n=1}^{\infty} n f_{ii}(n)$$

Depending on the value of μ_i, a state is *recurrent nonnull/positive recurrent* if μ_i is finite and *recurrent null* if μ_i is infinite. It is easy to see that for any positive recurrent state i, $\exists K \ \forall k > K : \ f_{ii}(k) = 0$, $f_{ii}(K) > 0$, i.e. the state will *always* be revisited after K or less steps.

For any recurrent state, its *period*, defined as the greatest common divisor of all $n > 0$ for which $p_{ii}(n) > 0$, can be computed. If the period is greater than 1, the state is called *periodic*, and *aperiodic* otherwise. The states S_b and S_w are both aperiodic; state S_i is transient and thus neither aperiodic nor periodic. The overall state classification of discrete-time Markov chains as outlined in [472] is displayed in figure 3.

8.3 Continuous-Time Markov Chains (CTMC)

Mathematical Foundations

A Continuous-Time Markov Chain (CTMC) allows state changes at *any* instance of time, leading to continous parameter space $T := [0, \infty)$, but state space I remains *discrete* as in DTMCs. Reformulation of the Markov property for CTMC, given an increasing parameter sequence $0 \le t_0 < t_1 < \ldots < t_{n-1} < t_n$, yields the requirement that

$$P(X(t_n) = x_n | X(t_{n-1}) = x_{n-1}, \ldots, X(t_0) = x_0) =$$
$$= P(X(t_n) = x_n | X(t_{n-1}) = x_{n-1})$$

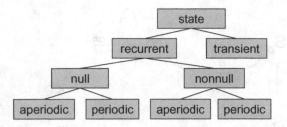

Fig. 3. State classification for discrete-time Markov chains according to [472]

As in the previous section, two structures completely define a Markov chain:

1. the vector $P(X_{t_0}) = \{k | k = 0, 1, 2, \ldots\}$ that contains the initial probabilities $P(X_{t_0} = k)$ for all states k at time t_0
2. the transition probabilities

$$p_{ij}(t, v) = P(X(v) = j | X(t) = i)$$

with $0 \leq t \leq v$ and the special cases $p_{ii}(t, t) = 1$ and $p_{ij}(t, t) = 0$ for $i \neq j$

Note that $\forall i,\ 0 \leq t \leq v$ the transition probabilities fulfill $\sum_{j \in I} p_{ij}(t, v) = 1$.

A CTMC is *homogeneous* with respect to time if for $p_{ij}(t, v)$, only the time difference $v - t$ matters, that is, if $\forall d > 0, p_{ij}(t, v) = p_{ij}(t + d, v + d)$. For a homogeneous CTMC and time difference (distance) τ, we define

$$\forall t \geq 0 : \ p_{ij}(\tau) := p_{ij}(t, t + \tau) = P(X(t + \tau) = j | X(t) = i)$$

The general probability to be in state j at a time t is defined as

$$\pi_j(t) := P(X(t) = j)$$

with

$$P(X(t) = j) = \sum_{i \in I} P(X(t) = j | X(v) = i) P(X(v) = i) = \sum_{i \in I} p_{ij}(o, t) \pi_i(0)$$

Since it is difficult to work with the dynamic *Chapman-Kolmogorov equation*

$$p_{ij}(t, v) = \sum_{k \in I} p_{ik}(t, u) p_{kj}(u, v) \ (0 \leq v < u < t)$$

the *rates of transitions for CTMC* are defined as follows: net rate out of state j at time t is

$$q_j(t) := q_{jj}(t) = -\frac{d}{dt} p_{jj}(v, t)|_{v=t} = \lim_{h \to 0} \frac{p_{jj}(t, t) - p_{jj}(t, t+h)}{h} = \lim_{h \to 0} \frac{1 - p_{jj}(t, t+h)}{h}$$

and the rate from state i to state j at time t (for $i \neq j$) is

$$q_{ij}(t) := \frac{d}{dt} p_{ij}(v, t)|_{v=t} = \lim_{h \to 0} \frac{p_{ij}(t, t) - p_{ij}(t, t+h)}{-h} = \lim_{h \to 0} \frac{p_{ij}(t, t+h)}{h}$$

$q_j(t)$ is the net rate out of state j at time t, while $q_{ij}(t)$ is the rate from state i to state j at time t. Over a series of transformations (cf. [472]), the *Kolmogorov Differential Equations* can be obtained (with $Q(t) := [q_{ij}(t)]$ and $q_{ii}(t) = -q_i(t)$):

$$\frac{dP(v,t)}{dt} = P(v,t)Q(t) \text{ and } \frac{dP(v,t)}{dv} = Q(t)P(v,t)$$

Rewriting this equations for a homogeneous CTMC, we obtain

$$\frac{dP(t)}{dt} = P(t)Q$$

and

$$\frac{d\pi(t)}{dt} - \pi(t)Q$$

The *(infinitesmal) generator matrix* $Q := [q_{ij}(t)]$ has the following properties: row sums are all equal to 1, $\forall i : q_{ii} \leq 0$ and the transition rates from state i to state j fulfill $\forall i \neq j, q_{ij} \geq 0$. For the discussion of semi-Markov processes as well as non-homogeneous CTMCs, we point to [472].

State Classification

While *recurrent null/non-null* and *transient* states have the same meaning in CTMCs as in DTMCs, a CMTC state i is *absorbing* if $\forall t \, \forall j \neq i$ holds $p_{ij}(t) = 0$. A CTMC is *irreducible* if $\forall i, j \, \exists t$ so that $p_{ij}(t) > 0$ (i.e., any state can be reached from any other state in a transition of suitable duration t with non-zero probability).

Steady-state values

$$\pi := \{\pi_j | j = 0, 1, 2, \ldots\}$$

of a CTMC are defined by

$$\pi_j := \lim_{t \to \infty} \pi_j(t)$$

and are subject to $\sum_j \pi_j = 1$ and to $\pi Q = 0$. An irreducible CTMC with all states being recurrent non-null will have *unique* π that do not depend on the initial probability vector; all states of a *finite* irreducible CTMC are recurrent non-null, so it is possible to compute the steady-state values for it.

Queues and Birth-Death Processes

Although the equations of continuous-time Markov chains look intimidating at first sight, they have a strong practical importance as the queuing theory is footed on them. We will introduce queues starting with the example from figure 4, and also briefly discuss *birth-death processes* which represent the abstract structures behind the queues.

The pictured queue shall have the properties that elements to it arrive one-by-one in a random manner and that there is only one "server position" where elements are processed on FCFS basis, after which the elements leave the queue. The elements arrive at the end of the queue with the *birth rate* λ; after being served, the elements leave the queue with the *death rate* μ. Equivalently, the *arrival times* are exponentially distributed

Fig. 4. A simple queue (M/M/1) as an example of a continous-time Markov chain

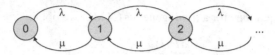

Fig. 5. The transition state diagram for the queue from figure 4

with mean $1/\lambda$ and the *service times* are exponentially distributed with mean $1/\mu$. In figure 5, the *transition state diagram* for this queue is pictured.

One of the quantities that a queuing model can help to determine the expected (average) number of elements in the system, $N(t)$, using the *traffic intensity* ρ

$$\rho := \lambda/\mu$$

of the queue. Considering the possible numbers k of elements in the system ($k \in [0, \infty)$, $k \in \mathbb{N}$), we need their probabilities π_k for weighting:

$$E[N] = \sum_{k=0}^{\infty} k\pi_k$$

Without citing the proof (which can be found in [472]), following formulas can be used if $\rho < 1$ (i.e. if the queue is *stable*) to compute the steady-state probabilities π_i for any state i:

$$\pi_0 = 1 - \frac{\lambda}{\mu} = 1 - \rho \quad \text{and (for } k \geq 1) \quad \pi_k = \left(\frac{\lambda}{\mu}\right)^k \pi_0 = \rho^k \pi_0 = \rho^k (1 - \rho)$$

As an example, consider a software component that compresses chunks of data with various sizes. The component is implemented as a single thread and sends/receives the data chunks asynchronously. The time between data chunks arrivals is exponentially distributed with mean 100ms ($= 1/\lambda$). Since the sizes of data chunks vary, the service time is also exponentially distributed with the mean 75ms ($= 1/\mu$). Thus, the traffic intensity ρ is $0.75 < 1$ and $\pi_0 = 0.25$, $\pi_1 = 0.1875$, $\pi_2 = 0.140625$ and so on.

Using ρ and given queue is in stable case, the mean and the variance of $N(t)$ can be computed without prior computation of all π_k (see [472]):

$$E[N] = \sum_{k=0}^{\infty} k\pi_k = \frac{\rho}{1 - \rho} \quad \text{and} \quad Var[N] = \frac{\rho}{(1 - \rho)^2}$$

For the above data compression example, $E[N] = 3$ and $Var[N] = 12$.

Another measure of interest in queues is the *response time* R, i.e. between the arrival of the element at the end of the queue and the time that element leaves the queue. To compute the mean of this random variable in the steady state case ($\rho < 1$), the *Little's formula* $E[N] = \lambda E[R]$ is used, as it creates the relation between the response time and the number of elements in the queue. Its interpretation is that the (mean) number of elements in the queue is the product of arrival rate and the (mean) response time. Using the above formula for $E[N]$,

$$E[R] = \sum_{k=0}^{\infty} \frac{k}{\lambda} \pi_k = \frac{1/\mu}{1-\rho}$$

can be derived. $\frac{1/\mu}{1-\rho}$ can be interpreted as the quotient of the (mean) service time and the probability of the queue to be empty. For the above example, $E[R] = 300$ms.

8.4 Markov Chains and Dependability Analysis

Markov chains will be used on several occasions throughout this volume. In Sect. 9.3, Markov process theory is used to calculate hardware availability through employment of continuous-time stochastic logic (CSL) and with possible application of model-checking algorithms.

In Sect. 9.4, assessing hardware reliability for complex, fault-tolerant systems with built-in redundancy is done, among other approaches, with Markov chains. Markov chains also permit to model systems that work if m or less out of n components have failed (with identical or distinct components as well as same or different failure/repair rates), and provide algorithms to compute the steady state probabilities of the parametrised Markov chains.

On the other hand, Markov chains can be used for modeling software reliability, especially for component-based systems (cf. Sect. 10.4). This approach is particularily suitable for reliability prediction during the design phase, even before a "black box" models of real components or software systems become available.

Markov models serve as the foundation for *Markov Reward Models* (MRMs), which are used in Sect. 24.2 to measure the effects of a system's performance degradation. This is done in a larger context of *performability*, i.e. the combination of performance and reliability and allows to *reward* the system for the time spent in states that representing readiness of the system.

Part II

Reliability Metrics

9 Hardware Reliability

Irene Eusgeld[1], Bernhard Fechner[2], Felix Salfner[3], Max Walter[4], Philipp Limbourg[6],
and Lijun Zhang[5]

[1] Swiss Federal Institute of Technology (ETH), Zurich, Switzerland
[2] University of Hagen, Germany
[3] Humboldt University Berlin, Germany
[4] Technische Universität München, Germany
[5] Saarland University, Germany
[6] University of Duisburg-Essen, Germany

Reliability is an important part of dependability. This chapter aims at supporting readers in the usage of the classical definitions, modelling and measures of (hardware) reliability metrics.

9.1 Introduction

In the IT field the term "fault tolerance" is often widely used as "reliability improvement". The question to be clarified is the relationship between reliability and fault tolerance. In a general sense *reliability* will be understood as ability of a component/system to function correctly over a specified period of time, mostly under predefined conditions. *Fault tolerance* is defined as the ability of the system to continue operation in the event of a failure. Fault tolerance means that a computer system or component is designed such that, in case a component fails, a backup component or backup procedure can immediately take its place with no loss of functionality. Reliability can be improved through fault tolerance. Metrics of "classical" reliability theory are well known and numerous. Metrics of fault tolerance are less common, e.g. number of tolerated faults, number of checkpoints, reconfiguration time, etc.

The most important method supporting fault tolerance/reliability is redundancy. *Redundancy* is duplication of components or repetition of operations to provide alternative functional channels in case of failure. Redundancy can be implemented in different ways: structural (hot and standby redundancy), temporal, functional, etc. Application of redundancy is always connected with an increase in cost and/or complexity as well as sometimes with synchronisation problems.

Predicting the system reliability by modelling during the design phase, and measuring the parameters of a real system are two completely different approaches. This chapter is sub-divided into five sections depending on the primary goal of the readers. The sections of this chapter are presented as set of references structured according to the various reliability metrics (RM).

An index is provided at the end of the book so that specific issues can be referenced directly.

The chapter is organised as follows:

- Sect 9.2 deals with the motivation on the application of reliability metrics. The reader should be able to define the reliability problem he/she is interested in.

I. Eusgeld, F.C. Freiling, and R. Reussner (Eds.): Dependability Metrics, LNCS 4909, pp. 59–103, 2008.

Depending on the goals the reliability measures will be chosen. In Sect. 9.2 the following problems are discussed: detecting design weaknesses and component failures that are critical to the proper functioning of a system, support in decision making in the case of alternative designs and implementations. Design modifications for an improvement of the system reliability are suggested. The readers interested in safety aspects as well as the readers interested in lifetime tests will find useful information in terms of RM in this section. Depending on the problem to be solved appropriate metrics are proposed which allow for an effective solution.

– Sect. 9.3 introduces definitions of terms to be used in the context of RM. Such widely used reliability metrics like availability, MTTR, MTTF, failure rate, repair rate, and more, are defined and basic formulas of Reliability Theory are given. The readers get also proposals when and how to use different distribution functions.

The terms reliability and availability are of special interest: the reader should be aware of both aspects, namely the qualitative and quantitative viewpoint. A qualitative definition of reliability is already given (see Sect. 9.2). As a metric reliability is the probability $R(t)$ that no failure will have occurred over a specified period of time. Accordingly, availability can be defined from the qualitative point of view as ability of the component/system to be in the operating state when required for use. From the quantitative point of view availability is a probability $A(t)$ of finding the component / system in an operational state at an arbitrary point in time. Some well-known types of availability are steady-state and time-dependent availability. Others are known as e.g. mission availability, overall availability etc. At the end of this section we discuss the logical characterisation of the estimation of availabilities.

– Sect. 9.4 gives an overview of necessary data to be collected for an estimation of RM. There are different ways to obtain data. The most helpful approach is to gather field data, including the measurement of real failure and repair time during operation.

Tests as wells as life time experiments allow for failure rate evaluation. The readers should be aware of the problem coming along with such experiments: data portability, real world conditions and so on. A physical model using empirical formulas can be applied, if the system structure is known. Another way to obtain missing data is expert judgement.

– Sect. 9.5 presents worthwhile methods to model a reliable system. In addition to state space methods like Markovian Chains, Stochastic Petri Nets and Stochastic Process Algebra, also structural models like Reliability Block Diagrams, Fault Trees and Reliability Graphs are described. In addition some special cases like inter-component dependencies, degraded states, failures with common causes, failures propagation etc., are considered. Necessary component data are specified.

In Sect. 9.5 the reader will be advised which model seems to be most suitable for his/her goals. Besides models this section introduces modelling support tools for solving practical reliability problems, including simulation-based tools and hybrid tools.

Assessment of the suitability of particular approaches is based on the research experience of the authors of proposals.

9.2   Objectives for Quantitative Evaluation: Why Do I Measure ?

The question imposed by the heading may not be answered entirely in this section. Reliability metrics may be used for an infinite number of different goals and questions. Yet this section tries to figure out the most common reasons.

Dependability metrics have gained a lot of importance in the technical practice. Current technical standards, such as the CENELEC EN 50126 / IEC 62278/79/80 [232, 233, 234] demand systematic "RAMS management" for rail systems starting with the specification of bounds on dependability metrics. "RAMS", a common abbreviation in technical reliability assessment is the abbreviation of "Reliability, Availability, Maintainability and Safety" and shows which goals are considered as important. While the first three may be primal contractual provisions, the fourth decides if the system may go on line at all.

Quite often, independent assessors such as the TÜV (Germany) or DNV (Norway) must be convinced that the specified requirements are fulfilled. Only after this step is passed, the authorities may approve the system operation (see e.g. Lovric [314]).

IEC 62308 [230] gives a broad overview of reasons for reliability prediction and reliability measurement. The listed methods may be grouped into four more or less fuzzy categories (see Fig. 1). System reliability modelling, higher-level modelling, requirement checking and actions.

System reliability modelling is the inclusion of the model output into another reliability model: We would like to assess the reliability of a higher-level system and thus need to assess the component reliability. System reliability predictions may be found in Sect. 9.5. Figure 1 lists e.g. Reliability Block Diagrams, Fault trees and availability models.

System modelling is a special case of the more general view of hierarchical modelling. Many other higher-level models may consider system reliability. Examples are e.g. Risk models, which model functions combining critical system failures together with their consequences (e.g. life loss) or Cost models (e.g. Life Cycle costs, LCC).

Of course, the first two groups are only means to the end (see chapter 6). The third group are evaluation purposes. Results may either be used to validate/verify that internal or external acceptance criteria are fulfilled. Or results may be used to find weak points and flaws in the design without formal requirements. Questions according to the GQM paradigm may e.g. be: Where are weak design points? Can the targeted MTTF be reached?

The fourth and final group are actions, which need reliability information as inputs. We have to consider a choice between different alternatives regarding several objectives, while at least one of them is the reliability of the system. This may contain the generation of maintenance or test plans, system redesign or calculation of an optimal number of spares. Most of this decision-making problems include another dimension, namely cost. If the number of alternatives is large, then the term "optimisation" is used. A popular branch in reliability engineering is the formulation and solution of such optimization problems. Perhaps the most important decision-making problems presented in literature are:

- Design of the system: How shall I build my system? Example: Where shall I put redundancy? [287, 337]

- Component selection: There is a set of different possible parts for each component of the system: What is the optimal combination? Which components must be improved? [102, 523, 529]
- Maintenance optimization: What is the best maintenance schedule to achieve high reliability with low cost? [141, 291, 339]
- Optimising the test programme: Which components shall be tested more intensive to guarantee high reliability (fulfil the requirements) with least effort.

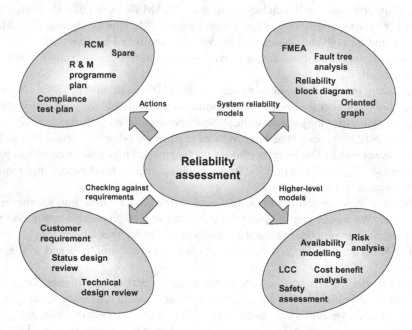

Fig. 1. Methods requiring a reliability assessment as input

Kochs and Petersen [281] describe a more detailed view on the reliability assessment process, which integrates assessment, decision-making and other factors to a cyclic model (Fig. 2). Thus, the dynamic aspect of changing models, data and goals is taken care of. Starting with the definition of preconditions, the core process consists of the modelling, calculation and assessment phase (review and utilisation of the results). Included into the modelling process is the environment of the system under consideration, which can not only influence the system itself, but also the modelling process (e.g. boundary conditions and acceptance values).

Another viewpoint of reliability modelling can be found in the British DEF Stan 00-42 [354]. In this document, reasons for reliability prediction in the product development process are treated. The statement is that the main reason for reliability modelling is the validation of the system according to acceptance criteria. This is defined as R&M (reliability and maintainability) case.

Definition 1 (R&M case [354]). *A reasoned, auditable argument created to support the contention that a defined system will satisfy the R&M requirements.*

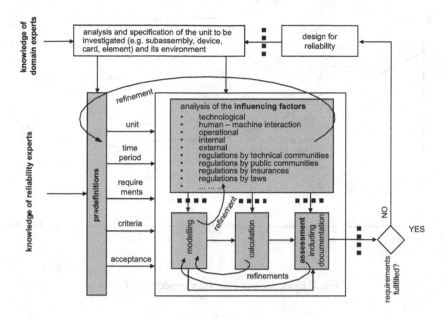

Fig. 2. Reliability framework [281]

All reliability models (simple, complex, qualitative, quantitative) thus may be considered as a "reasoned, auditable arguments" because they measure the reliability which can be compared to any threshold. As can be seen by this definition, reliability modelling has the purpose to demonstrate something: The ability of a system to match the reliability requirements given all evidence. This can be interpreted as the risk assessment perspective, as the risk of not achieving the reliability targets is measured. The most notable point of their position is the dynamic view of reliability prediction. Together with the R&M case comes the term "body of evidence", an entity which includes all necessary information and can be considered as both information about the input data and the model. This body of evidence is growing and shrinking over time (Fig. 3). We have to be aware that reliability models and accuracy grow over project time and system models may changes. Reliability growth analyses are examples of such dynamic techniques.

A similar approach has gained importance in the area of functional safety. As it is commonly known today, there is no absolute technical safety and each safety level may be improved a little more (with a corresponding effort). This raises the question which safety limit is adequate to be fulfilled by the manufacturer. The popular IEC 61508 [235] describes a risk-based approach to safety. Starting with hazard and risk analyses it is estimated how much effort has to be taken to reduce the risk to an acceptable level. This is quite a critical aspect, because it requires the definition of an "acceptable risk level".

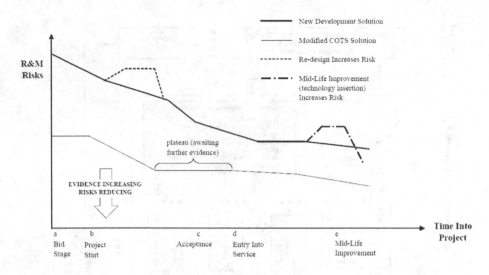

Fig. 3. Evidence in a reliability project [354]

Exemplary risks that may be analysed in this stage are:

– Railway: The train conductor is unobservant or suffers from a medical emergency. As a consequence, signals are ignored and collisions or derailings may occur.
– Automobile: The steering mechanism fails and a collision with oncoming traffic may occur.

Here, dependability metrics come into action. What is the reliability of a train conductor? What is the expected reliability of a system using a certain technology? How likely is the prevention / avoidance of a harmful event. In this stage, statistics and experiences from similar systems are utilised to estimate these parameters (see e.g. of Transportation [382]). The risk may e.g. be expressed in F/n curves (for examples of risk assessment and risk acceptance criteria see Lovric [317, 318]).

Based on an acceptable risk threshold the maximal risk contributed by each subsystem can be assessed. According to IEC 61508 one out of four "Safety Integrity Levels" (SIL) may be assigned. From SIL 1 (low risk) to SIL 4 (very high risk). The SIL defines which actions against random (hardware) and systematic failures have to be taken. To prevent the later, quality assurance measures are used. The possibility of the quantification of systematic failures is controversial and most often not required (but see Authority [24]). For preventing random faults, it is not sufficient to implement quality assurance or fault-tolerance measures. A quantitative demonstration that the requirements are fulfilled is necessary. Such quantitative assessments are done using the methods in Sect. 9.5 and Lovric [316]. In this stage, experimental measures such as fault injection (Sect. 9.4 and [315]) are utilised to validate the fault tolerance concept.

Many sectoral adaptions of the IEC 61508 have emerged or will emerge in the near future. For the automotive industry, this will be the ISO 26262 [164]. Other variants are [24, 167, 168, 420].

Quantitative reliability assessment of electronic components are since long state-of-the-art, supported by widely accepted standards and tools [231, 446]. These allow the prediction of reliability without actual field data. Being subsequently updated, they are much nearer to the "truth" than ancient "notorious" standards such as DoD [127].

In mechanics and hydraulics, this successful strategy has started to become increasingly popular and quantitative standards supersede the old "qualitative" philosophy as in für Normung e.V [168].

Based on these predictions, failure modes may be quantified to predict safety metrics such as Safe Failure Fraction (SFF), Diagnostics Coverage (DC), Probability of (dangerous) Failure on Demand (PFD) and Probability of (dangerous) Failures per Hour (PFH).

9.3   Common Measures and Metrics: What Do I Measure?

We will first review very briefly terms to be used in the context of Reliability Metrics. Subsequently we will introduce a particular class of distribution functions. We assume that the readers are familiar with probability theory (theory of random events) [185].

In the context of reliability metrics we are generally interested in nonnegative continuous random variables, in particular T (typically lifetime of the component). Then $F(t)$ is called the distribution function of T and is the probability that the component has failed with in time interval $[0, t]$. From the point of view of reliability theory, $F(t)$ is the unreliability (probability of failure) and is the complement of the reliability $R(t)$ (the definition of reliability see Sect. 9.1).

$$F(t) = 1 - R(t)$$

Its derivative $f(t) = dF(t)/dt$ is called the failure density function of t, which has the following properties:

$$\int_0^\infty f(t)\, dt = 1, \qquad F(t) = \int_0^t f(t)\, dt, \qquad \frac{dR}{dt} = -f(t)$$

The expectation value or mean of a random variable T is defined by

$$E(T) = \int_0^\infty t f(t)\, dt$$

and is called *mean lifetime*. When $R(t)$ is known, $E(T)$ can be calculated as follows:

$$E(T) = \int_0^\infty R(t)\, dt$$

The *Failure rate* (denoted by λ, also called hazard rate) can be estimated when $R(t)$ and $f(t)$ are known by

$$\lambda(t) = \frac{f(t)}{R(t)}$$

The failure rate can be interpreted as the conditional probability of a failure between t and Δt (with probability $f(t)\Delta t$) conditioned on the probability of surviving the first t units of time. The most simplified interpretation of $\lambda(t)$ is a mean frequency of failures.

The most simplified interpretation of the *repair rate* $\mu(t)$ is a mean frequency of repairs (renewal). The repair rate can be estimated analog to failure rate.

Assuming that $\lambda(t)$ is given, the reliability can be estimated from the equation

$$R(t) = \frac{1}{e^{\int_0^t \lambda(x)\,dx}}$$

Conditional reliability $R(t|t_1)$ is the probability of surviving $t > t_1$ units of time, under the condition that the component has already survived t_1 time units:

$$R(t|t_1) = \frac{R(t)}{R(t_1)} = \frac{1}{e^{\int_{t_1}^t \lambda(x)\,dx}}$$

Some Continuous Distribution Functions

We now define some commonly used distribution functions. The most commonly used distribution function is the exponential distribution.

Exponential distribution: Parameter λ, $\lambda > 0$
  Failure density function:
$$f(t) = \lambda e^{-\lambda t}$$

Reliability:
$$R(t) = e^{-\lambda t}$$

Mean lifetime:
$$E = \frac{1}{\lambda}$$

Failure rate (constant):
$$\lambda(t) = \lambda$$

Depending on the goals of the modelling, one of the following functions can be chosen.

Weibull distribution: Parameters $\alpha, \beta, \alpha > 0, \beta > 0$.
  The Weibull distribution can approximate a normal distribution ($\beta \approx 3.44$) and an exponential distribution ($\beta = 1$).
  Failure density function:
$$f(t) = \frac{\beta}{\alpha} t^{\beta-1} e^{-\frac{1}{\alpha} t^\beta}$$

Reliability:
$$R(t) = e^{-\frac{1}{\alpha} t^\beta}$$

Mean lifetime:
$$E = \alpha^{\frac{1}{\beta}} \Gamma\left(\frac{1}{\beta} + 1\right)$$

Some Γ values:

β	$\Gamma(\frac{1}{\beta}+1)$	β	$\Gamma(\frac{1}{\beta}+1)$	β	$\Gamma(\frac{1}{\beta}+1)$
0.5	2.000	2.0	0.886	3.5	0.940
1.0	1.000	2.5	0.887	4.0	0.906
1.5	0.903	3.0	0.893	4.5	0.913

Failure rate:

$$\lambda(t) = \frac{\beta}{\alpha}t^{\beta-1}$$

Normal distribution: Parameters $\mu, \sigma, \mu \gg 0, \sigma > 0$.
Failure density function:

$$f(t) = \frac{1}{\sigma\sqrt{2\pi}}e^{\frac{-(t-\mu)^2}{2\sigma^2}}$$

Reliability:

$$R(t) = \int_t^\infty \frac{1}{\sigma\sqrt{2\pi}}e^{\frac{-(t-\mu)^2}{2\sigma^2}}$$

Using $x = \frac{t-\mu}{\sigma}$:

x	$R(t)$	x	$R(t)$	x	$R(t)$
0.00	0.5000	0.75	0.2266	2.00	0.0228
0.25	0.4013	1.00	0.1587	2.50	0.0062
0.50	0.3085	1.50	0.0668	3.00	0.0014

Mean lifetime:

$$E = \mu$$

Failure rate:

$$\lambda(t) = \frac{f(t)}{R(t)}$$

Rectangle (uniform) distribution: Parameters $a, b, 0 \le a < b$.
The following formulas are applicable only in case $t \in [a, b]$.
Failure density function (constant):

$$f(t) = \frac{1}{b-a}$$

Reliability:

$$R(t) = \frac{b-t}{b-a}$$

Mean lifetime:

$$E = \frac{a+b}{2}$$

Failure rate:

$$\lambda(t) = \frac{1}{b-t}$$

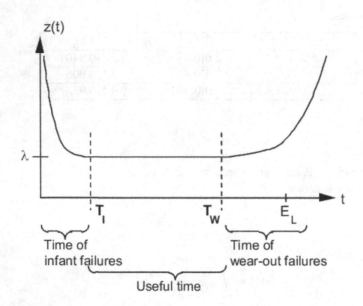

Fig. 4. Typical electronic component failure rate as a function of time (age)

The reader interested in learning more on distribution functions can be referred to [54, 185, 472].

We summarize some assessments on the suitability of particular distribution functions:

An exponential distribution can be applied when the failure rate is constant. Assumption: The component does not age. This distribution describes the component behaviour in the useful stage of lifetime (the middle phase of the "bath-tub curve", which describes the graph of the behaviour of the failure rate as a function of time (see Fig. 4).

When the failure rate is monotone decreasing (the first phase of the "bath-tub curve"), a *Weibull distribution* with $\beta < 1$ can be assumed. A Weibull distribution with $\beta > 1$ describes a monotone increasing failure rate (the last phase of the "bath-tub curve"). This distribution is also suitable for the modelling of repair time.

A *Normal distribution* can be recommended as well for lifetime modelling as for repair time modelling.

A *rectangle distribution* describes the wear-out process in the last phase of the "bath curve".

The choice of the distribution function is based on the field or test data (cf. Sect. 9.4), if available.

MTTF and MTTR

For calculating the steady-state availability two important reliability metrics must be also defined:

MTTF: For non repairable systems, the *mean time to failure*, abbreviated as MTTF, is the same as the *mean lifetime*. For repairable systems, MTTF can be thought of as the average time between a renewal point and the next following failure point. Particularly, if we assume that after each repair, the system is as good as new, i.e., with the same failure rate as before, then, for the random variable T, MTTF is equal to the *mean lifetime*:

$$MTTF = \int_0^\infty R(t)\, dt$$

MTTR: The *mean time to repair*, abbreviated as MTTR, is the mean of the repair time of a system. Let τ denote the positive random variable for the repair time with distribution function $G(t)$ and density function $g(t)$. The MTTR can be derived as follows:

$$MTTR = \int_0^\infty xg(x)\, dx = \int_0^\infty \int_0^x g(x)\, dt dx$$
$$= \int_0^\infty \int_t^\infty g(x)\, dx dt = \int_0^\infty (1 - G(t))\, dt$$

Availability

Instantaneous Availability: We assume familiarity with the renewal density function of repairable systems [58, pages 413–415]. We let $d(t)$ denote the renewal density function of the component at time t which can be calculated from the failure density function $f(t)$. Intuitively, for small h, $d(t)h$ denote the probability that a repair or a restore occurred in $(t, t + h]$.

The *instantaneous availability* (or *point availability*) [58, 472] $A(t)$ of a component is defined as the probability of finding it operating at time t. Considering that the component is new at $t = 0$, then:

$$A(t) = P\{\text{ component is up at } t \mid \text{component is new at } t = 0\}$$

It can be computed using the following equation:

$$A(t) = R(t) + \int_0^t R(t - x)d(x)\, dx$$

The first term is the probability that the component has not failed from the beginning. In the second term, $d(x)dx$ is the probability that the last repair occurred in time $(x, x + dx]$, and $R(t - x)$ guarantees that no further failure occurs in $(x, t]$. Note that these two events are mutual exclusive.

Steady-state Availability: Quite often we are interested in the equilibrium behaviour of the system. For this purpose we define the *steady-state availability* (or *limiting availability*) A as the limiting value of $A(t)$ as t approaches ∞. This measure is usually nonzero in contrast with the limiting reliability which is always zero. For systems provided MTTF and MTTR, A calculates to [472]

$$\frac{MTTF}{MTTF + MTTR}.$$

If we assume that we have a constant failure rate λ and repair rate μ (exponential distribution), we get $MTTF = \frac{1}{\lambda}$ and $MTTR = \frac{1}{\mu}$ respectively. Hence, $A = \frac{\mu}{\lambda+\mu}$.

Interval Availability: If we are interested in the expected fraction of time the component is up in a given interval $I = [t_1, t_2]$, we can use the *interval availability* (or *average availability*), which is defined by:

$$A_I(t) = \int_{t_1}^{t_2} A(x) \, dx$$

Joint availability: Assume that $t, t' > 0$ and $t \neq t'$. The joint availability $A(t, t')$ of a component asserts the probability that the component is up at time point t and t'. Formally,

$$A(t, t') = P(\text{component is up at } t \text{ and at } t' \mid \text{component is new at } 0)$$

Without loss of generality, we assume that $t < t'$. If the failure rate is constant, the two events "component is up at time t" and "component is up at time t'" are independent, and thus,

$$A(t, t') = A(t)A(t' - t)$$

Note that in addition to the above availabilities, there are several other kinds of availability measures like *Mission Availability* or *Workmission Availability* [58].

We can divide the systems into repairable and non repairable parts [261]. If a system is non repairable, it is not accessible after a single failure. On the contrary, if a system is repairable, it is continuously available for repair in case of failures.

For non repairable systems, the instantaneous availability reduces to the reliability. The steady-state availability is equal to zero, since we can assume $MTTR$ to be infinity. For repairable systems, to simplify the calculation of point availability, one assumes usually that the repaired part is as good as new after repair. This assumption is valid if we have constant failure rates. For more details, we refer to [58].

On the logical characterisation of the availability: If the failure rate and the repair rate are constant, Markov process theories can be applied to analyse measures of interests, including availabilities. Provided the Markov process for the systems, one can specify some measure constraints of interests using the continuous-time stochastic logic (CSL) [30, 33, 211]. Those properties can be verified automatically against the model, using the model checking techniques. Now we briefly review the definitions of continuous time Markov chains (CTMCs), the logic CSL, and how to specify properties, like availability measures, using CSL over CTMCs. For more detail, we refer to [33].

Let AP be a fixed, finite set of atomic propositions. We consider a CTMC (cf. Sect. 8) as a finite transition system (S, R, L) where S is a set of states, $R : S \times S \to \mathbf{R}_+$ is the rate matrix and $L : S \to 2^{AP}$ is the labelling function which assigns every state s a set of labels $L(s)$ which are valid in s.

For example, we consider the CTMC of the 2-out-of-3:G-system presented in Figure 5 (the same as the one in Figure 12 of subsection 9.5). The set of states S is given by $\{0, 1, 2, 3\}$. The rate matrix R is depicted on the edges, for example, $R(0, 1) = 3\lambda$. In

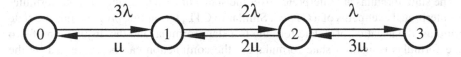

Fig. 5. Markov chain of the 2-out-of-3:G-system

state $i \in S$, i components of the system are failed. Let the atomic propositions up and $down$ denote that the system works or not respectively. Then, $L(0) = L(1) = \{up\}$, i.e., the states 0 and 1 satisfy the atomic proposition up. Similarly, $L(2) = L(3) = \{down\}$, i.e., the states 2 and 3 satisfy the atomic proposition $down$.

If $R(s, s') > 0$ for $s, s' \in S$, the transition from s to s' is enabled with probability $1 - e^{-\lambda \cdot t}$ with the next t time units provided that the system is in state s. If $R(s, s') > 0$ for more than one state s', a race between all of the outgoing transitions exists. More precisely, the probability that the transition from s to s' is taken before time t is given by $\frac{R(s,s')}{E(s)}(1 - e^{-E(s)\cdot t})$ where $E(s) = \sum_{s' \in S} R(s, s')$.

Given a sequence of states $s_i \in S$ of a CTMC and time points $t_i > 0$ for $i \geq 0$, let σ denote a path $s_0, t_0, s_1, t_1, \ldots$ with $R(s_i, s_{i+1}) > 0$ for all $i \geq 0$ in the CTMC, which indicates that the CTMC starts at state s_0, spends there t_0 time unit, and transits to state s_1, then spends there t_1 time unit etc. We use $\sigma@t$ to denote the state in path σ at time t. Formally, it denotes the state s_i where i is the smallest index such that $t \leq \sum_{j=1}^{i} t_i$. (Note that we consider here only infinite paths but the definition of $\sigma@t$ can be easily extended for finite paths.) Let $I_0, I_1, \ldots$ denote nonempty intervals on the nonnegative real line, and let $C(s_0, I_0, \ldots, s_{k-1}, I_{k-1}, s_k)$ denote the cylinder set consisting of all paths

$$\{\sigma = s_0, t_0, s_1, t_1 \ldots, s_k, \ldots \mid t_i \in I_i \text{ for } i = 0, 1, \ldots k\}$$

The cylinder sets induce the unique probability measure Pr on the set of paths, defined by: $\Pr(C(s_0)) = 1$, and for $k \geq 0$:

$$\Pr(C(s_0, I_0, \ldots, s_k, I_k, s')) = \Pr(C(s_0, I_0, \ldots, s_k))$$
$$\cdot \frac{R(s_k, s')}{E(s_k)} \cdot \left(e^{-E(s_k)\cdot a} - e^{-E(s_k)\cdot b}\right)$$

where $a = \inf I_k$ and $b = \sup I_k$.

CSL is a branching-time temporal logic which extends CTL [143] (Computational Tree Logic) with two probabilistic operators that refer to the steady state (S) and transient behaviour (P) of the system. The steady-state operator provides the probability of being in a state in equilibrium, whereas the transient operator gives the probability of the occurrence of set of paths in the CTMCs. The syntax of CSL formulas over the set of atomic propositions AP is is defined by:

state formulas: $\quad \Phi := a \mid \neg \Phi \mid \Phi \vee \Phi \mid S_{\geq p}(\Phi) \mid P_{\geq p}(\phi)$

path formulas: $\quad \phi := X^I \Phi \mid \Phi U^I \Phi$

where $a \in AP$, $p \in [0, 1]$ and I is an interval on the positive real line. The operator $\geq$ can be replaced by other compare operators.

The state formulas are interpreted over the states of a CTMC, and the path formulas are interpreted over paths of a CTMC. Similar to CTL, the atomic propositions are state formulas, the negation of a state formula is a state formula, and the disjunction of two state formulas is again a state formula. As the conjunction can be expressed by the negation and disjunction, i.e., $\Phi_1 \wedge \Phi_2 \equiv \neg(\neg\Phi_1 \vee \neg\Phi_2)$, the conjunction of two state formulas is also a state formula.

The state $s \in S$ satisfies the atomic proposition a if $a \in L(s)$, satisfies the formula $\neg\Phi$ if s not satisfies Φ. s satisfies the disjunction $\Phi_1 \vee \Phi_2$ if it satisfies Φ_1 or Φ_2. The state formula $\mathcal{S}_{\geq p}(\Phi)$ is true in a state s if the sum of the equilibrium probability to be in Φ-states meets the bound $\geq p$. More precisely, s satisfies $\mathcal{S}_{\geq p}(\Phi)$ if the following holds:

$$\lim_{t \to \infty} \Pr\{\sigma \mid \sigma@t \in Sat(\Phi)\} \geq p$$

where $Sat(\Phi)$ is the set of states satisfying Φ which can be calculated recursively. If we categorise the states into *up* and *down* states, i.e, $AP = \{up, down\}$, the steady-state availability can be simply expressed by $\mathcal{S}_{\geq p}(up)$. We note here that a CSL formula expresses a measure constraint, not the measure itself.

The state formula $\mathcal{P}_{\geq p}(\phi)$ is satisfied by the state s if $\Pr\{\sigma \mid \sigma \text{ satisfies } \phi\} \geq p$, i.e., the probability measure of the set of paths satisfying the path formula ϕ is greater equal than p. The interval I can be considered as a time interval. The path $\sigma = s_0, t_0, s_1, t_1, \ldots$ satisfies the next path formula $X^I \Phi$ if the first transition (s_0, s_1) occurs at time point inside I, i.e. $t_0 \in I$, and the second state (s_1) satisfies Φ. The path σ satisfies the until path formula $\Phi \mathcal{U}^I \Psi$ if there exists $t \in I$ such that $\sigma@t$ satisfies Ψ and for all $0 \leq t' < t$, $\sigma@t'$ satisfies Φ. The usual *eventually* and *henceforth* path formulas can be extended by $\diamond^I \Phi = true\mathcal{U}^I \Phi$ and $\square^I = \neg \diamond^I \neg\Phi$ respectively. Using the *eventually* path formula, the instantaneous availability at time t can be expressed by $\mathcal{P}_{\geq p}(\diamond^{[t,t]} up)$ where $I = [t,t]$ in this case. The time interval $[t,t]$ is restricted to a point t, which indicates that a up state is reached at time t, what happened earlier is of no importance.

To express the interval availability, we need the *henceforth* operator. Let $0 \leq t_1 \leq t_2$, the formula $\mathcal{P}_{\geq p}(\square^{[t_1,t_2]} up)$ indicates that for all time points in $t \in [t_1, t_2]$, the system must be in a up state. Hence, this formula corresponds the interval availability.

The *conditional instantaneous availability* at time t is simply $\mathcal{P}_{\geq p}(\Phi\mathcal{U}^{[t,t]} up)$, where Φ is a state formula. $\mathcal{U}$ is the usual until operator which indicates that Φ shall be always true before time t. A path in the CTMC satisfies the path formula $\Phi\mathcal{U}^{[t,t]} up$ if it is in a up state at time t, and all time point before t Φ is satisfied.

Using nested $\mathcal{P}$ and $\mathcal{S}$ operators more complicated properties can be expressed. The property $\mathcal{S}_{\geq p}(\mathcal{P}_{\geq p'}(\square^{[t_1,t_2]} up))$ is the steady-state interval availability, which is true in those states such that in the equilibrium with probability at least p, the probability that the system is available in the time interval $[t_1, t_2]$ is at least p'.

With the logic CSL, we are not able to express properties related to joint availability. Since for that we need to take the conjunction of two path formulas of the form $\diamond^{[t,t]} up$ and $\diamond^{[t',t']} up$. But $\diamond^{[t,t]} up \wedge \diamond^{[t',t']} up$ is not a valid path formula because of the definition of CSL path formulas.

If the availability properties can be specified using CSL formulas, the model checking algorithm [30, 33] can be applied to verify these properties automatically.

9.4 Techniques for Measurement: What Data Is Necessary?

Field Data

To gather field data is a very difficult task, since it is collected by observing parts failing while operating. If a part is well designed, dependent on the fault rate, it is likely to have a long life time. This leads to a long time for failures to occur and thus any useful information concerning part reliability. Therefore, there are relatively few field-data sources. The economic requirements of an industry affect prediction models, and consequently the reported field data for several reasons:

- There are few customers who need a generic field data source and the collection of field data is costly.
- Since the error prediction models look for different corrective factors (such as component placement), the gathered field data will focus on those factors and ignore others.

The EPRD (Electronic Parts Reliability Data) [406] and NPRD (Non-Electronic Parts Reliability Data) [407] offer a wide and very detailed variety of field data for electrical and mechanical parts. *NPRD-95* and [377] are data collections of non-electronic part reliability data. The EPRD-97 is unclear concerning the time interval on a part-by-part basis. The engineers are encouraged to use the in-depth data whenever possible, instead of using the average values. Error prediction rates are intended as a complement for a safety minded design, not as a substitute.

VZAP95 [408] contains electrostatic discharge (ESD) susceptibility data for 22,000 devices, including microcircuits, discrete semiconductors and resistors. A detailed section contains the commercial part number, device description, manufacturer, ESD classification (per MIL-STD-1686C [124] and MIL-STD-883F method 3015.7 [131]), date code, data source information, resistance and capacitance used in the discharge circuit, failure voltage, pin combination, failure criteria, and the version of method 3015 used. An interpretation of data and profiles of susceptibility levels for numerous device types and technologies is included.

The *IAEA-TECDOC-508* [226] offers a survey of ranges of component reliability data to use in probabilistic safety assessment. It contains failure rates and availability data for several hundred different types of non-electronic components. Among the component groups are battery, bus, diesel generator, inverter, motor, pump, rectifier, relay, switch, transformer, transmitter and valve.

The *Offshore REliability DAtabase (OREDA) [11]* is a project organization sponsored by several international oil companies. Reliability data is collected by the participating companies. OREDA has established a comprehensive database with reliability and maintenance data for exploration and production equipment from a wide variety of geographic areas, installations, equipment types and operating conditions. Offshore sub-sea and topside equipment are primarily covered, but onshore equipment is also included.

Physical Models

Error prediction models provide average system lifetime estimations and serve as a starting point for determining an expected (realistic) lifespan of a system. As described in the previous section, error prediction needs field data on failure rates. Prediction models depend on this data for several reasons:

- Prediction formulae are derived from field data and rely on observed lifetime data. Without some idea of the natural lifespans of the components, estimating their lifetime is meaningless.
- Engineers building new components based on components with known failure rates use existing field data in conjunction with their derived prediction models to make an estimate.

As the collection of field, prediction models are usually driven by the concerns of an industry. Safety standards used by the military are not necessarily appropriate for other industries, where models of use and the consequences of failure are radically different. E.g. military or aerospace applications stress reliability over long periods (months or years), while automotive reliability is based on an estimate of 400 hours of use per year. Thus, most data sources have some bias. Although the individual formulae describing the failure rate are quite different among the various reliability analysis handbooks, they have several aspects in common. One of the most characteristic parts of many models is the relation between effective device temperature and failure rate. These models use thermal stresses in a form related to the Arrhenius Law

$$k = Ae^{-E_{act}/RT}$$

which describes the temperature dependence from the reaction speed constant k. The fraction of collisions with proper orientation is represented by A. The fraction of collisions produced with activation energy in J/mol E_{act} is represented by

$$e^{-E_{act}/RT}.$$

$R = 8.314 J/molK$ is the gas constant, and T is the temperature in Kelvin. Activation energies used in this expression are often very different for similar components. Most other influence factors are modeled in the form of acceleration factors. The acceleration factors are often presented in the form of tables divided in classes. These classification tables are mostly based on practical experience and do not use an underlying physical model. The majority of the acceleration factors is either related to the effective device temperature, the device structure or is environment bound.

To be able to directly calculate and predict the reliability of a system, field data has been integrated in some of the following handbooks.

MIL-HDBK-217 [127]: The basis for error prediction models is the MIL-HDBK-217, listing various error prediction models for different systems. It is being developed since the late 1940's and periodically updated since. The handbook contains two basic methods of reliability prediction:

1. Part Count Analysis (PCA) and
2. Part Stress Analysis (PSA).

PCA only requires part quantities, quality levels, estimated values and the application environment, making it less accurate but more useful during the early development phase. The overall reliability is given by

$$\lambda = \sum_{i=1}^{n} N_i \lambda_i \pi_{Q_i}$$

where n is the number of part categories, N_i is the quantity of the i-th part, λ_i is the failure rate of the i-th part and Q_i is the quality factor for the i-th part. If the equipment consists of parts operating in more than one environment, the equation is applied to each portion of the equipment that is operating in a distinct environment. The sum of the failure rates of all environments represents the overall equipment failure rate.

PSA requires greater amount of information (calculated or measured values) and is used later in the development phase. A failure rate formula is computed by $\lambda_p = \lambda_b \pi_e \pi_q ...$, where λ_p is the part failure rate, λ_b the base failure rate which is dependent on temperature and applied stress. $\pi_e \pi_q ...$ are acceleration factors for the intended environmental conditions (π_e), the quality acceleration factor (π_q) and other parameters that will affect the part reliability. Other acceleration factors are modeled in terms of acceleration factors π. The data used to model acceleration factors is mostly obtained from the manufacturer and field data. Using this method, it is possible to model the effects of using a component under certain environmental conditions and the effect of using certain methods of component quality screening, etc.

New models have been developed by using the MIL-217 formulae, usually by applying the same form but introducing new correction factors. As close derivations to the MIL-217, CHINA299B based on GJB/z 299B, developed for the Chinese military, [49], [397], [445] and [466] can be mentioned.

The SAE-Model [55]: The SAE-Model is a reliability prediction model from the Society of Automotive Engineers (SAE). It is the standard prediction model for the automotive industry, based on equations similar to those in MIL-217 and provides insights into why the SAE would need a model distinct from the MIL-217 specification. The main difference is semantic: the modifying factors for a part are based on issues specific to the automotive industry. The failure rate can be calculated with $\lambda_p = \lambda_b \prod_{i=1}^{b} \pi_i$, where λ_p is the predicted failure rate, λ_p is the base failure rate for the component, and π_i are various modifying factors, such as component composition, ambient temperature and location in the vehicle. In [495] the model developed by [55] was reformulated and refined with the help of additional empirical evidence.

Telcordia SR-332 [465]/Bellcore: The Telcordia standard TR-332/SR-332 was developed by Telcordia Technologies Inc. It originated from the Bellcore standard developed by AT&T Bell Laboratories. Bell Labs modified the MIL-HDBK-217 equations to better fit their field, focusing on equipment for the telecommunications industry.

The most recent version of the SR-332 is issue 1, published May 2001. The second issue is available since March 2006. The basis of the Telcordia math models for devices is referred to as *Black Box Technique*. This parts count method defines the black box (BB) steady-state failure rate $\lambda_{BB} = \lambda_g \pi_q \pi_s \pi_t$, for different device types, where λ_g is the generic steady-state failure rate for the particular device, π_q the quality, π_s the electrical stress and π_t the temperature factor. The inputs contained in the Telcordia standard were obtained from statistical data collected over several years. For environments where temperature and electrical stress are unknown, Telcordia recommends using a value of 1 for π_s and π_t, assuming the electrical stress to be at 50% of the rated value and the temperature to be 40° C. The steady-state device failure rate, λ_{SS}, considers an adjustment to the black box failure rate depending upon the availability of laboratory and field data and device burn-in. For the simplest case where no data is available, it is assumed that $\lambda_{SS} = \lambda_{BB}$. In the Telcordia standard, the parts count steady-state failure rate for units is

$$\lambda_{PC} = \pi_e \sum_{i=1}^{n} N_i \lambda_{SS_i}$$

where λ_{SS_i} is the steady-state device failure rate of device i, π_e the environmental factor, N_i the quantity of device type i and n the number of device types in the unit. For the simplest case where no data is available, it is assumed that $\lambda_{SS} = \lambda_{PC}$. The system-level failure rate $\lambda_{SYS} = \sum_{j=1}^{M} \lambda_{SS_i}$ is the sum of all failure rates of the units contained in a system. The first-year multiplier, π_{FY} is defined on all levels (device/ unit/ system) as the ratio of the failure rate in the first year of operation to λ_{SS_i}. π_{FY} can be used to estimate the failure rate of the concerned items during the infant mortality period. For devices, the first-year multiplier calculation depends on burn-in time, device stress and burn-in temperature at device, unit, and system level. First-year multipliers for units and the system are calculated as weighted averages of the first-year multipliers at device and unit levels, respectively.

BT-HRD-4 [75]: The British Telecom Handbook of Reliability Data (BT-HRD-4) contains an approach quite similar to the MIL-HDBK-217. It replaces the term Part Stress Analysis used in MIL-HDBK-217 by *Part Stress Count Analysis*. Failure rates are calculated by formulae in the form: $\lambda_p = \lambda_b \pi_t \pi_q \pi_e$, where λ_p is the part failure rate, λ_b the base failure rate, π_t the thermal acceleration factor, π_q the quality correction factor and π_e the environmental acceleration factor. For most components λ_b is used as a constant which is independent from external stress. Table 1 shows the most common BT-HRD-4 parameters with their meaning, influence factors and origin.

The BT-HRD-4 is less detailed than the MIL-HDBK-217. The MIL handbook covers a wider range of environmental and application influence factors compared to the British Telecom handbook covering only equipment for telecommunication purposes. The next version of the HRD-4, the HRD-5 is based on the former RDF 2000 standard, CNET 93 [118].

IEC-62380 [231]/ RDF 2000/ CNET93/ RDF 93: RDF 2000 (UTE C 80-810) is a French Telecom standard that was developed by the Union Technique de l'Électricité

Table 1. BT-HRD-4 Parameter Overview

Param.	Description	Influence factors	Source
All parts			
π_e	Environmental Acceleration Factor	Environment	Heuristic
π_q	Quality correction factor	Component screening	Heuristic
Integrated circuits			
λ_b	Base failure rate, depending on number of bits/gates	Device structure	Heuristic
π_t	Thermal Acceleration Factor	Thermal, device structure	Arrhenius, Heuristic
Discrete semiconductors and passive components			
λ_b	Base failure rate	Device structure	Heuristic

(UTE). The previous version of RDF 2000 is referred to as CNET 93 [118]. CNET 93 itself was formerly known as RDF 93. It is a more comprehensive model similar to MIL-HDBK-217, providing a detailed stress analysis. RDF 2000 provides a unique approach to failure rate predictions without parts count prediction. The IEC 62380 TR edition 1 (formerly known as UTE C 80-810) is based on RDF 2000. Component failure is defined in terms of an empirical expression containing a base failure rate multiplied by factors influenced by mission profiles. It contains thermal behavior and steady-stress system modeling. The failure rate of the system is determined by summing all component failure rates.

Other Models: The *IEEE STD 493-1997 (Gold Book)* [134] is the IEEE recommendation for the design of reliable industrial and commercial power supplies. Data is provided for commercial power distribution supplies. Another IEEE standard for reliability prediciton is *IEEE STD 1413-1998* [237] which supports a framework for reliability prediction for electronic systems and equipment. Predictions based on *IEC-61709* [229] are not commonly used since it is internationally classified as *parts-count* method. It is only listed for completeness. Mechanical systems pose a special challenge with respect to reliability prediction because such systems have a large unit/device variety are thus often unique systems. The *Handbook of Reliability Prediction Procedures for Mechanical Equipment* [377], developed by the Naval Surface Warfare Center, contains reliability models for mechanical devices, e.g. motors, brakes etc.

Acquisition of field data to use with prediction models is difficult due to low failure rates of reliable systems. Two methods have been developed to accelerate the fault process: Environmental stress screening (ESS) and fault-injection experiments. Both can increase the probability of faults dramatically. Thus, the the amount of failure data can be increased. On the other hand, both techniques alter the system or its environment, making the translation of the results back to the original environment a difficult task.

Environmental Stress Screening

The reliability of a hardware system strongly depends on the working environment. Therefore the testing of equipment during design and production will have to take the environment into account in which the equipment is likely to function. Environmental stress screening (ESS) can be defined as a process or a series of processes in which environmental stimuli, such as rapid temperature cycling and random vibration are applied to electronic items in order to precipitate latent flaws or defects which are likely to create (intrinsic) infant mortality failures in field use, regarding the intended working environment. A screen is part of the manufacuring process, basically an added inspection step. Therefore, all components are subjected to the screen. Reliability screening increases the production cost for each component off the production line, but it is capable of producing valuable data for product improvement. The critical factor to control product reliability is to ensure that products have successfully passed through infancy, prior to their delivery. To ensure this, every product has to go through the following procedures and the associated environments:

- Storage: Products often have to be stored before being issued to the customer. The storage environment has an impact on the reliability of the product and is determined mainly by temperature, salt fog and humidity for most electronic components/products.
- Handling and shipping: The service and transportation environment consists of vibration, shock, bump and acceleration.
- Operating: The intended working environment of the product is mainly determined by the intended end-use of the product.

Environmental stresses are caused by following sources:

1. Natural: Stress is determined by the general geographic region and local climatic conditions. In VDI 4005, Fiches 1-5, 1981-1983 different environmental conditions are discussed with respect to the reliability of technical products.
2. Induced: Stress is created by man either directly or indirectly such as the mechanical stresses experienced during handling and transportation environment.

These environmental stimuli are used to ensure that new products are designed with generous margins of strength to:

- Improve reliability (MTBF). Most products will never have to endure the harsh environmental limits during the ESS. These limits help the product to withstand abuse and can lead to a longer average lifetime under normal conditions.
- Learn about product failure behavior to determine the type of environmental stimuli which may be used during manufacturing screens.
- Allow higher stress levels during manufacturing screens to substantially reduce the screening duration.

Higher stress levels can accelerate the duration of an ESS process, but the applied stimulation must not approach the mechanical, electrical, or thermal stress limits of any component to avoid damaging the component or accelerating the fatigue. Each screening profile must be adjusted for each module, unit, or assembly.

Standards for ESS are the DoD-HDBK-344 [123] from the US Airforce, the Navy MIL-STD-2164 [126] environmental stress screening process for electronic equipment and the [242] for environmental testing. It gives a general guidance and descriptions of environmental test methods for a range of conditions and is similar to the MIL-STD-810 [130], replacing BS2011 [74]

The ISO/IEC61163 [228] describes reliability stress screening in three parts regarding component application area:

- Part 1: Repairable items manufactured in lots.
- Part 2: Electronic components.
- Part 3: Reliability screening of repairable single items.

MIL-STD-781 [129] : The purpose of MIL-STD-781 testing is to show that the equipment meets the specified and contractually agreed performance levels within the specified risk levels. Therefore, the objective is not to induce failures by applying unrealistic stresses. MIL-STD-781 test plans are based upon the assumption of a constant failure rate, so MTBF is used as the reliability index. Therefore, MIL-STD-781 tests are appropriate for equipment where a constant failure rate is likely to be encountered, such as fairly complex electronic equipment, after an initial burn-in period.

A special case of ESS is *burn-in*, which is the screening of components and assemblies at elevated temperatures, under bias, to precipitate defects prior to shipment. If a burn-in should be performed, the following questions should be answered according to [258]:

- Which operating and environmental conditions should be used?
- Which duration should be chosen?
- Is it cost-effective? [57]

Most of the existing documentation of integrated circuit burn-in follow the guidelines by the MIL-STD-883 [131] series of documents. For discrete semiconductors the MIL-STD-750 [128] and MIL-S-19500 [125] are the main references. Practical guidelines are given by [68]. In contrary to the more classical definition of burn-in, the industry moved towards a re-assessment of the traditional burn-in approaches, to take corrective actions so that the costly burn-in tests can be eliminated. Here, burn-in tests consist of running the system over a more or less long period of time to overcome infant mortality.

Fault Injection

The goal of fault injection is to evoke faults that are as close as possible to faults that occur in a real environment. This involves two steps: First a fault model has to be defined that characterizes best the real faults that are to be evoked. The extent to which the fault model describes real faults is called *representativeness*. The second step is to set up technical modifications in order to evoke faults of the fault model. The ability of the modifications to emulate the fault model is characterized by *Fault Emulation Accuracy* Figure 6 visualizes the relationship.

The top level classification of hardware faults is the distinction between permanent and transient faults. Several injection techniques exist that try to emulate the stuck-at or

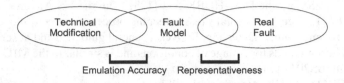

Fig. 6. Typical fault injector architecture

bit-flip fault model as accurate as possible. They can be grouped into two sets where one generates disturbances on the chip or system level that can lead to faulty pin levels and the other modifies the state of pins directly. General disturbances can be generated by, e.g., heavy-ion radiation, power supply disturbance or electromagnetic interferences. In general, they are hard to control and a gold unit is needed to check whether the disturbance lead to a change of a bit.

A *gold unit* is a reference unit to produce results which are assumed to be correct. A *golden run* is the period of time needed to produce the reference results by the gold unit before the fault-injection run.

Fault injection can be performed in order to achieve several goals (see [139]):

- *Verification and validation.* Verification uncovers differences between the specified and the real function of a system. Validation defines methods to resolve discrepancies between the realized and the system requirements. If a system is designed to tolerate a certain class of faults, or exhibit certain behavior in the presence of certain faults, these faults can be directly injected into the system to examine their effects. The system will either behave appropriately or not, and it's fault tolerance measured accordingly [23]. For certain classes of ultra-dependable untestable systems in which the occurrence of errors is too infrequent to effectively test the system in the field, fault injection can be a powerful tool for accelerating the occurrence of faults in the system and verifying that the system works properly.
- *Augment the trust in a system.* In context of a certification process safety-critical systems are tested with fault-injection. The execution of extensive fault-injection experiments can be a substantial certification requirement.
- *Determination of metrics.* Fault injection is a method to create unusual conditions to test the system for robustness. This quantifies a hard- or software prototype system. Thus, a metric for measuring the robustness of a system is provided. A classical metric is the *fault-coverage* of a fault-tolerant system. The fault-coverage is defined as the amount of detected errors divided by the amount of injected faults. In practice these metrics are hard to determine because the system must be observed over a long period of time. Such metrics (e.g. reaction times) can be determined experimentally through tests. There are two difficulties which must be addressed. The first is the diverse nature of systems, and the ways in which they can fail or experience faults. Unless two systems are set to accomplish the exact same task, determining the relative robustness is a difficult task. A good metric for robustness would be able to resolve this difference. Secondly, it is not yet certain the metric should be biased. A common practice is to have the test distribution mirror the real world distributions of fault occurrences. If we are truly testing the system's

response to unusual situations, however, it might be better to bias the test towards the less frequently encountered conditions.

Fault injection methods should exhibit the following properties:

Repeatability: Conducting the experiments several times should lead to the same results – at least in a statistical sense.
Reproducibility: Other parties should be able to come to similar results when conducting the experiments.
Portability: The fault injection method should allow to be applied to other systems.
Non-intrusiveness: Modification and influence / disturbance of the system under test should be minimal, although some modifications / influence is inherent in the approach of fault injection (see Figure 7).

Failure predictors typically contain the elements shown in Figure 7. A fault injection controller runs on a separate host injecting faults by use of a hook at the target system. In order to verify that the injection really caused a fault and to record other data, a readout collector sends measurements to the fault injector host where they are stored.

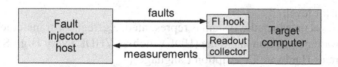

Fig. 7. Typical fault injector architecture

Fault injectors can be classified by the FARM model considering the set of *F*aults, *A*ctivations, *R*eadouts, and *M*easures.

- The set of faults is basically the fault model and fault emulation technique of the fault injector. In most cases, it consists of a set of *fault triggers* and *fault types*. Triggers are conditions when a fault should be injected and types define the technical modifications that are performed once a trigger condition is met. Chapter 10 covers of software and operator faults in more detail.
- The set of activations defines how the system under test is exercised. It covers a definition of workload profiles etc.
- Readouts are the raw measurements that are recorded.
- Measures are the metrics that are derived from readouts.

General disturbance techniques can only be used to emulate the bit-flip fault model representing transient faults, while direct pin-level modifications can emulate both fault models. Pin-level fault injection can be implemented by all injection techniques: physical techniques, simulation-based, software-implemented and hybrid approaches. The drawback of pin-level techniques is that for bit-flip emulations they have to operate on high frequencies (at least system rate).

Four main types of fault injection techniques exist: Hardware implemented, simulation-based, software implemented and hybrid tools. Physical fault injection uses heavy-ion radiation, electromagnetic interference, power-supply disturbance or altering of pin-levels. Simulation-based tools need a simulation model of the system under test and simulate the effects of faults, software implemented fault injection (SWIFI) interrupts the system and executes fault injection code. Hybrid approaches are a mixture of the previously mentioned, for example, debugging interfaces can be used to interrupt the processor on the hardware layer and to execute fault injection software. Fault-tolerance techniques can only be applied if the correctness of counter measurements against possible errors in safety-critical systems can be proven against an issuing authority. To do this, appropriate fault-injection techniques are used.

Fault injection can be performed on either simulations and models, working prototypes or systems in the field. There are two main issues in fault injection.Along these axes that different fault tolerant techniques may de divided.

Simulation-based Fault Injection Techniques. Simulation-based fault-injection offers the possibility to inject faults in a model of the system to be examined. Fault-injections are done through modification of the model. These can be only carried out in the design process. A complete simulation can only be done with high additional time complexity.

Points of accessibility are:

- The transistor level,
- The logic level on which the system is represented, e.g. register-transfer level (RTL) or a hardware description language (HDL) such as VHDL (Very High Speed Integrated Circuit Hardware Description Language),
- The functional level.

The fault model directly determines which faults are allowed. The most detailed injection concerning fault-types and location is at transistor level. Faults can be injected by e.g. modifying the netlist of the concerned circuit. By manipulating the VHDL-sources, faults can be induced in the logic level. The injection of faults on the functional level consists of modifying the output of the circuit. Furthermore, state changes within a model (*saboteur*) and structural changes (*mutation*) are distinguished. A fault-injection run consists of a program execution on the modified hardware. In principle, each modeled hardware component can be used as access point for fault-injection (probe).

The level of detail in which system and fault-injection probe are modeled, determines if fault effects - including the expected fault propagation - are modeled correctly so that it matches the final system realization and environment. No matter what type of fault-injection is applied, the system environment determines fault types within the fault-injection. Ideally a complete model of the hardware component e.g. in VHDL is available which covers all circuit details on logic level. Each detail of the circuit can be seen as a fault-injection probe. Since any modifications can be done within the model, it is possible to model various fault-types and to determine any fault duration and cause of a fault.

A high level of detail means a low injection speed since all modeled hardware components must be simulated. In practice detailed fault-injection experiments can lead to unacceptable simulation times. Besides the needed computing power to do the simulation, another disadvantage of simulation-based fault injection is that detailed hardware models of e.g. commercial microprocessors hardly exist or are not available to the public. Simulation-based approaches enable the injection of almost any fault type and the injection of permanent faults. Hardware simulations typically occur in a high level description of the circuit. This high level description is turned into a transistor level description of the circuit, and faults are injected into the circuit. Typically these are stuck-at or bridging faults, as software simulation is most often used to detect the response to manufacturing defects. The system is simulated to evaluate the response of the circuit to a particular fault. Since this is a simulation, a new fault can be easily injected, and the simulation re-run to evaluate the response to the new fault. It consumes time to construct the model, insert the faults, and then simulate the circuit, but modifications in the circuit can be more easily accomplished than later in the design cycle. This sort of testing would be used to check a circuit early in the design cycle. Simulations are non-intrusive, since the simulation functions are normally separated from those doing the introduction of the fault. For hardware simulation most tools will take a hardware specification and inject faults into it for simulation. One example of such tool is MEFISTO [257], which injects faults into VHDL description of a circuit and simulates them. It takes advantage of the manner in which systems are specified in VHDL to alter signals and values in the circuit - [257] details the operation of the VHDL fault injection. If special circuitry be included to cause or simulate faults in the finished circuit, these would most likely affect the timing or other characteristics of the circuit, and therefore be intrusive. In contrary to simulation-based fault-injection, physical fault-injection injects faults into the component to be tested while running.

Physical Fault Injection Techniques. Hardware fault injections occur in the actual implementation of the circuit after fabrication. Using this method, tests generally proceed faster than in simulations. The circuit is subjected to some sort of interference to produce the fault, and the resulting behavior is examined. Typically it is performed on VLSI circuits at the transistor level, because these circuits are complex enough to warrant characterization through fault injection rather than a performance range, and these are the best understood basic faults in such circuits. Transistors are typically given stuck-at, bridging, or transient faults, and the results examined in the operation of the circuit. Such faults may be injected in software simulations of the circuits, or into production circuits cut from the wafer.

Injectors can use the following different techniques:

– Direct manipulation of signals
– Parasitic induction (e.g. radioactive source, generators to create electromagnetic interferences).

For hardware execution, several tools exist. One is pin level testing, which manipulates the voltages at the pins in order to induce faulty or unusual conditions. The MESSALINE [23] project is an example of this sort of testing regime. The injection through direct manipulation of signals is a broadly used fault-injection technique. At the access point of the hardware (e.g. the pins of a microprocessor) the applied signals are manipulated. This can be done by directly accessing the pins or by usage of special test sockets which are inserted between processor and processor socket. By using a special test bus (JTAG-Bus) the limitation to signal manipulation at the pin-level can be overcome. The JTAG (Joint Test Action Group) or IEEE 1149.1 [236] boundary-scan standard has been

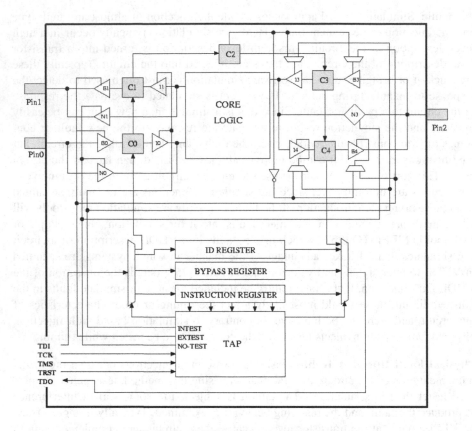

Fig. 8. The JTAG boundary scan interface

adopted industry-wide. Via the JTAG interface, boundary-scan solves test access problems introduced by advanced IC packages such as BGAs (Ball Grid Arrays). Figure 8 shows the basic JTAG interface structure.

Since the JTAG is a serial bus, fault-injections take a long period of time. In the last years, the industry tried to overcome this problem by introducing higher clock rates for TCLK.

Another technique is based on the artificial injection of fluctuations in the operating voltage of the examined circuit. Injections based on parasitic induction rely on the injection of faults through radiation with heavy-ions, lasers or electromagnetic radiation. The FIST project [202] used heavy-ion radiation to project random transient faults into the interior of a chip for testing. The MARS project [171] extended this to include electromagnetic fields to create faults in the interior of the chip. These methods tend to produce random temporary and permanent errors on more or less random locations in the hardware rather than targeted faults [223]. A new method of fault injection addresses this concern. Laser Fault Injection (LFI) uses a laser to inject faults precisely into the interior of the chip at specific times [425]. This allows a higher level of control and a much better data set than the other two methods. It is possible to manipulate the bitstream being send to an FPGA (Field Programmable Gate Array) in such a way that transient or permanent faults can be injected. The fault can be precisely located, but the effect of the fault is often unclear. Futhermore, the FPGA could be damaged, if no counteractive measures are taken. As JTAG, FPGA-fault injection is strongly hardware dependent. See [155] for details. Newer FPGA types enable the injection of delay faults by reprogramming the concerned units [156] so that the direct manipulation of signals becomes obsolete.

Software-implemented Fault Injection Techniques. While injectors of physical faults can confront the hardware more with the cause of a fault, software-implemented injectors mainly model the causes of a fault in software. They are popular, since they offer a low-priced and flexible alternative to physical fault injection.

Software fault injection is used to inject faults into the operation of software and examine the effects. This is generally used on code that has communicative or cooperative functions so that there is enough interaction to make fault injection useful. All sorts of faults may be injected, from register and memory faults, to dropped or replicated network packets, to erroneous error conditions and flags. These faults may be injected into simulations of complex systems where the interactions are understood though not the details of implementation, or they may be injected into operating systems to examine the effects. Software simulation typically is a high-level description of a system, in which the protocols or interactions are known, but no implementation details. These faults tend to be mis-timings, missing messages, replays, or other faults in communication in a system. The simulation is then run to discover the effects of the faults. Because of the abstract nature of simulations, they may be run at a faster speed that the actual system might, but would not necessarily capture the timing aspects of the final system if it is not asynchronous. This sort of testing would be performed to verify a protocol, or to examine the resistance of an interaction to faults. This would typically be done early in the design cycle. Simulations are non-intrusive, as they are simulated, but they may not capture the exact behavior of the system. Software fault injections are more oriented towards implementation details, and can address program state as well as communication and interactions. Faults are mis-timings, missing messages, replays, corrupted memory or registers, faulty disk reads, and almost any other state the hardware provides access to. The system is then run with the fault to examine its behavior. These simulations tend to take longer because they encapsulate all of the operation and detail of the system, but they will more accurately capture the timing aspects of the system. This is done later in the design cycle to show performance for a final or near-final design. Simulations are non-intrusive, especially if timing is not of a concern. If timing is not involved the time required for the injection mechanism to inject the faults can disrupt the activity of the system. This can cause timing results that are not representative of the final system without the fault injection mechanism deployed. A known fault in injected and the results examined to see if the system can respond correctly despite the fault.

Please note that for software-implemented fault injection, the shortest time for bit-flips is the duration of one cycle, hence the effect of glitches cannot be emulated. Additionally, software implemented techniques can only modify the level of bits within the processor or its memory and not of other hardware units that are, e.g., on the same board.

The following disadvantages exist:

- Assumptions must be made on which hardware faults can occur in practice.
- The exact effects of an assumed internal hardware fault are probably not known and can only be modeled approximately.

Software-implemented fault-injection is divided in pre-runtime and runtime. With pre-runtime fault-injection, faults are injecte before the simulation starts. Runtime fault-injection will inject faults into the system while running.

Most of the software tools that exist are for testing of actual systems, and not a simulation. This is probably due to the difficult task of correctly capturing high level behavior without the implementation being finished, and the relative ease of inserting faults into operating systems due to the debugging facilities provided by modern hardware. Ferrari is a testing system that introduces CPR, memory, and bus faults through CPU traps during normal execution. Ftape is a system that introduces CPU, memory, and disk faults through altered drivers and OS modifications [223]. DOCTOR [208] is a tool for introducing faults into a distributed real time system under synthetic workloads, introducing CPU, memory, and network faults through time-outs, traps, and code modification. Xception [87] causes multiple sorts of faults through hardware exception triggers. ORCHESTRA [113] is a distributed system testbed that tests protocols by inserting faults through the introduction of a Fault Injection Layer between the protocol and the communication layer beneath it [223].

Table 2 exemplarily lists some fault-injection tools.

Table 2. Different Fault-Injection Tools

Simulation-based	Physical	Software-implemented
VERIFY [444]	JTAG [236]	ProFI [319]
MEPHISTO [257]	MESSALINE [23]	FERRARI [175]
	RIFLE [326]	FIAT [39]
	FIST [202]	Xception [87]
		ORCHESTRA [113]

Further reading. Introductory material can be found in [448], [86], [223] and [139]. [100] an [223] additionally list several tools currently available for fault injection. [491] discuss fault injection as a testing and verification tool, rather than a debugging tool while [490] describe the inversion of test pattern frequencies from the usual observed workload to putting the emphasis on the unusual cases. [23] describes basic theory and describes interpretation of results.

Discussion. The results of fault injection need to be given meaning. At an absolute level, it described the system's ability to resist certain faults, and fall prey to others. This can be thought of a way of testing the robustness of the system, and its ability to operate under unusual conditions. If it is to be used as such, though, then its relationship to robustness needs to be better defined, and a framework for understanding the numbers that result needs to be built. While some of the theoretical underpinnings are there, the actual interpretation of the practice is not.

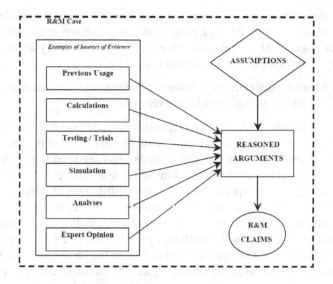

Fig. 9. Sources of reliability evidence [354]

Having answered the first question about the goal of the prediction, one should concentrate on the available information. It is dangerous to start the modelling process without having a look onto special properties of the input. The Defence Standard 00-42: R&M Case [354] lists a number of different sources of reliability evidence (a quite general term for model input) as depicted in Fig. 9. Evidence includes not only what one would consider as facts (test data, field data), but also other sources like expert opinions. The listed data sources may be divided into different categories: On one hand, we deal with "hard" data, e.g. from the field or experiments (e.g. accelerated life testing) or physical models. On the other hand, there are "soft" sources as e.g. expert opinions/estimates or similar component/forerunner data. These data types may vary in their availability, accuracy and uncertainty, but reliability engineers can't afford to waste away any of these sources.

In conclusion, reliability modelling data can be obtained from the following sources:

- Soft sources
- Field data from published sources
- Physical models that provide formulas to estimate reliability data
- Environmental stress screening
- Fault injection

Each source will be discussed separately in the following sections.

Uncertainty in Data Sources

As outlined, different types of sources may contribute to the model with information of different quality. Information sources may provide uncertain data, or they may be conflicting.

One of the most controversial scientific discussions in uncertainty analysis are the various forms of uncertainty. Perhaps most common is the separation into two categories: epistemic uncertainty and aleatory uncertainty [378]. Aleatory uncertainty arises from variability of the system or environment considered.

Definition 2 (Aleatory uncertainty - Noise). *Inherent variation associated with the physical system or the environment under consideration [378]*

Aleatory uncertainty (often referred to as repetition uncertainty) may e.g. be observed in random experiments as dice throws or chaotic system behaviour. Aleatory uncertainty regarding a quantity of interest can often be distinguished from other types of uncertainty by its characterisation as a random value with known distribution. The exact value will change but is expected to follow the distribution. A simple example for aleatory uncertainty is the uncertainty about the outcome of a coin toss $X \in \{0, 1\}$. We are uncertain about head ($X = 0$) or tail ($X = 1$) of a single throw, but we are sure that each of the numbers will occur with a probability $P(X = 0) = P(X = 1) = 1/2$. Infinite repetitive executions of this experiment will lead to the observance that the relative frequency converges to the given probability values. Traditional reliability engineering applications tend to model only aleatory uncertainties, which can lead to dangerous underestimations of the project risk.

On the contrary, epistemic uncertainty describes not uncertainty about the outcome of some random event due to system variance but the uncertainty of the outcome due to lack of knowledge or information.

Definition 3 (Epistemic uncertainty - Imprecision). *Uncertainty of the outcome due to any lack of knowledge or information in any phase or activity of the modelling process [378]*

This shows the important distinction between this two types of uncertainty. Epistemic uncertainty is *not* an inherent property of the system. A gain of information about the system or environmental factors can lead to a reduction of epistemic uncertainty. Focussing again on the dice example, lets imagine we know that the coin is biased and our knowledge about the exact probabilities therefore limited. We might expect that the probability is limited by $p(X = 0), p(X = 1) \in [1/12, 7/12]$ or may itself be described by a second-order probability. Of course, the coin follows a distribution and if we carry out multiple runs, evidence would grow (i.e. shrinking the intervals on $p(X = 0)$ and $p(X = 1)$. After an infinite number of experiments, we would find out that it is e.g. $p(X = 0) = 1/3, p(X = 1) = 2/3$. However, before doing so, there is not enough evidence to assume any possible distribution on X without neglecting that reality may be anywhere else. Hence, epistemic uncertainty is our inability to model reality.

Epistemic uncertainties occur in large amounts in almost all system reliability models, especially if large software systems are considered. Either it is impossible to carry out enough experiments for gathering informations about the quantity of interest. Or it is possible, but the resources (time, budget, manpower...) necessary surpass the constraints. While the application of probability theory is unquestionably the right choice for modelling aleatory uncertainties, this is not necessarily the case for epistemic quantities. It has been heavily discussed if probabilities are an adequate representation for degrees of belief and assumptions that are put into a model. The behavioural or Bayesian interpretation claims this and associates probabilities with degrees of belief, transferring probability theory to belief modelling. This opposes to other theories as e.g. fuzzy sets and imprecise probabilities.

Walley [496] describes several sources of imprecision in the model. He distinguishes between "indeterminacy" and "incompleteness". Indeterminacy reflects limitations of the available information, which might e.g. be the unknown value of a Weibull shape parameter. Incompleteness is caused by a simplifying model which allows to use only a partial amount of information the experts could provide. Incompleteness is caused by difficulties in the elicitation or modelling process. In this case, the engineer may know the exact values of the Weibull shape and form parameter. However the model allows only the estimation of a constant failure rate. Walley [496] gives a list of sources of imprecision, which he groups into "indeterminacy" and "incompleteness".

Lack of information. The absence of evidence concerning the quantity of interest

Conflicting information. Different sources of information do not necessarily lead to a reduction of imprecision, if these sources are conflicting (e.g. $\beta \in [1.2, 1.5]$ and $\beta \in [2, 2.3]$ by two test runs). Can be reduced by investigating prior probabilities or information source quality.

Conflicting beliefs. In contrast to the conflicting information, conflicting beliefs are not based on evidence but on expert opinion. Either the experts have access to different sources of information or they assess the information in different ways. Can be reduced by iterative elicitation.

Information of limited relevance. If the information that the model is based upon is only scarcely usable for prediction. E.g. if similarity estimates are based upon strongly different components, this should be reflected by a high amount of imprecision.

Physical indeterminacy. The quantity of interest is simply not precisely predictable with infinite information. This may be the case for prediction problems, either the problems are physically indeterminate or the underlying processes are too complex to be modelled in detail, or the parameters are not estimable from data (e.g. if only censored lifetime data is available). Walley groups this point to indeterminacy while it could reasonably argued that it belongs to incompleteness of the model.

Lack of introspection. Experts do not have time or resources to reduce the amount of uncertainty in their estimate. Walley calls this the "cost of thinking".

Lack of assessment strategies. There is a lot of relevant information available, but it is not straightforward to construct probabilities from it (e.g. textual reports or excessively detailed damage statistics). If the data is simplified, imprecision should be added.

Limits in computational ability. Imprecision introduced by lack of computational power.

Intractable models. The probabilistic model might be inconvenient or too complex. If replacing it by a simpler one, imprecision should be introduced.

Choice of elicitation structure. Depending on the experience of the assessor and the assessment technique, there may be a limit on the accuracy of the elicitation.

Ambiguity. The "fuzzy" characteristics of linguistic estimates as e.g. "pretty likely" and "almost impossible" introduce uncertainty if translated to probabilities

Instability. Using different elicitation methods or even the same method twice may lead to different assessments, because beliefs are unstable (e.g. underlying information is remembered or weighted different) or estimates are overly precise (which is often the case in reliability prediction, when the notion of imprecision is not correctly understood). Walley suggests to use a conservative aggregation strategy as e.g. enveloping for this case.

Caution in elicitation. Engineers may tend to give much higher imprecision ranges than necessary in case they e.g. fear to be blamed for wrong estimations.

Table 3. Sources of uncertainty [496]

Indeterminacy	Incompleteness
Lack of information	Lack of introspection
Conflicting information	Lack of assessment strategies
Conflicting beliefs	Limits in computational ability
Information of limited relevance	Intractable models
Physical indeterminacy	Choice of elicitation structure
	Ambiguity
	Instability
	Caution in elicitation

Soft Sources

Data from similar components are normally introduced in the model via a qualitative analysis [230, 237]. Similarities between new and in-field components are determined. The failure data from in-field components (e.g. probabilities of special failure modes) is then transferred to the new model. Either the data is left untouched (both components have the same properties) or is modified (both components have similar properties). For constant failure rates of electronic components, this modifications may be done by physical model-based similarity analyses.

Expert judgement has its greatest advantage in its omnipresence. Everywhere you build a model, you will find at least one expert who is willing to give a statement about the input parameters. Most often, there will even be a large number of estimates from various experts. Unfortunately, expert estimates are by nature uncertain and conflicting, and thus they need to be introduced with care. Aggregation methods, uncertainty propagation and reduction techniques have to be used as e.g. described in Cooke [105] and Sentz and Ferson [437].

Soft data may require special uncertainty propagation methods. Dealing with uncertainties in "hard" data (e.g. physical variance) is quite straightforward and requires standard probabilistic methods. However, the question how to model gradual belief and lack of knowledge seems much more controversial. Methods to propagate expert uncertainties through reliability models include e.g. Fuzzy probabilities [522], Bayesian (subjective) probabilities [52] and imprecise probabilities [116], [496]. Walley [496] argues and compares some of these methods and lines out their merits and limits. Klir [278] shows the different mathematical properties and lists imprecision and entropy measures for each of the proposed methods. Very useful practical comparisons can e.g. be found in [160] and [457].

All of these methods are concurrently applied in modern reliability science. Perhaps the most popular approach is Bayesian modelling (e.g. applied in Groen et al. [196]). Fuzzy probabilities are most often the tool of choice if it comes to the capturing of linguistic / verbal estimates (reliability is "high") due to the traditional use of fuzzy logic in AI. Perhaps most influential on practical reliability prediction were the PREDICT methodology [272], [353]. Other approaches include Hryniewicz [222], which apply a variety (shadowed sets) and Leuschen et al. [299], which fuzzify classical Markov models. The most recent "trend" in reliability prediction are imprecise probabilities, uniting interval and probabilistic calculations. Applying imprecise probabilities to propagate uncertainties through physical models [471] and logical models, such as RBDs [300, 479] has become more popular in the past. Applications in software reliability [203] are also available. But this field is still developing, as Rakowsky [410] and Coolen [106] line out.

9.5   Modelling Complex, Fault-Tolerant Systems

The dependability of large systems consisting of multiple components like circuit boards, integrated circuits, disks, and network devices is usually estimated by the use of dependability models. In this section, we will exemplify this with the measure availability. Similar (or in many cases identical) techniques exists for reliable systems (Reliability and availability are the same for non-repairable systems). In recent publications, even the security of systems was analysed using similar approaches as described here [499, 500].

The idea behind modelling complex High-Availability systems is to first quantify the availability of the components (possibly by first decomposing them into their subcomponents) and to calculate the system's overall availability in a second step, according to a well-defined set of assumptions. These assumptions are called an *availability model* of a fault-tolerant system.

Example: If we assume that a system is composed of n components $comp_1$, $comp_2$, $comp_3$, ..., $comp_n$ and

- all failures and repairs are exponentially distributed events,
- components are either fully working, or completely failed,
- the failure and repair rate of component $comp_i$ are λ_i and μ_i, respectively,
- all failure and repair events are assumed to be pair-wisely stochastically independent, and
- the system is available if and only if all its components are available

we can compute the overall system's steady state availability A by:

$$A = \prod_{i=1}^{n} Pr\{comp_i \text{ is available}\} = \prod_{i=1}^{n} \frac{\mu_i}{\lambda_i + \mu_i}$$

As the system is available if and only if all components are available, the steady state availability of the system is the probability that all components are available at the same time. As these events are stochastically independent, this probability can be computed by multiplying all the individual availabilities.

In the following, we will use the abbreviations below:

$$c_i := \textit{"comp}_i \textit{ is available", and} \tag{1}$$

$$a_i := Pr\{c_i\} := Pr\{\textit{"comp}_i \textit{ is available"}\} \tag{2}$$

Redundancy Structures

Per definition, a fault tolerant system does not necessarily fail as soon as one of its component stops working but will continue operating as long as not too many components are failed at the same time. The number and kind of failures which can be tolerated depends on the redundancy degree which was chosen for the system. In general, a redundancy structure formula is used to define the combination of component failures which lead to a system failure.

Example: A system consists of 2 servers ($c_{1,2}$) and a network (c_3). The system is assumed to be available, if the network is available and at least one of its servers is working. The redundancy structure ϕ of this system can be specified by the following boolean expression using AND ($\land$) and OR ($\lor$) operators:

$$\phi = (c_1 \lor c_2) \land c_3 \tag{3}$$

In general, arbitrary boolean functions with variables $c_1, c_2, \ldots c_n$ representing the basic events "component c_i is available" can be used to specify the redundancy structure of a system.

The example above is a special case, because every basic event appears at most once in the formula. In this simple case, we can apply the following formulas which are known from basic probability calculus for independent events ($\phi_{1,2}$ are arbitrary boolean terms):

$$Pr\{\phi_1 \land \phi_2\} = Pr\{\phi_1\} \cdot Pr\{\phi_2\} \tag{4}$$

$$Pr\{\phi_1 \lor \phi_2\} = Pr\{\phi_1\} + Pr\{\phi_2\} - Pr\{\phi_1 \land \phi_2\} \tag{5}$$

$$Pr\{\neg\phi_1\} = 1 - Pr\{\phi_1\} \tag{6}$$

Using the definition $Pr\{c_i\} = a_i$, we can express the availability of the system defined in Equ. 3 in terms of the availabilities of its components:

$$Pr\{\phi\} = Pr\{(c_1 \lor c_2) \land c_3\} =$$
$$= Pr\{(c_1 \lor c_2)\} \cdot Pr\{c_3\} =$$
$$= (a_1 + a_2 - a_1 \cdot a_2) \cdot a_3 =$$
$$= a_1 a_3 + a_2 a_3 - a_1 a_2 a_3 \tag{7}$$

The amount of work which has to be done for such a computation grows linearly with the number of operators in the structure formula which in turn is bounded by the number of components of the system (We assumed that each component can only appear once in the formula). Models of this simple kind can therefore be evaluated in linear time with respect to the number of their components.

However, not all systems can be modelled with a structure formula containing each component only once:

Example: A k-out-of-N:G-system consists of N components. The system is available, if k or more components are available (or *good*). For the case $N = 3$ and $k = 2$, we can specify its redundancy structure ϕ by

$$\phi = (c_1 \wedge c_2) \vee (c_1 \wedge c_3) \vee (c_2 \wedge c_3) \tag{8}$$

In this case, the sub-terms of the formula are *not* stochastically independent. For instance, the sub-terms $c_1 \wedge c_2$ and $c_1 \wedge c_3$ are not independent as they both contain the variable c_1. However, applying Equ. 4 implies (by definition) independent events.

An alternative approach of analysing structure formulas which also works with repeated events is based on the so called Shannon Decomposition. This approach comprises n steps, one for each component of the system. In each step, two Boolean terms are derived from the structure formula. In the first term $\phi_{c=\text{true}}$ the variable c is substituted by *true*, whereas in the second term $\phi_{c=\text{false}}$ the variable c is substituted by *false*. For example, the probability of the formula in Equ. 8 can be written as:

$$\begin{aligned}
Pr\{\phi\} &= a_1 \cdot Pr\{\phi_{c_1=\text{true}}\} + (1 - a_1) \cdot Pr\{\phi_{c_1=\text{false}}\} = \\
&= a_1 \cdot Pr\{c_2 \vee c_3 \vee (c_2 \wedge c_3)\} + (1 - a_1) \cdot Pr\{c_2 \wedge c_3\} = \\
&= a_1 \cdot (a_2 \cdot 1 + (1 - a_2) \cdot a_3) + a_2 a_3 - a_1 a_2 a_3 = \\
&= a_1 a_2 + a_1 a_3 + a_2 a_3 - 2 a_1 a_2 a_3
\end{aligned} \tag{9}$$

Using this technique, the variables are repeatedly substituted, until no term contains repeated variables anymore. In the worst case this has to be done for each variable, and for every substitution two terms have to be recursively computed. Thus, the computational effort grows exponentially with the number of components. In fact, it can be shown that computing the availability of a system is an NP-complete problem if it has an arbitrary redundancy structure.

In practice, efficient solution methods exists for the most common classes of redundancy structures. Most modern approaches are based on binary decision diagrams (BDDs [412, 430]) and can cope with very large systems comprising thousands of components.

Fault Trees and Reliability Block Diagrams

In practice, the redundancy structure is usually defined by using either *fault trees* or *reliability block diagrams*. Fig. 10 shows a fault tree and a block diagram of the structure formula of Equ. 8.

The fault tree is an explicit graphical representation of the structure formula. Its leaves (shown at the bottom of the tree) represent the negated variables of the formula.

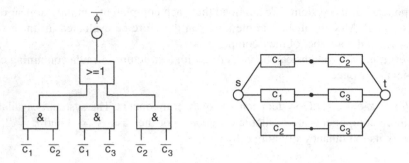

Fig. 10. Fault tree (left) and reliability block diagram (right) of the 2-out-of-3:G-system

In other words, they represent the unavailabilities of the individual components. The root of the tree is called top event and represents the event "system unavailable". Operators (AND and OR) are represented by so called gates. Evaluating a fault tree means computing the probability of its top event form the probabilities of its leaves. Again, this can be done fast and easily, if each component appears only once in the tree. In this case, the calculation is performed from bottom to top, applying Equ. 4 at each AND-Gate and Equ. 5 at each OR-gate.

Despite their name, reliability block diagrams (RBD) can be used for both reliability and availability analysis. They define a structure formula in an implicit way. An RBD is a undirected graph, whose edges are labelled with components. Two nodes of the graph, called s and t, play a special role. The system is assumed to be available, if and only if there exists at least one path (i.e. a subset of the edges of G) from s to t, which comprises available components, only. Thus, the structure formula of an RBD can be obtained by finding all minimal paths from s to t. In this context, *minimal* means that no edge can be removed from the path without disconnecting s and t. In the worst case, the number of paths from s to t grows exponentially with the number of edges. In some cases (but not always), it is therefore better to find the number of *minimal cut sets* to obtain the redundancy structure. A cut set is a subset of edges, which, if removed from the graph, will separate s from t. A minimal cut set is a cut set from which no edge can be removed without connecting s with t.

Obtaining the redundancy structure from an RBD is – again – an NP-complete task. In practice, fast methods exist to obtain a BDD from the RBD [91, 289]. This has the advantage that these BDD can be quickly evaluated as mentioned before.

Many systems are k-out-of-N-systems or contain such systems as subsystems. k-out-of-N:G system were already defined before as systems comprising N components which are working as long as at least k components are available. Likewise, k-out-of-N:F systems comprise N components, and are unavailable, if at least k components are unavailable. As it was exemplified in Equ. 8 and Fig. 10, k-out-of-N-systems can be modelled using regular AND and OR gates. However, to avoid the large trees or diagrams which are necessary to depict large system (try drawing a fault tree for a 50-out-of-100:F system!), special edges and gates are used in the graphical representations. Fig. 11 shows how the diagrams from Fig. 10 can be simplified by using k-out-of-N:F-gates and k-out-of-N:G-edges, respectively.

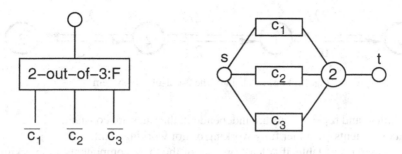

Fig. 11. Simplified fault tree (left) and reliability block diagram (right) of the 2-out-of-3:G-system

The structure formulas of fault trees and block diagrams containing k-out-of-N sub-systems can be obtained by replacing the gates by conventional AND and OR gates, respectively. However, there also exist more efficient solution methods which avoid the potentially large classical representations [13].

State-Based Methods

The classical solution methods for combinatorial modelling methods can deal with arbitrary redundancy structures, but work only under the assumption, that the failure and repair behaviour of all their components is stochastically independent. In practice, this is hardly ever true. For example, catastrophic events can destroy several components at once.

These failures with a common cause are a major threat to fault tolerant systems, as they may affect all redundant components of the system at the same time and lead to a complete system failure. Other examples for inter-component dependencies are failure propagation, failures due to improper repair, and delayed repair if too many components are failed at the same time and the repair personnel is overburdened.

All these dependencies decrease the dependability of a fault tolerant system. Thus, if they are not included in a model, the model is over-optimistic, sometimes by several orders of magnitude. To avoid this kind of over-optimism, state-based methods can be used.

State-based methods enumerate all possible failure states of the system in a so-called state space.

Example: A 2-out-of-3:G-system with identical components has four states $S = \{s_0, s_1, s_2, s_3\}$. In state s_i, i components of the system are failed. As all components are equal, no distinction has to be made *which* component is failed. If one knew the probability p_i that the system is in state i, one could compute the availability by adding p_0 and p_1, as these are the states where the system is available.

The system can be modelled using a Markov chain (see Sec. 8) shown in Fig. 12.

Using this Markov chain as a system model implies the following assumptions:

– All three components have an equal failure and repair rate, denoted by λ and μ, respectively.

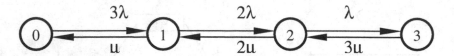

Fig. 12. Markov chain of the 2-out-of-3:G-system

- All failure and repair events are independent, the rates are constant.
- All components are either fully working or not working at all.
- The system is available, if at least two out of the three components are working.

The Markov model is therefore equivalent to the fault tree from Fig. 10. Indeed, an evaluation of the Markov chain yields the same results:

A steady state distribution of the state vector $\phi = (s_0, s_1, s_2, s_3)^T$ can be computed by solving the linear equations

$$\phi \cdot Q = 0, \text{ and } \sum_{i \in 0,1,2,3} s_i = 1. \tag{10}$$

As the corresponding generator matrix Q is

$$Q = \begin{pmatrix} -3\lambda & 3\lambda & 0 & 0 \\ \mu & -\mu - 2\lambda & 2\lambda & 0 \\ 0 & 2\mu & -2\mu - \lambda & \lambda \\ 0 & 0 & 3\mu & -3\mu \end{pmatrix} \tag{11}$$

Equ. 10 can be written as an equation system:

$$-3\lambda s_0 + \mu s_1 = 0 \Rightarrow s_0 = \frac{\mu}{3\lambda} s_1$$

$$3\lambda s_0 - (\mu + 2\lambda)s_1 + 2\mu s_2 = 0 \Rightarrow s_2 = \frac{\lambda}{\mu} s_1$$

$$2\lambda s_1 - (2\mu + \lambda)s_2 + 3\mu s_3 = 0 \Rightarrow s_3 = \frac{\lambda^2}{3\mu^2} s_1$$

$$\lambda s_2 - 3\mu s_3 = 0$$

$$s_0 + s_1 + s_2 + s_3 = 1 \Rightarrow s_1 = \frac{3\mu^2\lambda}{(\mu + \lambda)^3}$$

This yields:

$$s_0 = \frac{\mu^3}{(\mu + \lambda)^3}; \quad s_1 = \frac{3\mu^2\lambda}{(\mu + \lambda)^3}; \quad s_2 = \frac{3\mu\lambda^2}{(\mu + \lambda)^3}; \quad s_3 = \frac{\lambda^3}{(\mu + \lambda)^3}; \tag{12}$$

Applying $a = \frac{\mu}{(\mu+\lambda)}$ and $1 - a = \frac{\lambda}{(\mu+\lambda)}$, the availability of the system is:

$$A = s_0 + s_1 = 3a^2 - 2a^3, \tag{13}$$

which is equivalent to Equ. 9 for the special case $a_1 = a_2 = a_3 =: a$

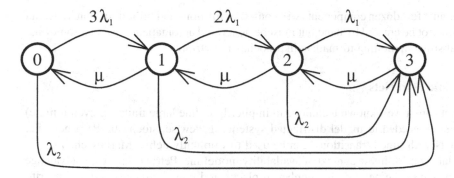

Fig. 13. Markov chain of the 2-out-of-3:G-system and inter-component dependencies

Thus the Markov model shown in Fig. 12 is equivalent to the Boolean models from Fig. 10. However, the Markov model is not limited to stochastically independent components. For example, it is possible to extend the Markov model by a common cause failure as shown in Fig. 13.

In this figure, three additional transitions with rate λ_2 model the occurrence of a catastrophic event which destroys all components of the system at once. In this case, the system will be put into state 3 immediately.

The problem with Markov chains is the possibly huge number of states which, in general, grows exponentially with the number of components the system consists of. For example, a more general model of the 2-out-of-3:G system, this time with non-equal components, already consists of 2^3 states (see Fig. 14). As a consequence, systems with

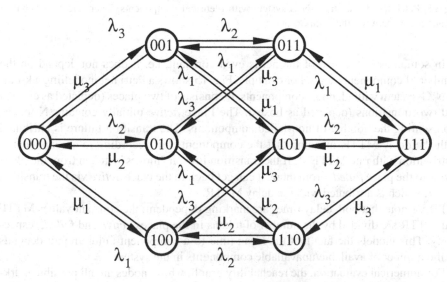

Fig. 14. Markov chain of the 2-out-of-3:G-system. Each component has a different failure- and repair rate

more than a few dozen components will consist of millions and billions of states and can therefore not be created by hand but must be generated automatically using a somewhat more abstract modelling formalism like stochastic Petri nets.

Stochastic Petri Nets

Petri nets are a well known technique to implicitly define large finite (or even infinite) automatons needed to model distributed systems. Likewise, stochastic Petri nets, i.e. Petri nets with timed transitions, can be used to implicitly define Markov chains with large state spaces. In the context of availability modelling, Petri nets have the advantage that the size of the net, i.e. the number of places and transitions, grows only linearity with the number of components.

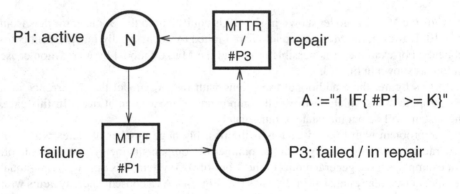

Fig. 15. Petri net of a k-out-of-N:G system with identical components. There are no stochastic dependencies between the components.

In some cases, the size of the net is even constant, i.e. it does not depend on the number of components at all. For example, Fig. 15 shows a Petri net modelling a k-out-of-N:G-system with identical components. It consists of two places (depicted as circles) and two transitions (depicted as boxes). The Place *active* initially contains N tokens representing the number of non-failed components. The transition failure is attributed with the delay MTTF, meaning that the components fail according to an exponential distribution with rate $MTTF^{-1}$. If the transition fires, it "moves" a token from the place *active* to the place *failed*. From there, it can get back to the place *active* via the transition *repair*, which is attributed with the delay MTTR.

Please note that both delay times are marking dependent: the constant values MTTF and MTTR are divided by the number of tokens in the places *active* and *failed*, respectively. This models the fact that the mean time to a component failure/repair depends on the number of available/unavailable components in the system.

For numerical evaluation, the reachability graph, whose nodes are all possible markings which can be reached from the initial marking, is generated. It is easy to see that the number of nodes in this graph is finite and depends on the parameter N. For $N = 3$, the reachability graph is equivalent to the Markov chain in Fig. 12.

To define in which states of the reachability graph the system is available and in which states it is not, a so-called reward function is used. In Fig. 15, the reward function A evaluates to 1 if and only if there arc at least K components in the place P1.

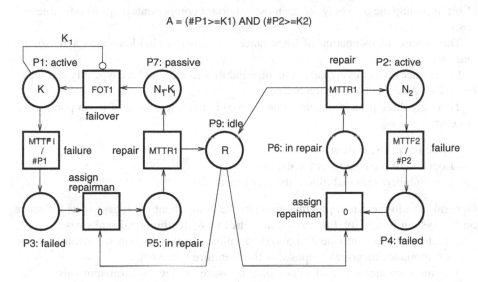

Fig. 16. Petri net of a system comprising 2 k-out-of-N:G subsystems with identical components. All components are repaired by a repair-group with capacity R. One subsystem (modelled on the left side of the net) is a standby-redundant system: passive components cannot fail and the activation of a passive component takes some fail-over time (FOT).

Fig. 16 shows a more complex Petri net modelling a system comprising two k-out-of-N:G subsystems. All components are repaired by the same repair group with capacity R. Thus, the number of components which can be repaired in parallel is limited by R. The left k-out-of-N:G system is build using cold standby-components. This means that the redundant components cannot fail. After the failure of an active component, a passive component will be activated (due to the "inhibitor arc", the transition *fail-over* can only fire if there are less than K_1 components in the place *active*). This takes some fail-over time (FOT) during which the overall system is not available.

Importance Measures: How Can I Find the Weak-Point?

Importance Measures are metrics which help to identify the weakest areas of a system and moreover they do give hints to modifications, which will improve the system reliability. Importance measures are useful as well by assisting system design and optimization as by diagnosing failures, generating repair checklists and development of inspection and maintenance strategies. Importance measures provide information for making various decisions to improve the system reliability. It should be noted that the application of importance analysis does not take the costs of all these events into account.

At the first design phases usually only the structure of the system is known, but not the component parameters (failure rate, repair rate, MTTF, etc., see Sect. 9.4). In some cases the developer can start with the importance analysis. Components with very low importance value will probably have a negligible effect on the system reliability. The effort in finding the data only for the most important components helps to safe time and costs.

The process of estimation of Importance Measures is also known as a *sensitivity analysis*.

Importance measures are defined upon reliability models and are typically applied in Fault Tree Analysis (see section before).

There are three principal factors that determine the importance of a component in a system:

- Structure of the system.
- Location of the component in the system.
- Unreliability/unavailability of the component.

General: The higher an importance value of the component the bigger is its influence on the system reliability. Importance measures provide numerical ranks based on the contribution of the component to a system failure. In this section we summarize the major importance measures proposed in the literature [56, 380].

The most commonly used importance measure is due to Birnbaum (also called marginal) importance. Birnbaum importance is the probability that the system is in such a state that a basic event A_i (component fails) is critical for the occurrence of the top event (system fails). It can be obtained by the partial derivation of the unreliability system function $F(\underline{q})$:

$$I_B(A_i) = \frac{\partial F(\underline{q})}{\partial q_i}, i = 1, 2, ..., n.$$

Birnbaum defined the importance of a component as the difference between two conditional probabilities:

$$I_B(A_i) = P(X/A_i) - P(X/\overline{A_i}),$$

where the first one is the probability, that the top event X has occurred, given that the event A_i , whose importance is being measured, has occurred. The second one is the probability, that the top event X has occurred, given that the event has not occurred $\overline{A_i}$. The Birnbaum importance measure determines the maximum increase in risk when component A_i has failed compared to the case where component A_i is operating state. Another view on Birnbaum importance is to see it as a rate at which the system reliability improves as the reliability of component A_i improves. The Birnbaum importance measure plays an important role in defining and calculating several other importance measures. In case no information is available about the components characteristics (unreliabilities / unavailabilities), then the Birnbaum importance measure can be computed by setting event unreliabilities to 0.5, that allows us to consider the relative importance of various components when only the structure of the system is known. This importance measure is known as *Structural importance* measure:

$$I_{STR}(A_i) = I_B(A_i), \text{where } q_i = 0.5.$$

The Structural importance establishes the probability of system failure due to a given component when we consider that all states have the same probability.

The Birnbaum importance does not directly consider how likely an event A_i is to occur. This measure is independent of the actual unreliability of event A_i, which can result in assigning high importance measures to events that are very unlikely to occur. To improve this, Criticality importance can be considered, which is the probability that the component is responsible for the system failure before time t:

$$I_{CR}(A_i) = I_B(A_i) \cdot \frac{q_i}{F(\underline{q})}.$$

Therefore, the Criticality importance measure modifies the Birnbaum importance measure by adjusting for the relative probability of a basic event A_i to reflect how likely the event is to occur and how feasible it is to improve the event reliability. These modifications enable the Criticality importance measure to focus on truly important basic events and make it possible to compare basic events between fault trees. Criticality importance measure is typically used to determine the next basic event to improve. The Criticality importance measure is defined as:

$$I_{CR}(A_i) = \{P(X/A_i) - P(X/\overline{A_i})\} \cdot P(A_i)/P(X)$$

The Criticality importance measure of event A_i is the probability that the top event has occurred given that component is critical for the system and has occurred. While the Birnbaum importance measure considers only the conditional probability that event A_i is critical, the Criticality importance measure also considers the overall probability of the top event occurrence due to event A_i.

If the objective is to minimise the individual contributions of basic events, then the *Fussell-Vesely* importance measure should be used to select the basic event to improve. In order for a basic event to contribute to the top event, at least one cut set (see section before for the definition) containing this event should occur. The Fussell-Vesely importance measure is the probability that at least one minimal cut set containing component, whose importance is being measured, has failed at time t, given that the system has failed at time t:

$$I_{FV}(A_i) = \frac{\sum_{j=1}^{m_i} F_j^i(\underline{q})}{F(\underline{q})},$$

where $F_j^i(\underline{q})$ denotes the probability that minimal cut set j among those containing component, whose importance is being measured, has failed at time t. In cases where event A_i contributes to the top event but is not necessarily critical, the Fussell-Vesely importance measure can be used.

Each situation will dictate the appropriate measure to apply.

Importance Measures Usage [380]: If all importance measures yield the same rank ordering of basic events, then the strategy for using the importance measures is straight-forward. However, when the three importance measures yield different rank orderings of basic events, the following guidelines suggest how to select an appropriate solution:

- If the decrease of the unavailability of each component is possible with the same effort, then use Birnbaum importance measures.
- If improvements can be made only to events that have high unavailabilities, use Criticality importance measures. (It may be impossible to de-crease the unavailability of events after a certain limit, and the unavailability of some events may already be very low.) Additionally, if the object is to prioritise maintenance efforts, use Criticality importance measures.
- If the objective is to minimise the individual contributions of basic events, use Fussell-Vesely importance measures.

The reader interested in learning more on novel techniques e.g. Fricks and Trivedi [169] and further classical importance measures can be referred to Fussell [174] and of Intellect in cooperation with Relex Software Corporation [380].

Tool Support

Fault trees, Markov chains and stochastic Petri nets of non-trivial systems cannot be analysed manually. Therefore, computer aided tools were created for model design and solution. Most of these tools were written with a certain kind of modelling method in mind. For instance, there exist a wider variety of tools for fault tree evaluation, Markov chain analysis, or the transformation of Petri nets into the corresponding Markov chains as well as other stochastic processes.

Some tools also combine several techniques in an integrated modelling environment. This allows for using the outcome of one model type as an input for another model type. Most tools also support the parametrisation of models and solving it with varying parameters. Commercial tools also offer import and export features to combine and support the file formats of standard office software packets.

More recently, some tools focus on disguising the complex evaluation process to the users. For example, the tool OpenSESAME takes a collection of reliability block diagrams as its input. These diagrams are enriched with inter-component dependencies. As traditional solution methods for reliability block diagrams cannot be applied to RBDs with dependencies, OpenSESAME transforms the input model into a set of semantically equivalent stochastic Petri nets. However, this transformation process is transparent to the users, who must not be familiar with Petri nets or Markov chains. For more information on OpenSESAME, the reader is referred to Walter and Schneeweiss [498].

9.6 Summary

The chapter "Hardware Reliability" addresses the issues quantitative evaluation, common measures and metrics, techniques for measurement and modeling of complex fault-tolerant system. The first issue deals with the goals of reliability evaluation and the choice of appropriate reliability metrics. In the next section reliability terms are defined with an emphasis on availability. Afterwards follows a discussion of the essential problem of properly collected data for further reliability analysis. The methods considered include - among others - field data gathering, stress screening and fault injection. Field data is used as an input for almost every physical reliability model such as the well-known MIL-217. There are a couple of rule-of-thumb techniques that can be used to estimate the relative reliability between different components such as the parts count, power consumption, heat and more complex ones, e.g. the parts stress analysis. Where field data is not available or fault-tolerance mechanisms aught to be validated, fault-injection must be used. Fault-injection basics and multiple fault-injection tools are presented and categorized (software-implemented, physical, simulation-based). To test the behavior of a system before delivery, stress screening is used during the manufacturing process. The problem to deal with uncertain data is briefly sketched. The chapter ends with a presentation of models for reliability metrics estimation. The described approaches include Fault Trees, Reliability Block Diagrams, Petri Nets, Sensitivity Analysis and Markov Chains.

10 Software Reliability

Irene Eusgeld[1], Falk Fraikin[2], Matthias Rohr[3], Felix Salfner[4], and Ute Wappler[5]

[1] Swiss Federal Institute of Technology (ETH), Zurich, Switzerland
[2] Darmstadt University of Technology, Germany
[3] University of Oldenburg, Germany
[4] Humboldt University Berlin, Germany
[5] Dresden University of Technology, Germany

Many concepts of software reliability engineering can be adapted from the older and successful techniques of hardware reliability. However, this must be done with care, since there are some fundamental differences in the nature of hardware and software and its failure processes. This chapter gives an introduction into software reliability metrics.

10.1 Introduction

Software reliability is often defined as "the probability of failure-free operation of a computer program for a specified time in a specified environment." [363, p. 15]. In this part, the three major classes of *software* reliability assessment are presented (Section 10.4):

Black box reliability analysis (P. 111): Estimation of the software reliability based on failure observations from testing or operation. These approaches are called *black box* approaches because internal details of the software are not considered.
Software metric based reliability analysis (P. 115): Reliability evaluation based on the static analysis of the software (e.g., lines of code, number of statements, complexity) or its development process and conditions (e.g., developer experience, applied testing methods).
Architecture-based reliability analysis (P. 119): Evaluation of the software system reliability from software component reliabilities and the system architecture (the way the system is composed out of the components). These approaches are sometimes called *component-based reliability estimation* (CBRE), or *grey* or *white box* approaches.

Many concepts of software reliability engineering are adapted from the older and successful techniques of hardware reliability. The application of hardware dependability methods to software has to be done with care, since there are some fundamental differences in the nature of hardware and software, and its failure processes. Therefore, well-established hardware dependability concepts might perform differently (usually not very well) for software. It was even proposed that "hardware-motivated measures such as mttf, mtbf should not be used for software without justification" [306].

Today, software reliability engineering is a separate domain. Research on software reliability measurement (e.g., the work of Cheung [95], Littlewood [305], and

I. Eusgeld, F.C. Freiling, and R. Reussner (Eds.): Dependability Metrics, LNCS 4909, pp. 104–125, 2008.
© Springer-Verlag Berlin Heidelberg 2008

Musa et al. [363]) addressed the characteristics of software reliability and adapted hardware reliability metrics. However, empirical evaluation is important before dependability concepts, derived from hardware-approaches, can be applied to software. For instance, such an empirical evaluation of component-based reliability estimation was presented by Krishnamurthy and Mathur [284].

Despite major advantages, software reliability assessment (with models such as the reliability growth models) is not powerful enough to address very high reliability demands (such as 10^{-9} of failure probability per hour) [308].

Software Faults Are Design Faults

The main difference between "hardware" and "software" failures is the underlying fault model. Traditionally, the largest part of hardware failures is considered as result from physical wearout or deterioration. Sooner or later, these *natural faults* [26], *will* introduce faults into hardware components and hence lead to failures.

Experience has shown, that these physical effects are well-described by exponential equations in the relation to time. Usage commonly accelerates the reliability decrease, but even unused hardware deteriorates. Physical separation and fault isolation (e.g., high-impedance electrical connections and optical couplers, such as applied by Wensley et al. [509]) made it possible to assume (approximately) statistical independence of the failure processes (of natural faults). The fact that this so-called *independence assumption* holds for physical faults, does not only highly reduce the complexity of the reliability models. Moreover, it makes the use of redundancy very effective in the context of hardware fault tolerance. Concepts, such as "hot" redundancy in combination with voting, or standby redundancy (reconfiguration upon failure detection), made it feasible to design systems with high hardware reliabilities.

Design faults are a different source for failures. They result mainly from human error in the development process or maintenance. Design faults will cause a failure under certain circumstances. The probability of the activation of a design fault is typically only usage dependent and time independent. By the increasing complexity of hardware systems, design faults become more and more an issue for hardware reliability measurement, so that "the division between hardware and software reliability is somewhat artificial" [362, p. 38].

Software is pure design [309] and consequently, software failures are caused by design faults [362, p. 38], [363, p. 7]. Note, the term "design" is used in a broad sense in software dependability and refers to all software development steps from the requirements to realization [294, p. 48]. Therefore, faults that are introduced during the implementation are also considered as design faults. In contrast to hardware, software can be perfect (i.e. fault-free). Unfortunately, it is usually not feasible to develop complex fault-free software, and even then, it is rarely feasible to guarantee that software is free of faults. Some formal methods can prove the correctness of software - this means it matches to a specification document. However, today's formal verification techniques are not designed for the application to large software systems such as consumer operation systems or word processors. Furthermore, correctness does not ensure reliability because the specification document itself can already be faulty. As it is not feasible to develop complex software systems free of faults and the absence of faults cannot be guaranteed, the reliability of software needs to be evaluated in order to fullfill high dependability requirements.

The failure process of design faults is different from the one of ("hardware") natural faults. Obviously, copies of (normal) software will fail together, if executed with the same parameters. This shows that the independence assumption does not hold. More precisely, the failure probabilities of software copies are completely dependent. This makes many hardware fault tolerance principles ineffective for software. Instead of using redundant copies, software reliability can be improved by using design diversity. A common approach for this is the so called N-version programming (surveyed in Avižienis [25], introduced by Chen and Avižienis [94]). However, the reseach of Knight and Leveson [279] indicates, that design diversity is likely to be less effective for software than N-modular redundancy is in hardware reliability engineering.

Some studies have shown that for complex systems, the majority of failures are typically caused by software faults (see, for example, Gray [194]). Although software faults are design faults, their behaviour in dependable systems is similar to transient hardware faults. This is due to the stochastic of their activation conditions [193].

Software Usage Profiles

Littlewood and Strigini [309] state that software reliability has to be a probabilistic measure because the failure process, i.e. the way faults become active and cause failures, depends on the input sequence and operation conditions, and those cannot be predicted with absolute certainty. Human behaviour introduces uncertainty and hence probability into software reliability, although software usually fails in the same way for same operational conditions and same parameters. An additional reason to claim a probabilistic measure is that it is usually only possible to approximate the number of faults of complex software system.

To issue different ways of usage, the concepts of *user profiles* [95] and *operational profiles* [360, 363] are common for (black box or white box) software reliability measurement. These models use probabilities to weight different ways of software usage. Usage profiles can be used for hardware as well. For software designers, it is easy (and often practice) to include "excessive extra functionality" [309]. From this point of view, the weighting of service requests seems especially important for software.

Besides software usage, other context information might have to be included into reliability assessment. This is required because software reliability is more sensitive to differences in operational contexts than hardware reliability [309, p. 179]. In other words, a piece of software that was reliable in one environment, might be very unreliable in a slightly different one.

10.2   Common Measures and Metrics: What Do I Measure?

Many software reliability metrics differ from hardware reliability metrics primarily in the models that are used for the computation (Section 10.4). Hardware reliability metrics are usually time dependent. Although the failure behavior of (software) design faults depends on usage and not directly on time, software reliability is usually expressed in relation to time, as well. Only as intermediate result, some reliability models use time-independent metrics such as the reliabilities of paths, scenarios, or execution runs. A major advantage of time dependent software reliability metrics is that they can be combined with hardware reliability metrics to estimate the system reliabiliy [363, p. 229]. For the evaluation of software design alternatives, time independent reliability metrics might be easier to compare.

For reasons of completeness, we repeat the relationships between the basic reliability metrics from Musa et al. [363, p. 228] (as said before, these are very similar to the hardware reliability metrics in Section 9.3, Page 65):

- Reliability $R(t)$:

$$R(t) = 1 - F(t) \tag{1}$$

- Failure probability $F(t)$:

$$F(t) = 1 - R(t) \tag{2}$$

- Failure density $f(t)$ (for $F(t)$ differentiable):

$$f(t) = \frac{dF(t)}{dt} \tag{3}$$

- Hazard rate $z(t)$ (also called conditional failure density):

$$z(t) = \frac{f(t)}{R(t)} \tag{4}$$

- Reliability $R(t)$ (derived from the hazard rate):

$$R(t) = exp[-\int_0^t z(x)dx] \tag{5}$$

- Mean time to failure (MTTF) $= \Theta$ (with t as operating time):

$$MTTF = \Theta = \int_0^\infty R(t)dt \tag{6}$$

- For clock time as approximation to execution time, $M(t)$ presents the random process of the number of failures experienced by time t, and $m(t)$ denotes the realisation of $M(t)$. The *mean value function*, which represents the expected number of failures at time t is given by:

$$\mu(t) = E[M(t)] \tag{7}$$

- *Failure intensity function* or *failure rate function*:

$$\lambda(t) = \frac{d\mu(t)}{dt} \tag{8}$$

- Note that the term "failure intensity" is used as a synonym for "failure rate" by foundational work in software reliability research (e.g., Musa et al. [363]). Musa [362] states that the term "failure intensity" was chosen to avoid common confusions between "failure rate" and "hazard rate".

Other relations between hardware and software reliabilities are:

- The *probability of failure per demand* can be suitable for terminating software. It is given by $1 - R$, with R as the reliability of a single execution [192].
- Availability related metrics such as downtime, uptime, or reboot time are more related to combined hardware-software-systems.
- Terms such as "*lifetime*" are less common in the context of software reliability.

Dependability Benchmarks

Performance benchmarks such as SPEC have become a powerful tool to evaluate and to compare performance of computer systems. This approach has not been adapted to dependability aspects until recently. Silva and Madeira [448] give an overview on the role of dependability benchmarks.

The objective of dependability benchmarks is to standardize ways how dependability of computer systems can be assessed. Since it is difficult to objectify dependability evaluation, an important part of the benchmark developing process is to set up an evaluation workflow that is accepted by a wide range of companies and customers of computer systems. Acceptance can be described by the attributes representativeness, usefulness and agreement.

The principle structure of a dependability benchmark is shown in Figure 1. In addition to a workload usually defined in performance benchmarks, there is a fault load which is basically a set of faults and stressful conditions, and there are measures that are related to dependability. The measurements of the benchmark can either be used directly in order to compare different systems or it can be used as input for dependability models (see Section 10.4) in order to derive dependability metrics that have a scope beyond the benchmark's measurements.

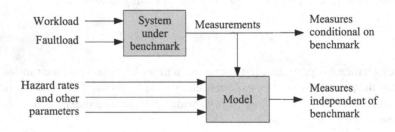

Fig. 1. Dependability Benchmarks

Silva and Madeira [448] also give references to dependability benchmarks that have been published recently.

10.3   Techniques for Measurement: What Data Is Necessary?

Just as a reminder, the title's question is worth repeating: What data is necessary? Data should not be collected only because it can be done. This would be just wasteful. First of all a purpose, a goal should be defined that leads to questions that can be answered by collecting data. One method to achieve this is the GQM method described in Chapter 6.

The corresponding section on hardware reliability (s. Section 9.4) was divided into subsections on field data and fault injection among others. For software those terms have a slightly different meaning and significance. Furthermore, in the context of hardware reliability modeling, research and practice focus almost only on data about observed failures. For software the data used is much more diverse.

Program Size

Several models use the size or complexity of a program as input. A well-known metric for measuring program size is the *lines of code* metric (LOC) which is deceivingly simple. One problem with LOC is the ambiguity of the operational definition. Which lines are to be counted? Surely executable lines are counted, but what about two executable statements in one line? Lines containing data declarations only? Empty lines? Comments? Obviously, this problem can and has to be handled by a clear definition of LOC that is adhered to throughout the project.

Another problem is the obvious dependency of LOC on the programming language used which is typically a disturbing property in this context. An alternative measure for program size that abstracts from the programming language is the *function point* (FP). Developed in the late 1970s by Albrecht [16] function points basically are a weigted sum of the numbers of the following components of an application: external inputs, external outputs, user inquiries, logical internal files, and external interface files. This weighted sum is refined by the estimated complexity of those components and furthermore by 14 weighted general system characteristics. As FPs thus rely much more on the functional requirements of an application and not on the implementation, FPs are much more useful for doing comparisons across different programming languages and also across different companies. A common metric involving FPs, e.g., is "defects per FP".

Test Phase

Data collected during the test phase is often used to estimate the number of software faults remaining in a system which in turn often is used as input for reliability prediction. This estimation can either be done by looking at the numbers (and the rate) of faults found during testing [197] or just by looking at the effort that was spent on testing. The underlying assumption when looking at testing effort is "more testing leads to higher reliability". For example, Nagappan et al. [364], Nagappan [365], Nagappan et al. [366] evaluated the following metrics (and more) in this context:

- Number of test cases / source lines of code
- Number of test cases / number of requirements
- Test lines of code / sourcelines of code
- Number of assertions / source lines of code
- Number of test classes / number of source classes
- Number of conditionals/ number of source lines of code
- Number of lines of code / number of classes

Failure Data

Of course, information about observed failures can also be used for software reliability assessment. Data collected includes, e.g., date of occurence, nature of failures, consequences, fault types, and fault location [266].

In the case that field data is not available and testing does not yield a sufficient amount of failure data, *fault injection* can be applied. An introduction is given in Chapter 9.4. Fault models for software faults exist but are not as common as hardware fault models, yet. A well-known example is Orthogonal Defect Classification (ODC) [97]. It divides software faults in six groups: *assignment, checking, timing, algorithm,* and *function.* For emulation by an injector, these faults have to be "generated", which means that even if there is no fault in the code, the code is changed. For example, if a checking fault should be generated, a check in the code could be changed such that a less-or-equal check is replaced by a less check. When the running program reaches the particular location in the code, a false check is performed resulting in a checking fault. Note, that the goal of fault injection is to acquire data about *failures* – not the data about the fault that was injected should be observed but the ability of the rest of the system to handle the fault. An implementation of a software fault injector was described by Durães and Madeira [137, 138].

Another use case for software fault injection not directly related to reliability is the assessment of test suites. The basic idea is to inject a number of faults into a system, run the corresponding test suite, and use the percentage of injected faults detected by the test suite as an indicator for the coverage achieved by the test suite.

10.4   Modeling: How Do I Model?

Although hardware and software reliability is similar, they have to deal with failure rates of diverse characteristics. Under the assumption that the program code is not altered and the usage profile stays constant, software lacks the typical wear-out phase where failure rates rapidly increase after a long time of being quasi-constant (see Figure 4 in Chapter 9). However, the assumption that the code stays the same for the lifetime of a system does not hold. Typically, a software is under permanent development, testing and bug fixing. This affects failure rates in several ways. Smaller updates reduce the failure rate in most cases, except for those where the fix of one bug introduced others increasing the failure rate. On the other hand, the majority of software offers major updates from time to time that offer a bunch of new functionality introducing a lot of code that shows high failure rates. This often leads to jumps in the overall failure rate. Figure 2 sketches the effect.

A bunch of models have been developed trying to get a grip on the specifics of software failure rates. Some of the models will be introduced in the following sections. They are grouped by the amount of internal knowledge about the software and its structure. Black box reliability models do not rely on internal specifics of the software. Another group of models builds on software metrics such as complexity measures and a third group analyzes the internal structure of the software under consideration.

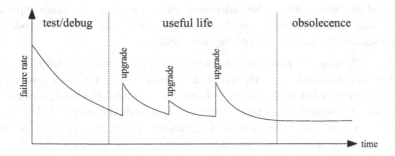

Fig. 2. A rough sketch of software failure rate over lifetime

Black Box Reliability Models

Software reliability estimation with black box models dates back to the year 1967 when Hudson [225] modeled program errors as a stochastic birth and death process. In the following years, a lot of models have been developed building on various stochastic properties. In their book "Software Reliability", Musa et al. [363] introduce a more general formalism that is able to capture most of the models that have been published. Farr [154] reiterates the overview of Musa et al. [363] but focuses more on the explicit description of each of the reliability models. The classification scheme of Musa et al. [363] groups software reliability models in terms of five attributes:

1. *Time domain:* Is the time base for the model calendar time or execution time?
2. *Category:* Is the number of failures that can be experienced in infinite time finite or infinite?
3. *Type:* What is the distribution of the number of failures experienced by time t?
4. *Class (for finite category only):* What is the functional form of the failure intesity in terms of time?
5. *Family (for infinite category only):* What is the functional form of the failure intensity in terms of the expected number of failures experienced?

The objective of this section is to sketch the major attributes in order to give an impression what properties are addressed by the attributes. A small set of well-known models will be described later in this section.

Time Domain. Musa [361] introduced a new notion of reliability modeling that was based on a software's execution time rather than calendar time. Times between failures are expressed in terms of computational processing units aiming at incorporating the stress induced on the software. Since execution time seems to be rather arbitrary for project managers, Musa added a second model component that relates execution time to calendar time by expenditures for human and computational resources.

Finite and Infinite Category. The *category* attribute classifies software reliability models according to the property whether the number of encountered failures tends to infinity or not in infinite time. Sounding rather theoretical, it classifies whether the software under consideration tends to be fault-free in infinite time or not. For example, if correction of a fault leads to other faults, the software may never be fault-free.

Poisson and Binomial Types. The distribution of the number of failures experienced by time t plays a major role in the classification of software reliabiliy models. The following section discusses both types in more details.

Distribution Class and Family. Reliability models of the finite and infinite category can each be subclassified according to the functional form of failure intensity modeling. *Failure intensity* is the number of failures per time unit. For models of the finite category, the functional form of failure intensity is described in terms of *time* by a distribution of a certain *class*. As models of the infinite category require an description of failure intensity in terms of the *expected number of failures*, it is described by a distribution of a certain *family*.

The intention of this section is not to provide a comprehensive overview of existing software reliability models but to sketch the basic ideas and to give some reference to the most well-known models.

Poisson and Binomial Type Models. Musa et al. [363] identified two types of models that differ in the underlying failure process. Whereas binomial type models assume that there is an initial number of faults u_0 in the program, Poisson-type models assume the initial number of faults to be a random variable with mean ω_0.

Binomial type models. Assume that there is a one-to-one correspondence between fault and failure. After each failure, the causing fault is repaired instantaneously and repair is perfect, which means that repair eliminates the problem and does not cause new ones. This assumption leads to the notion that each fault in the software occurs exactly once and that it is independent of other faults. It is assumed that each fault/failure occurs randomly in time according to a per-fault hazard rate $z_a(t)$, which is assumed to be the same for all faults.

Since the hazard rate is defined as

$$z_a(t) = \frac{f_a(t)}{1 - F_a(t)} \tag{9}$$

where $F_a(t)$ is the cumulative distribution function of the random variable T_a denoting time to failure of fault a and $f_a(t)$ is its density. By solving the differential Equation 9 we obtain

$$F_a(t) = 1 - \exp\left[-\int_0^t z_a(x)dx\right] \tag{10}$$

By conditioning on time t' we have

$$F_a(t|t') = \frac{F_a(t) - F_a(t')}{1 - F_a(t')} = 1 - \exp\left[\int_{t'}^t z_a(x)dx\right] \tag{11}$$

The essential notion for binomial-type models is that due to the hazard rate, by time t each fault a is removed with probability $F_a(t)$ and remains in the software with probability $1 - F_a(t)$. Since there are u_0 faults at $t = 0$ the probability that m out of u_0 faults are removed until time t is the value of the binomial distribution

$$P[M(t) = m] = \binom{u_0}{m} \left[F_a(t)\right]^m \left[1 - F_a(t)\right]^{u_0 - m} \tag{12}$$

This is why models building on the above assumptions are of binomial type.

In order to obtain an equation for reliability, we need to determine the probability

$$P[T_i > t_i | T_{i-1} = t_{i-1}] \tag{13}$$

where T_i is the random variable of the time of i-th failure. It denotes the probability that the next failure i occurs at time t_i given that the last occurred at t_{i-1}. The fact that $i-1$ failures have occurred implies that only $u_0 - i + 1$ faults remain in the software yielding:

$$P[T_i > t_i | T_{i-1} = t_{i-1}] = [1 - F_a(t_i | t_{i-1})]^{u_0 - i + 1} \tag{14}$$

Using Equation 11 yields

$$P[T_i > t_i | T_{i-1} = t_{i-1}] = \exp\left[-(u_0 - i + 1) \int_{t_{i-1}}^{t_i} z_a(x)dx\right] \tag{15}$$

Replacing the absolute time t_i by the temporal difference δt_i, which is the time from failure $i-1$ to failure i, we obtain an equation for reliability, that is dependent on the number of remaining faults $(u_0 - i + 1)$ and the time of the last failure t_{i-1}:

$$R(\delta t_i | t_{i-1}) = \exp\left[-(u_0 - i + 1) \int_{t_{i-1}}^{t_{i-1}+\delta t_i} z_a(x)dx\right] \tag{16}$$

If the hazard rate $z_a(t)$ is constant then the integral and hence reliability are independent of t_{i-1}.

Poisson-type models. Assume that the initial number of faults in a software is not known as is the case with binomial type models, but rather is a Poisson random variable with mean ω_0. Therefore, u_0 is being replaced by the random variable $U(0)$ and Equation 12 is transformed into

$$P[M(t) = m] = \sum_{x=0}^{\infty} \binom{x}{m} \left[F_a(t)\right]^m \left[1 - F_a(t)\right]^{x-m} \frac{\omega_0^x}{x!} \exp(-\omega_0) \tag{17}$$

where the first part is the binomial distribution for an initial number of x faults and the second part is the poisson distribution, yielding the probability that there are actually x faults given the mean ω_0.

This equation can be transformed into

$$P[M(t) = m] = \frac{[\omega_0 F_a(t)]^m}{m!} \exp[-\omega_0 F_a(t)] \tag{18}$$

showing that the assumption of a Poisson distribution of the number of initial faults leads to a Poisson distribution for the number of failures that have occurred until time t, which equals the number of faults removed.

Comparison. The two types of models described above are obviously similar. Both models assume that the hazard rate are the same for all faults. The Bayesian model of Littlewood and Verrall (see below) gives up this assumption. Since for Poisson-type models the number of failures is a random variable, they are able to accomodate, in an approximate fashion, for imperfect debugging that eventually introduces new faults during repair actions.

Having a closer look at the characteristics of the hazard rate of the entire program (not to be mixed with hazard rate of the single faults), it can be observed that binomial-type models have discontinuous program hazard rates. Each time a failure occurs it is removed and the program hazard rate decreases discontinuously, which seems realistic since the correction of a bug causes an immediate decrease. Poisson-type models do not show this property. However, in a real environment failures are not repaired immediately but at some random time after failure which is an argument in favour of the Poisson approach.

Besides from the number of failures experienced until time t, which was denoted by $M(t)$, and reliability $R(\delta t_i | t_{i-1})$, other reliability metrics such as mean time to failure (MTTF) can be derived from the stochastic process.

A Brief Overview of Existing Models. In the equations above, neither the fault hazard rate $z_a(t)$ nor the distribution of the time to the next fault/failure $f_a(t)$ and $F_a(t)$ respectively, have been specified. This is where many of the models that have been proposed differ. Since many of the models share assumptions about the characteristic of the hazard rate, Musa et al. introduced the "class" attribute. For example, the models proposed by Jelinski and Moranda [256] or Shooman [440] belong to the class of binomial type models with exponential hazard rates while the model proposed by Schneidewind [431] is a Poisson-type model with exponential hazard rates. Other classes include Weibull, Pareto or gamma distributions.

One well-known model should not be forgotten, even if it leaves the sketched framework in various ways: the model proposed by Littlewood and Verrall [310]. The authors postulated that software reliability is correlated with the belief that a software works correctly leading to the consequence that reliability changes even if no failure occurs. Therefore, reliability increases within failure-free time intervals and changes discontinuously at the time of failure occurrence. The model incorporates both the case of fault elimination and of introducing new faults. An additional assumption is that faults do not have equal impact on system reliability since some are more likely to be executed than others. Littlewood and Verrall use a Bayesian framework where the prior distribution is determined by past data (e.g., from previous projects) and the posterior incorporates past and current data. By this approach, both small updates including bug fixes as well as major upgrades that most commonly introduce new bugs can be modeled. As might have become visible, the model is very powerful covering a large variety of software projects, however, it is quite complex and more difficult to apply.

Fitting Black Box Reliability Models to Measurement Data. Brocklehurst and Littlewood [72] assessed the accuracy of some reliability models such as Jelinski-Moranda or Littlewood-Verrall based on industrial datasets and observed that the reliability prediction of the different models varied heavily. The authors also provided an overview of several techniques, how the divergence of predictions and real data can be measured. The techniques will be reiterated shortly, here.

From test data, two sets of data need to be extracted: Time to next failure and the model's reliability predictions. A straightforward way of comparison would be to take the predicted median time to failure and to count how many times the predicted median time was larger than the real time to next failure. If this is the case in approximately 50% of all predictions, the prediction could be valued accurate *in average*.

A more sophisticated approach is to draw a u-plot and to assess predictive accuracy in terms of divergence from the line of unit slope measured by, e.g., the Kolmogorov-Smirnov distance, which is the maximum vertical distance between both lines. Since the u-plot does not account for trends, a y-plot can be used instead of the u-plot.

The u-plot can be used to improve black box reliability models by fitting them to the MTTF values that are observed for a running system. The approach is also presented in Brocklehurst and Littlewood [72]: For the time between two successive occurrences of real failures, it is assumed that the cumulative reliability distribution estimated by the model $\hat{F}(t)$ can be linearly transformed by G such that $G[\hat{F}(t)]$ is equal to the true cumulative reliability distribution $F(t)$. Since G is also unknown, its estimate $G^{\star}$ is calculated by use of the u-plot obtained from previous observations: $G^{\star}$ is the polygon formed by successive u-plot steps. In Brocklehurst et al. [73] the same authors propose to replace the polygon by an SP-line yielding further improved prediction accuracy at the cost of more complex computations.

Software Metric Based Reliability Models

The objective is to reason about residual fault frequencies or failure frequencies which have to be expected when executing the software. Therefore, either static analysis of software using metrics such as lines of code, number of statements, or metrics measuring complexity can be used. On the other hand the development process and conditions under which software was developed influence its quality and such can also be used to estimate reliability.

Classification and Clustering Methods. The objective of *classification* methods is to learn how to assign data items to predefined classes. Clustering is the organization of data items into clusters based on similarity [248] without predefined classes.

A lot of research has been done and also is currently going on to investigate how classification and clustering methods can be used to assess the reliability of software and also hardware. For example Zhong et al. [526] describes how semi-supervised clustering is used to identify software modules as either fault-prone or not fault-prone. Classification methods are also useful to assess system reliability, e.g., Karunanithi et al. [268] use neural networks to predict the number of failures of a system after a given execution time based on time series information.

All classification and clustering methods have in common that the used data items are feature vectors $x = (x_1, ..., x_n)$ where x represents a single data item and every x_i with $i \in [1..n]$ is one measurement describing the data item, e.g., one could measure lines of code, number of methods and lines of comments for programs. This would result in one feature vector for each program. In principle every measurement described in Section 10.3 can be used as input data.

The usual procedure is that a set of data items–called training data–is used to train the clustering or classification algorithm. This phase is called training or learning phase of the algorithm. Afterwards the algorithm can be used to classify new unclassified data items, i.e., associate it with a class or cluster.

The literature distinguishes classification and clustering methods depending on the information used to train the algorithm:

Unsupervised: All clustering methods use unsupervised learning. Apart from the data collection and maybe depending on the algorithm the number K of clusters to be formed no information is available [195]. This only allows the partioning into clusters based on similarity and thus limits its usefulness for reliability assessment. Because of this unsupervised learning clustering is also called unsupervised classification [248].

Supervised: Supervised learning is required for classification. A data collection with additional knowledge about the data items, e.g., class labels is available for training.

Semi-supervised: A small amount of knowledge about the data collection is available, e.g., labels for some data items. The available data is not representative and thus cannot be used for a supervised algorithm [195].

There exist numerous algorithms for classification and clustering. For an introduction to clustering algorithms have a look at Jain et al. [248]. The current research dealing with classification of software or systems with respect to their reliability is using artifical neural networks as classification method. These have the advantage that they are able to develop the required model on their own in contrast to classical analytical models which have to be parametrized depending on the solved problem [269]. This parametrization is no trivial task. Karunanithi et al. [269] show that the neural nets which result from the training process are more complex than the usually used analytical methods by means of number of required parameters. Thus neural networks are easier to use and capture the problem complexity more accurate. For an introduction to artifical neural networks use Anderson and McNeil [18].

The most used approach for reliability assessement using classification is to take a set of data items somehow describing a program or a part of hardware and to label these data items with reliability information, e.g., number of residual faults or failure rates. This data collection is used to train a classification algorithm which later on is used to classify unknown software or hardware with respect to the used class labels. The following research follows this principle: Karunanithi et al. [268], Karunanithi et al. [269], Tian and Noore [469], Khoshgoftarr et al. [274], and Pai and Lin [387].

Karunanithi et al. [268], and Karunanithi et al. [269] were the first who used neural networks to realize a reliability growth prediction. As a training set pairs of execution times (input to the net) and observed fault counts (expected output) are used. These pairs represent the complete failure history of a system since the beginning of its testing up to some point. The trained net could be used to predict fault counts for future executions. Two types of prediction are distinguished: next-step and longterm prediction. The first predicts the output for the next point in a time series and the second predicts fault counts for some point in the future. Comparing the neural network approach to traditional analytical methods led to the observation that for longterm prediction the neural network approach resulted in significant better predictions and for next-step prediction the results were insignificant less accurate.

Since these first approaches for reliability growth prediction many contributions in this direction were done: Some of the newer papers dealing with reliability growth prediction using neural networks are Tian and Noore [469], and Pai and Lin [387].

Neural networks could not only be used to predict failure/fault rates using time series data. Khoshgoftarr et al. [274] used a collection of classical software metrics such as number of lines of code, Halstead's effort metric, or McCabe's Cyclomatic complexity to determine how many faults are contained in a program. Since this approach does not consider environmental conditions such as problem complexity, and development environment the obtained results should be treated with caution (see Fenton and Ohlsson [159]).

The research described up to now uses supervised approaches for training the algorithms. Since this requires extensive labeled data collection to train the algorithm current research aims at using semi-supervised approaches. Seliya et al. [436] and Zhong et al. [526] describe an approach which uses clustering methods to partition data collections describing software modules. Afterwards an expert estimates for each cluster if the described software modules are fault-prone or not fault-prone. The assumption is that software modules within one cluster partition have similar properties with respect to fault-proness.

Bayesian Belief Nets. *Bayesian Belief Nets* (BBNs) are an old concept for graphically representing and reasoning about logical relationships between variables. It enables us to handle the uncertainty in the dependency between these variables by using conditional probabilities [447]. Reliability of software is mainly influenced by the quality of its development process which is very difficult to judge objectively. Thus, it is not possible to determine its influence with certainty. Fenton and Ohlsson [159] showed that to assess software quality more is required than using classical software metrics such as lines of code. They proposed the usage of BBNs to take further influences, e.g., quality of the development process, into account [157, 158]. Prinicpially, BBNs are also usable for assessing reliability of hardware. But since design faults are not the major issue with hardware, they are rarely used in this context.

Furthermore, BBNs are usable when other reliability prediction methods are not, because not enough data is available. For example in safety critical systems usually reliability growth models are not applicable, because the number of observed failures is far too low [71].

A BBN is a directed acyclic graph. Every node represents a discrete random variable,i.e. the predicate or statement which is represented by this variable is true or false with a certain probability. Edges represent causal dependencies between variables. For an example have a look at Figure 3.

Nodes which have only outgoing edges and no incoming ones are called root nodes. The variable represented by a root node is not influenced by any other variable. Nodes at the end of an outgoing edge are called children and the nodes with outgoing edges are parent nodes. The meaning is that children somehow depend on their parents. How a variable depends on other variables is determined by conditional probabilities. Every node with incoming edges has a node probability table (NPT) assigned to it. This table

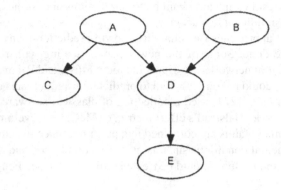

Fig. 3. Sample BBN [447]

contains conditional probabilities determining how a child depends on its parents. Root nodes are just assigned the probability for being true. Obviously, the probability for being false is the negation of the probability to be true.

To construct a BBN requires three stages [447]:

1. *Problem structuring:* In this step relevant variables are identified and the network structure is determined, i.e., the dependencies between the variables.
2. *Instantiation:* After defining the structure of the net, the probabilities have to be assigned. These may be derived from collected data or elicited from experts. For reliability predictions both is done. Amasaki et al. [17] extract the used probabilities from collected data, whereas Sigurdsson et al. [447] and Bouissou et al. [71] use expert knowledge.
3. *Inference:* In this step the net is evaluated using the baseyian theorem and theory of conditional probabilities. Known evidence about the state of variables is used to update the probabilities of the other variables and thus make statements about the probabilities of these variables becoming true or false. For example if we know that code reviews were made the probability that the software has no residual faults will increase. This statements are possible without using BBNs, but using BBNs makes them quantifiable, describes them more formal and prevents fallacies in reasoning due to misunderstanding of probability theory [71].

The main objective of BBNs is a what-if-analysis. On the one hand one can enter observed evidence, e.g., which tools are really used to improve design quality, and determine probabilities for all variables depending on this evidence. One of these variables usually will describe the reliability of the developed software, e.g. a predicate *residualFaultsExist*. This type of evaluation is called forward propagation.

On the other hand one could determine how big the influence of some variables onto others is. Thus, one can determine the benefit of methods such as code reviews or applied development models and use this knowledge to decide which methods are benefical and which not. This is called backward propagation since one first assumes that a reliable software was developed and with this evidence the conditional probability

$p(reliableSoftware|codeReview)$ can be computed,i.e. one goes from the dependen child node to its parent.

In reliability assessment BBNs are mostly used to model subjective knowledge about environmental conditions such as used development methods and tools, experience of developers and so on. For the first time this was done by Fenton and Neil [157, 158].

Advantages of BBNs in general are [447]:

– Easy to understand graphical representation.
– Combination of separate evidence sources.
– Easy to use.
– Takes uncertainty into account.
– Explicit modeling of dependencies.

In comparison to fault trees BBNs allow easier use of multistate variables, can model the undertainty in noisy gates and can capture sequentially dependent failures. In comparison to reliability block diagrams with BBNs common-cause failures can be modeled more naturally [447].

BBNs can also be used to complement already used mechanisms for predicting reliability. Amasaki et al. [17] observed that software reliability growth prediction sometimes predicts that a software is reliable, i.e. has few enough residual faults, for software which has no good quality at all. Thus, they proposed a solution where BBNs complement software reliability growth prediction by determining the probability that a software can be of high quality. For building the BBN the following data is used: product size, effort in the sense of person-day, detected faults, and residual faults.

For a deeper introduction into the theoretical foundations of BBNs refer to Pearl [391]. For learning how to use BBNs practically have a look at Jensen [259]. Bouissou et al. [71] gives a short less abstract introduction. Sigurdsson et al. [447] summarizes current work about using BBNs to represent expert knowledge in reliability assessment. The paper also gives advice how to obtain this expert knowledge.

Architecture-Based Reliability Models (White Box)

This subsection presents the basic approaches for reliability prediction of component-based software systems. Large software systems are often composed from smaller blocks that bundle functionality. In architecture-based reliability prediction, these blocks are named components. Without the need to refer to a special definition, components are just considered as basic entities of the software architecture. The architectural reliability models allow to predict the system reliability from the software architecture (containing components and connections between them) and the component reliability data.

The black box approaches, summarized above measure the reliability of a piece of software only based on observations from the outside. Intuitively, some software quality attributes, such as performance or reliability are compositional - the quality of a larger system seems to be derived from the quality of smaller parts and their relationship to each other. Architecture-based approaches follow this intuition by looking at the coarse-grained inner structure of software to measure the reliability.

A major advantage of architectural reliability (or performance) prediction approaches is that it is possible to predict the system reliability already early during the software design phase [441]. Failure data of the composed system is not required, as it is the case for the black box approaches. Therefore, potential quality problems might be discovered before a running system or prototype is implemented and black box approaches could be used.

The independence assumption is a major assumptions in reliability engineering. In the context of architectural reliability models, it assumes that the component reliabilities (as probability) are statistically independent. This allows to compute the reliability of a sequence of components as product of the component reliability. The independence assumption can lead to overly pessimistic reliability estimates, when the same components are executed multiple times in (large) loops.

The reuse of software components can affect the system reliability in both directions. Reuse of components plays a major role in making software development more effective. It is hoped to reduce development time and costs by reusing already developed and tested components. Reusing components can have a positive effect on the reliability of composite system because the components have already been part of a software product and taken part in its associated reliability growth. Therefore, the remaining number of failures might be smaller than that of newly developed components. However, reusing components can also be a reliability risk when some implicit assumptions about operation are not documented or ignored during reuse. As stated before, software (and therefore software components) is more sensitive to changes in their operational environment than hardware [309]. Software that has shown good reliability before, might perform bad in a slightly different context.

The following subsections are intended to provide a first idea on how the reliability of component-based software systems can be predicted, and which data is required. Surveys on architectural software reliability models have been published by Goševa-Popstojanova and Trivedi [192] and by Dimov and Punnekkat [120], focusing on the analysis of some more recent approaches. We limit this overview to provide simple examples for the three major classes, and describe only major conceptual extensions of later approaches.

We follow the structure of Goševa-Popstojanova and Trivedi [192], that distinguishes between three different classes of architecture based reliability models based on the way of combining the failure behaviour and the software architecture: state-based, path-based, or additive (using component reliabilities, omitting the architecture).

State-based Models. State-based approaches use probabilistic state representations, such as Markov chains, to model the transfer of control between components.

The early approach (for not continuously running applications) by Cheung [95, 96] uses a discrete time Markov chain (DTMC). It is created from a directed graph that represents the control flow between the software components. Without the loss of generality, N_1 is the single entry node and N_n is the single exit node. Matrix P contains the probabilities $P_{i,j}$ as possible transfer of control from node N_i to N_j.

As next step, the two absorbing states C and F are added, representing the states of correct and incorrect system output. This leads to the set of nodes $\{C, F, N_1, \ldots, N_n\}$. Absorbing states have no outgoing transitions to other states.

Matrix $\hat{P}$ is derived from P with $\hat{P}(i,j)$ by including the probability R_i that a component i produces the correct result. As shown in Figure 10.4, direct transfers of control from a component back to itself are not allowed (except for C and F). Furthermore, N_1 (as start state) has no ingoing transactions, and when N_n is reached, there are no transfers of control back to the other nodes (except to C and F).

	C	F	N_1	N_2	$\ldots$	N_j	$\ldots$	N_n
C	1	0	0	0	$\ldots$	0	$\ldots$	0
F	0	1	0	0	$\ldots$	0	$\ldots$	0
N_1	0	$1-R_1$	0	$R_i P_{12}$	$\ldots$	$R_1 P_{1j}$	$\ldots$	$R_1 P_{1n}$
$\vdots$	$\vdots$	$\vdots$	$\vdots$	$\vdots$		$\vdots$		$\vdots$
N_i	0	$1-R_i$	0	$R_i P_{i2}$	$\ldots$	$R_i P_{ij}$	$\ldots$	$R_i P_{in}$
$\vdots$	$\vdots$	$\vdots$	$\vdots$	$\vdots$		$\vdots$		$\vdots$
N_{n-1}	0	$1-R_{n-1}$	0	$R_{n-1}P_{(n-1)2}$	$\ldots$	$R_{n-1}P_{(n-1)j}$	$\ldots$	$R_{n-1}P_{(n-1)n}$
N_n	R_n	$1-R_n$	0	0	$\ldots$	0	$\ldots$	0

Fig. 4. Structure of the matrix $\hat{P}$ [95] as Markov model representation of correct transfer of control between components

$\hat{P}(i,j)$ represents only a single correct step in a execution sequence. The Markov Model has the nice property that $\hat{P}^n(i,j)$ denotes the probability of reaching the states $j \in \{C,F\}$ within n steps. Therefore, $\hat{P}^n(N_1,C)$ is the probability of correct termination in n or less steps.

Let the reduced matrix Q be created from $\hat{P}$ by removing the states C and F. The overall system reliability R is computed by

$$R = S(1,n)R_n \text{ ,with } S = I + Q + Q^2 + \cdots = \sum_{k=0}^{\infty} = (I-Q)^{-1} \qquad (19)$$

A variety of similar state-based models have been presented for terminating applications:

- The model of Kubat [285] uses *task-dependend* reliabilities for each component. These are derived from probabilistic component execution times. The component reliabilities are exponentially distributed with a constant failure rate.
- The failure rates in Gokhale et al. [186]'s model are time-dependent. Instead of using tasks (as Kubat [285]), different utilisation is modeled though the cumulative expected time spent in the component per execution.
- Hamlet et al. [207] use so-called *input profiles* as reliability parameter for each component. The input profiles are used to compute output profiles, which might be the input profiles for other components of the architecture.
- A similar parametrisation of usage is applied in the model of Reussner et al. [414], which computes the component reliability as a function of the usage profile. In addition, it enhances the approach of Hamlet et al. [207] by applying the idea of

parametrized contracts [413], which addresses the problem that functional and non-functional component properties highly depend on conditions of the deployment context. This idea is realized by making the properties of the services required (in the deployment context) a parameter of the component reliability function.

The reliability prediction of *continuously* running applications uses slightly different models. The required types of data are the exact or approximate distributions of the number of failures $N(t)$ in time interval $(0, t]$, the waiting time to first failure, and the failure rate [192]. The major approaches can be summarized as follows:

- Littlewood [305] models the architecture with an irreducible continuous time Markov chain (CTMC). A Poisson process predicts the occurrence of failures in the components using a constant failure rate.
- Ledoux [296] adds a second failure behaviour model to Laprie [292]'s approach. In addition to the failure behaviour model that assumes instantaneously restart, the second one addresses recovery times by delaying the execution for some time.
- Littlewood [307] generalises the earlier approach Littlewood [305] by characterising the system by an irreducible semi-Markov process (SMP).

Path-based Models. Path-based models abstract modularised system as paths. A path is understood as (mostly independent) sequence of components or statements.

Shooman [441] consider a path as a black box. This means that only f_i as the relative frequency of the execution of a path i of k total paths, and q_i as the probability of failure for a path are required. The number of failures to expect n_f in N system executions (= path runs) is given by

$$n_f = N f_1 q_1 + N f_2 q_2 + \ldots + N f_k q_k = N \sum_{i=1}^{k} f_i q_i \tag{20}$$

For the number of paths N approaching infinity, the probability of failure of a execution run is given by

$$q_0 = \lim_{N \to \infty} \frac{n_f}{N} = \sum_{i=1}^{k} f_i q_i \tag{21}$$

Given the execution time t_i, assuming a rectangular time to failure distribution for a path ($t_i/2$ hours in average), the average system failure rate z_0 is computed as

$$z_0 = \frac{\sum_{i=1}^{k} f_i q_i}{\sum_{i=1}^{k} f_i (1 - \frac{q_i}{2}) t_i} = \frac{q_0}{\sum_{i=1}^{k} f_i (1 - \frac{q_i}{2}) t_i} \tag{22}$$

A similar path-based approach is presented and evaluated in Krishnamurthy and Mathur [284]. The concept of operational profiles [360] is used to generate a representative set of test cases T. This moves the weighting of b (f_i in the approach presented above) into an earlier step. The system reliability R can be computed as

$$R = \frac{\sum_{\forall t \in T} R_t}{|T|}, \tag{23}$$

where the reliability R^t of the path t is given by

$$R^t = \prod_{\forall m \in M(t)} R_m. \tag{24}$$

R_m denotes the reliability of a component m. $M(t)$ is the *component trace* of the test case t. A component trace can contain multiple invocations of the same component.

Krishnamurthy and Mathur [284] evaluate the problem of intra-component dependencies, which is the dependency between multiple invocations of the same component. The authors use an approach to "collapse" multiple occurrences of a component in a trace to a lower number. The degree of this process is referred as degree of independence. A DOI of ∞ means that no collapse is done at all. The DOI decreases the maximum number of component occurrences in component trace to k. For instance, the component trace t containing n executions of component j, the path reliability would be

$$R_c^t = R_j^{min(n,DOI)} \tag{25}$$

The work of Cortellessa et al. [109] is similar to the path-based approaches. Scenario-dependent component failure probabilities are derived from annotated UML Use-Case Diagrams and UML Sequence Diagrams. Component and connector failure rates are assumed to be known. The annotations of UML Deployment Diagrams allow the computation of component interactions probabilities between components in different deployment contexts. The failure probability of components and the one of the connectors failure probability are combined to determine the reliability of the whole system.

Additive Approaches. According to the characterisation of Goševa-Popstojanova and Trivedi [192], additive approaches are not explicitly using the software architecture, but still base the computation on component failure data. It is assumed that the component reliabilities can be modeled as nonhomogeneous Poisson Process (NHPP). Thus, the times between the occurrence of component failures are independent. The presented models combine the NHPPs of the components to a single NHPP for the system.

Assuming parallel component testing, Xie and Wohlin [514] estimate component reliabilities from component failure data (from independent testing). As the system is considered as a series system, every component failure leads to a system failure. This is a pessimistic assumption for fault tolerant system designs, because these might not show a system failure for every component failure. An other major assumption of additive models requires that the time t is set to zero for all components at the same time. This requires the introduction of the components at the same time point. This assumption allows to compute the system failure rate $\lambda_s(t)$ at time t simply by summing up the subsystem (component) failure rates $\lambda_i(t)$

$$\lambda_s(t) = \lambda_1(t) + \lambda_2(t) + \ldots + \lambda_n(t). \tag{26}$$

The corresponding cumulative number of system failures $\mu_s(t)$ (also known as mean value function) at time t is

$$\mu_s(t) = \sum_{i=1}^{n} u_i(t) = \int_0^t (\sum_{i=1}^{n} \lambda_i(s)) ds. \tag{27}$$

A similar approach is presented by Everett [152]. It is argued, that the approach can be used before the system testing starts, because system failure data is not required for first predictions. Everett's model [152] differs from Xie and Wohlin [514] in determining the component reliabilities by an approach called Extended Execution Time (EET) model (see Everett [151]). The EET is in parts identical to Musa et al. [363]'s Basic Execution Time (BET) model. Both estimate component reliabilities from product and process properties such as the fault-density (e.g., estimated from earlier projects), lines of code, and other program and performance metrics. The EET extends the BET in using an additional parameter for modelling varying probabilities for the execution of instructions. For certain parameter values, the EET (and the BET) is a NHPP to model failure occurrence. This simplifies the computation, because the NHPP model allows to compute the cumulative failure rate function as sum of the corresponding component functions (as in Xie and Wohlin [514]'s Equations 26 and 27).

10.5 Proactive Schemes

In 1995, a new dependability technique called "rejuvenation" attracted attention, which is essentially a special preventive maintenance technique that tries to set components back to a "healthy", "young" state before they fail [224]. This approach differs from traditional fault tolerance techniques in that the system is not reacting to faults that have occurred but rather is trying to proactively deal with them, and it differs from traditional preventive maintenance approaches where maintenance implies manual check or replacement of field replaceable units. In the early 2000s, after publication of articles by Tennenhouse [467] and the autonomic computing manifesto by Horn [217], the new direction of proactive dependable computing gained importance.

In contrast to the attention that the topic attracted in terms of technical implementation, it is not thoroughly covered by dependability metrics. One exception is Garg et al. [179] where the authors modeled a system with rejuvenation by a Markov Regenerative Stochastic Petri Net (MRSPN) and solve it by use of a Markov Regenerative Process (MRGP) yielding the probability of being in an unavailable state. In 2005, Salfner and Malek [424] proposed a more general method to assess availability of systems employing proactive fault handling schemes. The proposed approach divides proactive fault handling into two parts: the *prediction* of upcoming failures and the *action* that the system performs upon prediction in order to deal with the fault. Two types of actions can be identified: Preventive actions try to prevent the occurrence of failures but also traditional repair actions can benefit from failure prediction by preparing for the upcoming failure in order to reduce time to repair. The accuracy of failure prediction, the effectiveness of countermeasures and the risk of introducing additional failures that would not have occurred without proactive fault handling are taken into account in order to compute the change in availability. However, the paper presented only a formula for steady-state availability. Metrics or models that cover other dependability metrics such as reliability are not available, yet.

10.6   Summary

This chapter covers dependability metrics that refer to software reliability. Although software and hardware reliability are related, several characteristics in which they differ are identified and discussed. Following the "goal-question-metric" paradigm, proper data collection is addressed including issues of testing, failure data and program attributes. The main focus is on models for software reliability assessment; the approaches are presented include black-box reliability models, reliability models that are based on other software metrics and white-box reliability models that build on knowledge about the internal structure of the system. For each group several models are described and compared. A brief survey on proactive schemes concludes the chapter.

Part III

Security Metrics

11   Introduction to Security Metrics

Felix C. Freiling

University of Mannheim, Germany

In one of his well-readable and instructively provocative newsletters [434], Bruce Schneier elaborates on the role of the insurance industry within the field of network security. He argues that eventually the insurance industry will run the computer security just like any other field which has risks: If you want to protect yourself from the damage caused by denial-of-service, simply buy insurance against this kind of attack.

Obviously, that article is very polemic. Schneier addresses two common objections from the security field: First, that it is impossible to calculate the premiums because it is hard to calculate the probability of an attack. Second, that large scale attacks, e.g. viruses, lack failure independence. These objections are blown away by the argument that insurance companies are able to "insure satellite launches and the palate of wine critic Robert Parker" [434]. So eventually, this will be no problem. But why is it a problem and probably will be for some time in the future? The core of this question boils down to whether or not it is possible to come up with meaningful ways to measure security. The following part of this book contains a collection of articles that survey the state of the art in security measurement.

Security is only a recent addition to dependability attributes which were discussed in the beginning of this book. In the orginal work edited by Laprie [293], security was treated only on roughly half a page (out of 40). However, security has gained importance and managed to get into the title of the 2004 revision of Laprie's work by Avižienis et al. [26]. There, security is defined as the combination of three attributes: confidentiality, integrity, and availability. This combination, sometimes referred to as the "CIA taxonomy" seems to have its origin in a paper by Voydock and Kent [493] and later appeared very prominently in the harmonized IT security criteria of France, Germany, the Netherlands, and the United Kingdom which are known as "ITSEC" [381]. If we want to measure security, the CIA taxonomy tells us that we should measure confidentiality, integrity and availability. But from a practical viewpoint, security is more than just CIA: Security is a continued effort to contain risk. To speak again with Schneier: Security is a process [432]. So if we want to measure security, we must measure in some way an organizational process.

In the following chapters we will see that many aspects of security interact: On the one hand, there are "hard" and objective measurements of restricted aspects of security as defined by the CIA taxonomy. For example, the notion of availability can be adapted from the notion with the same name from the area of reliability, i.e., the probability of delivering service at some time t (see Chapter 9). On the other hand, due to the complexity of organizations which must be assessed regarding their security, there are also "soft" and subjective measurements. These measurements often take seemingly hard measurements as input. But equally, available resources for security which are often determined by "soft" factors often influence the amount of effort spent on "hard" measurements.

I. Eusgeld, F.C. Freiling, and R. Reussner (Eds.): Dependability Metrics, LNCS 4909, pp. 129–132, 2008.
© Springer-Verlag Berlin Heidelberg 2008

The field of security metrics is academically old which can be seen from the amount of research invested in measuring the strength of cryptographic systems (see Chapter 12). Looking at metrics for *operational* security, Littlewood et al. [311] in a classic paper investigate the relations between reliability metrics and security metrics. They pose many questions which are still relevant and unanswered today, for example, how well can probabilities express the uncertainty about the security of a system? The area of *intrusion tolerance* today has revived the area relating reliability/fault-tolerance and security: It tries to carry established fault-tolerance methods over to the area of security. This starts with assimilating the relevant terminology (*faults* are extended to *attacks*, *errors* are *intrusions*, as in the AVI model of the MAFTIA project [485]). But there are also fundamental differences, which were already observed by Littlewood et al. [311]: While it is feasible to estimate the failure rate of a hardware component, it is hard to estimate the probability that a system will be attacked in the future. These issues were also discussed at a Dagstuhl seminar in 2006 [79] entitled "From Security to Dependability". Overall, measuring security seems to be more similar to measuring software reliability (see Chapter 10). Here many open questions remain and we have collected the research literature on the similarities and differences between reliability and security in an annotated bibliography in Chapter 25.

Hard quantitative metrics have only been defined for restricted areas of security (small components, protocols etc. and restrictive assumptions on the attacker) and they are always "looking into the past" (see for example Chapter 12 on metrics for cryptographic systems or Chapter 13 on metrics for malicious network traffic). A notable exception is work by Jonsson and Olovsson [262] which evaluates student "hacking" experiments and looks for patterns in the attack data. For larger entities like organizations best practices approaches dominate which we report on as qualitative metrics (see Chapters 14 and 15). They usually give limited confidence in predictions. Some authors, like McHugh [344] and again Schneier [433], are very sceptical whether it is possible to give any meaningful predictive measures for security at all. The only predictive security metrics which are surveyed in this part of the book are economic (market-based) metrics (see Chapter 15).

Today, practical considerations dominate security metrics research: Computer security is a giant market estimated to around $ 40 billion, half of which is in the U.S. [478]. Companies need ways to estimate the security of their products, their computer networks and their organizations and so the area is currently driven by efforts which have direct industrial benefit [250, 253]. However, efforts like the *security metrics consortium* [204] were announced early 2004 but have vanished from the web at time of writing.

We are only aware of a couple of academic events which have focused primarily on security metrics:

- The first seems to have been a workshop called *NIST CSSPAB workshop on security metrics* [103] which was hosted jointly by NIST and the Computer System Security and Privacy Advisory Board in June 2000 in Gaithersburg, MD, USA. While its website seems to be offline, the papers are still available through the Internet Archive.
- Often considered the first event, the *Workshop on Information Security System Scoring and Ranking* was held on March 21–23, 2001 in Williamsburg, Virginia,

USA. The event was sponsored by the Applied Computer Security Associates and the MITRE Corporation and the proceedings, a collection of position papers, were published online [20]. The conclusions of the workshop, as published on the workshop homepage [21], state that it will probably always be necessary to combine multiple measures to assess the security of a system and that more research is needed in this area. We are unaware of any followup event of this workshop.

– The *Workshop on Security Metrics* (MetriCon) has seen two iterations. The first was held on August 1, 2006 co-located with the 15th USENIX Security Symposium in Vancouver, B.C., Canada. There were no formal proceedings but presentations as well as extensive notes are available online [251]. Similarly, the second workshop of this series held in Boston, MA in August 2007 has its collection of material online [252].

– The *Workshop on Quality of Protection* (QoP) goes in its second iteration in association with the ACM CCS 2006 security conference in Alexandria, VA, USA. The 1st QoP workshop was held in Milano in September 2005 and was affiliated with the 10th European Symposium on Research in Computer Security (ESORICS 2005) and the 11th IEEE International Software Metrics Symposium (METRICS 2005).

Most of these events have been dominated by industrial participants and views. This could be interpreted as lack of academic interest in this area.

The following part of this book surveys the state of the art in security metrics and is structured on the one hand historically and on the other hand with increasing level of abstraction:

– Chapter 12 starts with an overview of metrics for cryptographic systems.
– Chapter 13 looks at approaches to measure malicious network traffic and the quality of intrusion detection systems. Measurement is used here as a means to detect malice.
– Chapter 14 surveys the large body of work in the area of security standards, best-practice and risk management approaches.
– Chapter 15 looks at economic measures of security. This covers measures to justify security investment like the well-known *return on security investment* (ROSI) as well as new streams of work in market-based metrics like vulnerability markets. As mentioned above, these metrics are currently the only mechanisms that have the potential to look into the future.
– Finally, Chapter 16 surveys metrics in the area of human factors, i.e., how to measure security knowledge and security awareness.

The contributions of this part cover a wide spectrum of security metrics. But since the individual chapters cover only the interests of the respective contributors, not the entire field has been covered. Here are some of the fields which deserve separate surveys in future work:

– The emerging area of *security testing* is only covered briefly in Chapter 14. Its relation to the area of software testing is still rather unclear and deserved special attention.
– Metrics for anonymity (like the anonymity set size) and unlinkability in privacy enhancing techniques have not been covered allthough there is a substantial body of work in this area.

- Similarly, metrics for information hiding like *detectability* (in stegoanography), *distortion measures* and *complexity of attack* (in digital watermarking), or *likelihood of false framing* (in biometric fingerprinting) have not been covered.

Work in these and other areas should be considered as contributions in future revisions of this volume.

As a final note, the economic emphasis in large parts of this part of the book mirrors the importance of security metrics in practice: The decision to dedicate entire sections to security metrics in business and economics is justified by the fact that organisations of any kind demand tools to quantify the security properties of their information systems. Both profit-oriented companies and publicly funded institutions need valid indicators for their decision of optimal resource allocation in security technology. The existence of valid and comparable measurements for security is thus a prerequisite for responsible decision-making in a cyber-world. The value of each security metric is, apart from academic beauty, eventually defined by its capability of supporting business decisions and containing risks, be it with participation of the insurance industry or not.

Acknowledgment

The authors of this part wish to thank Hanno Langweg for helpful comments.

12 Cryptographic Attack Metrics

Zinaida Benenson[1], Ulrich Kühn[2], and Stefan Lucks[3]

[1] University of Mannheim, Germany
[2] Sirrix AG security technologies, Germany
[3] Bauhaus-Universität Weimar, Germany

When evaluating systems containing cryptographic components, the question arises how to measure the security provided by the cryptography included in the system. In this chapter we highlight the difficulties involved and show that, while measuring cryptographic security is desirable, the opposite point of view, i.e. measuring cryptographic *insecurity* using *attack metrics*, yields useful results and behaves reasonably under composition of cryptographic components.

12.1 Introduction

This chapter is concerned with the difficulty of measuring the security of cryptographic protocols and of the primitives these protocols are based on. Examples for such primitives include hash functions, symmetric and asymmetric encryption algorithms, message authentication codes, digital signatures, and cryptographic pseudo-random number generators. Cryptographic protocols typically involve communication between two or more entities in order to achieve a particular security goal. For example, the goal of key establishment protocols is to make a secret key available to all participants while keeping it secret from any adversaries.

Any computer system which incorporates security mechanisms, such as password-based access control, authentication with public key certificates, or protection of data sent over a public network by encryption and authentication, implements and combines cryptographic primitives and protocols. In practice, it is often of interest to know the security properties of such a system, which involves rather complex concepts and notions.

Thus, typically, security experts are asked the much simpler and straight-forward question whether a given system is secure, or which level of security it can achieve, or, formulated in a third way, how much security the system provides. At first sight these are reasonable questions to ask. However, having a closer look, there are severe problems involved.

In particular, the underlying assumption of such questions is that there is a usable metric that can measure the security of a system quantitatively on a one-dimensional axis. However, although rare attempts at developing such a cryptographic metric have been made (see, e.g. Jorstad and Smith [263]), cryptographic research is very far from defining it, and it is not clear whether this can be done at all.

In the following, we will see that there is no simple answer, and, in fact, we argue that these questions are asking for the wrong thing, that these questions are too simplistic and miss the point.

I. Eusgeld, F.C. Freiling, and R. Reussner (Eds.): Dependability Metrics, LNCS 4909, pp. 133–156, 2008.
© Springer-Verlag Berlin Heidelberg 2008

Chapter Outline. In the remainder of this chapter we will explain why the simple way to ask the security question leads up a dangerous path to false positives, such that an insecure system is identified as secure. Instead, we propose metrics for the *insecurity* of systems, which are safer to use. We call such metrics *attack metrics*. Later, we will show an example based on key lengths, and touch the area of provable security, which is an area of active research and therefore still evolving.

12.2   Asking the Security Question the Wrong Way

To understand why the frequently asked general questions such as "Is this system secure?" or "How secure is this system?" are too simplistic and miss the point, we start with an example. Assume that a system is using a good block cipher like AES (Advanced Encryption Standard) in CBC mode to encrypt some information, e.g. for transmission or storage. Further, assume that all the details of key generation, key management as well as generation of the initialisation vector necessary for CBC mode are handled with state-of-the-art methods.

Coming back to the question "Is such a system secure?", we notice that this question lacks one important detail: secure against what? Essentially, the threats against which the system should protect are left out. However, in order to obtain a meaningful answer these threats must be implicitly or explicitly understood.

At a first look, one would be tempted to implicitly add "against any reasonable threat". However, this is a not a well-defined notion, as can be easily seen by considering again the example above.

In the example, the privacy of the data is protected by state-of-the-art methods. Nevertheless, a common misunderstanding is to assume that this also protects the authenticity (integrity) of the data. The false reasoning behind this is "It is encrypted, so it cannot be changed". Integrity protection here means that unauthorised changes will be discovered by the decrypting entity. As already mentioned, this assumption is, however, wrong. With CBC encryption, the limited error propagation during decryption gives changes in the *ciphertext* only a very local influence on the plaintext. The ability of the system to detect whether the plaintext is still meaningful depends very much on the higher levels of the system that deal with this data. And some changes can be even fully predictable by the adversary, e.g. when the initialisation vector is changed. To summarise, the cryptographic layer in the example does not guarantee anything about the authenticity of the data. Generally, when integrity protection is not explicitly included in an encryption mode, it *is not* included[1]. Furthermore, it might be the case that the data does not need to be kept private, but its authenticity must be protected. Then the system is protecting the wrong thing, namely the privacy instead of the authenticity of the data.

Making the Security Goals Explicit

Now we get back to the question "Is this system secure?" and to possible implicit additions of reasonable threats and security goals. The key point we have seen above is that,

---

[1] Note that there are modes of operation proposed in the literature that explicitly include integrity protection, and do so provably under sensible assumptions on the employed block cipher.

when they are added implicitly, the security goals are not well-defined. In the example, is protecting the data authenticity necessary? Or is it even essential? These questions can only be answered if one knows exactly what kind of data is involved, and how it is handled by the upper system layers.

As a consequence, the security goals of a system need to be stated *before* making design choices for the security layers of a system, i.e. selection of cryptographic algorithms, modes, parameter sizes like key lengths, etc.

This process of selecting and stating security goals of a system is a delicate task. The discussion above should have made it clear that usually a system is designed to protect against certain threats, while other threats might not have been addressed.

Indeed, the analysis and selection of threats a system needs to protect against must be an integral part of the system's design phase[2]. This analysis of threats is called *threat analysis*. During the threat analysis the whole system to be designed, especially the involved entities, the data, and the functionality, is examined to discover the threats that the system and its components may face.

From Threat Analysis to Cryptography

The discussion above highlights that it is necessary to clearly state the security goals of a systems before one can evaluate its security. The security goals should be derived from a threat analysis during the design phase of a system. Indeed, an initial threat analysis and explicit mentioning of the threats the system shall protect against is a necessity in order to design secure systems, with possible several iterations through the design and analysis cycle.

Typical security goals, especially in networked or distributed systems, include goals like confidentiality and authenticity of transmitted data, or authenticity of involved entities. To reach these and other goals, usually cryptographic methods are employed.

On the one hand, selecting the right general cryptographic method to solve a given security problem, e.g., message authentication code or digital signature for authenticity of data, is in many cases rather straight-forward. On the other hand, the selection of concrete algorithms, mode of operations, and parameters like key sizes can be a very delicate task. Examples include the mode of operation of a block cipher, along with the key size, to protect confidentiality of data, selection of a block cipher with key length and a message authentication code along with a suitable size of the authentication tag for data authenticity. A further and in practice important example is the selection of an asymmetric cryptographic algorithm for key transport or digital signatures, along with a key size, that does not put an unnecessary computational burden on the system, but keeps the data secure for the required amount of time.

The current chapter aims at providing some general help to this end. However, it turns out that providing a metric for cryptographic *security* is not well-defined. Instead, a metric for cryptographic *insecurity*, which we call the *attack metric*, makes sense. The

---

[2] However, this process is often neglected in practice, such that people start adding security functions only after the basic functionality of the system is established. Consequently, this can place problematic constraints on the security subsystem. These constraints result from prior design choices, and could have been avoided if the design of the system did include security functions.

idea is to measure the effort, such as time or computational expenses, an adversary has to invest to break a system.

12.3   On Measuring Cryptographic Insecurity

In this section we describe a metric for the efficiency of cryptographic attacks. The reader might reasonably have expected a metric to measure the security of cryptosystems, rather than some kind of attack metric. However, as we will explain in more detail below, a cryptographic security metric could yield falsely positive indicators of security of a system. Consequently, a cryptographic *security* metric can actually be dangerous.

What Would Be Wrong with a Cryptographic Security Metric?

Ron Rivest [416] described cryptography as being *"about communication in the presence of adversaries"*. Here, the word "communication" is used in a very general sense. For example, when storing some data to a file, the CPU communicates with the file system. If the data in question are confidential, and there is any possibility of an adversary reading these data, one should encrypt them. Thus, there is an application running in an adversarial environment, and there are cryptographic algorithms and protocols (in short, "cryptosystems") as a defence against adversaries. Any "cryptographic metric" has to measure attributes of cryptosystems. The most important attribute of a cryptosystem is its *security* – how well does the cryptosystem defend against adversarial attacks?

Assume a top-down approach, similarly to the Goal-Question-Metric paradigm, see Chapter 6. The global goal is a tool for the design and analysis of secure cryptographic applications. The question thus is, *how much security does a given cryptosystem contribute to the security of a given application?* Applications usually employ one or more complex cryptosystems, composed from some simpler cryptosystems, in turn composed from simpler cryptosystems, etc. ... This top-down approach stops at some cryptographic primitives such as, e.g. block ciphers, which cannot reasonably be decomposed into lower-level cryptosystems. To measure cryptographic security at the application level, we thus have to go bottom-up: estimate the security of complex cryptosystems based on the security of its components. So far, however, this approach does not provide reasonable results because of the following regrettable fact:

> *Cryptographic security is not preserved under composition.*

For a somewhat surprising example, consider combining a secure encryption (to ensure privacy) technique with a secure authentication method (for authenticity, obviously). It may be counter-intuitive, but in this case, it matters a lot for security whether (on the originator's side) the plaintext is first encrypted and then the ciphertext authenticated, or the plaintext is first authenticated, and then encrypted. With the wrong order the composed scheme may be insecure. The right order, however, ensures both privacy and authenticity, if the components, i.e. the encryption and the authentication method, both are secure [283].

A minor issue for any cryptographic security metric is that estimating the security of a primitive is mostly educated guesswork. After the publication of a primitive, cryptanalysts try to find good attacks. Most primitives are broken pretty soon after their publication. If, after a decent amount of time, no major attack has been found, and there seems to be no more progress in finding better attacks against this primitive, the cryptographic community gains confidence in such a primitive, assuming that no significant improvement over the best attacks against it will be found. This is a reasonable approach, and in order to do any practical cryptography, one has to accept this as a fact of life. But in principle a primitive is either known to be insecure, or of unknown security (and, after years of unsuccessful analysis, assumed to be secure).

As we indicated above, the major problem for any cryptographic security metric is going bottom-up from the primitives to the complex cryptosystems. One can compose some cryptosystem from secure components, and even without any flaw in the composition itself, the composed cryptosystem turns out to be insecure. Replace a secure primitive by another one, and the composed cryptosystem turns out to be secure. So far, no cryptographic security metric can describe the cryptosystems' attributes sufficiently well to make secure predictions about the security of their composition.

Paradoxical Security Properties of Complex Cryptosystems

In this section, we will briefly describe some examples of apparently "paradoxical" security results concerning complex cryptosystems, and how seemingly reasonable choices cause insecurities. For simplicity, we focus on cryptosystems where we need one single primitive, namely a block cipher.

An n-bit block cipher with a k-bit key space is a function

$$E : \{0,1\}^k \times \{0,1\}^n \to \{0,1\}^n,$$

such that for all $K \in \{0,1\}^k$ the function

$$E_K(x) = E(K,x) : \{0,1\}^n \to \{0,1\}^n$$

permutes over $\{0,1\}^n$. Given K, one can efficiently compute both the permutation E_K and its inverse E_K^{-1}.

As concrete examples for block ciphers, we consider AES (Advanced Encryption Standard), a 128-bit block cipher, which comes with key sizes of 128, 192, and 256 bits, and three-key triple-DES (Data Encryption Standard), a 64-bit block cipher with 168-bit keys.

Considering "m Bits of Security" as a Security Metric. There is a multitude of different attacks against block ciphers. However, *chosen ciphertext* attack is considered as some kind of a "standard" attack a good block cipher should resist.

It is usual to define attacks as some kind of a game between the adversary and a "challenger". A chosen ciphertext attack against a block cipher E works as follows. The goal of the adversary is to distinguish the block cipher (with some fixed but random key, unknown to the adversary) from a random permutation.

– First, the challenger devises a permutation π. To do this, the challenger flips a fair coin to generate a bit $b \in \{0,1\}$.
  • If $b = 0$, the challenger chooses a random permutation π over $\{0,1\}^n$. This fixes also its inverse π^{-1}.

- If $b = 1$, the challenger chooses a random key $K \in \{0,1\}^k$ and sets $\pi = E_K$ and $\pi^{-1} = E_K^{-1}$.
- Further, the challenger gives the adversary oracle access to the permutations π and π^{-1}, which works as follows. The adversary is allowed to ask some queries. Each query is either a chosen plaintext query (choose $x \in \{0,1\}^n$ and ask for $\pi(x)$), or a chosen ciphertext query (choose $y \in \{0,1\}^n$ and ask for $\pi^{-1}(x)$).
- At the end, the adversary has to deduce b.

It is easy to guess b with a probability $1/2$. An attack is "good", if the adversary can efficiently deduce b with a probability significantly exceeding $1/2$.

For AES, there is no better chosen ciphertext attack known than exhaustive key search over all 2^{128} to 2^{256} keys. For three-key triple-DES, there are more advanced chosen ciphertext attacks known, the best one runs in time equivalent to 2^{108} encryptions [321]. In any case, no chosen ciphertext attack against either AES or three-key triple-DES is known to be even remotely practical, so both block ciphers appear to be secure.

As some people would put it, *AES has 128 bits of security*, and *three-key triple-DES has 108 bits of security*. The notion of "m bits of security" appears in the literature as some kind of security metric. If m exceeds, say, 100, this indicates quite a strong cipher.

Now, wouldn't this "m bits of security" make a good security metric? How does this metric behave under composition?

For a simple composed cryptosystem, think of an (unkeyed) cryptographic hash function

$$H : \{0,1\}^* \to \{0,1\}^n.$$

The standard attack – as an exception from the general rule not an interactive game between adversary and challenger – is a *collision attack*: The adversary succeeds if it can find any $X \neq Y$ with $H(X) = H(Y)$. One could say, this hash function has "m bits of security", if the best attack we know of takes m steps of computations.

A classical (and extremely simple) composition technique is to define a hash function from an n-bit block cipher as follows:

- Fix some initial value $H_0 \in \{0,1\}^n$.
- Split the message $M \in \{0,1\}^*$ into k-bit blocks [3]$M_1, \ldots, M_L \in \{0,1\}^k$, with some padding in the last block M_L (as the length of M may not necessarily be a multiple of k).
- Iterate $H_i = E_{M_i}(H_{i-1}) \oplus H_{i-1}$.
- Output the final result $H(M) = H_L$.

Observe that $H_0, H_1, \ldots, H_L \in \{0,1\}^n$ – so the output size of our hash function is n.

In some idealised formal model for block ciphers, there is a proof that this construction is approximately as secure (i.e., collision resistant) as any n-bit hash function could ever be [59]. Thus, if we use AES with 128-bit or even 256-bit keys – does this imply that our hash function, which we have composed from AES, has "128 bits" or even "256 bits of security"? Unfortunately, the answer is a definitive *no*. Our AES-based hash function is a 128-bit hash function, and against all n-bit hash function one can

---

[3] Note that k is the key size of the block cipher, not its block size.

mount the so-called "birthday attack" with a workload of $2^{n/2}$. With whatever variant of AES we instantiate this hash construction, we will get (at most) 64 bits of security.

Even worse, if we think of "m bits of security" as a security metric. We may replace AES by a much weaker cipher, but with a block size $n > 128$, and improve the security of our hash construction! (Beware – there could be other attacks than the birthday attack!) As an extreme case, set $k = 1$ and $n = 256$. A chosen ciphertext attack against such a block cipher is very efficient, as one can easily search the entire key space with both of its keys. Nevertheless, such a block cipher might be used in the context of a hash function as described above, and actually provide "128 bits of security" – in spite of being extremely weak with one single bit of key space.

Thus, if we used the notion of "m bits of security" as a security metric, the composition of cryptosystems would provide very surprising and seemingly paradoxical results, contradicting the following rule, which can be derived from the properties of a meaningful metric as introduced in Chapter 2:

> *A reasonable security metric should behave monotonely: if we replace an insecure component by a more secure one, the composition's security should at least remain constant, but not decrease.*

Choosing Right Primitives for Composed Cryptosystems. There exist quite a number of further attacks against block ciphers. We will describe just one more, namely chosen ciphertext *related-key* attacks. Here the adversary is given access to several permutation oracles which, in the case of being derived from the block cipher, are related. The adversary's goal is to distinguish this from the case of an equal number of (unrelated) random permutations.

– The challenger flips a fair coin to generate a bit $b \in \{0, 1\}$.
  • If $b = 0$, the challenger chooses a family of 2^k random permutations π_K over $\{0, 1\}^n$. We write π_K^{-1} for the respective inverse permutation.
  • If $b = 1$, the challenger chooses a random key $K \in \{0, 1\}^k$ and sets $\pi_L = E_{K \oplus L}$ and $\pi_L^{-1} = E_{K \oplus L}^{-1}$ for all $L \in \{0, 1\}^{k}$.[4]
– The adversary is allowed to ask some queries. Each query is either a chosen plaintext query (choose $d \in \{0, 1\}^k$, $x \in \{0, 1\}^n$ and ask for $\pi_d(x)$), or a chosen ciphertext query (choose $d \in \{0, 1\}^k$, $y \in \{0, 1\}^n$ and ask for $\pi_d^{-1}(x)$).
– At the end, the adversary has to deduce b.

As before, an attack is "good" if the adversary can efficiently deduce b with a probability significantly exceeding $1/2$.

For AES, the best related-key attack is, again, to exhaustively search through the entire key space. But this type of attack really distinguishes AES from three-key triple-DES, which actually is insecure against such attacks [270].

Initially, related-key attacks had mostly been considered a theoretical tool to analyse the so-called "key schedule" of a block cipher. However, it turned out that some composed cryptosystems actually expose an underlying block cipher to related-key attacks.

---

[4] This is the special and quite common case of a related-key attack with $\oplus$ as its key transformation. There are more general definitions for related-key attacks in the literature, see Lucks [322] and references therein.

Two examples are tweakable block ciphers, see Liskov et al. [304], and the RMAC message authentication code by Jaulmes et al. [254]. In general, the designer of a composed cryptosystem should specify which attacks the underlying components actually are required to resist.

Clearly, if one uses such a composed cryptosystem, one needs to employ an underlying primitive (here, a block cipher) which is "secure" against such specific attacks. It is easy to overlook this. Even though the security proof in Jaulmes et al. [254] explicitly assumed security against related-key attacks, NIST proposed RMAC instantiated with three-key triple-DES for standardisation [369]. Fortunately, an attack by Knudsen and Kohno [280] by employing a well-known related-key attack against three-key triple-DES was published in time before the proposed standard was confirmed.

Composable Cryptography

There exists an important research branch about "provable security" in cryptography, studying how to securely compose a cryptosystem from abstract components, assuming certain requirements on these components. At first glance, answering the question "Does the component satisfy these requirements?" would make a reasonable security metric, allowing its user to deduce the security of composed cryptosystem. However, in general, these requirements are specific for each composed cryptosystem. So this approach would give us lots of different metrics, each for one specific purpose.

In the past few years, some theoretical approaches for "composable" cryptography have been studied, see Canetti [84] and Backes et al. [31] for some of the early papers on this. Cryptographic components need to satisfy certain conditions to be theoretically "composable", i.e. to provably preserve their security under composition. The composition itself is not arbitrary, but follows certain rules. This improves the traditional approach of provable security and may possibly lead to some useful cryptographic security metric in the future. So far, however, only few components of practical interest have been found to be "composable", and some are even known to not be "composable".

Actually, the goal of the theoreticians dealing with different notions of composability is defining something which could be used as a cryptographic metric. Thus, building an acceptable metric is a research goal far away on the horizon. So far, too few cryptographic schemes fit into any composability notions. For example, these notions are asymptotic by measuring the attack time as a function of the parameter size. Primitives with a fixed set of parameters, such as AES or SHA-1, are asymptotically weak, as one cannot arbitrarily increase their parameters. For these primitives, exhaustive key search, or collision or preimage search all can be done in constant time.

The Attack Metric under Cryptographic Composition

As we have seen above, when it comes to measuring the security of composed cryptosystems, any cryptographic security metric will frequently result in flawed conclusions. We could claim to provide only a metric for cryptographic primitives and not to measure the security of composed cryptosystems at all. But such a metric would be useless, as any "meaningful operation on attributes of a system should have a corresponding operation on the measurements of that attribute", as required in Chapter 2 of this book. Clearly, handling the composition of cryptosystems is meaningful – and even essential – to measure the security of complex cryptosystems and applications.

Moreover, we anticipate our readers' temptation to draw conclusions on the security of composed cryptosystems, nevertheless. Inaccurate measurements are regrettable, but not every metric needs to be perfect to be useful. So why not accept some flawed measurements as a fact of life and live with them?

The core point is – *the error goes to the wrong side!* An error would be a *false positive* by falsely classifying a composed cryptosystem as "secure". Such errors are potentially harmful, which makes such a metric an *insecurity tool*.

Thus, it is insufficient to choose cryptographic components seemingly secure against "standard" attacks. Before finally committing to a composed cryptosystem and some underlying primitives, one must understand precisely what component need to resist to which types of attack. This task should be left to expert cryptographers. A cryptographic attack metric can be useful, however, to sort out some apparently "bad" choices in advance, before asking the expert. This is what we will provide below.

These are the basic rules for using our *attack metric*:

1. A primitive is either insecure (there is a feasible attack known), or of unknown security.
2. A freshly published primitive is considered insecure for some time.
3. A composed cryptosystem is insecure if there is an attack against its structure, or if it is freshly published.
4. A composed cryptosystem is insecure if any of its components is insecure.
5. A composed cryptosystem is of unknown security if neither rule 3 nor rule 4 applies.
6. Avoid the use of insecure cryptosystems.
7. Before using a cryptosystem of unknown security, ask an expert.

The above rules assumed a metric with a dichotomic scale: A cryptosystem is either *insecure* or of *unknown security*, i.e. either an attack is feasible or no feasible attack is known. In practice, this may often be too restrictive. These rules can straightforwardly be adapted to an ordinal scale by quantifying the workload for the best known attack. The attack metric of a composition is the minimum workload of all relevant attacks.

Note that, when comparing our attack metric with a security metric, we find that they both make errors. However, with the attack metric, such an error results in a *false negative*. For example, if there is a certain attack against some component, this attack may or may not be applicable if the component is integrated into a complex cryptosystem. In fact, composition in the attack metric can only lead to false negatives. Such errors are, although regrettable, harmless and acceptable for a security tool.

12.4   An Attack Metric Using Key Size

We have seen in the previous section that measuring attack effort yields meaningful results even under composition. These results indicate the insecurity of a system. In this section we will apply this approach to the widely used notion of the key size of a cryptographic primitive, protocol, or system. Indeed, one of the most straight-forward and also popular approaches to assess the security of the cryptographic primitives is the notion of *key size*.

Most cryptosystems depend on some sort of a secret key. If the key is too short, the cryptosystem is insecure. In the sequel, we will discuss the question of how to set the key size threshold. In particular, the goal of the key size metric is to determine which key sizes are to be considered inadequate to reach a given security goal until some year y against a given type of adversary. More concretely, this metric helps to answer questions like:

– Assume that today all key sizes below a certain limit are considered inadequate for protecting data with respect to confidentiality or integrity. How will the situation be in a future year y with respect to the same protection?
– Assume that a symmetric cryptographic key size below s bits is considered insecure. Which asymmetric key sizes (e.g. for Diffie-Hellman key exchange to set up the symmetric keys) must be considered insecure as well?

A direct corollary from the answers to those questions is a limit on a minimal acceptable key size in a future year y.[5]

The first report which systematically considered adequate key lengths for symmetric cryptosystems is Blaze et al. [61]. The authors estimate, among other things, the effort needed for the brute-force attack on the 56-bit keys of DES, and conclude that this key size is not enough for protecting commercial information in the year 1996. They give recommendation to use at least 90-bit keys if the encrypted information should still be protected in 20 years time, i.e. until 2016.

The influential paper by Lenstra and Verheul [298] offers the first systematic analysis of symmetric as well as asymmetric key sizes. Since then, other researchers and organisations calculated the key size metric using slightly different approaches and arriving at slightly different results, see Silverman [449], the NESSIE report [372], Lenstra [297], the NIST recommendation [370], and the ECRYPT report [149]. Nevertheless, in most cases the results are close enough to each other, such that the key size can be considered a well established metric with clear methodology.

Note that the approach taken here differs slightly from the obvious statements of the previous works, although we use their results. Here, we show how to use this approach as an attack metric. We consider an attack metric that indicates which key lengths are not appropriate, instead of expressing which key lengths are adequate, as such a metric is not composable (see Section 12.3).

Key Size and Effective Key Size

It is clear that the actual key size of a cryptographic object, e.g. a block cipher, sets a lower bound on the key size. Further, by using this as an attack metric, we do not have to assume anything about the security of the cryptographic object at hand against other

---

[5] We note that usually the key size of a symmetric algorithm is fixed. Thus, there is no possibility to gradually increase it. However, the approach of this section still yields meaningful results insofar as it gives a good hint at when a given key size has to be considered inappropriate for a given security goal.

possible cryptanalytic attacks beyond the generic attacks that always work. Instead, this metric will give us a tool to determine when the key size is too short to achieve a specific security goal. Additionally, from the paradigm of attack metrics we obtain the same kind of results for more complex cryptographic systems, although with the same caveats of false negatives.

For example, the generic attack class that is measured with key-size metric for symmetric ciphers is brute-force key search. Here the adversary attempts to recover the key by trying out all possible keys. The resources, e.g. time or storage, required to the brute-force attack on an n-bit symmetric key yield a bound on the adversary's ability to break the primitive. Although the time needed depends on the actual primitive, the speed differences have been found to be rather insignificant for this kind of resource estimation.

As another example, asymmetric cryptographic primitives often rely on problems that are assumed to be hard to solve, such as the integer factorisation or the computation of discrete logarithms. Here the generic attack on an asymmetric primitive involves solving the underlying hard problem.

Symmetric and asymmetric algorithms are often used in combination. For example, symmetric keys can be exchanged or transmitted using an asymmetric algorithm. Thus, we need to be able to compare the breaking efforts for these algorithm classes. Here we follow the approach from Lenstra [297] which takes into account the generic attacks, i.e. brute force for symmetric ciphers, birthday attacks for hash functions, the best generic mathematical algorithms for integer factorisation etc.

The notion "key size" (or "key length") refers to the bit-size of security-critical parameters of cryptographic primitives, which are not necessarily the real keys. Examples include the size of the output of the hash function, the size of the RSA modulus, and the sizes of groups and subgroups in systems based on discrete logarithms. In order to make this comparable and have a clear notion we define the effective[6] key size.

Definition 1 (Effective Key Size). *Let A denote a cryptographic algorithm with k-bit keys with a specific security goal. For a given k, write $f_A(k)$ for the expected running time of the best known attack, i.e. the fastest algorithm to successfully undermine the security goal. Then $s = \log_2(f_A(k)) + 1$ is the effective key size of A.*

For an *ideal* block cipher with k-bit keys, the best known attack to undermine the usual security goals is exhaustive key search, which needs time 2^{k-1} on average. So in this case, the nominal key size k and the effective key size s are the same. For AES, no attack better than exhaustive search is known, so again we have $s = k$.

But not all symmetric algorithms have $s = k$, not even all which are used in practice and considered secure. One famous counterexample is three-key triple-DES, the application of three instances of DES in a sequence, using three independent keys. As the key size of DES is 56 bits (not counting some additional parity bits), the *nominal key size*

---

[6] The ECRYPT report [149] uses the term "equivalent" instead, and only for asymmetric cryptographic primitives, using the expected strength of symmetric cryptosystems to describe the security of asymmetric cryptography. Our notion of "effective" key size is similar in spirit, but applies to symmetric cryptosystems as well. Essentially, we use the strength of an "ideal" symmetric primitive to measure the security (or insecurity) of both symmetric and asymmetric cryptosystems.

of three-key triple-DES is $3 \cdot 56 = 168$ bits. It had long been known that the so-called meet-in-the-middle attack for three-key triple-DES runs in the time equivalent to 2^{112} encryptions, which implies an effective key size of only 113 bits. About ten years ago, it turned out that one can speed-up this attack to about 2^{108} encryptions [321], which implies an effective key size of only 109 bits.[7]

As the above example highlights, the effective key size s of a given cryptosystem can change over time, but it can only shrink, never grow. This is because we may discover new or improved attacks, but we assume that a good attack, once known, cannot be forgotten. As we bound the effective key size to the "best known attack", it is a quantified attack metric.

How about asymmetric algorithms and their effective key size? For example, for RSA the best known algorithm to break the general instance of the underlying number-theoretic problem is the general Number Field Sieve with an heuristically expected running time of $L(N, 1/3, \alpha) = e^{\alpha(\ln N)^{1/3}(\ln \ln N)^{2/3}}$ for a number N of bit-length $k = \lceil \log_2(N) \rceil$. This expression hides some constants, which are only known approximately. But the experts in the field agree that the effective key size for, say, 1024-bit RSA (i.e., $k = 1024$) is actually between 72 bits and 80 bits, as explained in the next section.

On a side note, in the case of asymmetric cryptography, the nominal "key size" is not always a well-defined notion. Even in the case of RSA, one considers the length of the modulus N as the determining parameter, but N is only a part of the public key, and the length of the public and private exponent may also matter for the security. Sometimes, we just write "parameter choices" for families of asymmetric cryptosystems.

Key Size Threshold as a Function of Adversarial Power

Obviously, some adversaries have more power (money, computational resources) than others. Accordingly, if your adversary is powerful, the key size threshold for the attack metric needs to be larger than if you only have to defend against a weak adversary. For example, defending against attacks from a well-funded government agency is much more demanding than defending against a casual criminal trying to break the system on his own. Thus, it makes sense to distinguish several classes of potential adversaries.

However, when designing a system one should not underestimate the abilities of an adversary, although from an economic point of view, overestimating these abilities may result in a stronger-than-necessary protection. Nevertheless, this argument is dangerous, as what is necessary usually turns out only in hindsight, so it is important to be conservative here.

Blaze et al. [61] consider adversaries undertaking brute-force attacks on symmetric keys protecting commercial information. These adversaries are classified by the amount of resources which they invest into the effort. The unit of measurement used is US-\$, based on the assumption that this money is invested in hardware to facilitate the attack, see Table 1. It should be noted that these figures are based on the year 1996, and would need a correction to accommodate advances in computational power since then.

---

[7] We remind the reader that we talk about certain types of attack which are "usual" in the context of block ciphers. If one allows some more unusual types, such as, e.g. related-key attacks, three-key triple-DES is quite vulnerable.

Table 1. Estimates on time and cost of successful attacks on 56-bit keys in 1996 for different classes of adversaries (from Blaze et al. [61])

Attacker Type	Budget [US-$]	Tool	Time	Amortised Cost per Recovered Key
Hacker	tiny	PC	infeasible	
	400	FPGA	38 years	$5,000
Small Business	10 k	FPGA	18 months	$5,000
Medium	300 k	FPGA	19 days	$5,000
Organisation		ASIC	3 hours	$38
Big Company	10 M	FPGA	13 hours	$5,000
		ASIC	6 minutes	$38
Intelligence	300 M	ASIC	12 seconds	$38
Agency				

The slowest and cheapest attacks can be mounted using off-the-shelf commodity PC-hardware. This approach can be used by virtually anyone, even a single "hacker". It should be noted, however, that in recent years serious cryptographic challenges were solved by exploiting parallelism using a large number of PCs and workstations connected via Internet, see the Distributed Net Project [122]. This suggests adding a new class of distributed adversary, as in the ECRYPT report [149].

More wealthy individuals and small organisations can buy Field Programmable Gate Array (FPGA) chips which allow much faster attacks. Organisations with large budget can even afford the development of custom chips, called Application-Specific Integrated Circuits (ASICs) which are several times faster than FPGAs.

It should be noted that the time-money relation remains roughly constant in Table 1: An attack which can be carried out in d days and costs c US-$ can also be carried out in d/w days at the cost cw US-$. This is due to the high parallelism of the key search attacks: the key space can be divided into arbitrary small parts (down to the individual keys) which can be searched independently (not taking into account possible communication and trustworthiness issues).

Based on the above budget classification, and on a classification of the intended duration of the cryptographic protection into short-term, middle-term and long-term protection, the ECRYPT report [149] suggests 8 security levels (including one legacy level) for parameter sizes of cryptographic primitives (Table 2).

For our attack metric these security levels and their respective "bits of security" should be considered as a kind of lower bound below which a system or component becomes increasingly insecure against the indicated type of adversary.

Key Size Metric as a Function of Time

It is a well-known fact that computers get more powerful over time. Thus, a key which was sufficient to defend against a certain class of adversaries ten years ago may be insufficient today, and a key size or parameter choice which is acceptable today can be too small in ten years. An influential work on determining adequate key sizes was done by Lenstra and Verheul [298]. In brief, and using our definition of the "effective

Table 2. Security levels from the ECRYPT report [149, Table 7.4]

Security Level	Bits of Security	Protection Type
1.	32	Attacks in real-time by individuals
2.	64	Very short-term protection against small organisations
3.	72	Short-term protection against medium organisations, Medium-term protection against small organisations
4.	80	Very short-term protection against intelligence agencies, Long-term protection against small organisations
5.	96	Legacy standard level
6.	112	Medium-term protection
7.	128	Long-term protection
8.	256	"Foreseeable future", Good protection against quantum computers

key size", it is based on choosing an effective key size s' which is considered to give "adequate protection" in some year y'. This is followed by an estimation (based on Moore's law, see below) of the effective key size s needed in the target year y for adequate protection. Finally, one estimates the parameter choices for the target family of cryptosystems such that its effective key size is at least s.[8]

Inspired by Lenstra and Verheul [298], there where a number of similar approaches to measure the effective key sizes, see the ECRYPT report [149] for a comparison. Further, a popular website keylength.com [184] allows to directly view and compare the results from different measurement methods. Below we will recollect the approach and measurement method suggested in Lenstra [297] (which refines on Lenstra and Verheul [298]) using the examples of symmetric and asymmetric algorithms as well as hash functions. As already mentioned above, if some attack can be carried out in d days at cost c, then this attack can also be carried out in d/w days at cost cw. Therefore, the attacker's effort is measured in *dollardays*.

Adequate Protection. As an example, Lenstra [297] defines the notion of "adequate protection" as *the security offered by DES in the year 1982*. This security level is 56 bits, the effective size of DES keys. Calling this "adequate" was a very deliberate choice, a given system may need a higher level of security, for another system a lower level may be sufficient. As we will elaborate below, 56 bits in 1982 is equivalent to 72 bits in 2006, which implies the security level 3 in Table 2.

To follow this approach, one needs to determine the amount of dollardays which was needed to break DES in year 1982. The rationale behind this definition is that DES was published in the year 1977 [368], and was brought up for reaffirmation once every 5 years thereafter. DES was widely adopted, and in the year 1982, at the time of the first reaffirmation, was considered to offer adequate protection for commercial applications.

---

[8] The name "adequate protection" is, perhaps, slightly misleading. In the spirit of our attack metric, we consider any key length or parameter choice below the level required for "adequate protection" as inadequate.

We stress that it is perfectly possible to measure the attacker's effort in some other way, to define adequate protection differently, or to use another starting point than the one used by Lenstra [297].

The Cost of Breaking Adequate Protection. The cost of attacking a system providing adequate protection, i.e. the dollardays needed in 1982 to break DES, needs to be estimated or determined next. Lenstra [297] reports that in 1980 the cost of breaking DES was estimated as 100 M dollardays. In 1993, the design of a DES-cracking device for about 150 k dollardays was proposed by Wiener [511], and, finally, in 1998 a DES-cracking machine able to recover a DES-key in several days was built at hardware costs of about 130 k US-$ [140]. Note that the latter value was found in practice by actually running the brute-force search.

This progress was made possible by advances in technology which can be described by *Moore's law*, an empirical rule stating that the computing power per area available on a chip doubles roughly every 18 months. In the context of attacking the cryptographic primitives, this rule can be reformulated as follows:

Moore's law. The cost of every fixed attack effort drops by a factor 2 every 18 months.

Now, to find the estimated costs of breaking DES in 1982, this rule is applied to the estimated cost of 100 M dollardays in 1980, resulting in $2^{-24/18}$ times the initial value, i.e. about 40 M dollardays.[9] We say that the cryptosystem offers adequate protection until year y if the cost of the successful attack on this cryptosystem in this year can be expected to be approximately 40M dollardays.[10]

Symmetric Key Sizes. Above we have outlined how to determine the cost in year y to break a cryptographic primitive offering adequate protection. The effort of a generic attack on a symmetric primitive with an n-bit key is about 2^n cipher operations, i.e. the cost of brute-force key search.

Leaving other cryptanalytic progress aside[11], there are twofold influences on the symmetric key size for providing adequate protection. One is that the required effort of brute-force key-search doubles with every additional bit in the key, the other is the above-mentioned technological progress described by Moore's law.

According to the latter, the adversary's resources double every 18 months, and therefore, in the year y the adversary can be assumed to have $2^{(y-1982)/1.5}$ times more resources for the same cost as in 1982. Therefore, in the year y, the cost of breaking an n-bit key would be $2^{(y-1982)/1.5}$ times less than in 1982. In order not to be considered insecure, it should still be more than 40 M dollardays:

$$\frac{2^n}{2^{56}} \cdot 40 \cdot \frac{1}{2^{(y-1982)/1.5}} \geq 40 \Rightarrow n - 56 \geq (y - 1982)/1.5 \tag{1}$$

---

[9] We note that this estimate does deviate from the practical data point in 1998 [140]. By this time, the initial 100 M dollardays in 1980 would have dropped to 24 k dollardays, a factor of about 15 below the real data of 130 k US-$ and and average search time of about 3.5 days. However, the error made is to underestimate the real costs and overestimate the adversary. Thus, the estimation errs on the conservative side.

[10] The effect of inflation could be taken into account, but we do not consider it here, as it is quite small compared to the technological progress (about a factor of 2 every 10 to 25 years).

[11] We may do so as we are later using these results in an *attack* metric.

From this we can compute the minimal necessary key length for providing adequate protection in the year y:

$$n = 56 + \frac{2(y - 1982)}{3}, \tag{2}$$

as well as the year from which on an n-bit key fails to offer adequate protection:

$$y = 1982 + \frac{3(n - 56)}{2}. \tag{3}$$

Examples

- The key size of 72 bits did offer "adequate protection" until the year $y = 1982 + 3(72 - 56)/2 = 2006$. Thus, "adequate protection" implies a security level 3 as defined in Table 2, i.e. *"short-term protection against medium organisations and medium-term protection against small organisations"*.
- Similarly, Table 2 defines *"medium-term protection"* (security level 6) as 112 bits in the year 2006. Thus, if we increase the key size to 124 bits, we get medium-term protection until the year $2024 = 2006 + 3(124 - 112)/2$.
- If we stick at security level 3 ("adequate protection" as above), then 80-bit keys offer this level of security at most until the year $y = 1982 + 3(80 - 56)/2 = 2018$.

Hash Functions. The generic collision attack, which applies to any hash function with H-bit output, uses the birthday paradox and has the cost proportional to $2^{H/2}$. Therefore, if the effective key size we need is s, any hash function with less then $2s$ output bits is insecure.

Parameter Sizes for Asymmetric Cryptosystems. Most estimates of the appropriate key sizes consider schemes based on the difficulty of integer factoring (such as RSA), the systems based on the difficulty of computing discrete logarithms in finite groups (such as Diffie-Hellman, ElGamal, elliptic curves), and those based on the subgroup discrete logarithm systems (such as Schnorr's signature scheme or DSA). For the sake of brevity, only the factoring based systems are considered here, as the aim of this section is to provide examples of the key size calculation.

The generic attack on RSA is the factoring of its modulus. The fastest publicly known factoring algorithm is the general Number Field Sieve algorithm which can factor a number N at costs of approximately

$$L(N, 1/3, \alpha) := e^{\alpha(\ln N)^{1/3}(\ln \ln N)^{2/3}} \tag{4}$$

where $\alpha = 1.976 + o(1)$. According to Lenstra [297], the cost of factoring a 1024-bit RSA modulus in 2004 can be estimated as $400\,\mathrm{M}$ dollardays. Analogous to the symmetric key case, the cost of the factoring of an b-bit RSA modulus in 2004 can be estimated as

$$\frac{L(2^b, 1/3, \alpha)}{L(2^{1024}, 1/3, \alpha)} \cdot 400\,\mathrm{M} \text{ dollardays.} \tag{5}$$

When b is reasonably close to 1024, one can assume that the factors $o(1)$ cancel out, making this an acceptable approximation.

As in the symmetric case, the resources of the adversary satisfy Moore's law, and therefore, in the year y, are $2^{(y-2004)/1.5}$ times higher for the same cost as in 2004.

In contrast to the symmetric key case, the cryptanalytic progress in the factoring algorithms developed continually over the years and decades, and therefore, can also be estimated with Moore's law. This leads to the estimation that in the year y, an adversary could factor $2^{(y-2004)/1.5}$ times faster than in 2004, and therefore, the cost of factoring in the year y can be estimated to be a fraction of $2^{-4(y-2004)/3}$ of the costs in 2004.

Based on these estimates it is now possible to find the length b of an RSA modulus such that it should at least not have to be considered insecure by the year y:

$$\frac{L(2^b, 1/3, 1.976)}{L(2^{1024}, 1/3, 1.976)} \cdot 400 \geq 40 \cdot 2^{4(y-2004)/3} \qquad (6)$$

For example, a 1024-bit modulus would have to be considered insecure after 2006, which corresponds to the symmetric key size of 72 bits, see Formula (2). This is in contrast, e.g., to the NIST recommendation [370] to use 1024-bit moduli in conjunction with the 80-bit symmetric keys until 2010. Nevertheless, these two estimations are close enough to each other.

Summary: Using the Key-Size Metric as an Attack Metric

So far, the description of the key-size metric focused on cryptographic primitives. In Section 12.3 we have seen that a metric measuring the security of a system composed of such primitives is rather dangerous. Instead, applying the key-size metric in our paradigm of an attack metric for composed systems yields meaningful results, such that errors are false-negatives. That is, for composed systems the resulting key-size based attack metric yields recommendations for key sizes of the components that do not make the complete system insecure.

12.5   (In)Security Metrics from Provable Security Results?

In recent years, there is a clear trend towards having security theorems[12] for cryptographic primitives, constructions, or protocols. In this section we aim at explaining the implications of such theorems, raise attention regarding possible pitfalls, and argue that, while such results could ultimately be used for a metric, it is actually still too early to do so.

Provable Security

In modern cryptography, constructions like modes of operation for block ciphers or padding schemes for RSA encryption / signatures used to be designed and analysed in a rather ad-hoc manner, i.e. without a formal framework or proofs that these constructions

---

[12] Usually one speaks about proofs of security. Here however, we focus not on the existence of such a proof, beyond establishing a theorem, but on the theorems themselves, which gain only the status of theorems by having a valid proof. Therefore, we adopt the language of speaking about security theorems.

were sound. This changed in recent years as more and more constructions underwent a rigorous formal analysis yielding proofs of security. Further, new constructions are usually designed with provable security results in mind and are proposed in conjunction with such results.

While a security theorem for a cryptographic primitive, construction, or protocol is certainly desirable, the evaluation of the implications of the resulting security theorem must be done with great care. One danger here is to treat the existence of a theorem in a black-or-white manner, like a box on a check-list that is to be ticked.

In fact, when evaluating the theorems, one needs to pay attention to three issues: (1) the model or set of axioms, (2) the assumptions as a prerequisite of the theorem, and (3) the conclusions. In the following, we will speak of security theorems as mathematical objects, consisting of axioms, assumptions, conclusions, and a proof. We will assume here that the proof is correct, so that we really can speak about a theorem.

Axioms and Assumptions. The security theorems come with a number of assumptions. Like any mathematical statement, the theorem holds only if the assumptions are met. Otherwise the theorem with its proof does not apply, and therefore does not say anything about the security of the cryptographic object at hand.

Furthermore, security theorems are usually constructed in a certain security model. Such a model formalises a further number of axioms on some building blocks of the cryptographic object at hand. Typical models and their axioms are listed below.

Standard Model: This model uses the standard axioms of theoretical computer science as they are used for analysis of the efficiency of algorithms.

Random Oracle Model: This model uses the axioms of the standard model, and additionally that certain functions can be modelled as a random oracle, i.e. they return upon input of a new value a new random value. Each output value can be modelled as a uniformly distributed random variable that is independent of the other result values.

This abstraction tries to model the use of cryptographic hash functions, which are unkeyed functions. While this model gives some idea about the security about cryptographic constructions, it is a bit controversial, as the available and commonly employed cryptographic hash functions are far from being random oracles. Further, there are schemes that are secure in this model, but cannot be instantiated such that they remain secure, see Canetti et al. [85].

Ideal Cipher Model: This model (sometimes referred to as the "Shannon Model") uses the axioms of the standard model, plus the axiom that block ciphers behave like a family of random permutation where a member of the family is selected by the key. One can think of this as selecting (without repetition) at random a permutation from the family of all permutations of the input values.

This abstracts from all properties of real block ciphers (usually consisting of data randomisation part, the round functions, and key scheduling), so this model essentially presupposes that the block cipher is secure in any way that one might reasonably expect.

Generic Group Model: Many asymmetric cryptosystems employ a group in which the discrete logarithm is assumed to be infeasible. On the other hand, the group operation needs to be performed efficiently on a computer. The computer-based implementation thus needs to represent group elements somehow – and the adversary might take advantage of such a representation. As a trivial example, consider the set of integers in $\{0, \ldots, n - 1\}$, with addition modulo n as the group operation. A natural (and even canonical) way to represent these numbers would be as $\lceil \log_2(n) \rceil$-bit binary numbers, representing zero as $0 \ldots 0000$, one as $0 \ldots 0001$, etc. But in this case, computing the discrete logarithm is tantamount to division – and thus feasible.

The generic group model treats groups as cryptographically ideal, using the standard axioms and an additional one, which allows the adversary to apply the group operation and to compare group elements for equality, preventing all other ways to derive any information from the representation of group elements. This axiom excludes large classes of potential attacks, such as using the division in the trivial example above, or the index calculus technique to compute the discrete logarithm in certain groups. In fact, the most efficient way to compute the discrete logarithm in a generic group with n elements takes approximately $\sqrt{n}$ group operations, if n is prime. For certain groups, e.g. a carefully chosen subgroup of the point group of a carefully chosen elliptic curve, the index calculus attacks do not work, and the best attacks known so far actually are the generic attacks – and thus need the time of roughly $\sqrt{n}$ group operations, where the prime n is the number of points on the subgroup.

To summarise, the prerequisites of security statements can be classified into two types of preconditions:

– One type is the model involved, which actually bundles a set of axioms. As they are mathematical axioms, they are true by definition. Security results in the standard model are more meaningful than security results in more "demanding" models, such as the random oracle model, the ideal cipher model, or the generic group model, because the additional axioms abstract away certain real-world properties.
– The other type describes the assumptions actually made and stated explicitly in the security theorem. These can be true, or false. If an assumption is false, the theorem is logically correct but meaningless.

Evaluating the Conclusions. Typical security statements use reductions in their proofs. That is, they relate the security properties of the cryptographic object at hand to some security properties of their building blocks or underlying mathematical problems. These reductions can be stated in an asymptotic (depending on some freely scalable security parameter) or a concrete manner where security parameters such as block length of block ciphers are treated as fixed. An example for the latter is the security theorem of the CBC-MAC message authentication code by Bellare et al. [47], and a recent advancement by Bellare et al. [48].

Typically, security theorems contain statements about the advantage that any adversary can have in breaking the cryptographic object at hand, including parameters and the advantage of any adversary against the underlying building blocks. To use such a result in a meaningful way, it is important to come up with a reasonable setting for the parameters, and to check that the theorem bounds the advantage of an adversary to a probability of breaking the system that is acceptable for the application at hand.

We elaborate the above with an example. We employ the theorem on CBC-MAC for equal-sized messages from Bellare et al. [48]:

Theorem 1 ([48], Theorem 3). *Let* $\pi : \{0,1\}^n \to \{0,1\}^n$ *be a random permutation. Let q be the number of queries an adversary can make to a MAC-oracle using* $\text{CBC}[\pi]$, *each query with exactly l blocks. Then*

$$\text{Adv}_{\text{CBC}[\pi]}(q,n,l) \leq \frac{lq^2}{2^n} \cdot \left(12 + \frac{64l^3}{2^n}\right) \quad . \tag{7}$$

Note that the advantage of an adversary to break π is not included here, so it is implicitly assumed that π is instantiated with a secure block cipher. Further, the theorem holds only for *equal*-length messages, regardless of what the length l is.

Let us now instantiate the scheme and check what security bounds we get from the theorem. Assume that we use AES with a random 128-bit key K for π (assuming this meets the requirements), and try to compute message authentication codes for each block of 512 bytes of a hard disk of about 60 GB. Then $n = 128, l = 32, q = 60 \cdot 2^{30} \approx 2^{36}$. Then Theorem 7 tells us that

$$\text{Adv}_{\text{CBC}[\text{AES}]}(2^{36}, 128, 32) \leq \frac{2^5 2^{72}}{2^{128}} \cdot \left(12 + \frac{2^6 2^{15}}{2^{128}}\right) \approx \frac{2^{77}}{2^{128}} \cdot 2^4 = 2^{-47}.$$

This bound is certainly acceptable, as it is an upper bound for the probability that *any* adversary can break the integrity protection, *provided AES under key K behaves like a random permutation*.

If instead we instantiate π with three-key triple-DES, i.e. $n = 64, l = 64, q = 60 \cdot 2^{30} \approx 2^{36}$, we obtain

$$\text{Adv}_{\text{CBC}[\text{3DES}]}(2^{36}, 64, 64) \leq \frac{2^5 2^{72}}{2^{64}} \cdot \left(12 + \frac{2^6 2^{18}}{2^{64}}\right) \approx \frac{2^{77}}{2^{64}} \cdot 2^4 = 2^{17},$$

which is *completely meaningless* as a bound on a probability. In fact, triple-DES with its rather short block size is not suitable to protect this amount of data under a single (triple-length) key. Thus, this second instantiation has to be considered insecure, even though we have a security theorem.

The big advantage of having security theorems is not that things are necessarily secure, but that we can do the math and get bounds on the security or insecurity of instantiations!

Proofs. The proof is the basis for a security theorem. Without the proof no such theorem is valid. Common proof methods make use of simulation-based arguments or of so-called hybrid arguments, now usually known as the game-based approach. In the latter proof technique the security properties are modelled as games which the adversary can win if it can break the cryptographic construction at hand, see Bellare and Rogaway [46], Shoup [443]. The original game is then transformed step by step into a similar game where the adversary deals only with random data, so that its advantage in reaching a winning condition can be bounded.

However, the transformation has to be done in a way that the adversary can distinguish the transformation only with a negligible probability.

A proof of security in the right model for the problem at hand rules out the existence of all possible attacks breaking the cryptographic construction or protocol with an advantage better than stated in the theorem. However, there are further pitfalls. When ultimately implementing cryptography, a proof of security of a certain construction or protocol does not guarantee that the implementation is correct and secure.

An example for such a problem is given by an attack on PKCS#1 v1.5 and subsequently on PKCS#1 v2.0, more specifically on Optimal Asymmetric Encryption Padding (OAEP). In 1998 Bleichenbacher [62] presented an attack on PKCS#1 v1.5 encryption padding that could exploit certain reactions of the decrypting party, if the decryption was implemented incorrectly. In order to protect against this problem, the PKCS#1 standard was augmented by the OAEP method [45] . This padding method comes with a proof of security[13]. However, later Manger [333] showed that an attack similar to the one of Bleichenbacher can be mounted against some implementations of the newly standardised method. It turned out that this new attack was even much more efficient. In fact, Manger did not attack what was proven secure, but routed around the proven properties of the cryptographic scheme. The bottom line here is that provable security results do give assurance about security properties and that these results guarantee only what is covered by the security theorem. This last point is important, as there are potentially many other things that can go wrong when employing a cryptographic construction or protocol in practice.

Using Provable Security Results to Construct a Metric

Here we take a closer look at the status of the area of provable security in general with regard to defining an attack metric from these results.

Concrete Security: the Quantitative Approach. The area of provable security is split up into two different approaches:

- The *qualitative approach* essentially distinguishes "efficient" from "inefficient" algorithms, where "efficient" often means that the amount of resources is "bounded by a polynomial" (in the security parameters), while "inefficient" means "superpolynomially". This approach is useful for simple theorems and proofs, and as a first step towards understanding security properties, but not quite useful for our purposes.

  The good news is that the proofs in the area of provable security are typically so-called algorithmic "reductions". These can often be turned into proofs for quantitative statements. The typical costs are a lot of tedious work done by the proof author, and a much longer proof at the end.
- The *quantitative approach*, also denoted as *concrete security*, actually quantifies the resources needed for an attack, just as we showed above for the CBC-MAC.

---

[13] We presupposed above that the proof of a security statement is correct. However, for OAEP it turned out that the proof provided in Bellare and Rogaway [45] had a gap that went unnoticed for some years until it was exposed in Shoup [442]. While Shoup could show that the gap cannot be closed under general security assumptions, OAEP could be proven secure when used in combination with RSA, see Fujisaki et al. [172].

Typically, concrete security theorems bound an adversary's advantage and resources when attacking a compound system based on the advantage and resources for breaking the components. In order to give an example we need a semi-formal definition:

Definition 2. *Let $\mathcal{A}$ be an adversary trying to break a cryptographic component $\mathcal{C}$. The attack consists of making queries of certain types to the components of $\mathcal{C}$ and computations based on the results. Assume that the adversary $\mathcal{A}$ makes up to q_1 queries of a first type, up to q_2 queries of a second type, ..., and up to q_n queries of an n-th type. Further assume that the running time of $\mathcal{A}$, including the time for reading the code of $\mathcal{A}$, is bounded by t units of time. Then we say that $\mathcal{A}$ $(t, q_1, \ldots, q_n)$-breaks $\mathcal{C}$.*

Considering any possible adversary that $(t, q_1, \ldots, q_n)$-breaks $\mathcal{C}$ we say that $\mathcal{C}$ is $(t, q_1, \ldots, q_n, \epsilon)$-secure with

$$\epsilon = \sup_{\mathcal{A}} \{\Pr[\mathcal{A}\ (t, q_1, \ldots, q_n)\text{-breaks } \mathcal{C}]\}.$$

Now an example structure of a concrete security theorem can be described as follows.

Let component 1 be (t_1, q_1, ϵ_1)-secure, let component 2 be $(t_2, q_2, q_3, \epsilon_2)$-secure. Then a certain compound cryptosystem built from these components is (T, Q, ϵ)-secure, where

$$T = t_1 + t_2 O(\ldots),$$
$$Q = q_1 q_2 + q_3, \text{ and}$$
$$\epsilon = \epsilon_1 + q_1 \epsilon_2.$$

where t_i, T bound the respective adversary's running times, q_i, Q the number of certain oracle queries, and ϵ_i, ϵ bound the respective adversary's advantage in breaking the components resp. the compound system.

Note that such results usually hold in general, i.e. not only against certain attacks, but show that the given security property is kept up against *any possible* adversary trying to break the system.

The Dolev-Yao Model. There are a few other approaches to formalise and prove cryptographic security. A rather influential one is based on the Dolev-Yao model for cryptographic protocols [133].

This model considers entities which communicate over an insecure network. The Dolev-Yao adversary has full control over the network which connects the entities. Thus, the adversary can read all messages, but also decide what to do with these messages (send them to the intended receiver, send them to the wrong receiver, manipulate them, suppress them, invent fake messages, ...). Informally, one could describe the adversary as an untrustworthy Internet service provider. Specifically, the adversary can always mount a denial-of-service attack against the communicating entities by simply suppressing all messages they send. The adversary's goal, however, is more advanced than just denial-of-service, such as learning the content of some encrypted message, or making entity A believe that a certain message has been sent by B, while it actually has been faked or modified by the adversary, or sent by C. The adversarial goals are always to break the security properties which to preserve the protocol in question has been designed to address.

Assuming idealised cryptographic operations (such as symmetric or asymmetric encryption, authentication or digital signatures), one can analyse a given protocol and hopefully derive a formal logical proof that the protocol serves its claimed purpose. In contrast to other areas of cryptography, these proofs are often generated automatically, by appropriate analysis tools. The ability to automatically generate such proofs is a major benefit of the Dolev-Yao model.

From the point of view of an attack metric, there are two serious drawbacks of the Dolev-Yao approach. One is that the theorems in the Dolev-Yao model are qualitative, while we would like to have quantitative statements. The second one is that the proofs are not algorithmic reductions, but are of a logical nature. This seems to defend against deriving quantitative statements from the proofs, instead of just qualitative ones.

The Dolev-Yao model has been a landmark in theoretical cryptography. Further, it was an important step towards automatically analysing cryptographic protocols. But for the purpose of our metric, it seems not to be useful.

Composability or Simulatability as a Security Metric. As we have seen, cryptographic security is not preserved under composition. One way to resolve this may be to impose some restrictions on the cryptosystems in question. One may require the underlying cryptosystems to have some "extra" features, in addition to their native security features, one may restrict the composed cryptosystem to follow certain composition rules. If all these constraints are maintained, then security actually (and provably) is preserved under composition. Since about the year 2000, this idea has been studied intensively in theoretical cryptography, initiated by Canetti [84] and Pfitzmann et al. [394], developing frameworks for "composability" and "simulatability".

As security properties are preserved under composition, this approach actually allows to define a reasonable cryptographic security metric. The disadvantage is that any such metric is always only applicable to a very limited number of cryptosystems. The constraints imposed by the frameworks are severe, most underlying cryptosystems one would like to use in practice just do not provide the "extra" features required by the frameworks.

Outlook on Provable Security. In the area of provable security, the hope is that one can build up in a bottom-up manner concrete (i.e., quantitative) security theorems for ever more complex systems. In this case the theorems would allow to assess the security of a very complex security system based on known or assumed simple security properties of its components. This would indeed be a very comfortable metric.

However, while in a certain sense such security results yield a metric that could be evaluated by non-experts (although very carefully), it turns out that things are actually much more complicated and less beautiful.

Usually, there are many different assumptions on the components of compound systems, not only a single one for each component. Thus, there are many bottom-up hierarchies growing at the same time, which makes combining them at higher levels rather difficult. However, we need precisely this in order to achieve the goal of a single metric that can be used by non-experts. Up to now, the assumptions made and the results achieved provide a rather complex set of rules that needs a lot of experience to be judged correctly.

In fact, provable security is a very active research area which ultimately aims at building up complex security systems from simpler components and bounding the advantage any adversary can possibly have in breaking the systems. For the present, however, the research results here mark only a very promising beginning.

12.6 Summary

In this chapter we examined metrics related to cryptographic security. Starting from considerations about *security* metrics, two issues turned out to be important: first, one has to be very careful to specify against which attacks security is sought, and second, cryptographic security is not preserved under composition. A severe consequence of the latter finding is that the security of complex systems cannot be established from the security results on the components the system consists of. In fact, errors in the measurement add up in such a way that the combined error goes to the wrong side, i.e. suggesting that a combined system is more secure than it actually is.

Taking on the opposite point of view, namely, measuring cryptographic *insecurity* using *attack metrics*, turns out to be fruitful. With this approach, any possible measurement errors add up in a conservative way, therefore underestimating the security of a composed system. One example of such an attack metric is a metric based on the cryptographic key size.

Finally, we investigated whether results on provable security can be used as some kind of security or attack metric. Researchers in the field clearly follow an approach well in line with establishing some security metric. Some of the results could indeed serve as the foundation for building up a security metric. However, the current state of the art in provable security makes the application of its results to actually measure the security of complex cryptosystems difficult and error-prone. Currently, we believe that provable security cannot be used to establish a useful metric. On the other hand, provable security is a very active research area. We hope that future results in this area will allow people to build up security metrics.

13   Security Measurements and Metrics for Networks

Thorsten Holz

University of Mannheim, Germany

This chapter surveys research in two areas of security metrics: The first area is the field of malicious network traffic. The measurements made there are used to estimate the "health" of a network. The second area is the field of intrusion detection systems. These measurements can be taken as indicators on the quality of the system, i.e., its assurance to reliably detect intrusions.

13.1   Measuring Malicious Network Traffic

In today's Internet, we observe more and more security threats. Examples of these malicious attacks include network attacks against vulnerable services, host based attacks such as privilege escalation, unauthorised logins and access to sensitive files, data driven attacks on applications, or many other attack vectors. Up to now, there is no real metric to classify this malicious network traffic. In this section, we try to come up with at least some possibilities to *measure* malicious traffic. This data can then hopefully be used in the future to establish metrics for this area.

Currently, there are several different attempts to measure security-related network activity. Measurement is the first step towards a real metric, so we present in this section the basics. On the one hand, there are tools to measure actual malicious network traffic. These tools include amongst others *honeypots*, *network telescopes / Internet Motion Sensor*, and *flow-based techniques*. On the other hand, there are several attributes that help us to describe malicious network traffic, e.g., *backscatter*. In the following, we will describe each of these tools and attributes in detail and elaborate how the results can be used as a metric. We start with *honeypots* and *honeynets*.

Honeypots and Honeynets

A honeypot can be defined as an information system resource whose value lies in unauthorised or illicit use of that resource. Honeypots are used to learn more about attack patterns and attacker behaviour in general. The concept is rather simple: electronic decoys, i.e., network resources deployed to be probed, attacked, and compromised, are used to lure in attackers. A honeypot is usually a computer system with no conventional task in the network. This assumption aids in attack detection: every interaction with the system is suspicious and could point to a possibly malicious action.

In honeypot-based research, there is a distinction between two fundamental methodologies: *high-interaction* and *low-interaction* honeypots. A high-interaction honeypot is a conventional computer system, e.g., a commercial off-the-shelf (COTS) computer, a router, or a switch. This system does not offer any production-related services in the network and no regularly active users access it. Thus it should neither have any unusual

I. Eusgeld, F.C. Freiling, and R. Reussner (Eds.): Dependability Metrics, LNCS 4909, pp. 157–165, 2008.
© Springer-Verlag Berlin Heidelberg 2008

processes nor generate any network traffic, besides regular daemons or services running on the system. These assumptions aid in attack detection: every interaction with the high-interaction honeypot is suspicious and could point to a possibly malicious action. Hence, all network traffic to and from the honeypot is logged. In addition, system activity is recorded for later analysis. Several honeypots can also be combined to a network of honepots, a *honeynet*. Usually, a honeynet consists of several honeypots of different type (different platforms and/or operating systems). This allows the operator to simultaneously collect data about different types of attacks. Usually high-interaction honeypots help to learn in-depth information about attacks and therefore qualitative results of attacker behaviour [400, 494]. An example of this type of honeypot is the so-called *GenIII honeynet* [36].

A honeynet creates a fishbowl environment that allows attackers to come, while giving the operator the ability to capture all of their activity. This fishbowl also controls the attacker's actions, mitigating the risk of them doing harm to any non-honeynet systems. It is within this fishbowl environment that the operators place any honeypots they want, real systems with real services. The key element to a honeynet deployment is called the *Honeywall*, a layer-two bridging device that separates the honeynet from the rest of the network. This device mitigates risk through data control and captures data for analysis, known as data capture. Tools on the Honeywall allow for analysis of attacker's activities. Any inbound or outbound traffic to the honeypots must pass the Honeywall. Information is captured using a variety of methods, including passive network sniffers, Intrusion Detection System alerts, firewall logs, and the kernel module known as "Sebek". The attacker's activities are controlled at the network level, with all outbound connections filtered through both an Intrusion Prevention System and connection limiter, to mitigate outgoing attacks.

A similar approach in the area of high-interaction honeypots is more lightweight: instead of deploying a physical computer system which acts as a honeypot, it is also possible to deploy one physical computer which hosts several virtual machines which act as honeypots. This leads to easier maintenance and lower physical requirements. Usually VMware [488] or User-mode Linux (UML) [477] are used in order to set up such *virtual honeypots* [403]. These tools allow the operator to run multiple operating systems and their applications concurrently on a single physical machine, thus enabling an easy way of data collection which can eventually be used as a basis for a metric.

If the operator of a honeynet is primarily interested in quantitative results, it is possible to even go one step further and pursue the deployment of a whole computer system. This approach is called *low-interaction honeypot* in contrast to the high-interaction honeypots described above. This type of honeypot does not simulate all aspects of a system, but only simulates specific services or some parts of an operating system, e.g., the network stack. Low-interaction honeypots can primarily be used to gather statistical data about attacks and to collect high-level information about attack patterns. Furthermore, they can be used as a kind of intrusion detection system where they provide an early warning, i.e., a kind of burglar alarm, about new attacks (see Sect. 13.2 for more information about intrusion detection systems). Moreover, low-interaction honeypots can be deployed to lure attackers away from production machines, to detect and disable worms, distract adversaries, or prevent the spread of spam e-mail [32, 402]. Low-interaction honeypots can also be combined into a network, forming a *low-interaction honeynet*.

In the context of the project *eCSIRT.net*, several European Computer Security Incident Response Teams (CSIRTs) set up a network of network sensors across Europe [183]. This network collected data about attacks in a central database for further analysis and helped in vulnerability assessment. After the project ended, some teams decided to continue the then established sensor network across Europe, which has been providing information about network attacks since September 2003. A similar project is *leurre.com* [401]. Several low-interaction honeypots are deployed on different networks and collect data about malicious network traffic in a central database. The collected information can be analysed and enables a comparison between several different parts of the Internet in terms of malicious network traffic.

High- and low-interaction honeypots enable a way to measure malicious network traffic. With low-interaction honeypots, the measurements are rather quantitative since the resulting data sets are typically statistics about the type of traffic, e.g., how much traffic has been observed at a particular port during a specified time frame. In contrast to that, high-interaction honeypots lead to qualitative measurements of malicious network traffic. The operator can learn about particular types of attacks or new attacking techniques. The collected data could be used to form a metric to classify traffic according to certain patterns. However, up to now there is no such metric, the research in this area concentrates currently on data collection. The following quantitative statistics could for example help to form metrics for this area of research:

– Most attacked network ports.
– Number of observed, unique IP addresses.
– Sequences of attacked ports.
– "Mean time between attacks".

Large-Scale Monitoring of Networks

Today, many solutions exist to observe malicious traffic on a large-scale base, e.g., on large parts of the Internet. These solutions often consist of monitoring a very large number of unused IP address spaces to monitor malicious activities. Several names have been used to describe this technique, such as *network telescopes* [81, 358], *blackholes* [104, 454], *darknets* [112], or *Internet Motion Sensor* (IMS) [34]. All of these projects follow the same approach: they use a large piece of globally announced IPv4 address space and passively monitor all incoming traffic or – to a very limited extend – also respond to incoming packets. For example, the network telescope run by the University of California, San Diego, uses 2^{24} IP addresses. This is 1/256-th of all IPv4 addresses. The telescope contains almost no legitimate hosts, so inbound traffic to nonexistent machines is always anomalous in some way, i.e., the principle of honeynets is also used in this context. By analysing all packets, the operator is able to infer information about attackers. Since the network telescope contains approximately 1/256-th of all IPv4 addresses, it receives roughly one out of every 256 packets sent by an Internet worm with an unbiased random number generator. Thus the monitoring of unexpected traffic yields a view of certain remote network events, the so called *backscatter*. This can for example be used to study the threats posed by Denial-of-Service attacks [358].

Another approach in this area is to passively measure live networks by centralising and analysing firewall logs or IDS alerts [239, 517]. Especially the *Internet Storm Center* (ISC) / *DShield.org* [239, 240] is a well-known project in this area. In this project, the collected data is simple packet filter information from different sources all around the world and no "high-level" data is included. Reports are published on a daily basis. They include information about attack patterns and take a closer look at unusual events. A report combines 8 – 20 million records per day with 200,000 – 400,000 source and 300,000 – 450,000 target IP addresses per day. The results are statistics like "Most Attacked Port" or for each port the number of observed source addresses. However, the data contains no detailed information about the source which has collected the packet since this kind of information is anonymised. Therefore a comparison of different attacks is not easily possible. Nevertheless, the huge amount of collected data could enable a way to form metrics. Since the collected information can be compared on different scales, it would be possible to measure the impact of certain malicious events or other metrics could be applied.

Coarse-grained interface counters and more fine-grained flow analysis tools such as *NetFlow/cflow* offer another readily available source of information. A *flow* is an abstraction of individual packets and a summary of packet data between two sites. It can be defined as IP traffic with the same source IP, destination IP, source port and destination port, since this quadruple describes the IP traffic between two devices on the Internet. A flow record typically also contains some additional data, e.g., the number of bytes sent, the duration of the flow, or the timestamp of the first packet. However, the actual payload of the connection is not included within a flow. This is mainly due to logistical reason: if also the payload would be stored, this would quickly result a unmanageable amounts of data. A router which is capable of monitoring flows will only output a flow record when it determines that the flow is finished, e.g., either by explicit connection shutdown or timeout. The flows are stored in a central database and can be analysed from a high-level point of view. With this aggregation of data, it is often possible to draw conclusions about unusual events within a network. Moreover, this concept is often used for visualisation of network traffic. Spikes at certain network ports or certain anomalies can be detected via flow-based analysis techniques. And again, the collected data can enable metrics to analyse the current state of a network in terms of malicious network traffic. However, also this area has up to now no real formalism or model as foundations of metrics.

13.2   Metrics for Intrusion Detection Systems

An *Intrusion Detection System* (*IDS*) generally tries to detect unwanted manipulations to information systems resources. An IDS is required to detect as many types of malicious network traffic and computer usage as possible. Each of these malicious events can be described with the help of an *attack vector*, i.e., a path or means by which an attacker can gain access or modify an information system resource. So the basic task of an IDS is to classify an event as normal or malicious. In general, there are two fundamentally different approaches to build an IDS:

– *Misuse detection systems* (or *signature-based Intrusion Detection Systems*) identify malicious attacks by comparing actual network traffic or executing flow of an application with *patterns of malicious attacks*. Therefore, this kind of systems needs to know the signature of an attack in advance. The main drawback is that these signatures have to be updated regularly to adapt to new attack vectors. In addition, a *zero day attack*, i.e., an attack vector for an unknown vulnerability, can not be detected with such an approach.

– *Anomaly-Based Intrusion Detection Systems* identify malicious attacks by detecting network traffic or executing flow of an application that deviates from "normal" network or system activity. In most cases, this "normal" state is learnt during a training period in which the IDS observes the regular behaviour of the information system resource, the *baseline/threshold*. Afterwards, the IDS can detect whether the current behaviour differs from the learned behaviour.

Orthogonal to this classification is the differentiation between *host-based IDS* (*HIDS*) and *network-based IDS* (*NIDS*). A HIDS monitors and analyses the behaviour of a computer system and is typically also installed on this system. The HIDS could for example monitor system calls, modification of the filesystem, or other changes in the operating system or application. In contrast to that, a NIDS examines the network traffic within a computer network. It tries to detect malicious activity, e.g., Denial-of-Service (DoS) attacks or exploitation attempts, at the network layer. Moreover, both approaches can be combined to build a *Hybrid Intrusion Detection System* to enhance the effectiveness.

A survey on intrusion detection systems can be found in the paper by Hervé Debar and Wespi [214] or Axelsson [29]. A preliminary taxonomy of IDS and attacks is a result of the MAFTIA project [327].

Binary Classification

In order to compare different IDS solution, we need metrics to evaluate them. Firstly, these metrics should be able to objectively measure the effectiveness of the solution in terms of its ability to correctly classify a certain behaviour as normal or malicious, i.e., measure the *accuracy* of the IDS. Secondly, an IDS can also be evaluated on the basis of its *performance*, i.e., how many packets per second can be examined or how large the memory usage is. For more information on this kind of metrics, please see Part IV of this book. Thirdly, an important metric is the *resilience* of an IDS. The resilience measures how the IDS reacts on stress tests or attacks against the IDS itself. In this area, there are currently no established metrics since this is rather an arms-race between attackers and defenders and this area is changing quickly. So we will focus in the following on metrics to measure the accuracy of an IDS solution.

The most simple — and most often used — accuracy metrics for IDS come from the area of binary classification. Since the IDS has the task to classify an event or behaviour as malicious or normal, we can use the results obtained in the area of statistics. The first metrics we introduce are thus *False Positive Rate* (*FP* or *Type I Error*) and *False Negative Rate* (*FN* or *Type II error*). The FP is the probability that the IDS outputs an alert although the behaviour of the system is normal. This means that the IDS incorrectly outputs an alert. In contrast to that, the FN is the probability that the IDS does not output an alert although the behaviour is malicious. FP and FN can be computed as the proportion of false positives from the number of negatives, and vice versa:

$$FP = \frac{\text{number of false positives}}{\text{number of negatives}}$$

$$FN = \frac{\text{number of false negatives}}{\text{number of positives}}$$

Consequently, we can also define *True Positive Rate* (*TP*) and *True Negative Rate* (*TN*) as metrics for an IDS. TP is defined as the probability that the IDS outputs an alert when there is an intrusion and can be determined as TP $= 1 -$ FN. Similarly, TN is defined as the probability that the IDS outputs no alter when the behaviour is not malicious. This can be expressed as TN $= 1 - FP$.

When developing an IDS, there is always a trade-off between false positive rate and false negative rate: we can make the IDS more sensitive at the risk of introducing more false positives, or can deploy it more restrictively at the risk of rejecting false negatives. The risk of false positives must be balanced against the risk of false negatives when selecting the best IDS configuration.

Similar to the above metrics, we can also use the *sensitivity* of an IDS as a metric. The sensitivity is defined as the proportion of normal behaviour.

$$\text{Sensitivity} = \frac{\text{number of true positives}}{\text{number of true positives} + \text{number of false negatives}}$$

A sensitivity of 1 means that all malicious events are detected. But this is not very meaningful since this can be trivially achieved by classifying all behaviour as malicious. Therefore, another metric that we need to determine is the *specificity*. This is the proportion of true negatives of all the negative behaviour examined:

$$\text{Specificity} = \frac{\text{number of true negatives}}{\text{number of true negatives} + \text{number of false positives}}$$

Here, a specificity of 1 means that all normal behaviour is classified as such. Again, specificity alone does not help us much since specificity of 1 can be trivially reached by classifying all behaviour as normal. To combine these two metrics, we can use the *F-measure*. This is the harmonic mean of sensitivity and specificity:

$$\text{F-measure} = \frac{2 \times \text{sensitivity} \times \text{specificity}}{\text{sensitivity} + \text{specificity}}$$

Moreover, there are additional metrics that are similar to the metrics presented up to now, but which bear some slightly different information:

- *Positive Predictive Value* (*PPV* or *Bayesian Detection Rate*) is the probability that there is an intrusion when the IDS outputs an alert.
- *Negative Predictive Value* (*NPV*) is the probability that there is no intrusion when the IDS does not output an alert.

Both PPV and NPV can be calculated similar to specificity and sensitivity:

$$PPV = \frac{\text{number of true positives}}{\text{number of true positives} + \text{number of false positives}}$$

$$NPV = \frac{\text{number of true negatives}}{\text{number of true negatives} + \text{number of false negatives}}$$

In contrast to specificity, PPV yields a measurement of actual normal behaviour in the whole observation set. The important difference between both concepts is that specificity and sensitivity are independent from the total number of samples in the sense that they do not change depending on the fraction of malicious traffic in the whole observation set. In contrast to this, PPV and NPV are sensitive to this fraction. PPV is called Bayesian detection rate [28] since it can also be expressed by using the Bayes theorem (accordingly for PNV):

$$PPV = P(\text{actual intrusion}|\text{IDS alert})$$

To determine these metrics for an IDS system, the common way is to use some standardised data set. An example of such a set is the 1998 DARPA Intrusion Detection Evaluation Program [302]. The whole DARPA data set is a test bed that contains normal traffic data similar to that of an organisation with hundreds of users and thousands of hosts. In addition, it contains more than 300 instances of 38 different attack vectors. There is also the 1999 DARPA Off-Line Intrusion Detection Evaluation during which a similar test bed with even more data was generated [303]. These two test beds were used for the most comprehensive evaluation of research in intrusion detection systems. Nevertheless, the results and the methodology are not without controversy, see for example McHugh [343] for a criticism of that work. The main criticism for these two data sets is that they contain *artifacts* due to the way the data was generated.

Receiver Operating Characteristic (ROC) Curves

Another possible approach to define a metric for intrusion detection systems is to use a *Receiver Operating Characteristic (ROC)* curve and plot the true positive rate (*detection rate*) versus the false positive rate. ROC curves can be used to evaluate the results of different IDS systems. An example of such a curve is given in Fig. 1 (taken from Eskin et al. [144]). Three different algorithms perform unsupervised anomaly detection on a training data set taken from the KDD Cup 1999 Data [9]. This data set consisted of a subset of the 1998 DARPA Intrusion Detection Evaluation Program [302]. The three curves were obtained by varying the baseline of the underlying algorithms and plotting the corresponding false positive/true positives rates.

But which of these three IDS systems is now the best one? Since the ROC curves of the systems cross, there is no easy way to compare them. If the ROC curve for one IDS is always above (i.e., closer to the top left corner) the ROC curve of another IDS, then this means that the first IDS performs better than the second one: for every false positive rate, it has a higher detection rate. But if both curves cross, it is unclear which IDS has the better overall performance. Regarding the figure, we can tell that in certain areas

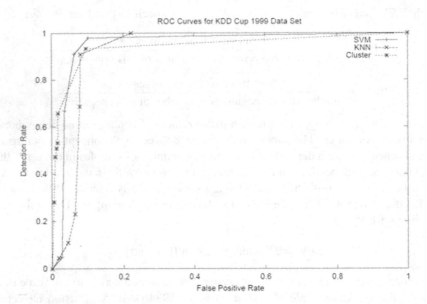

Fig. 1. Example of ROC curve for three different IDS setups

each of the three algorithms has its advantages, e.g., if a false positive rate of about 0.1 is tolerable, then KNN is worse than the two others.

A possibility to extend a metric based on ROC curves is to measure the *Area Under (ROC) Curve (AUC)* and use this as a metric. An area of 1 represents a perfect detection rate of malicious attacks. And an area of 0.5 represents a worthless IDS since the false positive rate always corresponds to a true positive rate. Again, this metric has some limitations since it measures the overall performance of an IDS at all baselines. In practice, however, the IDS would be deployed with the best baseline possible.

Cost-Based Approaches

In order to integrate the notions of false positive rate and true positive rate, it is possible to assign a *cost* to each of them. This *cost-based analysis* yields a metric that considers the trade off between false negative rate and false positive rate in terms of a (possibly estimated) cost measure. This cost measure can be individually adjusted to differentiate between the damage caused by a successful intrusion or the costs corresponding to a false alarm. For example, a company with lots of sensitive information will presumably prefer a very low false negative rate even if the false positives rate could be high. Ulvila [476] and Gaffney [176] use such a cost-based analysis to combine ROC curves and cost-based estimations to determine the expected cost of several IDS baselines. The expected costs can be used as a metric to identify the best baseline and also to compare different IDS implementations. The difficulties and caveats to assign a cost to false negative rate and false positive rate will be further examined in Sect. 15.

Information-Theoretical Approaches

It is also possible to transfer concepts from another research area to build a metric for intrusion detection systems. The concept of information theory can be used to motivate an *information theoretic metric* [201] for IDS. This metric is based on the following observation: at an abstract level, the purpose of an IDS is a binary classification of the input data X (i.e., events that the IDS observes) as normal or malicious. From an information theoretic point of view, this means that we should have less *uncertainty* about the input given the IDS output Y. This metric – called *Intrusion Detection Capability* (C_{ID}) – is the ratio of the mutual information between IDS input and output $I(X, Y)$, and the entropy $H(X)$ of the input:

$$C_{ID} = \frac{I(X, Y)}{H(X)}$$

This metric provides a normalised measurement of the amount of certainty gained by observing IDS outputs. Besides the information given in this paragraph, more information can be found in the technical report by Gu et al. [201].

Another metric for intrusion detection systems is proposed by Helman and Liepins [213]. They model network activity as generated by two stationary stochastic processes, one being malicious and the other legitimate. They formally demonstrate that the accuracy of an IDS is bounded by a function of the difference of the densities of the two processes over the space of transactions. The according metric is called *prioritisation*.

14   Industrial Approaches and Standards
for Security Assessment

Steffen Weiss

University of Erlangen-Nuremberg, Germany

This chapter surveys the work on security standards and best-practices approaches for the security of entire organizations.

14.1   Introduction

Attacks against organizations are becoming more frequent and more severe as recent studies show [22, 474]. As a consequence the risk for an organization to be target of attacks and to suffer substantial losses cannot be neglected. In order to avoid such loss, organizations try to secure their systems by implementing security measures. These measures can be policies, procedures, guidelines, practices or organizational structures, which can be of administrative, technical, management, or legal nature [7]. In the literature, these means are often called *controls*. Organizations need to select appropriate security controls and decide how much should be invested for security and where to invest. Installing these controls can on the one hand lead to an improved security, but also to high installation and maintenance costs. On the other hand, installation of too few or the wrong controls could lead to large and expensive security incidents.

In the context of security metrics, two questions arise:

1. How *effective* are the security controls of an organization? This question aims at evaluating the security status of an entire organization.
2. How *efficient* is the investment in security controls? This question aims at evaluating the economic return of security measures.

It should be clear that both questions are closely interrelated. In this chapter, we aim at discussing the first question. The second question is investigated in the chapter on economic measures of security (Chapter 15).

The security status of an organization is a complex thing which is influenced by many things like attacks, controls, assets etc. Ideally, taking all these aspects together, it should be possible to "calculate" a statement about security. But organizations are complex structures and so in practice results of such calculations are often rather qualitative and imprecise. In this chapter we review general methods to perform such calculations. These include well-known standards like ISO 17799 [7] as well as risk management approaches. We first present a basic categorization and taxonomy of these approaches and then present existing approaches following the taxonomy.

I. Eusgeld, F.C. Freiling, and R. Reussner (Eds.): Dependability Metrics, LNCS 4909, pp. 166–175, 2008.
© Springer-Verlag Berlin Heidelberg 2008

14.2   Basic Categorization

In theory, an organization can be structured hierarchically from low-level structures like offices, employees, hardware to high-level ones like departments, company branches, or divisions. So ideally the security status of an organization can be computed by a hierarchical process: first calculate *basic indicators*, i.e., security values of low-level structures and then combine them to more complex security values following the hierarchical structure of the organization. (In practice there are some effects like missing independence making this process quite difficult.) This calculation can be done with different levels of rigor, i.e., precisely and quantitative on the one hand and more qualitative on the other. This gives rise to two basic dimensions in which the domain of organizational security metrics can be structured.

The first dimension refers to whether one is interested in basic indicators or in the calculation process from basic indicators to global indicators:

- *Measurement approaches* specify how to measure the basic security indicators of an organization.
- *Combining approaches* specify how to measure a whole organization's security given values for basic indicators.

The second dimension refers to the level or rigor in which measurement is performed:

- *Algorithmic approaches* rely on a formal representation of the calculation, i.e., an algorithm, a program or a mathematical formula.
- *Guidelines* give a rather high-level and abstract description of how to carry out the calculation.

These two dimensions structure the domain of security metrics for organizations into four categories. Table 1 shows these categories and points to the sections of this chapter in which these categories are treated in detail. Two categories turn out to be more relevant than the others: On the one hand algorithmic approaches to measure basic indicators, on the other hand guidelines to combine basic indicators to an overall security evaluation. This corresponds to the observation that with growing complexity security measurements become more qualitative. We treat the main two classes of metrics in own sections (Sections 14.4 and Section 14.5) while we discuss the other two in a basic overview only (Section 14.3).

Table 1. Taxonomy of security metrics for organizations

	Measurement approaches	Combining approaches
Algorithmic approaches	Section 14.4	Section 14.3
Guidelines	Section 14.3	Section 14.5

14.3   Overview

We now give a brief overview over all four classes of security metrics for organizations as introduced in Section 14.2. The two main classes are treated in more detail in the following sections.

Algorithmic Approaches for Measuring Basic Indicators

Algorithmic approaches measuring an organization's security properties rely on tools like scanners for weak passwords. Also statistical output of intrusion detection systems, and virus scanners can be mentioned. There are already quite a lot of approaches like this and the number seems to be growing steadily. We give an overview over this area in Section 14.4. Additional information on this area can be found for example in Chapters 13 and 15.

Algorithmic Approaches for Combining Measurement

Algorithmic approaches for combination of indicators and measurement of whole organization´s security are very often derived from the reliability domain. One of the most commonly used approaches are (fault-)trees. Even if these security metrics are mathematically correct and theoretically well founded there is usually lack of applicability. As a result these metrics are not very useful in the real world. Useful hints on this area are also given in the annotated bibliography on the combination of reliability and security (Chapter 25).

Guidelines for Measuring Basic Indicators

Guidelines for measurement of an organization's security indicators are approaches used to get information about security of specific elements which can not or not solely be described by an algorithm. Penetration testing is probably the best known approach in this area. An expert simulates an attack of a malicious cracker. It involves an active analysis of the system for any weaknesses, technical flaws or vulnerabilities. Sometimes people make use of tools to simplify work. Nevertheless, the whole process cannot be completely described by an algorithm. This part is not established as well as for example the algorithmic measurement approaches, yet it seems to be growing.

Guidelines for Combining Measurement

Guidelines for assessment of a whole organizations's security are based on values of single security indicators. This category is the most relevant one in practice. This area is the domain of best practices and standards. There are many standards telling how one can principally perform this "measurement". One very common approaches in this area is the Baseline Protection Manual [3]. Another approach is BS 7799-2 [2] the "measurement standard" for ISO 17799 [7]. (BS 7799-2 as well as ISO 17799 will be included in the ISO 27000 series in future.) Usually, these approaches rely on intensive use of consultants. We discuss this class of metrics in more detail in Section 14.5.

14.4   Algorithmic Measurement of Basic Indicators

There is a large body of work aimed at measurement of basic indicators. Some of this work is surveyed in detail in other chapters of this book. For example, the evaluating the strength of cryptosystems is treated in Chapter 12, the quality of firewalls, intrusion detection systems and virus scanners is discussed in Chapter 13 while measurement of the security knowledge of personnel is presented in Chapter 16. Here we briefly mention two additional approaches to get indicators about an organization's security:

- Vulnerability analysis.
- Security testing (also known as penetration testing).

Vulnerability Analysis

There is a large body of tools that can be used to gain insight into the level of security of a system in an automated fashion. These tools have often evolved from software which was originally designed to break into networks. These tools aim at finding known vulnerabilities in a network. Examples of such vulnerabilities are:

- Known software vulnerabilities and missing security updates.
- Weak passwords.
- Bad security configuration settings (like open guest accounts or disk volumes with insecure file systems).

Thus, vulnerability analyzers give a quick overview of the current security status of networked systems.

An example of such a vulnerability analysis tool is the Microsoft Baseline security analyzer (MBSA) [10] which is available for free download. The security analyzer works on most currently available versions of the Windows operating system (including Windows XP, Windows 2000, Windows 2003 Server) and covers the three directions mentioned above. Figure 1 gives an impression of how the MBSA works.

Another well-known tool that does vulnerability analysis is Nessus [373]. Nessus originally evolved as an open source project but has now forked into a commercial version and a non-commercial open source version called OpenVAS [468]. Another well-known commercial product is the Internet Security Scanner [241].

Security Testing

For security testing or penetration testing (terms are used as synomyms) evaluators attempt to circumvent the security features of a system. This is one of the oldest methods used for assessing computer system's security [136]. The primary aim is attaining control over the target system and evaluating the difficulty of doing this.

The usual way of proceeding is described for example by Shinberg [439]: Penetration testing starts with determining the IP address of a host on the network of interest and investigation who owns the address space allocated. Knowing enough details about the network to attack, the actual test or penetration can start: Usually, scans are used to determine the services which are running on the hosts. Afterwards tools are used to scan for vulnerabilities in the network (e.g. routers and firewalls) or the telecommunication equipment (e.g. PBX, fax, and modem) Additionally tests of physical security can be launched or social engineering can be applied to disclose important network details like passwords or gain physical access to important hardware. Penetration testing can also be applied to single security controls like firewall systems.

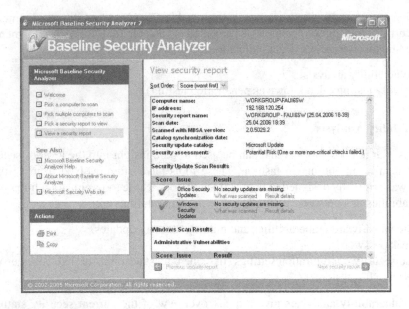

Fig. 1. Screen shot of the Microsoft Bazeline Security Analyzer

Today, security testing is a low-key high-volume business. Superficial security testing can be done in an automated fashion using vulnerability scanners. In-depth security analysis requires a team of highly-skilled experts that may test a system against unusual and even unknown breaches. Result of a security testing procedure is a detailed report on the weaknesses of the system.

14.5 Guidelines for Combining Approaches

In this section we survey the area of informal metrics to measure the security of whole organization. The basic principle is combination of diverse data and data types like values about attacker's strength and information about rates of occurrence to meaningful values for the whole organization.

Questionnaires

Questionnaires available over internet are usually a marketing instrument of security product vendors. They aim to make people more aware about IT security. Visitors are asked some questions, e.g. whether they have installed a firewall. Afterwards some (usually very simple) mechanisms are used to calculate a "total security scoring". The result – for example on a scale of 0 to 10 – is afterwards presented to the user. Even if the assessment mechanism usually is rather guesswork, these questionnaires provide at least a first impression about an organization's security. Nevertheless one cannot speak about a real metric.

There are quite a lot of questionnaires or "security (self) assessment tools" - which is another well known term used in literature. A good overview can be found in [392].

Selection of Security Indicators

The primary standard in this field is NIST SP 800-55 [462]. This approach provides guidance on how an organization, through the use of metrics identifies the adequacy of in-place security controls, policies, and procedures. A suggested metric is for example whether there is a system security plan and whether it is up to date. The metric presented in NIST SP 800-55

- Describes the roles and responsibilities of the agency staff that have a direct interest in the success of the IT security program.
- Provides guidance on the background and definition of security metrics, the benefits of the implementation etc.
- Presents an approach and a process for the development of useful IT security metrics.
- Discusses those factors that can affect the technical implementation of a security metrics program.

Special effort is laid upon the integration into the management system of the organization. All single metrics base on IT security performance goals and objectives, which state the desired results and should be validated with stakeholders. The approach is a quite abstract, management-oriented approach. It does not really say something about how to measure security. The basic statement made by this standard is that if the guidelines are followed, then the organization is more secure than without following the guidelines.

Best Practice Approaches

Best practice approaches contain suggestions for security controls to improve information security. Usually suggestions are subdivided according to the domains where these suggestions are useful. ISO 17799 [7], the most common approach in this direction, contains for example:

- Asset management.
- Human resources security.
- Physical and environmental security.
- Access control.

Beside a control objective, stating the intended achievements, each main security category contains one or more controls that can be applied to achieve the control objective.

Each control description provides detailed information to support the implementation of the control. For example, the control "Addressing security in third party agreements" contains topics, important to be included in agreements with suppliers like responsibilities regarding hardware and software installation and maintenance. Nevertheless details about these topics are not defined.

Even if the list of controls can be seen as some type of binary metric (if fulfilled security is good - if not security is not so good) it is not intended to be a real metric. To be exact ISO 17799 does not contain any measurement approach itself. Instead BS 7799-2 [2] is suggested to be used (for more details about BS 7799-2 see chapter "management system assessment").

Beside ISO 17799, there are other best practice approaches: BS 7799-1 [1] (which is nearly identical to ISO 17799) and the NIST SP 800-53 [418]. But even NIST SP 800-53 does not significantly differ from ISO 17799 at the concept level, the only difference is a rudimentary selection schema. For additional introduction to BS 7799 see [492].

All together, best practice approaches are useful as a starting point for security measures in organizations. Unfortunately, they mainly focus on providing sets of controls and thus one can not actually speak about a metric apart from claiming that if these controls are in place, then the security of the organization is higher than without the controls.

Baseline Protection

The *Baseline Protection Manual* (Grundschutzhandbuch) of the German Federal Office of Information Security (BSI) [3] contains standard security safeguards, which are applicable to virtually every IT system providing basic security.

An IT baseline protection analysis is carried out by accomplishing the following steps:

- The structure of the existing IT assets is analyzed.
- Adequate protection requirements for information and IT assets used are identified.
- Assets are modeled with the help of existing modules of the IT baseline protection manual.
- A test plan is established using a target versus actual comparison.

A certificate aligning with this manual allows saying whether an organization has implemented the needed IT baseline protection standard security safeguards. The certificate can be awarded if an audit [5] is successfully performed. The audit mainly relies upon the documented results of the four steps mentioned above. Criteria are given to check the adequacy of the documentation, for example:

- Comprehensiveness of the analysis of existing IT.
- Plausibility of defined protection requirements.
- Conceivability of the model of the IT system.

The auditor's judgment about this check is the basis for the decision whether the regarded object of investigation fulfills the discussed requirements and, thus, awarding an IT baseline protection certificate is acceptable.

Additional information about management aspects and technical application of this approach can also be found in [376].

Assessment of Security Management Systems

Another type of metric is measurement of security management system's fitness. This approach is integrated into BS 7799-2 [2] and will be integrated into an ISO-standard in future.

This standard specifies the requirements for the implementation of security controls, customized to the needs of individual organizations or parts thereof. Core of this standard is an information security management system (ISMS), a mainly administrative framework of processes and procedures used to ensure that an organization can fulfill all tasks required to achieve information security.

A management system is the framework of processes and procedures used to ensure that an organization can fulfill all tasks required to achieve its objectives.

This system is designed to ensure adequate and proportionate security controls that adequately protect information assets and give confidence to customers and other interested parties.

The main aspects of BS 7799-2 and the comparable ISO standard are:

- Establish the ISMS.
- Implement and operate the ISMS.
- Monitor and review the ISMS.
- Maintain and improve the ISMS.

Additionally, management responsibility and documentation requirements are elucidated.

Nevertheless it is not a metric in the classical form. It is some kind of indirect metric saying "if the ISMS is established according to the given rules then an adequate selection of controls can be assumed".

Information Security Risk Management

The main part of (classical) information security risk assessment or risk management approaches is the assessment of the security in single scenarios. Even if there is some difference between the approaches, the general principle is always the same. In the following, we will explain the primary working principle on the example of NIST SP 800-30 [460]:

For the calculation of severity of single scenarios, threat likelihood and threat impact are taken as input. Both are assessed on a scale with 3 units: 1.0 for high, 0.5 for medium, and 0.1 for low likelihood, 100 for high, 50 for medium, and 10 for low impact. The product of these two factors along with the predefined thresholds for the product determines the resulting risk level.

Besides NIST SP 800-30 there is also the Mehari [114] approach. In addition to the guideline for metric establishment in an organization, it defines which values to estimate and how to combine. This assessment incorporates more assessment steps as for example the NIST SP 800-30 standard and is more detailed. Nevertheless it follows the same principle.

In conclusion, risk assessment approaches provide a good overview about the threats of an organization and, even if the approach is not very detailed, it is a good starting point.

Between Classical and Extended Information Security Risk Assessment

An approach lying between classical information security risk assessment and an "extended" information security risk assessment is proposed in the PhD thesis of

Soo Hoo [456]. The actual metric is based on the annual loss expectancy (ALE) (see Chapter 15). Soo Hoo sees risk modeling as a decision-driven activity.

The advantages of this approach are incorporation of probability theory and capture tools to deal with uncertainty. Most important, decision analysis utilizes influence diagrams as a common graphical language for communicating the collective knowledge of an organization. This language is written down in diagrams. These diagrams are composed of nodes, representing variables, and arrows, representing influence between variables.

As argued by Schechter [426], there are mayor limitations within this model: It overstates the reduction of risk resulting from the use of safeguards that act as substitutes for each other. Additionally the model fails to capture effects of complimentary safeguards and does not provide a procedure for producing forecasts.

Extended Information Security Risk Assessment

Recent work [506, 507] presents an approach similar to classical information security risk assessment but extending it. The main idea is to perform a more detailed assessment of security. It is also based on scenarios and allows a more detailed and more objective assessment of security.

Basically, three indicators are calculated within this metric: First, there is the basic indicator (also called "expectation"). It is calculated by

$$S = 100\% - [\text{percentage of lost assets}]$$

This formula signifies that security is higher if less assets are lost. As the term "percentage of lost assets" suggests, the basic indicator is based on incidents.

An example shall demonstrate that this aligns with the intuitive understanding of security: There are two organizations, both possessing 100 computers. In the first organization, 1 of these computers is stolen over a year, in the other 10 computers are stolen over a year. Assuming that all thefts are detected and reported, the first organization would probably be regarded to be more secure.

This single value gives a first impression on information security, but it does not tell something about the distribution of the damage over the years. In other words, it does not say whether security varies between "very good" and "very bad" or whether there are only minor differences. Additionally, it does not tell something about very big damages in one incident. Therefore, two additional indicators are necessary: on the one hand, the distribution of the security over the time and, on the other hand, an indicator telling something about the occurrence of very big damages. These two distributions are the "likely security" and the "minimum security":

- Likely security is the probability that at least a given security is reached (being equal to the probability that a given percentage of loss is not exceeded). This value is good for getting an impression about the *expected distribution* of the information security over the time.
- Minimum security is the probability, that no scenario occurs, which (on its own) leads to a security less than a given threshold. This value is equal to the probability that no *single scenario* occurs which leads to a loss bigger than a given percentage of assets. This indicator helps to recognize probability of occurrence of very big incidents.

It should be mentioned that these three indicators (expectation S, likely security, minimum security) are calculated for each of the three attributes of security (availability, confidentiality, and integrity) [4, 114, 426, 525] separately.

The calculation of this metric is carried out in the following steps:

- *All relevant scenarios are identified.* For that, all threats, vulnerabilities, and possible damages of an organization are regarded. The resulting scenarios which are possibly occurring (like viruses, fire, theft etc.) are listed. Making identification easier, a generic list of scenarios is provided. It can be taken as a starting point for modeling scenarios of an organization.
- *Assessment of scenarios.* On the one hand the rate of occurrence of the scenario is assessed. On the other hand the damage if the scenario occurs is assessed. Available internal and external statistics should be used to make these assessments more objective. Nevertheless scenarios make assessment already more reliable because they are covering only a small scope of the whole organization.
- *Mathematical modeling techniques are used to combine these results.* For this, Poisson processes are used to calculate the three indicators (per dimension) presented above. In opposite to the first and the second step, this proceeding is described in very detail. There is no room for interpretation in this step. Only results of scenario assessment are taken as input. This makes assessment quite objective.

Nevertheless, quality of the approach depends on quality of available data. As argued by Soo Hoo [456], this quality is not satisfactory. Even if some years have passed by, no significant changes in the data situation have been observed.

14.6   Summary of Presented Approaches

In this chapter, we presented the following approaches:

- Questionnaires (or security (self) assessment tools) giving a rough feeling about security but lacking a founded basis.
- An approach directed to selection of security indicators producing very subjective results (NIST SP 800-55).
- Best practice approaches which are no actual metric approaches themselves.
- The German Baseline protection approach incorporating a well founded but very laborious and quite subjective metric.
- Assessment of management systems, which does not assess security directly but by assessing the procedures established to implement security measures.
- Information security risk assessment as an abstract approach for combination is presented.

The common problem about these approaches is that they are rather informal and very subjective. This problem is solved to some extent by the extended information security risk assessment approach presented at the end.

15 Economic Security Metrics

Rainer Böhme[1] and Thomas Nowey[2]

[1] Technische Universität Dresden
[2] University of Regensburg

This chapter surveys economic approaches for security metrics, among which we could identify two main areas of research. One has its roots in investment and decision theory and is mainly pursued in the field of information technology-oriented business administration. It has yielded a number of quantitative metrics that can be applied as guidelines in investment decisions as well as for the evaluation of existing security measures. The second area of research has ancestors in micro-economics. It deals with market concepts to gather security-relevant information and extract quantitative indicators on information security properties.

15.1 Metrics for Security Investments

The previous chapter has demonstrated that it is essential to measure organisations' security at different levels of detail. This also applies to the investment perspective. In the recent years, organisations see an increasing demand for determining the cost and benefit of IT security investments. Possible reasons include compliance with regulatory requirements, emerging information security threats, or increased dependence of business processes on information technology. Apart from definitions for metrics, this section will show the motivations behind metrics as well as challenges in quantifying the value of IT security investments.

Basics

When assessing investments one can basically take two different perspectives. First, the ex ante perspective tries to assess the costs and benefits of possible future investments and helps to decide whether an investment project is profitable or not. Second there is the ex post perspective for the retrospective judgement of past investments. The first perspective can help to decide whether to invest in a certain security measure or not, or to choose the best alternative out of different possible security measures ("What measures should we implement?"). The second perspective should provide a target-performance comparison and answer the question if the firm's resources were spent effectively ("Did we do the right things?").

The overall goal of the investment perspective on IT security is to measure the influence of investments in IT security on a firm's success and to determine the cost and benefits of different security solutions. Thus metrics for IT security investments should support both of the perspectives explained above. And they should also fulfill some additional requirements, such as allowing for comparisons between firms. It is reasonable to assume that the law of diminishing marginal returns holds true for IT security investments as well (see [189]). Thus from a cost-benefit-perspective there can be a "too

I. Eusgeld, F.C. Freiling, and R. Reussner (Eds.): Dependability Metrics, LNCS 4909, pp. 176–187, 2008.
© Springer-Verlag Berlin Heidelberg 2008

much" of IT security. So as Soo Hoo [456] put it the question to answer could also be "How much is enough?".

One could assume that it is easy to adapt the metrics of classical investment theory to IT security. However there are some major differences between investments in IT security and ordinary investments. The first main difference between usual investment considerations and investments in IT security is, that it is hard to determine the economic utility of those investments. This lies in the nature of IT security measures. Investing in IT security processes or products usually will not provide direct returns in the sense of a measurable positive cash flow. Their main utility rather lies in reducing potential risks. Second, determing the cost of IT security can also be quite hard. Besides direct costs (e.g. installation, maintenance, training) there are also indirect costs (e.g. through changes in employee motivation or changed workflows).

It is widely accepted to regard IT security risks as *operational risks*. According to the Basel Committee, operational risk can be defined as "the risk of loss resulting from inadequate or failed internal processes, people and systems, or from external events" [40]. Thus, many recent standards and other publications apply risk management theory and techniques to IT security (see for example [460], [8], [173]). To understand the metrics presented below it is useful to know some basic taxonomies and concepts of IT security risk management. Nevertheless a broad introduction is beyond the scope of this book and can be found in literature (see above).

An important determinant in risk management is the so called risk exposure, which is formally the product of expected likelihood vs. expected severity of an unwanted event. Investments in IT security aim either at reducing the probalility of occurence or on reducing the potential loss from an unwanted event or both. Gordon and Loeb [190] have shown that information security managers regard those parameters as critical determinants in budgeting for information security. Hence most metrics for security investments survey how efficiently a certain security measure can change those parameters.

Metrics

The concept of *annual loss expectancy* (ALE) represents one of the building blocks of quantitative metrics for IT security. It has been used in risk management since the 1970s and was adapted for IT security risks in the FIPS publication #65 in 1979 by the National Bureau of Standards [367]. The ALE for a single type of security event can be computed as the product of *single loss expectancy* (SLE) and the *annual rate of occurence* (ARO). SLE represents the expected financial consequences of an unwanted event, while ARO is equivalent to the number of occurences of that type of event per year.

$$ALE = SLE \times ARO \tag{1}$$

ALE can also be an aggregation of the annual loss expectancies of several undesirable events (see [456]).

$$ALE = \sum_{i=1}^{n} S(O_i)F_i \tag{2}$$

where O_i is the harmful outcome i, $S(O_i)$ is the severity of outcome i (in monetary units) and F_i is frequency of occurence of outcome i.

Being regarded as too complicated for a long time, this concept has been rediscovered shortly after the turn of the millenium and quickly gained popularty. An article by Berinato [53] presented it as a part of an easily understandable metric called *Return on Security Investment* (ROSI).

Meanwhile ROSI is a collective term for various modifications of the original concept. The basic idea of ROSI is derived from the classic *return on investment* (ROI) and represents the financial gain of a project compared to its total cost [101]. A report written by the French CLUSIF gives examples for the various possible interpretations of the term ROSI [101]. It also includes some definitions that are rather qualitative than quantiative. We will leave out this type and concentrate on calculatable concepts here.

The original ROSI-calculation is derived from an example by researchers at the University of Idaho [504] who performed a cost-benefit-analysis for IDS. The equation can be formulated as

$$ROSI = ALE_0 - ALE_1 - cost \tag{3}$$

where $ALE_0 - ALE_1$ represents the change in the annual loss expectancy due to the security measure with ALE_0 and ALE_1 being the ALE without and with a security measure that costs a certain amount of money (*cost*). This ROSI can be used to support the decision in favour or against a security measure. If ROSI is positive then the investment is judged as advantageous, otherwise the costs are higher than the benefits and thus the firm should not implement the measure. However this concept lacks the relation to the capital employed and thus cannot be used to compare different alternative IT security investments [313].

Other authors [60, 404, 455] give a ROSI-definition that puts the absolute value of a security measure in relation to its costs:

$$ROSI = \frac{(\text{risk exposure} \times \% \text{ risk mitigated}) - cost}{cost} \tag{4}$$

It is worth mentioning that the product (risk exposure × % risk mitigated) is very similar to the differential $ALE_0 - ALE_1$. This metric does not lead to a monetary unit but to a ratio (usually expressed in percent). This has two advantages. First, it enables the comparison of different security measures. Second, the firm can see how efficiently its capital is used since IT security investments can be compared to other investment projects.

Pfleeger and Pfleeger [395] introduce a quite similar metric called risk leverage that can be used to demonstrate the efficiency of a security measure

$$\frac{(\text{risk exposure before reduction}) - (\text{risk exposure after reduction})}{\text{cost of risk reduction}} \tag{5}$$

The risk exposure can be computed by multiplying the risk impact by the risk probability.

The basic concepts assume a planning interval of one year. Since in reality most investment decisions not only affect the current period but also have impact on the future an extension to multiperiod investment seems necessary. For that purpose we take a closer look at investment theory (see for example [419]). According to the economic theory of time preference, investors prefer receiving an inflow from an investment project now to receiving the same nominal amount in the future. Consequently, they prefer spending a certain amount in the future to spending it at present. Thus decision makers aim at calculating the present value of future inflows and outflows. This can be done by discounting the expected future cash flows to the present with an appropriate risk adjusted interest rate.

Gordon and Loeb [190] found that security managers increasingly try to use some form of economic analysis in budgeting for information security. The *net present value* (NPV) is a well established approach for determining the cost or benefit of a decision. It can be calculated as the difference between the present value of future inflows minus the present value of outflows of an investment project. An investment project is judged as profitable if NPV > 0. Another possibility would be to calculate the *internal rate of return* (IRR) of a security project and then compare it to the cost of capital as well as to other investments. The ROSI could then serve as IRR of the security investment project and could be applied for residual concepts and profitablitiy measurement methods(see [313]).

In a recent paper Faisst, Prokein and Wegmann [153] present a sophisticated calculation formula for the NPV that has been particularly developed for the evaluation of security investments in a financial services company:

$$NPV_0 = -I_0 + \sum_{i=1}^{T} \frac{\Delta E(L_t) + \Delta OCC_t - C_t}{(1 + i_{calc})^t} \qquad (6)$$

Their approach includes many of the aspects mentioned above. Besides the change in expected losses $\Delta E(L_t)$ their formula also considers the reduction in opportunity costs of capital charge for unexpected losses ΔOCC_t. Those benefits are compared to the initial investment I_0 and the current costs C_t. The approach is suitable for multiperiod investments and incorporates time preference by discounting with the interest rate i_{calc}. The original article presents further extensions of the concept (see [153]).

Most concepts focus on a single type of harmful event. Assuming that the losses are additive, the ALE and thus the ROSI can also be summed up over several harmful outcomes and their expected frequency of occurrence. Finally, some definitions also consider possible returns generated by a security investment as side effects[60, 404]. For example, single sign-on services may have positive indirect returns other than reducing the risk of false authentication [101].

Limitations and Challenges

Some constraints have to be considered when applying investment metrics for the evaluation of IT security investments. Gordon and Loeb [188] point out that the term ROSI is somehow misleading because it could easily be mistaken as an accounting metric. They differentiate clearly between accounting and economic rates of return. Accounting rates are indicators computed from the balance sheet and are used for backward-looking ex post considerations. This cannot be achieved by the ROSI concepts. The metric as defined by Berinato is not suitable for comparing different alternatives because it only regards absolute values and lacks a common denominator.

It is very difficult to determine a single number for the expected likelihood and the expected severity. Especially the expected severity can vary broadly. Thus the concept of *value at risk* (VaR) has been adapted to IT security recently. The VaR is defined as upper bound for the aggregated severity in a given period. This value is not exceeded with very high probability (typical values are 99 % or 95 %). Due to the lack of data and analytical intractability of parametric loss functions, many contemporary approaches in this area use simulations methods to generate the necessary parameters [264, 313].

As described in Chapter 14, the metrics for measuring the security of a whole organisation used today are based on relatively rough qualitative measurements. Of course it is desirable to aggregate the metrics for measuring single investment at a higher level to be capable of doing cost-benefit analyses of the whole organisation's IT security investments. There exists some tools to support a holistic view on the organisation's security status. Among the concepts proposed for that purpose are risk portfolios, scorecards, as well as decision theoretic concepts like those of Soo Hoo [456] or the AHP [64].

We have already pointed out some of the main advantages and shortcomings of the existing metrics. In addition to that there remain a number of challenges that have to be solved before those metrics become useful in practical contexts.

- *Reliable data.* All metrics require estimations for severity and probability of loss events. In traditional risk management those values are often deducted from historical data. This is barely feasible at the moment for two main reasons. First, there is a lack of historical data on information security related incidents, partly because firms prefer not to communicate their security issues (see Table 1 below). Second it is not clear whether historical data alone is sufficient to estimate future developments in a rapidly changing environment.
- *Quantification.* Historical data is scarce even within organisations that have been using IT technology for a long time because it is so hard to quantify data. Most existing procedures for risk assesment (e.g., OCTAVE [15]) use qualitative estimates only. For economic evaluation, however, it is necessary to have quantitative data or at least to be able to transform qualitative into quantitative data.
- *Complexity.* The area is highly complex. Already at the risk identification stage it is very hard to really get a comprehensive picture of possible threats to an organisation's security.

A main task for future research will be to find good quantification tools for IT security risks. This could be realized by going new ways of collecting historical incident data or by using alternative, indirect measures like the ones presented in the following section.

15.2   Metrics Based on Market Mechanisms

The approach to security metrics discussed in this section differs from the previous ones in the fact that these metrics are not necessarily employed in an economic or business context, but that their way of measurement is based on economic principles. Economics is a social science which studies decision-making processes by rational agents, such as people, firms, and states. Conversely, the observation of rational agents' decisions yields useful indicators for their expectations and can eventually be used to construct operable metrics.

A central element of economic studies is the concept of a *market*. Characterised as "invisible hand" by Adam Smith in 1776 for its self-regulating properties, a market is a negotiation platform for the exchange of goods, whereas goods are not restricted to physical goods but may well include information, securities (stocks) and other types of contracts. Rational agents can be observed in their negotiation process and since all relevant markets trade in money, the outcome of the negotiation process is a *price* denoted in a monetary unit. Markets thus implicitly quantify any tradable property. A profound discussion of the market principles can be found in almost any micro-economic textbook, for example chapter 1 of Varian [483].

As a limitation, market prices are not always accurate for different reasons: most market disturbances can be attributed to low liquidity or transaction volumes, false estimations (i.e., irrationality) of the participating agents, and imbalances in bargaining power between supply and demand-side. Though not perfect, market metrics usually provide a good approximation. They are, in contrast to above-discussed metrics, forward-looking because market prices are based on expectation about the future rather than on historical data.

The economic approach to information security is relatively young and was seeded by Anderson's seminal article "Why information security is hard – an economic perspective" in 2001. Its scope is far broader than the question of metrics, as can be seen from the papers presented at the interdisciplinary "Workshop on the Economics of Information Security" (WEIS), which reached its sixth iteration in 2007. As to security metrics, we can distinguish between research targeted on identifying the impact of security-related events in *existing markets* and the design of *specific markets* for information security.

Metrics Derived from Existing Markets

All studies reviewed in this section empirically analyse the impact of computer-security related news on financial market prices, typically the stock price of affected or involved publicly traded firms. The underlying methodology is a standard approach in finance research called *event study* [325]. In the analysis, the development of stock market prices before the event of interest—the *estimation window*—is fed into a prediction model for each individual stock. Then the prediction model is employed to forecast the most likely development of the stock price after the event date. It thus simulates the scenario as if the event would not have happened. The *abnormal return*, defined as difference between estimated and actual returns during the *event window*, can be interpreted as a measure for the impact of the event on the market valuation of a firm. Different types of event studies differ in the assumptions made in the prediction model, and in the sophistication of the derivation of asymptotic distributions to test the aggregated abnormal returns from a set of events for statistical significance. The abnormal returns are also sensitive to the choice of the estimation and event windows. In most explorative studies the exact magnitude of abnormal returns is less important whereas sign and relative sizes are central to the interpretation. Therefore estimates from different methods can be compared to assess the robustness of the results obtained.

The first, to our knowledge, event study related to information security was published by Ettredge and Richardson in 2002 [146]. The authors conducted a case study of the February 2000 denial-of-service attacks against popular websites. Even when excluding the directly affected firms (Amazon, Yahoo and eBay, among others) significant and negative abnormal returns have been identified for a sample of 287 firms. An additional breakdown revealed that business-to-consumer (B2C) firms suffered relatively more than firms with primary business-to-business (B2B) operations. This distinction is statistically significant and shows that markets not only consider security threats in their expectation of a firm's future value, but can also well capture qualitative information, such as the exposure to denial-of-service risk, which is very difficult to quantify with other means.

Two more studies test similar hypotheses with the same methodology, however with an extended sample of security incidents. Campbell et al. [83] find negative significant abnormal returns on the stock market prices of firms where computer security incidents have been reported in the press. A more detailed analysis showed that the losses are higher when the incident report contained statements about confidential data being exposed. This is another example for the market's capability to quantify subtle differences, though a very careful interpretation is still recommended since the methodology explains only average effects in a set of cases. Another study conducted by Cavusoglu et al. [89] coherently reports negative significant abnormal returns of about the same magnitude as in reference [83]. However, the authors analysed different breakdown and add two more interesting facts: they find that small firms suffer relatively more, which is intuitive from a risk management point of view but counters the common argument that computer security is an issue for big firms only. Second, applying the same methodology to the stock market prices of computer security firms showed *positive* reactions to news about security incidents.

Telang and Wattal [464] use the event study methodology to assess the impact of vulnerability disclosure on the stock market returns of the respective software vendors. This shifts the focus away from IT users and a step closer towards the origin of vulnerabilities in IT products. The results show statistically significant and negative abnormal returns, albeit considerably lower in magnitude than in the previously presented studies (though magnitudes are barely comparable). Moreover, they find that negative reactions to new vulnerability reports affect Microsoft stronger than average. This could be explained by the firm's prominent market position or a general sensitivity to security news among Microsoft investors. But it could also be a technical artefact of a nonlinear reaction function in combination with the firm's outstanding market capitalization. Similar results were also reported in another independent study by Garg et al. [178], although the latter is based on a considerably smaller set of security breaches (43 and 22, respectively). Hovav and D'Arcy analyse particular types of security events, such as denial-of-service attacks [219] and virus contagion [220]. They find negative impact in the short-term, although not statistically significant, which is in part due to the small sample size.

Financial market data has also been used to measure the impact of publicly announced privacy breaches. According to a preliminary report available at time of writing, Acquisti, Friedman and Telang [12] find significant and negative abnormal returns on the event day. A comparison between studies allows to conjecture that the cost of *privacy* breaches (in terms of loss in market valuation) seems to be lower than for *security* breaches in general.

Assuming the absence of a publication bias, particularly those event studies with large samples provide evidence for a market impact of information security news. However, the general utility of stock market prices as a direct metric for security properties is limited by two obstacles: first, event studies capture short-term losses only and it is very difficult to estimate the medium and long-term impact of security properties. Second, the occasions to conduct an event study are limited to the occurrence of extreme events, such as attacks and security breaches. So they are merely a post-hoc indicator of insecurity rather than a metric for security in a state where no incident happens. Both problems have a common source, namely that the stock market price aggregates too many diverse information to be useful as a valid security indicator. As a consequence, one could conceive markets that are closer to the object of interest and isolate the information security aspect in their price information. Those markets are discussed in the following section.

Design of Specific Information Security Markets

There exist, at least in theory, a number of different market concepts for information security related information. Most of them have been conceived for the purpose of countering the present *security market failure*. Due to several economic reasons, namely network externalities and information asymmetries, neither vendors have incentives to build sound security technology into their products nor are users willing to spend extra money on security technology [19]. This leads some scholars to the conclusion that the true causes for the lack of information security in nowadays IT infrastructure lie rather in economic obstacles—and thus in the regulatory framework—than in technological challenges [482]. Even though the actual extent of the security market failure and the relative contribution of technology and policy are difficult to gauge, many of the countermeasures proposed in the literature stimulate new markets and therefore are not only good tools to align incentives, but also to obtain a new class of security metrics.

The remainder of this section discusses three possible market solutions and comments the usefulness of derived metrics: bug challenges, cyber-insurance, and exploit derivatives. We refrain from including other vulnerability market types (see [65, 461]) that do not directly allow for the construction of meaningful security metrics.

Bug Challenges. Bug challenges are the oldest concept to "prove" the security strength of a product, or to signal invisible properties of traded goods in general. In the simplest scenario, the vendor allots a monetary reward for vulnerability reports in his product. Then the amount of the reward is a lower bound to the security strength of the product: it can be safely used to handle and secure assets totalling up to this amount because a rational adversary would prefer to report possible vulnerabilities and cash the reward over attacking the system and capitalizing the information gained. Schechter [426], in his Ph. D. thesis, coined the term *market price of vulnerability* (MPV) for this model.

In a common interpretation, the MPV is regarded as a lower bound of the cost to break a given system. Examples for simple bug challenges include the Mozilla Security Bug Bounty Program[1], the RSA factoring contests, and the Argus Security Challenges[2].

One of the main issues in bug challenges is the choice of the amount allotted. The sum is fixed by the demand-side for vulnerability reports, which consists in the majority of cases of just one entity (the vendor). However, a functioning market needs many participants on both sides, and frequent updates of price quotes are a prerequisite for the construction of timely and accurate indicators.

Several extensions to fixed-sum bug challenges have been proposed in the literature. For example, the reward could be initialized at a very low level and then gradually grow over time. After each vulnerability report, the reward is reset [426]. This scheme allows for a certain dynamic in price-setting, which is similar to market mechanisms designed as auctions[3] [386]. Even with this extension, the price quote is not always a reliable indicator for the true security of a product. Consider the case where two vulnerabilities are discovered at the same time. A rational agent would sell the first one and then wait with the second release until the reward has climbed back to a worthwhile amount. In the meantime, the mechanism fails completely in aggregating information about the security of the product (and prudent users should stop using it until the reward signals again a desirable level of security).

As to the operational aspects, it is still questionable whether the rewards can ever be high enough to secure the accumulated assets at risk for software with large installation bases. Indeed, the amount could be smaller than the assets at stake if we assume a risk-averse adversary (the reward is certain whereas making a fortune as black-hat is risky). However, even the so reduced sum requires a financial commitment of vulnerability-buyers which exceeds the tangible assets of many software vendors, let alone the case of open source software or legacy systems where the vendor ceased to exists.

Table 1. The data dilemma: reasons for not sharing security information

- Loss of reputation and trust
- Risk of liability and indemnification claims
- Negative effects on financial markets
- Signal of weakness to adversaries
- Job security and individual career goals

---

[1] http://www.mozilla.org/security/bug-bounty.html

[2] http://www.wired.com/news/technology/0,1282,43234,00.html;   the contest's aftermath demonstrates the need for a trusted third party to settle the deals: http://www.net-security.org/news.php?id=1522.

[3] This is the reason why bug challenges are sometimes referred to as "bug auction", which *should not be mistaken* as offering vulnerability reports on auction platforms such as eBay (http://it.slashdot.org/article.pl?sid=05/12/12/1215220). For a precise terminology, we propose to distinguish between *buyer-administered* bug auctions and *seller-administered* ones.

Cyber-Insurance. Cyber-insurance copies the idea of risk-transfer from the physical world to cyber-world: individuals can buy insurance coverage for unlikely events from an insurance company in exchange for a fixed price called *premium*. The insurance company, in turn, uses the premiums from many contracts to regulate losses where they occur, to cover their administrative expenses, and to extract a profit for its business risk. Cyber-insurance is not only a tool to mitigate risks and lower the financial impact of security incidents, but the level of the premiums—because the business is organized as a market—can be regarded as an indicator of security strength to construct security metrics for systems or organisations. Similar to real-world examples, where premium deductions come into effect if, say, sprinklers are installed or conventional locks are replaced by hardened ones, the cost of cyber-insurance could be adjusted according to the security technology and practices in place. See Gordon et al. [191], Kesan et al. [273], Varian [482], Rader [409], Grzebiela [200] and Yurcik [521] for further elaboration on cyber-insurance as a risk-management tool.

In theory, on a long-term average the premiums converge to the actual security risk (plus a constant overhead) because competition sets an upper and profitability a lower bound. Premiums are never completely ill-aligned (like in bug challenges after a reset of the reward) but the timeliness of a security metric based on premiums depends on the frequency of contract re-negotiation and (for the public) on the publication of quotes and statistics. In contrast to bug challenges and exploit derivatives (see below), premiums are adjusted to each individual insured's risk profile and not on the expected security strength of standard components. On the one hand, this tailored nature is an advantage, because an organisation or a system is measured on a whole and there is no need for sophisticated and error-prone aggregation to high-level indicators. On the other hand, it might be a disadvantage because the tailored datum becomes more sensitive and so declines the willingness to share or publish it. Hence, one might end up in the same trouble as with the collection of historical data on security incidents [88, 177] (see table 1).

Moreover, despite the presence of potent insurance companies, cyber-insurance business remains on a comparatively low volume. One of the reasons could be that insurance companies hesitate in underwriting cyber-risks, because the losses from information security risks are highly correlated globally—think about viruses and worms, and the lack of diversity in installed platforms. This concentration of risk is contrary to the insurance principle of portfolio balancing and requires additional safety premiums that render cyber-insurance policies financially uninteresting [66]. Apart from the fear of "cyber-hurricanes", there are other operational obstacles, such as the difficulty to substantiate claims, the intangible nature of cyber-assets, and unclear legal grounds.

Exploit Derivatives. Exploit derivatives apply the idea of binary options, as known in financial market research, to computer security events [67, 342]. Consider a pair of contracts $(C, \bar{C})$, where C pays a fixed amount of money, say 100 EUR, if there exists a remote root exploit against some specified server software X on platform Y at date D in the future. The inverse contract, $\bar{C}$ pays out the same face value if there is *no* remote root exploit submitted to a market authority—not a trusted third party in a strict sense—before date D. It is evident that the value of the bundle $(C, \bar{C})$ is 100 EUR at any time and that selling and buying it is risk-free (ignoring interest rate yield of alternative investment, which can be easily compensated for, but is omitted here for the sake of brevity). Therefore one or many *market makers* can issue as many bundles as demanded by the market.

Now assume that there is an exchange platform, where the contracts C and $\bar{C}$ can be traded individually at prices determined by matching bid and ask orders. Then the ratio of the market price of C and its face value approximately indicates the probability of software X being compromised before date D. Of course liquidity, and thus a high number of market participants as well as low transactions costs, are a prerequisite for this mechanism to provide timely and accurate estimates.

However, it is possible that quite a number of different interest groups would participate in such markets. Software users would demand C in order to hedge the risks they are exposed to due to their computer systems in place. The same applies for cyber-insurance companies underwriting their customers' cyber-risks. Conversely, investors would buy contracts $\bar{C}$ to diversify their portfolios. Software vendors could demand both types of contracts: contracts $\bar{C}$ that pay if their software remains secure as a means to signal to their customers that they trust their own system; or contracts C_{comp} that pay if their competitors' software gets compromised. One could even think of software vendors using exploit derivatives as part of their compensation schemes to give developers an incentive to secure programming.

Finally, security experts (a.k.a. "vulnerability hunters") could use the market to capitalize efforts in security analyses. If, after a code review, they consider a software as secure, they could buy contracts $\bar{C}$ at a higher rate than the market price. Otherwise they buy contracts C and afterwards follow their preferred vulnerability disclosure strategy. It is obvious that buyers of C are sellers of $\bar{C}$, and vice versa, if they acquire new contract bundles from the issuer. Since any interaction on the market influences the price, the quotes are constantly updated and can be used as reliable indicators for security strength. Note that this concept does not require the co-operations of the vendor, and the number of different contracts referring to different pieces of software, versions, localisations, etc., is solely limited by demand.

Figure 1 shows a hypothetical price development for an exploit derivative. Operable metrics can be derived from the price quotes, where a mapping to probabilities for security breaches is possible. In the baseline case, this is quite easy, but it gets more complicated if we consider alternative investments, risk-free interest rates, and non-negligible bid-ask spreads. Combining information from more than one contract allows for even more interesting metrics. Price differences between related contracts ("spreads" in financial terms) can be directly attributed to distinctions in security (or public scrutiny) due to underlying technical differences. In the figure this is illustrated as differences in the perceived security between two localisations of the same software. What's more, joint probabilities of failure can be computed from pairs of contracts to measure the total security of cascaded protection mechanisms.

Relation of Market Metrics to Other Metrics

We have seen that economic concepts in general and the market principle in particular offer a new class of metrics. They differ from other metrics in essentially two ways: first, they are expectation-based and such forward-looking, a property which some authors

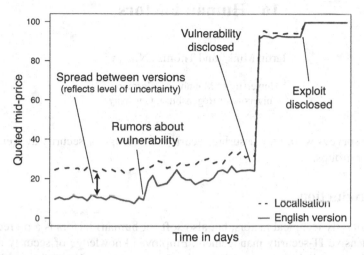

Fig. 1. Relation of events and price quotes of hypothetical exploit derivatives

consider as the sole possibility to cope with the problem of strategic adversaries [426] – in contrast to stochastic ones which can indeed be captured with probabilistic models (see Chapter 9 on hardware reliability) . Second, since almost all markets are settled in money, the often-difficult quantification is inherently implied in the market mechanism. On the downside, while most existing markets are good at predicting future states in the long run, the advantages go along with short-term frictions and, in the terms of metrics, with measurement error.

15.3   Summary

This chapter dealt with economic approaches to security metric. They comprise financial valuation techniques for information security risks that can be used as basis for security investment decisions. After an investment has been made and the ex ante uncertain future state has materialised, economic metrics can be used to assess the efficiency of past security investments. Apart from prescriptive investment metrics we have presented market mechanisms as tools to quantify security properties. We consider them as particularly powerful because their expectation-based and thus forward-looking nature might be an appropriate response to the strategic interplay between attacker and defender. In computer security, information about vulnerabilities are key, and it is hard to beat markets in aggregating and weighting information. However, markets by themselves cannot *create* new information that does not yet exist among the participants. So they can never replace all the other types of measurements discussed in this book, but rather complement them. And since markets reward those participants that contribute accurate predictions, there is also an incentive to improve on all kinds of measurement techniques.

16 Human Factors

Martin Mink[1] and Thomas Nowey[2]

[1] University of Mannheim, Germany
[2] University of Regensburg, Germany

This chapter surveys work on measuring security knowledge or security awareness of individuals or groups.

16.1 Introduction

Regarding not only technical factors, but also soft (or human) factors is a prerequisite for comprehensive IT-security management. Employee knowledge of security threats and mechanisms is vital to a secure electronic environment. As Yngström and Björck [519] state, "the human factor is one of the most significant determinants of the overall success of information security efforts in an organisation" and this fact "has been pointed out in several recent empirical studies on information security in organisations". Especially social engineering attacks (see Kevin Mitnick's book for some good examples [355]) illustrate that a certain amount of knowledge about IT-security is not only necessary for programmers and other IT-related staff but for all employees that somehow get in touch with information technology. This section will be about the human factor in IT security: knowledge about IT security.

Objectives of Using Metrics for Human Factors

As already stated, where IT security is considered, normally just the technical aspects are regarded. But security also concerns the people working with IT systems. By ignorance, carelessness, improper reactions and social engineering security is threatened. An attacker will generally attack the weakest link in a system, and this can be the people working with or being affected by the system.

The lack of proper security knowledge might – and most often will – create problems and can lead to security incidents. But if this kind of knowledge is measurable, it becomes possible to identify deficiencies and to take actions before critical events occur. Those metrics can be used as an early indicator that can be integrated in an organisation's measurement system for IT security like for example a security scorecard.

Another benefit of metrics in this area is the facilitation of benchmarking. This feature is important to both individuals and organisations. Using metrics can help individuals to perform tasks more efficiently or even to get a better job or obtain a better position by being able to prove a certain level of knowledge. Organisations can do a cost-benefit analysis, measure the effect of invested resources, compare candidates when hiring staff members, safeguard information assets, and have a competitive advantage through lower costs and new business opportunities

And, last but not least, metrics for human factors can help to achieve a holistic view of IT security.

I. Eusgeld, F.C. Freiling, and R. Reussner (Eds.): Dependability Metrics, LNCS 4909, pp. 188–195, 2008.

Problems and Challenges When Measuring Knowledge

When trying to measure knowledge a number of questions arise, that make measurement both a problem and a challenge. The first question is: How can one measure knowledge at all? Qualitative features are hard to quantify. And which is the "right" knowledge? What should be measured: what has been done (e.g. number of days of training) or what participants remember from training? Which kind of knowledge is measured by a certain method: explicit knowledge that is suitable for just a certain situation (or application), or the implicit knowledge being equivalent to the ability to transfer the knowledge to day-to-day business?

Some tests or metrics we already know from daily life. Take for example the use of passwords for authentication. Users of computer systems are asked to use "strong" passwords, because "poor" passwords are easy to break. Organisations normally have a password policy stating what criteria a good password should have, to measure the quality of a chosen password. Some applications exist, that have a tool integrated to give feedback about the strength of the chosen password (e.g. master password for password manager in Mozilla-based web browsers). These measure the quality of passwords by certain criteria, like type of characters used to form it. Riley assessed password usage practices among college students using a questionnaire [415].

When being faced with the task to assess knowledge, one has to distinguish the different objects which are being measured. There are metrics that measure

- the level of knowledge of individuals (evaluation of students),
- the realisation of training courses (evaluation of programmes),
- the imparting of knowledge (evaluation of trainers/teaching),
- the success of awareness campaigns and
- whole processes.

Security Awareness vs. Security Knowledge

The following sections deal with metrics for security awareness and security knowledge. How are the terms "awareness" and "knowledge" related and how do they differ? Several publications [512, 513] of the *National Institute of Standards and Technology* (NIST) introduce the terms *awareness*, *training* and *education* for different levels of IT security knowledge.

Awareness is defined as

Awareness is not training. The purpose of awareness presentations is simply to focus attention on security. Awareness presentations are intended to allow individuals to recognize IT security concerns and respond accordingly.

Training is defined as

Training [...] strives to produce relevant and needed security skills and competencies by practitioners of functional specialties other than IT security [...]

Education is defined as

> Education [...] integrates all of the security skills and competencies of the various functional specialties into a common body of knowledge [...] and strives to produce IT security specialists and professionals capable of vision and proactive response.

In these publications users are grouped into four groups: *All users, All users involved with IT systems, Functional roles and responsibilities relative to IT systems* and *IT Security Specialists and Professionals*.

We see security knowledge as the generic term and security awareness as part of it. In the following, "awareness" relates to the definition of *awareness* and "knowledge" relates to both *training* and *education*.

16.2 Measuring Security Awareness

In today's networked and IT-dependent organisations every single employee's behaviour can play an important role in ensuring IT security of the whole organisation. Therefore it is widely accepted, that all people in an organisation that are in contact with IT-systems should have at least a basic understanding of IT security [379]. For this purpose a number of guidelines for the implementation of so called security awareness campaigns have been developed (e.g. Wilson and Hash [512], Fox and Kaun [166]). Their goal is to sensitise users to the issue of IT security. Some of them also contain approaches towards a measurement of security awareness.

Examples for those security awareness metrics shall be described in the following:

NIST SP 800-50. NIST SP 800-50 [512] points out the importance of metrics for determining training needs as well as for assessing the effectiveness and efficiency of awareness and training programs. However just a "Sample Awareness and Training Metric" is presented in Appendix B. It aims to answer the question "Have employees received adequate training to fulfil their security responsibilities?" and can be computed by dividing the number of employees with significant security responsibilities who have received required training by the total number of employees with significant security responsibilities. The target for this measure is 100 %, the required data can be gathered from employee training records and course completion certificates. This metric can show if enough employees received security awareness training but it gives no evidence on the quality of the training. For that purpose further metrics are required. The construction and choice of additional metrics is left to the reader with reference to NIST SP 800-55 [463].

NIST SP 800-16. NIST SP 800-16 [513] presents a conceptual framework for providing IT security training. Moreover, chapter 5 describes ways for evaluating training effectiveness on different levels of complexity (End-of-Course Evaluations, Behavior Objective Testing, Job Transfer Skills, Organisational Benefit). Guidance on implementation of evaluation planning is given as well as two sample questionnaires but no real metrics are defined.

Information Security Culture. The Information Security Culture is part of the organisational culture and can be defined as the

assumption about which type of information security behaviour is accepted
and encouraged in order to incorporate information security characteristics
as the way in which things are done in an organisation. [338]
Security Awareness is an important building block of the security culture on the individual level. For their concept of an Information Security Culture Schlienger and
Teufel [429] developed the so called *Information Security Culture Radar*, a graphical representation of the results of a survey consisting of 10 questions on different
elements of the security policy. With a scale ranging from 0 % to 100 % it can be
used to get a quick overview of the acceptance, publicity and actual implementation
of the policy and to identify the areas where additional awareness measures have to
be carried out.

Mathisen. Using a slightly enhanced version of the NIST template (Swanson et al.
[463]), Mathisen [341] proposes nine different metrics for awareness in his master
thesis. Those metrics can be employed right away but since the list is far from being
complete they are mainly meant to serve as examples for other metrics. The target
of the majority of those metrics has to be set individually by each organisation.

Hansche. In 2001, Hansche [209] published a guideline on how to design and establish
a security awareness program. The article contains a section that describes ideas to
evaluate such a program. The author argues that for most organisations a qualitative
or quantitative analysis is not necessary. Thus the measures proposed are not real
metrics, but since the term awareness itself is somewhat fuzzy, some examples are
nevertheless worth mentioning. Among them are questionnaires on the user per-
ception of the awareness campaign, recording of the number of security incidents
before and after the awareness campaign as well as tracking the number of requests
to on-line resources with training material.

Commercial vendors. Various commercial vendors (e.g. *Brainbench*) offer programmes on employee and awareness testing, but do not disclose which metrics
they use.

16.3   Measuring Security Knowledge

Whereas there is a long history of IT security training or education and evaluation of
the programmes (see Yngström and Björck [519] or NIST publications [513]), there is
almost no effort to measure an individuals' knowledge of IT security. Here we try to
come up with some possibilities to measure security knowledge. These can hopefully
help to establish future metrics for this area. First, existing concepts are presented, that
were not designed with the goal of measuring security knowledge in mind, but that
could be used for it. Then, a new approach is introduced.

Adapting Existing Concepts

This Section gives an overview on existing methods that can be adapted to measure
knowledge. Possible downsides and limitations are discussed in short.

Market-based Approach. Following a market-based approach (see also Sect. 15.2),
security knowledge could be measured by the value received by organisations and society, e.g. on the job market. This can be the salary an employee gets paid by her employer

or the amount of time she needs to find a new job. The problem here is the influence of a number of non-controllable variables: e.g. one person might have a high knowledge in information security but is not good at negotiating his salary while another person with poor knowledge is good at presenting himself. We do not go further into the market-based approach here.

Certification Programmes for Professionals. For security professionals certification programmes as *CISSP* by *(ISC)*² or *Security+* by *CompTIA* are being offered (see Tab. 1 for two examples). Problems in this area are: Is the certificate necessary and relevant in respect to the knowledge required and to local standards and laws? Does it test for the skills that are needed in practise? And, in most cases it is just a binary metric (i.e. "passed" or "failed").

Table 1. Example certification programmes for professionals

Certificate	CISSP (*Certified Information Systems Security Professional*)
Introduced	1989
Organisation	*(ISC)*² (non-profit), `http://www.cissp.com`
Preconditions	3 to 4 years of work experience in IT security, pass test, endorsement by another CISSP, pass audit
Type of test	Multiple choice: 250 questions in 6 hours
Test content	10 domains (e.g. application development, cryptography, (US) law/investigations, network security)
Continuity	Need to earn continuing professional education credits every three years or retake certification examinations
Certificate	TISP (*TeleTrusT Information Security Professional*)
Introduced	2004
Organisation	German *TeleTrusT* (*Fraunhofer-Institute SIT, CAST*, and companies *Siemens, apsec, secunet, gits*), `http://www.tisp.de`
Preconditions	3 years of work experience in IT security, one-week training course, pass test
Test content	18 modules (e.g. network security, firewalls, standards, laws)
Type of test	Multiple choice: 180 questions in 4 hours
Continuity	No

Game-like. So called *Capture the flag* contests (CTF) and *Wargames* have a tradition among security enthusiasts and can also be seen as a means to measure practical knowledge of information security. CTFs are a special kind of live exercise where two or more teams compete against each other in a hacking contest with the goal "to test the security skills of the participants from both the attack and defense viewpoints" [486]. Each team is given a host with certain services running on it. The goal of the game is to exploit vulnerabilities on the other teams' systems in order to collect so called "flags" (usually certain strings placed on the system by the organizer) and to prevent the other teams from attacking that teams' system. Capture the flag contest can be centralized or distributed. Well-known CTFs include the *UCSB iCTF* [486], *C.I.P.H.E.R.* [398], *23C3 CTF* [90], *hack.lu* [206] or the *Cyber Defense Exercise* in military information security education

[132, 427]. Each CTF has its own scoring system. Teams get points for successfully securing their own system and attacking other teams' hosts. Consequently these scores could be used as a measure for the practical security knowledge of a certain team. Of course, some points have to be considered when interpreting these metrics:

- The measurements are always relative and never absolute. Only teams participating in the same contest can be compared.
- CTFs usually are a team exercise. Consequently it is not possible to assess the performance of a single participant.
- CTFs are games that obey to certain rules. Reality may be different. The scoring systems are mostly designed for an optimal flow of the game and not for measuring skills.

In general we see CTFs as an appropriate way to measure the knowledge of practical security. CTFs are for example used as a part of the grading system in several practical security courses at universities. More information on CTFs and other live exercises can be found in Vigna [487].

Another game-like form of measuring, which makes it possible to also assess the performance of an individual, can be provided by the use of *Wargames*. In Wargames the organizer creates a set of challenging scenarios of increasing difficulty which have to be solved by the participants. Challenges usually are modelled somewhat after the problems an attacker faces when attempting a system penetration. Wargames typically are level-based and can be web-based (accessed via a web browser) or shell-based (remote access). Examples for Wargames can be found at Hack this page [205], Next Generation Security Technologies [374][1]. The level reached by a person in a certain Wargame and the time invested can be used as a metric for that persons knowledge in information security. Some Wargame sites (e.g. Next Generation Security Technologies [374]) offer a ranking list of the participants, which gives a good metric. Still, it is just a measurement for the skills needed for that certain Wargame.

Empirical Approach

Apart from the ones mentioned in the preceding section, we are not aware of any approaches. Especially at university degree level we did not find any attempts to measure knowledge of information security. So we use a different approach: Taking methods from social sciences and humanities (pedagogical sciences, psychology and other). In these areas already exists a long history of and methods for measurement of knowledge. The classical – and most well-known – way to measure knowledge is via exams at school or university. The metric is the grade received in the exam (using an ordinal scale, see Sect. 2.2). But this is not a well defined metric, and normally there is no comparison between classes or courses and schools or universities (only between the members of a class). In Europe this might change with the Bologna Process [148].

Empirical Methodology. Here we give a short (and simplified) introduction into the empirical methods used in social sciences. See the books by Bortz and Döring [69] or Kerlinger and Lee [271] for more information.

---

[1] The famous site Digital Evolution [119] was shut down in 2006.

On one hand there is the *classical test theory*: it is still the most widely used model of psychometric testing theory. The model assumes that the result of a test is equivalent to the parameter-value, but that each measurement is afflicted with a measuring error. The quality of a test is defined by three test quality factors: objectivity, reliability and validity. On the other hand there are the (newer and more sophisticated) models of *item response theory* (IRT). IRT is based on the assumption that the probability of a certain answer on each item is dependent on the characteristic of a latent existing parameter-value dimension. The currently most used model in IRT is the *Rasch model* [35, 162].

To conduct a test basically two methods are possible: laboratory experiment and field experiment. A field experiment means gathering data in the natural "habitat" of the test-takers (e.g. in a lecture hall). It has the advantage of producing results that are closer connected to life but makes it difficult to control influences of the environment. A laboratory experiment is conducted in a controlled environment, disabling all negative influence, but has the disadvantage that it might not be related to real life.

Metrics for Measuring Practical Knowledge. How do we measure knowledge of information security? What cannot be observed cannot be measured; so we need to make knowledge observable – and then measure it. A test appropriate to the domain in question should be used: e.g. for practical knowledge a practical test is more suitable whereas for theoretical knowledge a questionnaire can be used.

Here we propose a hands-on test conducted as a laboratory experiment to measure IT security knowledge: Each test-taker is presented a computer system that is configured with a number of security holes (vulnerabilities) and misconfigurations. Then the test-taker is asked to identify and fix these security problems and to configure the system in a secure way, thus transforming the insecure computer system to a secure one. To form a metric, a number of criteria is observed, which include the number of vulnerabilities found, the amount of time needed to achieve a certain result, and the strategy used to achieve the transformation. A metric might look like this: a computer system is prepared with ten vulnerabilities (e.g. weak log-in password(s), installed root kit, and such) and five misconfigurations (e.g. log files writable by all users). If a test-taker identifies eight vulnerabilities and two misconfigurations on such a system she achieves a score of 10 out of 15, which is about 67 %. This score should be set in respect to the time used by the test-taker to finish the test. A more significant result is obtained by including the strategy of the test-taker (e.g. resetting weak log-in password in contrast to notifying users that have weak passwords).

The problem here – as always when measuring – is, that some criteria (as number of vulnerabilities and time) can be quantified, whereas others (as stratey) are hard to quantify. The limitation of the proposed test is, that it is oriented on tasks a system administrator is concerned with. Other important aspects of security as risk evaluation are not considered. So the test needs to be revised to also address other relevant aspects of security.

16.4   Conclusion

As we have seen, a holistic view of an organisation's IT security needs to encompass metrics for the human factor, or – to be more specific – metrics to assess the security awareness and security knowledge within an organisation. However this is quite a challenging task since knowledge consists of an explicit and an implicit part, and only the first can be easily measured, for example by exams. Even if one succeeds in defining metrics for security knowledge, they have to be carefully applied. Knowledge does not necessarily result in according behaviour. For that reasons metrics have been proposed that try to assess programmes or behaviour. Those approaches try to transfer experience in knowledge measurement from other areas.

Despite the challenges mentioned above, we are convinced that it is important to measure the soft factors. And even if those metrics are merely estimates, they can help to get an impression of the security knowledge of an individual or a whole organisation. In addition to that, the process of measuring itself can improve the overall security of an organisation by raising awareness and by rethinking processes.

Acknowledgements. Thanks to Hanno Langweg for a review of this chapter and for his helpful comments.

Part IV

Performance Metrics

17 Introduction to Performance Metrics

Heiko Koziolek

University of Oldenburg, Germany

This chapter defines simple performance metrics and gives an outlook over the remaining chapters of Part IV.

17.1 The Term Performance

Performance can be considered as a sub-characteristic of dependability, although the classical literature does not include it in their definitions [26]. If users perceive the performance of a system as bad, for example because of high response times or denied requests due to overload, they will not consider the services of the system as dependable. There are various definitions of the term *performance* in computer science. Sometimes, people talk about the *speed* of their systems, when they actually mean performance. In this chapter, by performance we refer to the time behaviour and resource efficiency (see Fig. 1) of a computer system. This definition is analogous to the term *efficiency* in the ISO9126 standard [244].

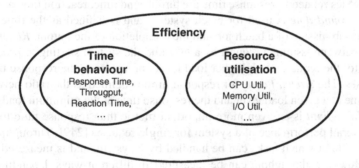

Fig. 1. Performance in Computer Science

17.2 Common Performance Metrics

Some of the most commonly used performance metrics are response time, throughput and utilization [249].

Response Time is defined as the time interval between a user request of a service and the response of the system. This metric is sometimes called responsiveness. As responses often cannot be delivered instantaneously, there are two possible implication of this definition (see Fig. 2): Either the response time is defined as the time interval between the user issuing a request and the system *starting* to respond or *finishing* to

I. Eusgeld, F.C. Freiling, and R. Reussner (Eds.): Dependability Metrics, LNCS 4909, pp. 199–203, 2008.

respond. The former is suitable for systems that deliver short responses, while the latter is best used, when the time interval between starting and finishing the request is rather long. In any case, before using this metric, it should always be made clear which of the two definitions is meant.

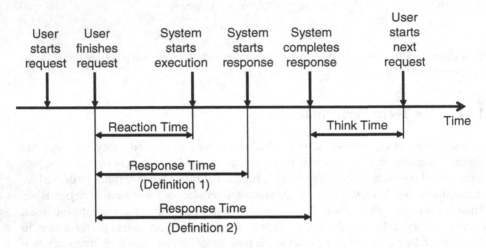

Fig. 2. Definition of Response Time [249]

Some metrics related to response time are turnaround time, reaction time and stretch factor. *Turnaround time* is used for batch systems and is defined as the time interval between the submission of a batch job and the completion of the output. *Reaction time* is the time between issuing a request by a user and the system starting to process (not to respond to) the request. With higher load levels of a system, the response time usually increases. The *stretch factor* for response time is defined as the ratio between the response time at a given load level and the response time at the minimum load level.

Often, *throughput* is an even more important metric than response time to characterise the overall performance of a system for single requests [249]. Throughput is defined as the rate at which tasks can be handled by a system, and is measured in tasks per time. However, throughput can be measured in different ways depending on the system and the devices involved in handling tasks: For batch systems, throughput is measured in jobs/sec, while in interactive systems request/sec and in transactions systems transactions/sec are used. The throughput of CPUs is often specified as MIPS (Million Instructions Per Second) or MFLOPS (Million Floating Point Operations Per Second). For network devices, throughput is either described in packets/sec or bits/sec. Bits/sec is also used to specify the throughput of memory and storage devices like hard disks or DVD drives.

The throughput of a system usually increases, when the load on the system is increased (see Fig. 3). However, at a certain load level, the usable capacity of the system has been reached. It is the maximum achievable throughput without exceeding a pre-specified response time limit. At a higher load level, some of the incoming requests may have to be refused due to full queueing buffers, possibly even causing a decrease of the throughput. The nominal capacity of a system is the throughput under ideal work-load conditions (i.e. with no queueing in the system), which is hardly ever reached in practice. For example, a network device with a bandwidth of 100 MBit/sec as nomi-nal capacity, usually only achieves a throughput of about 85 MBit/sec because of the overhead involved in the networks packets. As seen at the bottom of Fig. 3, the re-sponse time for requests does not increase significantly up to a certain load level. This is called the knee capacity of the system. Upon higher load than the knee capacity, a higher throughput can still be achieved until the usable capacity is reached. However, the responsiveness of the system decreases quickly after this point.

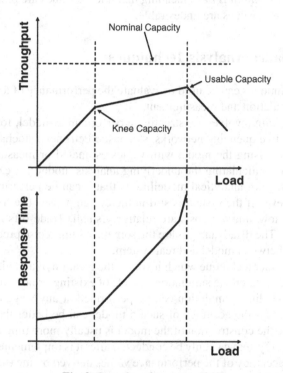

Fig. 3. Capacity of a system [249]

For each resource, the *utilisation* can be measured to characterise the overall perfor-mance of the system. For most devices, utilization is defined as the ratio of busy time of a resource and the total elapsed time of the measurement period. For example, if a CPU processes requests for 8 seconds during a 10 second period, its utilization is 80%. Opposed to processors, some devices can be used only partially. For example, only a fraction of memory may be used at a given point in time. In this case, utilization is defined as the average fraction the resource is used over a time interval. The resource with the highest utilization in a system is usually the bottleneck limiting the overall performance when the load on the system is increased. Because of this, performance analysts characterise the utilization of each resource, and then try to balance the load of the system to achieve a similar utilization on each resource.

When analysing performance measures, it is useful to state the utility function of the metric explicitly. For response time, *lower is better* as users and system administrators prefer short response times. System throughput shall be as high as possible so that the resources of the system are not wasted and a large number of users can be served, thus for throughput *higher is better*. The situation is different for utilization. With a very high utilization, the response times of the system might increase, which annoys users. A low utilization of the system resources can be considered as a waste, which is generally bad for system managers. System administrators try to optimise their systems to support a large number of concurrent users, while users would prefer no concurrent users at all. Thus, for utilization *nominal is best*, meaning that middle values are preferred and both very high and very low values are undesirable.

17.3   Performance Analysis Techniques

Three different techniques can be used to evaluate the performance of a system: analytical modelling, simulation and measurement.

Analytical modelling involves constructing a performance model, for example with known formalisms like queueing networks, stochastic Petri nets, stochastic process algebras etc., parameterising the model with values estimated or measured from existing systems and then calculating the underlying analysis model, for example Markov chains. The advantage of analytical modelling is that it can be performed in early development stages, even if the system is still in the design phase. The time required for analysis is usually low, and the costs are relatively small. Trade-offs in a system can be evaluated easily. The disadvantages are the sometimes imprecise predictions and the possible deviation between model and real system.

Simulation is another technique which involves the creation of a model. A lot of simulation software exists to create simulation models of existing or new planned systems. Like analytical modelling, simulation can be performed at any stage of the development. With some effort the accuracy of such a model can be better than in analytical models. In this case the construction of the model is usually more time consuming.

Measurement of a system can only be conducted after it is implemented or prototypes are available. The accuracy of the performance values derived by measurements can be significantly higher than in analytical modelling and simulation, if the actual workload of the system can be reproduced during measurements. To conduct a trade-off evaluation with measurements is difficult because for example different hardware parts would have to be already available (i.e. purchased) to analyse their impact on the performance of the system. If performance problems are encountered only during measurements that stem from the architecture of the system, it is often costly to solve these problems. For complex system, the costs of measurements may be high, however the saleability of the results of measurements to managers and customers is usually also higher than with analytical modelling or simulation. However, in some situations measurements of a system are difficult or even impossible to conduct (e.g., the control system of a nuclear power plant).

17.4   Chapter Overview

The following chapters about performance metrics elaborate on the metrics and techniques described above. Chapter 18 sums up the performance metrics defined in the ISO9126-standard.

A lot of work has been conducted in computer science to create analytical models to evaluate the performance of systems. A survey of analytical models is beyond the scope of this book and can best be retrieved from the respective literature [249, 295, 349]. Chapter 19 focusses on specific metrics that are used in such models, namely queueing networks and stochastic Petri nets.

A recent trend in performance engineering is deriving performance models from general software models, surveys can be found in Balsamo et al. [38], Becker et al. [44]. Today, the Unified Modelling Language (UML) [383] is often used to model object-oriented systems. In chapter 20, the process of performance evaluation starting from software design models is explained, and extensions to UML are introduced that allow the integration of performance metrics into this notation.

If performance metrics are collected with measurements from existing system, it is necessary to characterise the workload of the system adequately and to use different existing tools. This is the topic of chapter 21.

Some performance metrics are specific for certain domains or are used in a different way in those domains. Chapter 22 includes examples from web-based and real-time systems.

18 Performance-Related Metrics in the ISO 9126 Standard

Steffen Becker

University of Karlsruhe, Germany

ISO 9126 [243, 244, 245] is a standard which can be used to describe the quality of software systems. It is based on a quality model that is illustrated in part one of the standard [243]. This model distinguishes quality attributes into internal and external attributes. Internal metrics depend on knowledge on the internal details of the respective software. External metrics can be measured without knowing internal details. Furthermore, the quality model introduces characteristics and sub-characteristics which are abstractions of the actual attributes. For example, *Usability* is an abstraction of *Learnability, Understandability, and Operability* which each itself again abstracts from the different attributes.

The ISO 9126 standard has no characteristic *Performance*. The closest characteristic to our definition of performance is *Efficiency*. It is divided into two sub-characteristics: time behaviour and resource behaviour. Some people say this distinction is artificial as time is also a (rare) resource. Nevertheless, the timing behaviour is separated in ISO 9126. The important attributes of *Efficiency* in ISO 9126 are being described in the external metrics specification. Hence, the following is restricted to the second part of the standard describing the external metrics [244].

18.1 General Comments

The introduction to the efficiency metrics in ISO 9126 contains some interesting general comments. First, it is remarked that most of the metrics for efficiency vary over time and can only be measured with certain jitter. Therefore, the introduction recommends to use statistical means to characterise the respective attributes. It is recommended that at least the maximum and the distribution should be taken during measurements.

Additionally, the influence of the hardware and software environment is pointed out. Software running on different hardware platforms and/or different software platforms (operating systems, application servers, middleware platforms, ...) has different efficiency characteristics. The timing behaviour varies with the speed of the underlying system layers. Hence, ISO 9126 recommends to specify the environment on which the measurements have been performed exactly.

In some of the metrics a so called *task* is referenced. Task should be defined in the context of the application and should somehow correspond to typical tasks of the system. Examples stated are business or database transactions, sending/receiving a communication package, the processing and output of a chunk of data for a user application.

18.2 Time Behaviour Metrics

ISO 9126-2 defines the following timing related metrics:

I. Eusgeld, F.C. Freiling, and R. Reussner (Eds.): Dependability Metrics, LNCS 4909, pp. 204–206, 2008.
© Springer-Verlag Berlin Heidelberg 2008

Response time. The response time should measure the time consumption for completing the specified task. It should be recorded as the time span between the start of the task and its completion.

Response time (Mean time to response). The mean time to response should record the average response time under a specified system load in terms of concurrent tasks and system utilization. It is estimated by taking the response time several times and dividing the sum of all runs by the amount of measurements.

This can again be divided by the required mean response time so that the result is the ratio of fulfilling the requirements. The ratio should be less than 1.0, lower being better.

Response time (Worst case response time). The worst case response time is calculated using the ratio of the maximum response time of a set of measurements divided by the required maximum response time. Again, the value should be less than 1.0, lower being better.

Throughput. The throughput describes the amount of tasks which can be performed over a given period of time.

Throughput (Mean amount of throughput). For an amount of concurrent runs of the specified task calculate the sum of each of the throughputs divided by the amount of runs. Then divide this by the required throughput to get a ratio. The ratio should be less than 1.0, lower being better.

Throughput (Worst case response time). For an amount of concurrent runs of the specified task, take the maximum of the measured throughput values and divide this by the required throughput to get a ratio. The ratio should be less than 1.0, lower being better.

Turnaround time. The turnaround time is the waiting time an user experiences after issuing an instruction to start and complete a group of related tasks. It is the time span from starting the tasks until the last task finishes.

Turnaround time (Mean time for turnaround). For an amount of measures of the turnaround time under a given system load in terms of concurrent tasks and system utilization take the sum of all measures divided by their number. This value is again divided by the required average turnaround time to get a ratio. The ratio should be less than 1.0, lower being better.

Turnaround time (Worst case turnaround time ratio). For an amount of measures of the turnaround time under a given system load in terms of concurrent tasks and system utilization take the maximum of all measures divided by the required worst case turnaround time to get a ratio. The ratio should be less than 1.0, lower being better.

Waiting time. The waiting time characterises the proportion of the time the users spent waiting of the total time a set of concurrent scenarios takes to execute.

18.3   Resource Utilisation Metrics

We briefly summarize the resource utilisation metrics in the following. The resource utilisation metrics are divided into three main groups: I/O device utilisation, memory resource utilisation and transmission resource utilisation.

I/O Device Utilisation

The I/O device utilisation section offers several metrics to characterize the load of the specified resources with respect to the tasks defined. It contains metrics for the device utilisation, load limit, I/O related errors and the waiting time of the user resulting from device response times.

Note, that several of the metrics have to be taken under fixed conditions with respect to the concurrency of the tasks involved. Hence, those metrics can be adjusted to several situations and their interpretation highly depends on the conditions under which they have been measured.

Memory Resource Utilisation

The memory resource utilisation metrics can be used to determine the memory consumption during the execution of the specified tasks. The standardised metrics contain metrics for the maximum amount of memory consumed, the mean occurrence of memory errors and the ratio between memory errors and execution time.

Note, that the maximum memory utilisation is determined by evaluating the maximum number of memory related error messages during a set of experiments which is different from common sense (see ISO9126-2 [244, p.48]).

Transmission Resource Utilisation

The transmission resource utilisation is supposclsed to describe the load of communication related transmission channels. Metrics of this group contain the maximum transmission utilisation, the media device utilisation balancing, the mean occurrence of transmission errors and the mean of transmission errors per time.

Note again, that the maximum transmission utilisation is evaluated using the maximum of the transmission error count over a set of experiments (see ISO9126-2 [244, p. 49]). Additionally, the device utilisation balancing is supposed to capture the delay introduced by synchronisation constraints between the different media types.

18.4 Open Issues

The metric definitions in the ISO 9126 are quite vague. Additional information has to be supplied together with the metric: the system, on which the value was measured, workload, and the task performed. This sounds reasonable, however, it is a tough task to compare the results taken by one person with results from another person. In order to allow the comparison of the measured values, there is the additional need to have a common reference platform, reference setup and reference measurement instructions. Additionally, those instructions have to be clear and reproduceable, so that any two experts perform the same experiment. In so doing, the results become comparable and can be verified by third-parties.

19 Analytical Performance Metrics

Jens Happe

University of Oldenburg, Germany

This chapter summarizes queueing networks and stochastic Petri nets, two common mathematical tools to measure performance analytically.

19.1 Introduction

Design decisions during early development stages often have a major impact on the performance of the developed system. They can decide between success and failure of a project. Due to the importance of these decisions, system architects need support to reach the best decision under given constraints. To do so, the architect has to consider different aspects of a system, e.g. its performance. She or he has to identify a set of metrics that need to be optimised or have to fulfill certain standards. For performance, typical metrics are throughput of a system and its response time. Since the most important design decisions are made during the early development phases, there is no system to measure or evaluate. Analytical methods are one means to predict and/or estimate the performance metrics of intrest. Opposed to intuition and trend extrapolation, which require a high degree of experience and insight into the field to yield reliable results, analytical methods provide a framework for the definition, parametrisation, and evaluation of performance. This support is required, since even for experts, it is hard to find the right decision concerning performance based on intuition only [282]. On the other hand, experimental evaluation or prototyping yields sound results and detailed knowledge of system behaviour. However, the development of a prototype is expensive and time consuming. Analytical performance models are less laborious and more flexible than experimentation, since a model is an abstraction of the real system avoiding unnecessary details. They can provide the needed balance of accuracy and flexibility.

Since analytical methods abstract the real world, many assumptions have to be made to create a model that can be handled. Often it is unclear how the assumptions affect the predictions and whether the model is a valid abstraction of the system. Thus, it must be possible to compare the results of the model to the measurements of a real system. Furthermore, the relationships among quantities based on measurement or known data need to be established. This is known as *operational analysis* [117]:

> All quantities should be defined so as to be precisely measurable, and all assumptions stated so as to be directly testable. The validity of the results should depend only on assumptions which can be tested by observing a real system for a finite period of time.

The analytical models discussed within this part base on stochastic processes that describe the system behaviour and provide the needed mathematical framework. This is known as *Stochastic Hypothesis* [117]:

I. Eusgeld, F.C. Freiling, and R. Reussner (Eds.): Dependability Metrics, LNCS 4909, pp. 207–218, 2008.
© Springer-Verlag Berlin Heidelberg 2008

The behaviour of the real system during a given period of time is characterised by the probability distributions of a stochastic process.

This hypothesis is refined with assumptions on the kind of stochastic process (e.g. Markovian), which introduce concepts as steady state, ergodicity, independence, and distributions of specific random variables (see chapter 8). Observable aspects of the real system (states, parameters, and probability distributions) are associated to quantities in the stochastic model. Equations relate these quantities, so that some can be derived from others.

A major disadvantage of stochastic modelling is the impossibility of validating the Stochastic Hypothesis and the supplementary hypotheses that depend on it, since one cannot prove asserted causes by studying observed effects. Thus, the truth or falsehood of the stochastic hypothesis can never be established beyond doubt through any measurement [117]. Opposed to the general Stochastic Hypothesis, the performance models described in this part are operationally testable. Their veracity can be established by measurement.

The remainder of this chapter is organised as follows. Section 19.2 introduces queueing networks and their usage for performance prediction. We describe the metrics used as input (e.g. the workload specification) and derived as output (e.g. response time and throughput). Finally, we discuss some of the assumptions underlying queueing theory. Section 19.3 gives an overview on stochastic Petri nets for performance prediction. We describe some of the metrics that can be derived from stochastic Petri nets. As for queueing networks, we discuss the assumptions underlying the model.

19.2   Queueing Network Models

Queueing networks (QNs) have been introduced by Jackson [247] to analyse a multiple device system, whose devices contain one or more servers. From there, QNs evolved continuously so that many variants of QNs exist today. In this section, we focus on general metrics of QNs, which apply to most of its classes.

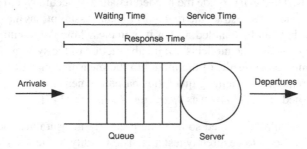

Fig. 1. A simple queueing network [349]

A queueing network consists of service centres and customers. Service centres (or servers) represent the system resources (e.g. CPUs and disks) and their queues. Customers are the active users or transactions in the system. They represent, for example, database transactions, HTTP requests, and batch jobs that receive service from different service centres in the QN [349]. Figure 1 shows a simple queueing network, which consists of a single server and its queue. Customers arrive at the service centre, wait in the queue if necessary, receive service from the server, and depart. In general, queueing networks consist of multiple service centres and customers circulate among these service centres until they leave the system.

Some of the performance metrics for QNs are illustrated in figure 1. When a customer arrives at a service centre, it first has to queue up and wait. The waiting time plus the service time yields the response time for the customer at the service centre. Additionally, we can determine the mean queue length, the throughput and the utilisation of a service centre. These metrics depend on the service demand of the customers at each service centre and their arrival rate.

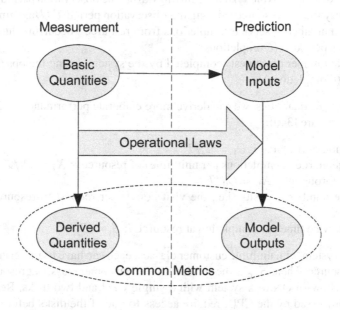

Fig. 2. Comparison of metrics from measurement and prediction

Before we describe performance metrics of QNs in more detail, the relationship between prediction and measurement for QN needs to be clarified, since both offer different alternatives to compute a metric. Figure 2 shows the relationship between different methods to obtain performance metrics of QNs. *Basic quantities* are metrics that can be directly measured on a real system. They are used to compute more elaborate metrics, so-called *derived quantities*. The derived quantities that are obtained on the basis of measurements, can also be computed in a predictive manner. Therefore, the modifiable parameters of the QN are characterised by the *model inputs*. These can be estimates or they can be derived from basic quantities. The *operational laws* are used to compute the *model outputs*. Based on the formulae for the derived quantities, they provide a mathematical framework to obtain the model outputs from its inputs. Thus, the metrics for measurement and prediction are easily comparable. In the following, we describe the metrics of basic and derived quantities, how the model inputs can be derived from basic quantities, and the operational laws, which include the computations for the outputs of the prediction model.

Basic and Derived Quantities

In operational analysis [117], a set of basic quantities, which can be observed at a real system, is defined.

T: Length of the observation period (Time).

A_i: Number of service requests (i.e. as arrivals) to service centre i during the observation period T (Arrivals).

A_0:   Number of arrivals to the system occurring during the observation period (Arrivals).

B_i: Total busy time of resource i during the observation period T (Busy time).

C_i: The total number of service completions from resource i occurring during the observation period T (Completions).

C_0:   The total number of requests completed by the system during the observation period T (Completions).

From the basic quantities, we can derive more elaborate performance metrics. Some of these metrics are [349]:

U_i: Utilisation of resource i: $U_i = B_i/T$

X_i: Throughput (i.e., completions per unit time) of resource i: $X_i = C_i/T$

X_0:   System throughput: $X_0 = C_0/T$

V_i: Average number of visits (i.e., the visit count) per request to resource i: $V_i = C_i/C_0$.

S_i: Mean service time per completion at resource i: $S_i = B_i/C_i$

If we have a system with multiple customer classes, each can have its on service demand for every resource. Then, $S_{i,r}$ is the service time of customer class r at resource i.

Figure 3 shows a QN of a system with a single CPU and two disks. Requests that have been processed by the CPU, require access to one of the disks before they leave the system. Assume, we measure the following quantities [349]:

$$T = 60 \text{ sec}$$
$$B_{CPU} = 36 \text{ sec}$$
$$A_{CPU} = A_0 = 1800 \text{ transactions}$$
$$C_{CPU} = C_0 = 1800 \text{ transactions}$$

From these, we can derive the average service time for each customer at the CPU: $S_{CPU} = B_{CPU}/C_{CPU} = 36 \text{ sec}/1800 = 0.02 \text{ sec.}$

Further performance metrics of QNs are discussed in the context of operational laws. The model inputs described in the next section can also be derived from the basic quantities and, thus, can also be considered as derived quantities.

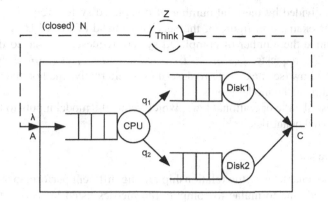

Fig. 3. A queueing network with multiple servers

Model Inputs

The inputs of a queueing network characterise the workload (see section 21.1) of the system, e.g. the rate at which customers arrive, and the service requirements of customers at the service centres. Figure 3 illustrates the input parameters of a QN with multiple servers. The QN contains a set of parameters, like the arrival rate λ, that have to be specified in order to solve the QN. We describe these parameters in the following.

Workload intensity. The workload of a system can be specified in different ways depending on the type of system that is modelled. If the system is *open*, customers that are finished leave the system and new customers enter the system continuously (figure 3 without the dashed part). This is a common way of characterising transaction processing workloads. The workload intensity is specified by λ indicating the rate at which customers arrive. The population of active customers (or jobs) varies over time. This allows a possibly infinite number of jobs within the system. For each resource i, the average arrival rate, λ_i, is given by: $\lambda_i = A_i/T$.

In *closed* systems, customers that are finished re-enter the system after a *think time* (figure 3 with the dashed part). This models interactive workloads. The number of customers in the system is fixed to a value N and the time each customer spends thinking is modelled by the parameter Z. Optionally, the think time can be zero. In this case, customers re-enter the system immediately. This is generally used to model batch workloads. Customers that have completed service can be thought of as leaving the model and being replaced instantaneously from the backlog of waiting jobs. The values for N and Z can be obtained using Little's Law described in section "Operational Laws".

Service demand. Additionally to the service time, the service demand of a customer at centre i, D_i can be specified. It is defined as the total amount of time a customer requires at a service centre. It can contain multiple visits to the same resource and, thus, is the sum of the service times for all visits. Opposed to the service time, it contains the complete time a customer spends at a resource during its lifetime in the system. The service demand can be computed from the basic quantities. It is the busy time of resource i, B_i, divided by the total number of completed system requests, C_0: $D_i = B_i/C_0$. For our example in figure 3, the service demand of the CPU is equal to its service time, since the number of completed system requests is equal to the number of completed CPU requests: $D_{CPU} = B_{CPU}/C_0 = B_{CPU}/C_{CPU} = S_{CPU}$. The Service Demand Law (see next section) describes an alternative method to compute the service demand from the model inputs.

Next, we describe the operational laws, which relate the model inputs to the metrics defined for derived quantities.

Operational Laws

Operational laws characterise the relationship among different performance metrics of QNs. They provide the formulae to compute the metrics listed in section "Basic and Derived Quantities" based on the model inputs instead of basic quantities. Thus, the input parameters can be estimated and no actual measurements have to be conducted. The operational laws base on a set of mathematical assumptions that characterise the underlying process, some of which are discussed in the end of this section.

Utilisation Law. So far, utilisation is defined as $U_i = B_i/T$. If we divide nominator and denominator by C_i, the total number of service completions from resource i, we get

$$U_i = \frac{B_i}{T} = \frac{B_i/C_i}{T/C_i} = \frac{B_i}{C_i} \times \frac{C_i}{T} = S_i \times X_i.$$

Thus, the utilisation of a resource i is the product of the mean service time of a customer at resource i and its throughput. In flow balanced systems, the number of arrivals A_i is equal to the number of departures C_i and, therefore, $X_i = \lambda_i$. In this case, the utilisation can be easily computed from the model inputs.

Service Demand Law. Service demand, D_i, is the total average time spent by a typical customer of a given type obtaining service from resource i. It is one of the input parameters of QNs. In section "Model Inputs", a formula to compute the service demand from basic quantities is given: $D_i = B_i/C_0$. We can modify this formula so that D_i can be derived from the model inputs

$$D_i = \frac{B_i}{C_0} = \frac{B_i/T}{C_0/T} = \frac{U_i}{X_0}$$

So, the service demand is the utilisation of resource i, U_i, divided by the system throughput, X_0. Intuitively, the service demand is the sum of service times S_i for each visit to resource i. This coherence can be expressed in a formula as well

$$D_i = \frac{B_i}{C_0} = \frac{C_i \times S_i}{C_0} = \frac{C_i}{C_0} \times S_i = V_i \times S_i.$$

The busy time of resource i is the number of completed requests at i multiplied by the service time of each request at i. The service demand is the service time, S_i, multiplied by the number of visits V_i, to the resource i. The average number of visits to a resource i is $V_i = C_i/C_0$. For the CPU in our example, the number of visits is $V_{CPU} = 1800/1800 = 1$. In this case, the service demand is equal to the service time.

The Forced Flow Law. The forced flow law relates the throughput of a device to the system throughput. Consider a system where for each system requests, two requests are issued to the CPU. If we have a system throughput of $X_0 = 5$ requests per second, then the throughput of the CPU must be $X_{CPU} = 10$, since each request to the system causes two requests to the CPU. Thus, the throughput of a resource is equal to the number of visits V_i to that resource multiplied by the system throughput X_0:

$$X_i = V_i \times X_0.$$

Little's Law. Little's law is probably the most important operational law for queueing theory. It basically states that the number of customers in a black box, a system whose internal structure is unknown, is given by the departure rate from the box multiplied by the average time spent in the box. This assumes that the system is flow balanced (the number of arrivals A_i is equal to the number of departures C_i) and that customer cannot be created or destroyed within the black box. With this formula we can compute the average number of customers in different parts of the QN. For example, we can look at a single service centre without its queue. There can be either one or no customer in the centre. The average number of customers of the service centre should yield its utilisation. If we apply Little's law to the service centre we get

$$N_i^S = X_i \times S_i = U_i.$$

The average number of customers in i is its throughput X_i multiplied the average service time, which is equal to its utilisation.

Appropriateness of Queueing Networks

Queueing network models provide the means to model complex systems in an abstract manner. However, the accuracy of QN is appropriate in most cases. For utilisation and throughput, the error is less than 5-10% in many cases. For response time, the accuracy is a lower bound depending on the compexity of the system. The error is mostly between 10% to 30% [295]. These numbers refer to systems build in the early eighties. At this time, batch system have been strongly used. So, one has to take care when generalising the results and applying QNs on today's software systems.

Assumptions. When using QN one has to be aware of the many underlying assumptions. So, even if the accuracy of QN is rather good in the general case, they might not be appropriate to model any kind of system. For each system, at least the most important assumptions have to be checked. We give only a list of the most important assumptions. A more detailed list can be found in Lazowska et al. [295].

- The system must be flow balanced - i.e., the number of arrivals at a given system must be almost the same as the number of departures from that system during the observation period.
- The devices must be homogeneous - i.e., the routing of jobs must be independent of local queue lengths, and the mean time between service completions at a given device. So, the load and the distribution of jobs in a system does not influence its behaviour.

– The system must have an equilibrium and/or stationary behaviour (see chapter 8). This assumption cannot be proved to hold by observing the system in a finite time period, since it is an assumption about the infinite system behaviour.

Actually, most of the assumptions can be disproved empirically: Parameters change over time, jobs are dependent, device to device transitions do not follow Markov chains, and systems are observable only for short periods. However, experience showed that queueing models can apply well to systems (especially batch systems), even if so many assumptions are violated [117].

19.3   Stochastic Petri Nets

Stochastic Petri Nets (SPN) represent a powerful tool to describe and analyse concurrent systems with synchronisation and locking mechanisms. Since their introduction in the early eighties by Natkin [371] and Molloy [357], they have been applied to many problems in the area of performance, reliability, and availability analysis of software and hardware systems. This includes real-time and embedded systems [528] as well as distributed systems [99, 227]. The granularity of the system description varies from coarse grained, abstract system descriptions to fine grained, low level descriptions.

A typical example of a Stochastic Petri Net is shown in figure 4. It consists of a set of *places* $P = \{p_1, \ldots, p_5\}$ represented by rounded rectangles and a set of *transitions* $T = \{t_1, \ldots, t_5\}$ drawn as black bars. The *arcs* between the places and transitions are

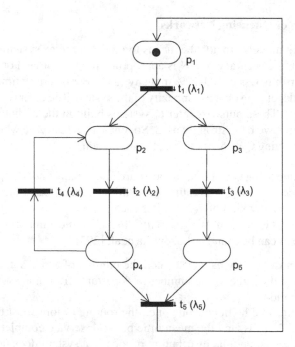

Fig. 4. Example of a Stochastic Petri net [43]

defined by a function $F : (P \times T) \cup (T \times P) \rightarrow \mathbb{N}$. $F(p,t)$ states how many arcs are going from place p to transition t and $F(t,p)$ analogously states how many arcs are going from transition t to place p. The *initial marking* M_0 of the Petri net in figure 4 is drawn as a black dot in place p_1. It represents a single token on this place. The entire Petri net is described by a tuple $PN = (P, T, F, M_0)$.

The dynamic behaviour of a Petri Net is determined by the movement of tokens. A transition t is *enabled* if the number of tokens in each of its input places is at least equal to the multiplicity of the corresponding input arc from that place. When the transition fires, tokens are removed from its input places and and put in each of its output place. For the example above, transition t_1 is enabled. Its firing would remove the token on p_1 and place a token on both places p_2 and p_3.

A *marking* of a Petri net can be represented by a vector that contains the number of tokens on each place. For example, the initial marking of the Petri net in figure 4 is $M_0 = (1,0,0,0,0)$, place p_1 contains one token and all other places are empty.

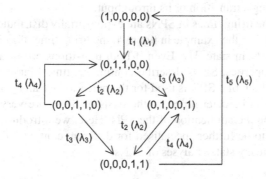

Fig. 5. Reachability Graph [43]

The set of markings that can be reached from the initial marking by any possible firing sequence is called the reachability set. Based on the reachability set a reachability graph can be drawn. The nodes of the graph represent the elements of the reachability set, while the arcs describe the possible marking-to-marking transitions. Figure 5 shows the reachability graph of the example in figure 4. The arcs are labelled with the transitions that fire, when the marking changes.

For continuous-time SPNs, the set $\Lambda = \{\lambda_1, \ldots, \lambda_5\}$ is added to the definition. Each λ_i is associated to a transition t_i and is the, possibly marking dependent, transition rate of transition t_i. Thus, the firing time of t_i is exponentially distributed. In figure 4 the transition rates are added in braces behind the transition labels. Once t_1 fired, the system is in state $M_1 = (0,1,1,0,0)$. In this state, transitions t_2 and t_3 are concurrently enabled. So, either t_2 or t_3 will fire next. This is a typical race condition.

In performance analysis, SPNs are used to model stochastic processes, which represent approximations to the dynamic system behaviour. These models are used to analyse qualitative and quantitative properties of a system. Quantitative properties include aspects, which can be derived from the underlying stochastic process, like the probability of firing a transition or the throughput at a transition. These properties can be derived by analysing the corresponding Markovian process. Qualitative properties are those, which can be determined from the structure of the Petri net, for example, if the Petri net is deadlock-free [43].

The analysis techniques of SPNs can either be transient or steady state analyses. Both are fundamentally different concepts. Transient analyses are applied to acyclic nets, which describe finite stochastic processes. These nets have a subset of markings, which describe the final states. The net terminates with a certain probability, if such a marking is reached. The transient analysis is used to make statements about, for example, the overall execution time of a system or the mean number of visits to a state or transition. Cyclic SPNs, which describe infinite stochastic processes, are analysed with steady state analysis techniques. The steady state of a system contains, for each state, the probability of being in that state at any point in time. So, if an observer looks into the system at a random time he will find the system in that state with the probability specified in the steady state. The steady state distribution is given by the probability vector $\pi = (\pi_1, \ldots, \pi_n)$, where $\pi_1, \ldots, \pi_n$ sum up to 1. This information can be used to determine the probability of firing a transition or its throughput.

As stated above, the firing times of SPNs exponentially distributed. Furthermore, they are independent. For the example in figure 4, the firing time of t_2 is not influenced by the firing time of t_3 in state M_1. Even if both transitions are in a race condition. Because of these properties, SPNs describe continuous-time Markov processes. The underlying Markov chain of a SPN is used for the performance analysis of the SPN.

The metrics that can be determined on the basis of SPNs are very broad and vary strongly depending on the application of the SPN. Here, we introduce a set of general metrics, which need to be further specialised for different contexts. The metrics listed below are based on steady state analyses of SPNs.

Probability of being in subset of markings. Given a subset $P \subset R(PN)$ of the reachability set $R(PN)$ of a Petri net PN, we can determine the probability of being in a marking of this subset by summing up the probabilities of the single markings:

$$P(B) = \sum_{M_i \in B} \pi_i,$$

where $\pi = (\pi_1, \ldots, \pi_n)$ is the steady state distribution.

Mean number of tokens. This metric can be used to determine the utilisation of system parts. Therefore, we divide the reachability set into subsets $B(p_i, n)$, for which the number of tokens in place p_i is n. Now, we can compute the mean number of tokens at place p_i summing up the number of tokens n multiplied with the probability of their occurrence $P(B(p_i, n))$:

$$\overline{m_i} = \sum_{n=1}^{\infty} n P(B(p_i, n)).$$

Probability of firing transition t_j. To compute the probability r_j that transition t_j is fired next at any given point in time, we need set of markings EN_j enabling transition t_j. EN_j is a subset of the reachability set R(PN). Given this set, we can compute the probability that transition t_j is fired in marking $M_i \in EN_j$. This is the fraction of the firing rate λ_j of transition t_j and the sum of the firing rates of all transitions $(-q_{ii})$ enabled in marking M_i. If we multiply the result with the probability of being in that marking π_i and sum up the results for all markings enabling transition t_j, we obtain the desired probability:

$$r_j = \sum_{M_i \in EN_j} \pi_i \frac{\lambda_j}{(-q_{ii})}.$$

Throughput at transition t_j. The troughput of a transition t_j is the mean number of firings at a steady state or, in other words, the mean firing rate of a transition. It is computed by multiplying the transition rate of t_j by the probability of being in the subset of markings EN_j, which contains all markings enabling t_j:

$$\overline{d_j} = \lambda_j P(EN_j).$$

The metrics listed above are very SPN specific. For the analysis of a real system the need to be associated with a semantic. For example, the probability of being in a subset of markings can be combined with a certain reward, i.e. response time to compute the performability of the system; the probability of firing a transition can be interpreted as the probability of failure; the throughput at transition t_j can be the throughput of a network connection. As you can see, there are many different ways to do so depending on how the system is modelled.

However, when modelling systems with SPNs one has to be aware of there properties and limits, since these strongly influence the interpretability of the results. SPNs describe a Markovian process and, therefore, allow the analysis of many performance aspects of a system. Furthermore, they provide easy means to describe concurrency and synchronisation problems. However, there are many open problems concerning the applicability of SPNs as stated by Balbo [37].

A well known issue, when analysing SPNs is the problem of *state space explosion*. With an increasing number of tokens, the size of the reachability set increases nearly exponentially. This leads to an increased complexity of the analysis, sine the underlying Markov chain grows at the same speed. Thus, the analysis of large systems with many tokens becomes infeasible.

With plain SPNs, only *exponentially distributed firing times* can be modelled. Even if the exponential distribution represents a good approximation for some applications of SPNs, it does not model the real world, where almost arbitrary distributions for time consumptions are possible.

SPNs describe Markovian processes, which have the property that the next state depends only on the current state and not on the history of the process. This so-called *Markov property* might be a valid assumption for some systems, but cannot be considered as a general truth. Hence, it has to be validated for each application of SPNs.

Several extensions have been proposed to overcome some of the limitations of SPNs. Generalised Stochastic Petri nets [335] introduce so-called immediate transitions, which complete in zero time. These permit the reduction of the state space of the embedded Markov chain. The resulting stochastic process is only semi-Markovian. Additionally to immediate and timed transitions, Deterministic SPNs (DSPN) introduce deterministic transitions, which have a constant firing time [334]. The stochastic process associated with a DSPN is a Markov regenerative process and an analytical method for steady state and transient analysis exists [98]. Generally Distributed Transitions SPN (GDT_SPN) extend GSPNs with timed transitions whose firing times are generally distributed [336]. Moreover, an execution policy has to be defined, which states how the next transition to fire is selected. Furthermore, SPNs have been combined with Queueing Networks [43]. This allows the representation of scheduling strategies. This is done by partitioning the set of places into two subsets: queued places and ordinary places. Many of the different variants of SPNs have been extended with reward rates to efficiently describe Markov Reward Models (MRM), which are mostly used in performabiltiy, reliability, and availability analysis [472]. The usage of Stochastic Reward Nets for performability analysis is described in section 24.2 of chapter 24.

20 Performance Metrics in Software Design Models

Antonino Sabetta[1] and Heiko Koziolek[2]

[1] Università di Roma, "Tor Vergata", Italy
[2] University of Oldenburg, Germany

This chapter summarizes two extensions of the Unified Modeling Language (UML) that allow to express performance characteristics.

20.1 Software Performance Engineering

Performance problems are hard and costly to fix in later development stages. In fact, from the point of view of performance evaluation, a successful (and even more an unsuccessful) implementation is mostly determined by the choices that are made at the architectural level, i.e. very early in the development life-cycle. As software systems get more and more complex, the inadequacy of the traditional fix-it-later approach becomes evident. It is impractical (and most of the times infeasible) to wait until an implementation is available before assessing the extra-functional characteristics of a system. In some cases, to meet the required performance characteristics, a major rework of the architectural design may be necessary, which causes a significant amount of additional effort to be spent. In many other cases the situation is even worse, as completely wrong architectural choices may render it impossible to meet the target quality level at all and can cause the entire project to fail.

To address these problems, the Software Performance Engineering (SPE) methodology was proposed in the early 1990s [451]. According to the SPE approach, the adoption of performance evaluation techniques should start from the early stages of the software life-cycle (i.e. from the architectural design) and continue throughout the whole development process.

The performance modelling approach of SPE is based on the identification of a set of key scenarios. The execution path of each scenario is modelled as a set of steps, each associated with a quantitative specification of its demand for resources and of the timing aspects of its execution. From the analysis of such a model, a number of performance metrics can be evaluated (response time, utilization of different resources by different software modules, throughput) and many performance-related design problems can be identified and solved before they are propagated to the detailed design or implementation phases.

The application of the SPE principles to the practice is hindered by the fact that the skills that are required from performance analysts are not usually possessed by software designers and developers. In fact, software design models and performance analysis models refer to different domains and are separated by a significant semantic gap.

To address this problem, and to bridge this gap, a number of proposals have been discussed in the literature. They are based on a variety of notations, spanning special-purpose formal languages (such as process algebras) and "semi-formal" graphical

I. Eusgeld, F.C. Freiling, and R. Reussner (Eds.): Dependability Metrics, LNCS 4909, pp. 219–225, 2008.
© Springer-Verlag Berlin Heidelberg 2008

languages, such as UML-based design specifications. What most of these proposals share, is the idea of automating the derivation of analysis-oriented models from design models, in order to relieve software designers of this complex task.

Approaches based on mathematical/logical notations are amenable to automated and/or formal reasoning. On the other hand, they usually require highly specialized skills and good mathematical background to be built or interpreted, and thus suffer from usability problems and lack of mainstream tool support.

Approaches based on graphical notations are considered more intuitive and convenient and for this reason are much more widespread and commonly used in the practitioners' community. Furthermore, as UML is in the position of being a "de facto" standard, UML-based notations that support performance modelling can benefit from a wide tool-base, thus being more usable and practical.

Especially when using visual languages, performance modelling, and in general the modelling of most non-functional properties of computer systems, is realized by means of annotations attached to "standard" design models. Such annotations are used to convey the additional quantitative information that is needed to derive an analysis-oriented model. It is critical to the acceptance of the methodologies supporting the analysis of extra-functional properties that the introduction of additional modelling activities should have the least possible impact on the "traditional"/usual established design activities and languages.

In the case of UML, this important requirement is addressed by using the mechanism of *profiles*, which allows tailoring the standard language to special modelling needs, turning it into a *domain-specific language* (DSL), without breaking the compliance with the standard definition of the language and, most important, without requiring the development of new special-purpose tools.

In the remainder of this chapter we present an overview of the most eminent examples of UML profiles for performance modelling in the software domain, namely the "UML Profile for Schedulability, Performance, and Time" (in short the "SPT profile") and the "UML Profile for Quality-of-Service and Fault Tolerance" ("QoS/FT profile").

At the time of writing, a proposal for a new standard profile by the OMG, called MARTE (Modelling and Analysis of Real-Time and Embedded systems) [145] is being worked on. This proposal is expected to merge the SPT and QoS profiles, addressing at the same time a few additional needs that have emerged after their introduction. In the final section of this chapter we will present an overview on the state of the new proposal, comparing it with the existing profiles.

20.2   UML SPT Profile

The SPT Profile [385] is an OMG standard that enables the application of the SPE methodology to the design of software systems specified with UML. The profile supports modelling those aspects of a computer system whose quantitative characterization is required for performance prediction or analysis at different levels of abstraction and from different analysis viewpoints.

A fundamental part of the profile deals with the description of resources, and their characteristics. Of course, any model dealing with performance issues must be able to suitably represent timing characteristics, spanning time values, events, timed stimuli and mechanisms such as timers and clocks.

The performance part of the SPT profile offers the support for defining the performance requirements of a system, associating QoS characteristics with elements of a UML design model, for specifying execution parameters (used by analysis tools to "evaluate" the model), and for feeding back the results of the analysis into the model. In this section we will give an overview of the key concepts related to performance modelling that are available in the SPT profile. For each of them, the most important characteristics and the relative metrics are summarized.

In accordance with the SPE principles, the performance of a system is investigated by analysing a set of scenarios. Response time and throughput are metrics typically used to specify the requirements imposed on scenarios. A scenario is associated to a host which supports its processing, and is executed by a "workload" (i.e. a class of jobs, see also 21.1). If the workload is open it is defined in terms of the rate and time distribution of the arrivals. If it is closed, the population and a think time (or external delay) value is given. Scenarios are characterized by steps, arranged in a graph by means of a predecessor-successor mutual association. A step can have a nested scenario, allowing arbitrarily complex nested scenarios.

Scenarios are specified referring to a *performance context* that is characterized by a set of resources involved and by a set of workloads that can be applied to its scenarios. Among other properties, scenarios have a response time property. It represents the total time required to execute the scenario. Usually the principal objective of the performance analysis is to determine (estimate) the value of this property.

Each step of a scenario is characterized by a host execution demand, i.e. the load that it imposes on the host where it is executed. Other properties of steps include: delay, caused for instance by a user interaction (think time); response time, i.e. the total time required by the step (which possibly involves completing nested scenarios); a time interval between successive repetitions of the step; number of repetitions or operations performed.

The resources, referred by steps, are defined by the three QoS attributes utilization, throughput and scheduling policy. Resources, in turn, can be active or passive. Both active and passive resources inherit all the attributes from the abstract resource class. The former also have the following properties: processing rate, expressed in relation to a reference processor speed; context switch time, i.e. the time required to switch from a scenario to another, and other more specific attributes. Passive resources have the following special attributes: capacity, indicating the allowed number of concurrent accesses to the resource; access time, i.e. the time spent by a step or scenario to acquire and to release the resource. The utilization property of passive resources indicates the (average) number of concurrent users of that resource. Giving numerical values for the QoS characteristics of the concepts presented so far is not sufficient if nothing else is said about their meaning. For this reason their specification is done by using a simple, purposely devised, language whose expressions takes the format shown in code fragment 8. There source-modifier can be one of required, assumed, predicted, or measured; type-modifier can be one of average, variance, k-th moment, maximum, k-th percentile, distribution;

```
<PA-characteristic> ::= <performance-value> [<performance-Value>]*
<performance-value> ::= <source-modifier> <type-modifier> <time-value>
```

Code fragment 8: Performance value specification

time-value is the actual time value, which may itself be complex (e.g., a probability distribution).

20.3   UML QoS/FT Profile

The "UML Profile for Modeling Quality of Service and Fault Tolerance Characteristics
and Mechanisms" [384] (short: UML QoS/FT profile) has been adopted by the OMG
in 2004 (latest working document from 05/02/05). It allows the introduction of extra-
functional aspects into UML models by associating UML model elements with QoS/FT
requirements or properties. The profile aims at real-time and fault tolerant systems. It is
split into a QoS part and a FT part. We will focus on the QoS part and specifically its
performance metrics.

The profile is intended to allow the specification of so-called *flexible software components*. Such components are able to trade off among the time and resources they
use, the quality of their input, and the quality of their output. The basic elements of
the QoS model are resource-consuming components (RCC) and QoS-aware specification functions (QASF). The interfaces of RCCs are specified according to the CORBA
component model (CCM). QASFs are used to specify the extra-functional behaviour of
component services.

Metrics are called *QoS Characteristics* within the profile and can be associated with
both RCCs and QASFs. Different QoS Characteristics are defined in the profile (for example latency, throughput, capacity, scalability, availability, reliability, safety, integrity,
accuracy, etc.). A *QoS Dimension* adds a scale to a QoS Characteristic. It is attributed
with a direction (increasing or decreasing depending on which is considered the better
value), a unit for the values of the dimension, and a statistical qualifier (like min, max,
range, mean, variance, etc.).

QoS Values instantiate QoS Characteristics and assign specific values to the associated element. If QoS Values depend on other QoS Values or on other model elements,
this dependency can be described by a *QoS Context*.

QoS Constraints add restrictions on QoS Characteristics, either by enumerating the
allowed QoS Values or by defining minimum and maximum values. QoS Constraints
can be defined for required and for provided services. An agreement between required
QoS and provided QoS has to be found forming a contract. If the provider of a service cannot deliver the required QoS, the contract between the two parties has to be
renegotiated.

QoS Levels describe modes of QoS supported by a component. For example, a component providing a video player may specify different QoS Levels by supporting different video resolutions.

Multiple QoS Characteristics can be grouped into a *QoS Category*. The QoS
Categories defined in the QoS/FT profile are performance (with the subcategories

throughput, latency, efficiency, and demand), dependability (subcategories reliability, availability), security, integrity, coherence, and scalability. Most of the QoS Categories contain *QoS Characteristics* with the same name. We will describe the subcategories of the performance QoS Category and also the scalability QoS Category in the following as they deal with performance metrics.

Throughput Category

A *throughput category* contains an abstract QoS characteristic named throughput, which represents throughput in general and is attributed by a rate without a unit and a direction. Three concrete types of throughput are distinguished: input-data-throughput, communication-throughput, and processing-through-put. inputdata-throughput describes the arrival rate of input data in bits/second and an increasing direction. Output data in bits/second and an increasing direction is represented by communication-throughput, while processing-throughput refers to the possible amount of processing in instructions/second and an increasing direction.

Latency Category

The QoS Characteristics in this category are latency and turnaround. latency is specified as the time interval during which the response to an event must be executed. It defines a window for this time interval with the QoS Dimensions minimum-Latency and maximumLatency. Moreover, the QoS Dimension jitter refers to the maximum variation in time between two subsequent outputs, and the criticality describes the importance of the event to the system with a priority. The other QoS Characteristic turn-around specifies the time interval between the event of receiving a request and the event of generating the final result.

Efficiency Category

The *effixiency category* contains the resource-utilization and the resourcepolicy QoS Characteristics. resource-utilization is defined as the "capability of the software product to use appropriate amounts of resources when the system performs its functions under stated conditions". It contains the QoS Dimensions worst-case-request and mean-case-request without specifying the unit. The units are added in the extensions resource-computation (seconds), resource-communication (byte), and resource-memory (byte). The QoS Characteristic resource-policy refers to the scheduling policy of a resource (e.g. rate monotonic, fifo, etc.).

Demand Category

In the *demand category* the resource-utilization characteristics are combined with the QoS Characteristic arrival-pattern via demand. The arrival pattern describes the occurrence of invocations and can be periodic, irregular, bounded, bursty, and unbounded), which can be specified by the QoS Dimensions period, jitter, and burst size.

Scalability Category

The *scalability category* contains as the only QoS Characteristic `scalability`. With this characteristic, it is possible to express that a service does not produce the same quality level, if the demand for the service is increased. QoS Dimensions are minimum and maximum number of elements representing the capacity of the service. Furthermore, the function `cost-per-unit` returns a value describing the cost of the service for a given number of demand units.

20.4   Conclusions

We have reviewed the UML SPT and QoS/FT profiles, two standardized extensions of the UML language that support the annotation of models with information regarding extra-functional properties of systems. The SPT profile is more specifically oriented towards scenario-based analysis (which is close to the approach of SPE) and poses a special emphasis on the domain of real-time systems. The QoS/FT profile on the other hand is more general in scope and defines a wider range of QoS characteristics. It also provides a flexible mechanism to define and store new user-defined characteristics. Unfortunately this flexibility comes at the cost of a higher complexity of the definition mechanism.

Furthermore the QoS/FT and the SPT profile follow a different approach to the annotation of models. While the latter uses plain annotations to carry the additional performance information, the former requires to augment the original model with additional objects for annotation purposes. This implies on one hand that with the QoS/FT profile, the annotation process is more complicated, but on the other hand its more verbose approach enables a fuller exploitation of the OCL (Object Constraint Language) to specify QoS expressions and constraints.

At the time of writing, the OMG is working on the definition of a new standard profile named "MARTE" (Modelling and Analysis of Real-Time and Embedded systems) [145] which is supposed to replace the current SPT profile, using the second version of the OMG family of standard (namely MOF 2.0 QVT, OCL 2.0, UML superstructure 2.0) and integrating features of the QoS/FT profile. The new profile will be designed so that it will give better support for the design and specification of time-critical and resource-critical systems, addressing several requirements coming from the domain of real-time and embedded systems. The principal guidelines for the specification of MARTE are the following:

- To support both software and hardware specification, and combinations of the two;
- To provide modelling constructs oriented to the design of RT systems, capturing both qualitative characteristics, such as parallelism, synchronization, communication, and quantitative characteristics such as deadlines and periodicity. The profile should enable the high-level description of systems (for specification purposes) as well as the description of implementation details at a lower level of abstraction.

- To leave the modellers free to choose the modelling style and constructs they prefer, without forcing them to adopt a predefined approach.
- To foster the use of predictive quantitative analysis along the development process, even starting from incomplete models.
- To enable the use of analysis techniques without requiring specific or deep knowledge of the underlying theory.
- To support the automatic derivation of analysis models from design specifications.

21   Measuring Performance Metrics: Techniques and Tools

Antonino Sabetta[1] and Heiko Koziolek[2]

[1] Università di Roma, "Tor Vergata", Italy
[2] University of Oldenburg, Germany

This chapter describes techniques for characterising workloads, which is a prerequisite for obtaining performance measurements in realistic settings, and presents an overview on performance measurement tools such as benchmarks, monitors, and load drivers.

21.1   Characterisation of Workload

An accurate workload characterisation is critical to any successful performance modeling, prediction and analysis activity. In fact, workload model inaccuracies have a strong impact on the accuracy of performance evaluation, even when a detailed system model is available. The task of appropriately characterising the workload of a system is not easy; it involves a number of skills, is difficult to formalize and automate, and it is largely based on expertise gained through experience.

The Workload Characterisation Process

Even though workload characterisation approaches that are specific to a particular domain or kind of application have been investigated in the literature, a few typical steps that are common to every approach can be identified. They are grouped in three main phases: requirement analysis, workload model construction, validation [82, 142, 348].

Requirement Analysis. The requirement analysis begins identifying the purposes of the study and deciding at what abstraction level the characterisation should be done. A hierarchical view of the system being investigated can often be useful to define the interesting quantities that should be modeled. The topmost layer in such a description is usually called the *functional level* whereas the bottommost layer is the *physical level*. At the functional level the analysis focuses on the types of requests addressed to the system classifying them according to the user-level functionality they refer to. At the physical level, the focus is on the load expressed in terms of low-level resource demand (cpu steps, I/O operations, memory). Of course intermediate levels can be considered in between, and for each of them specific metrics should be chosen as appropriate. The layered approach helps define, for each layer, what are the *basic workload components*, i.e. the the elementary units of work that external sources address to the system (layer) being investigated. The metric used vary with the layer: for instance, the number of calls to a high-level functional module and the number of cpu steps are good candidates as basic components for the functional level and the physical level respectively. The basic components are described in turn by their parameters, which usually refer to two

I. Eusgeld, F.C. Freiling, and R. Reussner (Eds.): Dependability Metrics, LNCS 4909, pp. 226–232, 2008.

types of information: the *workload intensity* and the *service demand characterisation*. The former spans the arrival rate of each request type, the time that passes between subsequent request (i.e. the *think time*), the number of clients that generate requests, and so on. The latter specifies the resource demand addressed to the system by each request type. In the first phase of the characterisation process, the criteria for assessing the representativeness of the workload model should be stated. These criteria will be used in the last phase to validate the model.

Model Construction. In the first step of this phase the workload data are collected and pre-processed. The pre-processing stage is necessary when the raw data are not ready to be used directly by the subsequent activities. For instance they may need to be translated in a more practical format, or some sort of filtering may be required, e.g. to remove the outliers from a time series or to reduce the skewness of a distribution by applying a logarithmic transformation. After the filtered data have been stored in a database, the static and dynamic features are extracted and the workload is partitioned in suitable classes. The obtained model can be further enhanced to derive an executable workload, that can be used, for instance, as a *benchmark*. Having an executable version of a workload model is especially useful to carry out the validation phase.

Model Validation. The basic idea behind model validation consists in comparing the behaviour of the system when it is presented with the real load and the modeled one. The validation is successful if the difference in the values of some predefined performance indices measured in the two cases is small enough (i.e. less than the threshold specified in the first phase, when the validation criteria were declared). If the validation fails, the model must be *tuned* calibrating some of its parameters or changing the mix of its components and then the validation can be repeated.

Workload Characterisation Approaches

The techniques for workload characterisation can be grouped in two categories: static and dynamic. The first comprises approaches like clustering, principal component analysis, averaging and correlations. They all study the intrinsic features of the workload that are independent of time, like the classification in transaction classes or the analysis of stochastic stationary characteristics. On the other hand the category of dynamic techniques includes approaches that aim to capture the time-dependent behaviour of the workload: the most widely used among such techniques are based on Markov models, user behaviour graphs and regression methods applied to historical data. They describe the time-dependent patterns followed by the requests addressed to the system. Static and dynamic techniques can be combined to obtain more accurate workload models.

Choosing Metrics

When modeling the workload, the choice of what metrics should be used is affected by a number of factors. First of all, it should be considered that characterising a workload starting from data collected from a running system requires a simplification of the collected information to obtain a more compact and manageable model from a possibly huge amount of rough data. One of the most important problem in workload characterisation is to understand how this simplification should be realized, i.e. how data can be aggregated, sampled, selected or discarded according to the specific objectives of the study, to the level of accuracy that is required and also depending on the level of abstraction at which the analysis must be done. For this reason it is fundamental to fix a level of abstraction for the system and workload models. To this end, a system can be considered as composed by a set of layers, each consisting of a network of resources that offer services to the upper layer. The services offered by a layer can require in turn those provided by the lower layers. In this framework, the requests that a layer receives from the upper one constitute its workload.

Client/Server Systems

As an example of the layered view presented above, we might consider the case (described in Calzarossa and Serazzi [82] as well as in Elnaffar and Martin [142]) of a Client/Server system. The topmost layer models the client; it addresses requests to the server (bottom layer) passing through an intermediate network layer. Depending on the layer that is being analysed the load is measured using suitable metrics. For instance, the load seen by the client and server layers can be characterised in terms of high level requests, whereas for the middle layer it is expressed in terms of the packets as seen by the network. If a more accurate representation is needed, one could include parameters that model the packet generation rate, inter-arrival time, size, routing (or other protocol-specific aspects such as the number of packets generated per high-level transaction) or transmission error rate. Especially when characterising network loads, the (related) notions of *self-similarity* and *burstiness* are often considered. In fact the arrival process of network packets is usually distributed so that a burst of packets arrives in a very short time-frame, whereas for relatively long periods a low network activity is measured. This obviously has a serious impact on the measured performance because of the non-linear dependency between the load and the typical performance figures such as response time and throughput.

Workload Models for Database Management Systems

Special workload models are widely used to understand and fine-tune the performance of Database Management Systems. They mostly refer to two kinds of load: online transaction processing (OLTP), which is typically characterised by a large number of concurrent clients who access and update a small fraction of the database, and online analytical processing (OLAP) that consists of long read-only queries that operate on data stored by OLTP processes. For both kinds of workload, the characterisation is based on the analysis of execution traces, containing information like the amount of data read/written, the number of locks the number of SQL statements executed or transactions completed per time unit, the mean transaction length. Other metrics concern the usage of memory and cache (cache miss ratio, overall memory footprint, locality or sequentiality of memory references) or the type of statements executed (ratio between static vs. dynamic statements, mean number of scanned/returned tuples).

Parallel Systems

A parallel application can be represented using a *task graph* whose nodes model functional units, each executed on a processor. The arcs of such a graph represent the data or control-flow dependencies among tasks. The static metrics for parallel systems describe the inherent parallel characteristics of the application, whereas the dynamic metrics describe the behaviour of an algorithm over time and are useful to study how effectively the parallelism is exploited in solving a class of problems. Both static and dynamic workload models use time-based metrics like the mean duration of computations, communications and coordination tasks as well as metrics about the amount of data processed and I/O activity. From a task graph, some interesting metrics regarding the application that is deployed on a parallel platform can be evaluated: they span the number of nodes in the task graph, the size of the problem (e.g. the size of the matrices involved in a scientific computation), the depth of the task graph (i.e. the length of the maximum path from the initial note to one of the final tasks) and the mean number of arcs that arrive/depart from the nodes of the graph, which indicates the complexity of communications and coordination. The maximum cut of the task graph indicates the maximum achievable degree of parallelism. Many static metrics are *single values* that usually refer to the execution of a given algorithm on a given set of processors. Other metrics are expressed as *signatures*, i.e. as plots of a metric as a function of some variable; for instance the *speedup signature* expresses the gain in performance obtained using p processors compared to the serial execution. Similar signatures can be defined to study how a change may impact the performance of the resulting system (e.g. the change in the actual degree of parallelism measured when an additional processor is added to the system). The most commonly used dynamic metrics are *profiles* and *shapes*. The former represent the number of used processors as a function of time; similarly the latter show the fraction of the overall running time during which a given number of processors is active.

21.2 Obtaining Performance Metrics: Measurement Tools

Performance analysts use different tools to measure and analyse the performance of existing computer systems. The metrics discussed before can be obtained with the help of these tools. We will briefly describe performance benchmarks, performance monitors, and load drivers.

Performance Benchmarks

Comparing the performance of several systems by measurements is called *benchmarking* [249]. The workloads used in these measurements are standardised and are called *benchmarks*.

Before the 1980s, it was often compared how many instructions a processor could execute over a given period of time. The metrics used were for example MIPS (Millions of Instructions Per Second) or MFLOPS (Millions of Floating-Point Operations Per Second) [249]. However, the execution of instructions by processors is highly dependent on addressing modes, cache hit rates, pipelining efficiency and interference from other devices. More complex instruction classes were often not reflected by these benchmarks. Moreover, the performance of a system does not depend on the processor alone, but on the bottleneck device present in the system. For example, a slow hard disk would invalidate a high processor performance and eventually slow down the whole system.

During the 1980s the Whetstone [111] and Dhrystone [505] benchmarks were often used. The *Whetstone* benchmark was originally written in ALGOL and later translated into different programming languages. It consists of 11 modules simulating the dynamic frequency of operations observed in over 900 ALGOL programs. The Whetstone benchmark is generally considered representative for small applications from the scientific or engineering domain, and primarily executes floating point operations. The results are measured in KWIPS (Kilo Whetstone Instructions Per Second). In 1984 the *Dhrystone* benchmark was developed at Siemens, and is available in C, Ada, and Pascal. This benchmark is representative for system programming environments. It does not execute floating point or I/O operations, but it is a popular measure of integer performance and string operations. The result of this benchmark are DIPS (Dhrystone Instructions Per Second).

In 1990 the first version of the SPEC (Systems Performance Evaluation Cooperative) benchmark suite was released [458]. The SPEC is a non-profit organisation formed by leading computer vendors. This benchmark suite has been popular in the 1990s. It consists of a number of benchmarks from different real-life applications, such as the GNU C Compiler or a chess program. The results for different tasks are weighted according to their assumed importance, and summed up into a single value (e.g. SPECint for integer operations or SPECfl for floating point operations). Compiler vendors are known to optimise their products to the SPEC benchmarks. There are also benchmarks in the SPEC suite to measure the performance of web servers, file servers, OpenGL graphic systems, or parallel computing systems. The next version of the SPEC suite is expected to be released in 2006.

Performance Monitors

A *performance monitor* is used to observe the performance of systems, gather performance statistics, to conduct a data analysis, and to display the results [249]. Performance monitoring tools are classified into hardware, software, firmware, and hybrid monitors, which we be described in the following individually. Furthermore, it is distinguished between event-driven monitors and sampling monitors, based on the trigger mechanism.

Hardware monitors consist of pieces of hardware attached to a system to conduct monitoring with probes [249]. During the early phases of computer development, this was a common methods to gather performance measurements [451]. Nowadays, probes cannot be attached to microcomputers, if special probing points have not been provided by the hardware. Therefore, today, hardware monitoring is mainly applied on networks and distributed systems (e.g. network cables). The advantages of hardware monitoring are the low system perturbation, and the possibility to monitor systems with a very high rate of events. A disadvantage is, that features only concerning the software cannot be detected.

Software monitors are used to monitor the operating system and higher level software [249]. Operating system monitors are usually sampling monitors and implemented by inserting routines into the operating system kernel. An example is the Windows XP Performance Monitor. Software monitors for individual programs are also known as profilers [451], program optimizers, program execution monitors [249], or program analysers [349]. The main purposes of using profilers is to find the most frequently used parts of a program, which is most critical for performance, and to analyse the memory footprint of a program. They can also be used for tracing, i.e. for extracting the execution path of a program from the measured data. Furthermore, they are used for coverage analyses in order to determine the adequacy of a test run. Different granularities are possible with profilers (e.g. module, subroutine, statement, machine instruction level). The overhead of monitoring heavily depends on the granularity. Usually, profilers are programming-language dependent [249]. The monitoring mechanism can be added to a program before compilation, during compilation, after compilation (before linking) or during run time. Examples for profilers are JProfiler (Java) or AQTimer (C#). An advantage of software monitors are the fine grained measurements. As a disadvantage, the system perturbation of software monitors is usually high and the recorded performance metrics are distorted by the monitoring process.

Firmware monitors are implemented by altering processor microcode [249]. Usually, they are similar to software monitors. They are mainly used in systems where probing points for hardware monitors are inaccessible and demanding timing consideration prevent the use of software monitors.

Hybrid monitors are a combination of hardware and software monitors [349]. A software routine is responsible for sensing events and storing this data in special monitoring registers. As hardware monitors have a high resolution and software monitors provide capability of reducing the recorded amount of data to practical results, hybrid monitors are considered the best of both worlds [249]. However, a hybrid monitor requires a special hardware and software design and has to be an integral part of the architecture of a system. Therefore, the practical use of hybrid monitors remains limited [349].

Event-driven monitors are activated if specific events occur in a system [349]. Events can be either globally for the system (e.g. I/O interrupts or read/write operations on a hard disks) or specifically for single program events (e.g. execution of a database access). To detect program events, the program under analysis has to be modified. This is also called instrumentation. After events are detected, the date, time, and the type of the event are recorded. The overhead for event-driven monitors is low if events occur only occasionally. If lots of events are detected, the monitoring procedure will influence the results and possibly invalidate the measurements.

Sampling monitors are activated at specific time intervals that are controlled by external timers and not by events [249]. Because not every event occuring in the system is monitored, but only the system state at specific points in time, this kind of monitoring is usually less precise than event-driven monitoring. However, the overhead for monitoring can be adequate even if a high rate of events occur in the system. Furthermore, the overhead can be controlled by adjusting the external timer. Monitoring based on sampling is often used for system level statistics (e.g. CPU or disk utilization) [349].

Load Drivers

Load drivers are software tools used in performance testing to simulate user behaviour in a reproducible way [451]. Usually they are used to test a system when executed by multiple users simultaneously, without the effort of actually having multiple users to perform the tests. As input these tools get one or more workload profiles. In this case, a workload profile consists of the number of users, arrival rates, frequency of transactions, and a distribution of input values. The techniques of workload characterisation discussed above are helpful in determining such a profile. A script that simulates user requests is produced as the output. The inputs produced by load driver scripts look like actual user requests to the system. Opposed to benchmarks, the workload is adjusted during several test runs to analyse the influence on the system and to determine its capacity.

Load drivers can also be used to certify hardware and software components by testing sequential and random combinations of workload demands [249]. Integrating components into an existing system can be supported by first testing the component in isolation under the expected workload conditions. By imposing very high loads on a system, a stress load analysis can be performed, to analyse the possibility of error-free behaviour at these load levels. Moreover, inputs produced by load drivers can be used in regression testing to demonstrate that an updated component still performs at least on the level of the older version.

22 Performance Metrics for Specific Domains

Heiko Koziolek and Jens Happe

University of Oldenburg, Germany

Some performance metrics are specific for certain domains or are used differently under different circumstances. In the following, performance metrics for Internet-based systems and embedded systems will be described.

22.1 Web- and Internet-Specific Metrics

Different stakeholders put different emphases on performance attributes of services offered over the Internet. Users expect fast response times and a low number of refused connections, for example, due to overload or errors. Administrators and managers of web-based services optimise their systems for high throughput and high availability. It is often more difficult to characterise the performance of web-based services compared to normal services because of their special characteristics. Web servers can potentially be accessed by hundreds of thousands of users, and requests by users are often randomly distributed. Furthermore, the infrastructure of the Internet, consisting of various interconnected networks with different hardware and usage characteristics, adds to the limited predictability of networks delays of web services.

General Metrics in a Web Context

For Menasce and Almeida [348, pp.115], the most important metrics to analyse web systems are response time, throughput, availability, and costs. They distinguish between three types of *response times* (see Figure 1):

Response time. The time between sending a request and the ending of the response by the server

Reaction time. The time between sending a request and the beginning of the response by the server

Think time. The time a client waits after a response before initiating the next request

Response times perceived by users can be determined for example by polling web services using geographically distributed servers. Response time is of less interest if streaming services are used. In this case, startup latency (i.e. the initial delay before starting to stream data) and jitter (i.e. the maximum variation in data transfer rates during the execution of a stream) are more significant performance metrics.

Throughput is defined as the number of requests executed per time unit. This metric has to be refined by specifying the type of requests and the used time unit for an actual measurement. For example, throughput of a NFS (Network File System) server can be measured in NFS IOPS (NFS Input/Output operations per second), while web-server throughput is for example HTTPops/sec (HTTP operations per second). Often,

I. Eusgeld, F.C. Freiling, and R. Reussner (Eds.): Dependability Metrics, LNCS 4909, pp. 233–240, 2008.
© Springer-Verlag Berlin Heidelberg 2008

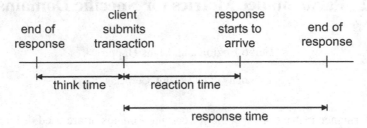

Fig. 1. Definition of think time, reaction time, and response time

throughput is simply measured as bits/sec on a network device. Some special throughput metrics have been established for web activity:

Hit/sec. A hit is any connection to a website, also including for example in-line requests and errors. To retrieve a single web page, usually multiple hits have to be performed, for example to retrieve additional images. However, hits/sec are no longer considered a valuable metric to measure web performance, because it is difficult to compare the importance of the number of hits across different websites.

Visits/sec. A visit is a series of requests by a user to a single site. It is also called a *session*. If a user does not use a website for a time-out period (e.g. 5 minutes), the old session is terminated.

Other important metrics considered by Menasce and Almeida [348] related to the performance are availability and costs. *Availability* is defined as the fraction of time a website is operational. *Costs* are in most cases connected with another metric, such as response time or throughput. The TPC-C benchmark from the Transaction Processing Performance Council (TPC) has a metric dollar/tpm (transactions per minute), while the TPC-W benchmark for e-commerce systems defines a metric dollars/WIPS (web interactions per second). In this case, costs include both hardware and software costs.

Burstiness and Heavy Tail Distributions

Traffic (i.e., throughput) in web-based systems resembles a bursty behaviour. In the randomly distributed traffic, there are often peaks, in which the average arrival rate of requests to the web system is exceeded by factors of eight to ten [356]. This *burstiness* of web traffic can be observed over multiple time scales (e.g., when evaluating web traffic for weeks, days, or hours [348]). Across different time scales, a self-similarity of the traffic bursts can be detected [110]. The load spikes occurring in bursty web traffic can lead to a performance degradation observed by the users. Such spikes are characterised with the performance metric *peak traffic ratio*, which is the ratio between the arrival rates during peak traffic and average traffic.

When analytical models like queuing networks (see Chapter 19.2) are used to characterise the performance of a web-based system, it is useful to include the burstiness of web workloads into the models [348]. The service demand (in seconds) at a resource in a queuing network has to be modified using the performance metric *burstiness factor*.

Therefore, first the burstiness factor b has to be determined using the arrival rates during normal and bursty periods. The arrival rate λ of requests to a web server is defined as $\lambda = \frac{L}{T}$, where L is the number of requests that have been performed during a time span T. This time span can be separated into n intervals, so called epochs. $Arr(k)$ is defined as the number of HTTP requests arriving during an epoch k. Then, the arrival rate λ_k for an epoch k is

$$\lambda_k = \frac{Arr(k)}{(T/n)} = \frac{n \times Arr(k)}{T}$$

The total number of request arriving in all epochs in which $\lambda_k > \lambda$ is defined as Arr^+, while analogously Arr^- is defined as the number of requests in all epochs with $\lambda_k \leq \lambda$. Now the burstiness factor b is defined as

$$b = \frac{\text{Number of epochs with} \lambda_k > \lambda}{n}$$

Notice that if the web traffic is uniformly distributed over the epochs (i.e., if it is *not* bursty), $Arr(k) = L/n$ and $\lambda_k = (L/n)/(T/n) = L/T = \lambda$ for all $k = 1, \ldots, n$. In this case $b = 0$.

The above average arrival rate λ^+ is defined as

$$\lambda^+ = \frac{Arr^+}{b \times T}$$

Now the peak traffic ratio a between the above-average arrival rate and the average arrival rate can be computed over the whole time span T as

$$a = \lambda^+/\lambda = [Arr^+/(b \times T)]/(L/T) = Arr^+/(b \times L)$$

The demands to service centers can then be adjusted according to the burstiness factor as follows: Service demand D (in seconds) is computed as $D = D_f + \alpha \times b$, where D_f is service demand independent from burstiness, α is proportional to the burstiness factor b and contains the portion of the service demand that is dependent to burstiness. Adjusted service demands can be used in queuing networks to account for bursty behaviour when modelling web systems.

Apart from burstiness, web workloads are different from traditional distributed system workload, because of the large variability in file sizes transmitted through web servers. Most requests for popular sites are for files between 100 Byte and 100 KBytes [110]. Only few requests are smaller or larger. However, very large file sizes are possible with a non-negligible probability and need to be accounted for when modelling the performance of web based systems. The highly variable distribution of file sizes is called *heavy tail distribution* [348]. These distributions can be included into queueing netwokrs by defining workload classes for different file sizes. An arrival rate can be assigned to each of these classes. Multiclass queuing networks [295] can then be used to derive the desired performance metrics (also see Chapter 19.2).

Internet Performance Metrics

Paxson [390] defines a catalogue of Internet performance metrics. He distinguishes between analytically-specified and empirically-specified metrics. Analytical metrics are defined in an abstract, sometimes mathematical way, while empirical metrics are defined in the context of a measurement methodology. For example, the "instantaneous route of a network path" is analytically specified as the sequence of links and routers comprising the path from A to B at a given point in time. Empirically, this metrics could be specified as the output of the `traceroute` program run on host A with argument B. Paxson lists the following analytical metrics without claiming completeness:

Propagation time of a link. Time difference (in seconds) between the point in time host X begins sending 1 bit to host Y on a link L, and the point in time Y receives the bit

Transmission time of a link. Required time (in seconds) to transmit n bits from X to Y on a link L, as opposed to 1 bit

Bandwidth of a network link. Capacity of a network link (in bits/second) without bits needed for link-layer headers. For links with variable sized transmission units, a transmission size also has to be specified, to make this metrics well-defined.

Flow capacity of a network path. Maximum rate (in bits/second) at which data can be transferred along a given Internet path from A to B. This is also called the *bottleneck bandwith*, because it is the capacity of the slowest link in the chain of linkings between A and B.

Maximum flow capacity of an IP cloud. An IP cloud is a black box consisting internally of a collection of routers and has well-defined entry and exit points on the outside. This metric measures the greatest achievable transmission rate (in bits/second) for a given entry and exit point of the cloud, if we could manage all the links and routers in the cloud, so that data could be sent along multiple, parallel routes.

Instantaneous route of a network path. Sequence of links and routers involved on the path from A to B at a given point in time

Hop count of a route. Number of routers a packet will take along the path from A to B

Buffer size of router. Number of bits available, to buffer queued packets in a router

Instantaneous queue size of router interface. Number of bits consumed at a router by packets queued for transmission on a particular interface at a given point in time

Instantaneous connectivity of an Internet path. Boolean value, stating whether host A can send IP datagrams to host B

Epoch connectivity of an Internet path Boolean value, specifying whether starting at a time T over a given interval S seconds host A can send IP datagrams to host B and have B receive one or more with non-zero probability.

Maximum jitter along an Internet path Maximum amount of variation (in seconds) that the end-to-end transmission time might vary when packets are sent from A to B

Mean NOC turn-around time. Expected time (in seconds) between the point in time when a trouble ticket is submitted to a Network Operation Center and the point in time the problem is resolved

22.2 Performance Metrics of Real-Time and Embedded Systems

A large variety of performance metrics for real-time systems can be found in literature. This alludes to the large number of different real-time and embedded systems existing in the real world, which range from small controller-based systems to networked arrays of powerful processors coordinating their activities to achieve a common purpose. High requirements concerning functional as well as non-functional properties like performance, reliability, safety etc. yield many challenges for developers of embedded systems as stated by Masters [340]:

> [...] no matter how fast the processor, meeting critical timelines always seems to be the paramount concern. Communication among system components is almost always a bottleneck. Low latency is usually more important than high throughput, and the two are not reciprocals of each other. If the system goes down during its active duty cycle, something expensive and/or awful happens. And, no matter how carefully the system is designed, someone will want to change it in ways not anticipated by the original designers.

This statement is particularly true for real-time systems, where "the correctness of a result not only depends on its logical correctness, but also on the time when it is delivered" as stated by Douglass [135]. This is not true for every real-time system. Basically, there are two variants of real-time sytems: Hard real-time systems and soft real-time systems. The terms hard and soft refer to the type of deadline important for the system.

Hard deadlines are performance requirements that absolutely must be met. A missed deadline constitutes an erroneous computation and a system failure. So, the correctness of an action includes a description of timeliness. For static real-time systems (fixed schedule, and arrival rate of events), the worst case execution times of all tasks are determined and their schedulability with a given algorithm on a given processor is proven. On the other hand, soft real-time systems are characterised by time constraints which can be missed occasionally, be missed by small time deviations, or occasionally skipped altogether. Soft deadlines are often stochastically characterised. For example, in 98% of all cases the next video frame is delivered within 1/30 second.

In this section, we describe different metrics for real-time and embedded systems. This includes some general metrics for performance as well as metrics used for the performance evaluation of special aspects of embedded systems like schedulers, memory systems, network connections, and distribution.

General metrics. It is hard to give a reasonable selection of performance metrics for real-time systems, since there is such a large variety. However, the list of metrics for adaptive real-time systems given by Lu et al. [320] seems to be promising. They emphasise that the performance of an real-time system in a varying environment can only be specified with respect to its workload. For a given system, they specify a set of representative *load profile*. The *system load* is defined as the resource requirement in percentage of the system capacity.

Performance is determined in terms of a *deadline miss-ratio* in response to a specific workload. The *miss-ratio function* $MR(t)$ is defined as the number of deadline misses divided by the number of task submissions in a specified time unit. The *average miss-ratio* $\overline{MR}$ is defined as the total number of deadline misses divided by the total number of task instances throughout the run-time. It represents the average system performance over a long time period. This metric can be inadequate in characterising the dynamics of the system performance. The miss-ratio can be further refined by a *miss-ratio profile*, which is a set of characteristics of $MR(t)$ in response to a specific load profile.

Lu et al. [320] distinguish *steady-state* and *transient state* of a real-time system. The first represents a state when the system performance is satisfactory, while the second represents a state with degraded performance upon overload. The steady-state is defined as a state when $MR(t)$ is bounded by a constant called steady-state miss-ratio bound (SMB) $(MR(t) \leq SMB)$, which depends on the tolerance of the application to the deadline miss-ratio. Based on this definitions the following metrics can be specified.

Stability: A system is said to be stable, in response to a step or ramp load profile, if the miss-ratio function converges to zero as time goes to infinity under any step or ramp loads. *Practical stability* is defined as the system's ability to return to a given small miss-ratio after the system experiences a step load or a ramp load profile. A stable system can always recover from the specified overload conditions and resume satisfactory performance; while an unstable system may fail to recover from an overload. Therefore, stability is an important requirement for real-time systems.

Overshoot M_o: The highest miss-ratio in the transient state. Overshoot represents the worst-case transient performance of a system in response to the load profile. Overshoot is an important metric because a high transient miss-ratio can cause system failure in many systems such as robots and media streaming.

Settling time T_S: The time it takes the system miss-ratio to enter a steady state after a load profile occurs. The settling time represents how fast the system can recover from overload. This metric has also been called reaction time or recovery time.

Steady-state miss-ratio $\overline{M}_s$: Average miss-ratio in the steady state. $\overline{M}_s$ characterises how well the system recovers after adaptation.

Sensitivity S_p: Relative change of the steady-state miss-ratio with respect to the relative change of a system parameter p. For example, sensitivity with respect to the task execution time set represents how significantly the change in the task execution time affects the system miss-ratio. Sensitivity describes the robustness of the system with regard to workload or system variation.

Distributed Systems. Welch and Shirazi [508] define a set of metrics for distributed real-time systems to evaluate adaptive resource management algorithms. These algorithms react if the Quality of Service (QoS), in this case performance, decreases below a specified threshold and then dynamically reconfigure the system. The authors implemented a set of host selection algorithms that choose the host on which to move or replicate an application in case of the violation of QoS requirements. The aim is to restore an acceptable QoS under the current workload. Common strategies are: *worst fit*, which chooses the host with maximum fitness, i.e. the best ability to perform; *middle and anti-worst fit*, which choose the host with medium and minimum fitness, respectively; *random fit*, which selects a random host; and *round robin*, which cycles through the set of hosts. The metrics specified by Welch and Shirazi [508] aim at assessing the quality of these adaptive resource management algorithms.

Improvement in QoS per reallocation action: This metric describes the impact of a reallocation action within the system on the performance of the applications. Welch and Shirazi [508] measured the absolute and percentage improvement in response time and/or latency per reallocation action. For the absolute improvement, the difference in latency before and after the reallocation is computed. The relative improvement is the latency before the reallocation divided by the latency after the reallocation.

Both metrics describe different aspects of the same attribute. In some cases, there were negative improvements by the anti-worst, random fit, and round robin. So, the reallocation actions lead to degradation in performance. This influences the metrics differently. The absolute performance improvement achieved by round robin was quite large, but it did only result in a small relative performance improvement, since the negative performance effects caused in previous cycles by the round robin allocation scheme were quite significant.

Two other metrics for the evaluation of reallocation algorithms are the *QoS violation rate* and the *sensitivity*. The QoS violation rate is the number of QoS violations per time unit. Sensitivity is measured with respect to increased tactical load. It represents the amount by which the amount of workload could be increased without causing a QoS violation.

Memory Systems. Uhlig and Mudge [475] evaluated different tools for trace driven memory simulation. Despite a detailed analysis of tools, they describe performance metrics used by tools to compare different memory systems. Here, common metrics for performance are *miss counts, miss ratios, misses per instruction (MPI), write backs*, and *cycles per instruction (CPI)*. The first four metrics are related to caches implemented in the memory unit. For example, the number of misses is defined as the number of total references minus the number of cache hits:

$$misses = totalReferences - hits.$$

The miss ratio is defined as the number of misses devided by the number of total references:

$$missRatio = \frac{misses}{totalReferences}.$$

The average number of misses per instruction is the total number of misses divided by the total number of instructions:

$$MPI = \frac{misses}{totalInstructions}.$$

In this case, 'total' always refers to a special trace for which the performance is analysed. Here, a trace is simply a sequence of memory addresses that is requested by an application.

Real-Time Operating Systems and Scheduling. Metrics concerned with real-time operating systems and schedulability are mostly concerned with the efficiency of a scheduling algorithm and its ability to schedule a set of tasks without causing any violations of hard and soft deadlines. Ramamritham and Stankovic [411] distinguish between static and dynamic real-time systems. While for static systems everything is known in advance, dynamic systems have to react on changes in the environment. These characteristics certainly influence the kinds of metrics defined. In the static case, an off-line schedule is to be found that meets all deadlines. If many such schedules exist, a secondary metric, such as maximizing the average earliness is used to choose one among them. If no such schedule exists, one which minimizes the average tardiness may be chosen. In general, it cannot be a priori guaranteed that all deadlines will be met for dynamic real-time systems. Therefore, maximising the number of arrivals that meet their deadlines is often used as a metric.

Panzieri and Davoli [388] define further metrics for scheduling algorithms. The *breakdown utilisation* is the degree of resource utilization at or above which the real-time operating system can guarantee that all the task deadlines will be met. This figure provides a metric for the assessment of the effectiveness of a scheduling policy, as the larger the breakdown utilisation, the larger the CPU time devoted to task execution. The *guaranteed ratio* is the number of tasks whose execution can be guaranteed versus the total number of tasks that request execution. The *normalised mean response time* is the ratio of the time interval in which a task becomes ready for execution and terminates, and the actual CPU time consumed for the execution of that task. This metric is another metric for the efictiveness of a scheduling policy.

Real Time Networks. Real-time communications refers to communication in local area networks that provides bounded channel access delay. The performance metrics mentioned by Panzieri and Davoli [388] are based on the percentage of messages that miss their deadlines, and the effective channel utilization.

Kim and Shin [277] propose metrics for real-time networks with dependable connections. The most important metric there is the average bandwidth reserved for each primary channel. Furthermore, the amount of change in the bandwidth reserved is considered to describe the performance of a network connection.

Part V

Overlapping Metrics

23 Introduction to Overlapping Attributes

Ralf Reussner and Viktoria Firus

University of Karlsruhe (TH), Germany

Research on software quality attributes is often focused on one attribute. For example, the software reliability community is rarely concerned with memory footprint and researchers dealing with performance are seldom interested in availability metrics. This leads to metrics and prediction models focusing on a single attribute. Although this approach is comprehensible for practical reasons of feasibility, we argue that unified models are of high relevance and should gain a much higher attention in research for the following reasons.

1. Intrinsic relationships between quality attributes are relations where one attribute is defined in terms of another. An obvious example is availability which is a function of reliability and mean time to repair (MTTR). Less obvious, but also related are reliability and performance, because reliability metrics include a notion of time (intervals). As a consequence, reliability predictions need to make assumptions or predictions on the timing behaviour of the software. Another example can be specific definitions of availability, as whether a system is available or not depends on what is considered a failure. As a failure could be defined as response time or throughput below a prescribed threshold, this definition of availability is intrinsically linked to a performance metric.
2. Extrinsic relationships between quality attributes occur in specific software designs. Often the optimisation for one quality attribute lowers another quality attribute. For example, the introduction of cryptographic measures lowers throughput and response time. However, whether two or more quality attributes have such an antagonistic relationship or not depends on the actual software design. For example, reliability and performance can have an antagonistic relationship (e.g., by checksums and retry-approaches) but can also be optimised simultaneously by replication. As these dependencies are not a property of the quality attributes themselves this kind of relationship is called *extrinsic*.
3. The application of several separate models for prediction results in repeated costs for staff training, tools purchases, model construction, computation and interpretation.

As we saw above, the quality attributes performance and reliability are be linked intrinsically in various ways. This leads to the notion of performability (an artificial word made from "performance" and "reliability"). Different to other pairs (or tuples) of quality attribute, a certain body of scientific literature for performability exists. Therefore, we devote a separate chapter to performability.

In principle, performability includes performance metrics by weakening the assumption of the absence of failures. While values of a performance metric (say response time) are only valid for normal (failure-free) system operation, the same metric, re-formulated as performability metric would state the probability distribution of response-times in different system modes which are induced by failures.

I. Eusgeld, F.C. Freiling, and R. Reussner (Eds.): Dependability Metrics, LNCS 4909, pp. 243–244, 2008.

In principle, this weakening of assumptions can be applied to other metrics. For example, one could talk about reliability in the presence of attacks. This would weaken the assumption that results of reliability metrics are only valid in the absence of attacks or intrusions. (One could coin the term "relurity" for this reliability metric weakened by a security assumption.)

24 Performability

Irene Eusgeld[1], Jens Happe[2], Philipp Limbourg[3], Matthias Rohr[2], and Felix Salfner[4]

[1] Swiss Federal Institute of Technology (ETH), Zurich, Switzerland
[2] University of Oldenburg, Germany
[3] University of Duisburg-Essen, Germany
[4] Humboldt University Berlin, Germany

Performability combines performance and reliability analysis in order to estimate the quality of service characteristics of a system in the presence of faults. This chapter provides an introduction to performability, discusses its relation to reliability and performance metrics, and presents common models used in performability analysis, such as Markov reward models or Stochastic Petri Nets.

1 Introduction

Performability metrics quantify the system's ability to perform in the presence of faults [351, 452]. It combines performance and reliability[1] to quantify the operational quality of a service between the occurrence of an error and its full recovery, or over the complete execution. The results from a performability evaluation are a supplement to other evaluations to assess the trustworthiness of a system. Performability evaluation was applied to all kinds of hard- and software systems or components that were subject to dependability evaluation, and especially to fault tolerant systems.

This chapter provides an introduction to performability and its metrics. Detailed surveys on performability have been provided by Meyer [351, 352], Trivedi and Malhotra [473], and Souza e Silva and Gail [115].

The remaining parts of this chapter are structured as follows: The introduction continues by analysing the relation between performance and reliability, and discusses why they are usually measured independently. General models and analytical metrics are discussed in section 24.1, such as Markov reward models, Multi-state System models, and Stochastic Petri Nets. Finally, the related metric of responsiveness is discussed in section 24.2.

The Relation between Performance and Reliability

To understand the motivation for performability, it is required to look more closely at what is covered by the common reliability and performance metrics. Reliability focuses on the event that an error becomes visible (as a failure) at the service interface. More precisely, it is the probability of failure-free operation in a specified period of time in a specified environment [363]. Only the occurrence of the failure is of importance. Availability can be seen as reliability in combination with repair, so two events influence the metric: the occurrence of the failure and the return to failure-free operation. From

---

[1] Some older literature used the term dependability as synonym for reliability.

I. Eusgeld, F.C. Freiling, and R. Reussner (Eds.): Dependability Metrics, LNCS 4909, pp. 245–254, 2008.
© Springer-Verlag Berlin Heidelberg 2008

an availability point of view, a system is in one of two states: failure-free ("up") or failure-"showing" ("down") [351]. So there are no levels of service quality covered by (typical) reliability and availability metrics.

Performance metrics quantify the level of service quality. Many performance metrics are related to time (e.g., the response time or execution time), while others quantify more general quality aspects (e.g., precision, confidence, or efficiency of an operation). Obviously, service quality can only be measured, if a service is provided. Most performance metrics can be seen as independent from faults and failures, because they simply measure a quality aspect of failure-free operation [351].

Reliability and performance are usually measured independently. As stated before, for reliability only the event of failures occurrence is relevant, and performance is only assessed during failure-free operation. This is sufficient for systems that have just the binary states "up" and "down", because there is literally no service quality to measure if the system is "down".

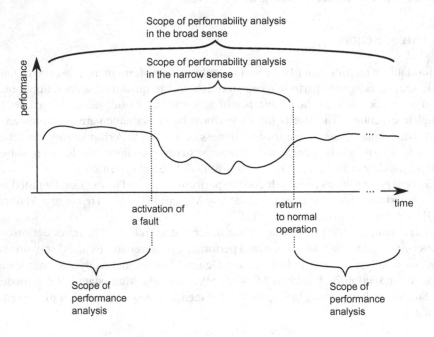

Fig. 1. Scopes of performability analysis

As shown in Fig. 1, performability analysis can have different scopes. *Performability analysis in the narrow sense* quantifies the quality of a service *only* between the activation of a fault (which causes an error) and the return to normal operation. *Performability analysis in the broad sense* quantifies the quality of a service over the complete operation. Consequently, the performability analysis in the broad sense overlaps in some way with normal performance analysis.

Performability is often misunderstood as combined replacement of performance metrics and reliability metrics. At first, this sounds reasonable and useful; both are relevant aspects of a trustworthy system, and one single value for performance and reliability would simplify the comparison between alternative designs. However, if performance and reliability are considered as separate issues, as presented above, it is not be recommended to "mix" them early into a combined metric (with a combined model) because performance and reliability models can already be complex. It is to expect that a meaningful combined metric will be more complex than both are together alone, and the resulting measurement might be even more difficultly to interpret. Instead, it seems more reasonable, to use a two (or more) step approach for dependability evaluation, as suggested by the Goal-Question-Metric approach (see Chapter 6). This means that performance and reliability are evaluated independently with own metrics. Only in a final step, both are combined (e.g., by explicitly weighting the values according to system requirements) with other dependability aspects.

The Need for Performability

The need for performability arises from a "gap" between reliability, availability, and performance measurement. Above we presented two reasons for the gap: (1) reliability has just a binary view on system operation, and (2) performance metrics (usually) assume that the system is in the failure-free state. Hence, performability (in a narrow sense), as metric for the ability to perform in the presence of faults, does not overlap with typical reliability and performance metrics. Although it shares concepts, it can be considered as additional class of metrics for the characterisation of the trustworthiness of a system.

Real world systems do not only crash-fail. A *degradable system* is able to survive the occurence of component failures and continue to provide service at a reduced quality level [423]. Such a system is is clearly superior to one that simply crashes, although both could have the same reliability and performance. A degradable system can have several reduced operational states between being fully operational and having completely failed. Each state provides some performance level (which would be 0 for a complete system failure).The concept of graceful degradation is of relevance for many fault tolerant systems, especial if higher reliability is hard to achieve. Therefore, performability metrics have been applied in particular for the evaluation of many fault tolerant hard and software systems [351].

The major open issue of performability is that the utilisation in practise is relatively low and that many approaches do not scale well in respect to the number of states of real world systems [351]. However, as both the number of degradable system and the need for high dependability increase, performability evaluation might become more important in the future.

24.1   Models for Performability and Analytical Metrics

Markov Reward Models

One way to measure the consequences of system performance degradation under failures is to reward the system for every time unit it is ready, at a rate proportional to its performance during that interval. The basic model is the so-called rate-based *Markov reward model* (MRM). When a system moves from one up state to another one (because of a failure or a repair/reconfiguration), the performance level can change. Such system behaviour is usually described by different states in a Markov chain. This way a framework for combined performance-reliability analysis is provided.

The MRM-concept is described by several authors. The follow definition is based on the work of Sahner et al. [423]: Formally, a Markov reward model consists of a continuous time Markov chain (CTMC) $X = X(t), t \geq 0$ with a finite state space S, and a reward function r where $r : S \to \mathbb{R}$. X is completely described by its generator matrix Q and the initial probability vector $\pi(0)$. For each state $i \in S$, r(i), usually written as r_i, represents the reward obtained per unit time spent by X in that state. In general, the reward associated with a state denotes the performance level given by the system while it is in that state. A negative value of the reward index is allowed; it denotes a loss rather than a gain in the total work done by the system. This model is called rate-based reward model because the system produces work at rate r_i for all the time it remains in state $i \in S$.

Different classes of performability measures are distinguished: steady-state performability, transient or point performability, cumulative measures and others [210].

For $i \in S$, let π_i denote the steady-state probability of residing in state i, and $p_i(t)$ the (transient) probability of residing in state i at time t. Steady-state performability (SSP) is defined as:

$$SSP = \sum_{i \in S} \pi_i r_i,$$

In words, SSP is the expected asymptotic reward.

Transient or point performability (TP):

$$TP(t) = \sum_{i \in S} p_i(t) r_i,$$

In words, TP(t) is the expected reward rate at time t.
Cumulative performability (CP):

$$CP(t) = \int_0^t r_x(t) ds,$$

Note that CP(t) is in general a random variable. Its distribution is called the performability distribution:

$$F_{CP}(t, y) = Pr\{CP(t) \leq y\} \tag{1}$$

The MRM is very good illustrated in Jawad and Johnsen [255], applied to a simplified 3-CPU multi-processor system (see Fig. 2 and 3), [255]) A failure of any one processor causes the system to degrade. This degradable system is fault-tolerant because the work still can be shared among the remaining operational one(s), should one or two CPUs fail. Thus the system has several different stages between fully functional and completely failed, with a reduced performance level. This provides the perfect opportunity for employing perfomability modelling and evaluation.

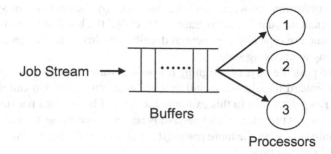

Fig. 2. Model of a multi-processor system

To reduce the state space of the problem, the follow assumptions are taken: There are no simultaneous failures of the CPUs, i.e. not more than one processor can fail at any point of time; all processors are identical, so that only a single state represents a failure of any CPU (Either processor 1, 2 or 3 failing, with the other two up); another assumption is that the buffers are ultra-reliable, so a buffer failure is not modeled; there are no limits on buffer capacity. The MRM is built up of two distinct models:

1. The behaviour model: The states and the transition links between the states representing failures and repairs, make up the behaviour model.
2. The reward structure: Each different state, representing a different number of processors 'up', is capable of a different amount of work. In other words each has a certain performance level associated with it. The amount of performance achievable has a certain reward related to it. This reward rate quantifies the ability of the system to perform. If the system goes to a state with a higher reward, a higher performance level is reached. The set of these rewards, associated to the individual states, make up the reward structure.

Together the behaviour model and reward model describe the MRM:

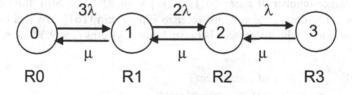

Fig. 3. The Markov Reward Model

The system above is described by four states:

- State 0 : 3 processors up, 0 processors down
- State 1 : 2 processors up, 1 processor down
- State 2 : 1 processor up, 2 processors down
- State 4 : 0 processors up, 3 processors down

The possible transitions between states are described by the arrows. The system will only spend a certain amount of time in each state, called the holding time. The holding times in each state are typically exponential distributed, therefore we can associate to each a probability of changing state.

There are two possible ways of assigning rewards: reward rates associating with state occupancies or reward impulses associating with state transitions (so called impulse-based Markov reward model). In this example the reward is assigned per time (a rate). It can be interpreted as the rate at which reward is accumulated in each state: The longer the system remains in a state, the more reward it accumulates; the higher the reward rate, the more reward per unit time.

The rates described in Fig. 3 are summed up below. The highest reward rate (R0) is associated with state 0, and the lowest (R3) with state 3:

- R0 : performance level = 3.0
- R1 : performance level = 2.0
- R2 : performance level = 1.0
- R3 : performance level = 0.0

By interpreting rewards as performance levels, the distribution of accumulated reward characterizes systems that evolve through states with different performance levels (degradable systems). The distribution of accumulated reward by time t is denoted by equation 1.

The reader interested in more advanced applications including examples from the field of fault tolerant multiserver systems is referred to Eusgeld and Müller-Clostermann [150].

By many applications there is a need for performability evaluation tools (e.g., Haverkort et al. [212]), because of the state space explosion problem. For an overview of various Markov reward models the reader is referred to Howard [221].

Multi-state Systems

Multi-state systems (MSS) are the extensions of binary network models with two states $\{0, 1\}$ to a larger number of states $\{0, 1, ..., M\}$ with $M \in \mathbb{N}$. Still, this models are discrete (for continuous-state systems, refer to Finkelstein [161]. We will only give a short introductions to the differences between binary systems (see 9.5) and MSS.

Notation

1. $x_i \in \{0, ..., M\}$: state of component i.
2. $\mathbf{x} = (x_1, ..., x_n)$: vector of component states.
3. $\phi(\mathbf{x}) = y \in \{0, ..., M\}$: System state, where ϕ is the structure function.

Using this notation, the extension to MSS can be seen in 1 and 3. Coherency may then be extended to the multi-state case as:

Definition 1 (Coherent multi-state system). *A MSS with n components is coherent, if ϕ satisfies:*

1. $\phi(\mathbf{x})$ is monotonically increasing in each argument.

2. *there exist two vectors* x, x' *with* $x_i = 0$ *and* $x'_i = M$ *for each* $i = \{0, ..., n\}$, *such that* $\phi(x) < \phi(x')$.

3. $\phi(j, j, j..., j) = j$ *for* $j = \{0, ..., n\}$.

What are the reasons for this requirements? Monotonicity is necessary and makes sense for the same reason as in the binary case. Achieving a better state in one component may not lead to a worsening of the system. Requirement 2 guarantees the importance of all components. If it does not hold for any component i, then i does not influence the system reliability (follows from monotonicity) and can be omitted. Requirement 3 guarantees that each system state can be reached. So far, we have dealt with the extension reliability models to multiple states. But where is the performability aspect? If we define a function $u(y) = z$ we can assign arbitrary levels of performance to each system state. This reward/risk/utility function represents the performance of each system state similar to Markov reward models.

Formulation and display of system reliability becomes increasingly difficult, as we cannot simply draw e.g. a block diagram for a MSS system. Thus it is necessary to define some common sense building blocks as e.g. k-out-of-n:G structures.

Definition 2 (k-**out-of-**n**:G system with constant structure**). $\phi(x) = j$, *if at least* k *components are in state* j *or above, but less than* k *components are in state* $j + 1$ *or above. A coherent MSS with this property is called* k-*out-of-*n*:G system with constant structure.*

This is a very restrictive way of defining k-out-of-n:G systems which is very close to binary models. Restrictive, because it is assumed that the k-out-of-n:G system has the same structure for each performance level. The more realistic case is that k varies for different performance levels. Let's assume performance of a web service running on 10 servers. Total system failure will be reached only if at least 9 machines fail (1-out-of-10:G system for $\phi(x) = 0$). Nevertheless, the performance decreases even if only one machine degrades or fails (10-out-of-10:G/series system for $\phi(x) = M$). Thus, it is feasible to extend k to a vector $\mathbf{k} = (k_1, ...k_M)$ and define k-out-of-n:G systems more flexible:

Definition 3 (k-**out-of-**n**:G system with flexible structure**). $\phi(x) = j$, *if at least* k_j *components are in state* j *or above, but less than* $k_l, j < l \leq M$ *components are in state* k_l *or above. A coherent MSS with this property is called* k-*out-of-*n*:G system with flexible structure.*

For analytical reliability calculations of k-out-of-n:G systems, the enthusiastic reader may refer to Pham [396].

Stochastic Petri Nets

Metrics of Stochastic Petri Nets (SPN), as defined in section 24.1, can be used to compute the performance, reliability, and availability of a system as well as its performability. The approaches existing to analyse performability with SPNs can be separated into different categories, two of which are interesting in the context of SPNs: Reward models and integrated models [473].

Reward Models. Reward models describe performance and reliability of a system separately. The performance model, in our case a SPN, is used to compute the performance metric of interest. Its results are the input to a reliability model, which, in case of Petri Net analyses, can be Stochastic Reward Nets (SRN). The reward rates of the SRN are given by the results of the performance analysis. An alternative approach is the computation of performance with different reward rates in dependence of available resources.

Ciardo et al. [99] introduce SRNs to analyse the throughput of a producer-consumer system and the availability of a multiprocessor system. SRNs extend Generalized Stochastic Petri Nets (GSPN), which itselves extend SPNs. GSPNs distinguish between immediate and timed transitions. Immediate transitions do not consume time, while the time consumption of timed transitions is, as in SPNs, exponentially distributed. Immediate transitions have a higher priority than timed transitions. If immediate transitions are enabled in a marking, these fire first. No time is spend in vanishing markings, which enable immediate transitions. On the other hand, time is consumed in tangible markings, which enable timed transitions only. Stochastic Reward Nets define reward functions for sets of tangible markings. Reward rates of SRNs are comparable to those of Markov Reward Models (MRM) introduced in section 24.1. For analysis, the reward functions and the SRN are transformed to a MRM.

SRNs, as described by Trivedi [472], not only add reward rates to GSPNs, but also guards, marking dependent multiplicities, and firing rates for transitions. Guards are marking-dependent, Boolean conditions. A transition is enabled in a marking only if its guard is satisfied. Marking-dependent arc multiplicities can be applied if the number of tokens to be transferred depends on the current marking. For example, all tokens can be flushed from a place by a single firing. Marking dependent firing rates allow the specification of firing rates as a function of the current marking. For example, the firing rate of a transition can be proportional to the number of tokens in its input place. Furthermore, the initial marking is a probability vector over a set of markings, which is often required for transient analysis when the initial marking is uncertain. Initial probabilities are realised by adding a vanishing initial marking that transfers to all markings in the initial set with the given probabilities.

Possible metrics of SRNs are described by Muppala et al. [359]. As done for SPNs and Markov chains they distinguish between steady state and transient analysis. In the first case, a general expression for the expected reward rate in steady-state is:

$$E[X] = \sum_{k \in \mathcal{T}} r_k \pi_k,$$

where X represents a random variable for the measure of interest, $\mathcal{T}$ is the set of tangible markings, π_k is the steady -state probability of the tangible marking m_k and r_k its reward rate.

The expression for the expected instantaneous reward rate at time t is:

$$E[X(t)] = \sum_{k \in \mathcal{T}} r_k \pi_k(t),$$

where $\pi_k(t)$ denotes the probability of being in marking k at time t and X(t) is the random variable corresponding to the instantaneous reward rate of interest.

In the transient case, so called absorbing states are introduced, which, once entered, cannot be left. Here, the metrics of interest are the accumulated reward rate in a time interval [0..t) (Y(t)) and the accumulated reward rate until absorption, which are given by:

$$E[Y(t)] = \sum_{k \in \mathcal{T}} r_k \int_0^t \pi_k(x)dx,$$

and

$$E[Y] = \sum_{k \in \mathcal{T}} r_k \int_0^\infty \pi_k(x)dx,$$

respectively.

The interpretation of the computed reward of the SRN certainly depends on the way a system is modelled with Petri nets. Common assignments of the reward rates are execution rates of tasks in computing systems (the computational capacity), number of active processors (or processing power), throughput, average response time and response time distribution. Furthermore, reliability models can be considered as a special case of performability reward models, where the reward rates are binary: If the Petri net is in a functional state the reward is one, otherwise, if the system is in a failure state the reward rate is zero.

Markov reward models use an approximation of the performance as reward for reliability model. The reward is the result of a steady state analysis and can be given as mean value or distribution function. The usage of approximations as rewards leads to a certain inaccuracy of the result. Integrated models overcome the shortage introduced by approximations through the creation of a combined system model.

Integrated Models. Integrated models combine performance and reliability descriptions in an overall system model. For analysis, it can be specified by any kind of stochastic model, like Markov chains, queuing networks, and of course SPNs. Here we focus on the usage of SPNs.

Since SPNs do not impose very strong restrictions on how a system can be modelled, many different approaches concerning performability modelling with SPNs can be found in literature. They vary in the degree of detail and the way a system is described as well as the metrics of concern. Basically, all metrics used are derivates of the ones described in section 24.1. In the following, we give two examples of performability modelling and the used metrics.

Bobbio [63] use SPNs to compute performance and reliability attributes of a parallel system with a finite input buffer. The system consists of a set of processing units, which access a buffer to read and write their data. First, the behaviour of the input buffer and processing units is modelled. The resulting Petri net is augmented with information (transitions and places) describing the failure and repair behaviour of both elements. The metrics computed on the basis of the resulting model are the mean fraction of arrived tasks processed in a given time interval, the mean number of failures and repairs, and the distribution function and mean number of active, idle, failed units or buffer stages.

Lindemann et al. [301] model an automated manufacturing system with deterministic SPNs (DSPN). The example is comparable with the well known production cell example for verification and/or validation of performance prediction techniques in embedded systems. The Petri net constructed to model the system consists of two main parts: The workflow and the system model. The first one describes how different items are processed within the system. The second one specifies the performance degradation of the system's tools over time and the machines failure and repair behaviour. Performance degradation is modelled discretely by encoding the efficiency of a tool in different places. For example, the performance of a drill is modelled by four places, which represent its efficiency in steps of 100%, 70%, 50%, and 40%. Transitions between these places represent the events of performance degradation or, in case of increased efficiency, replacement of the tool. The metrics of interest are the throughput of parts, the utilisation of the machine and the mean buffer length.

Integrated models usually yield a large state space, since each state in the reliability model needs to be combined with each state in the performance model (cross-product). Furthermore, the model is stiff, meaning that there is a large difference in the rates of events occurring in the reliability and performance model.

Reward vs. Integrated Models. The separation of concerns, as done by reward models, yields two small models: One for performance and one for reliability. This leads to a less stiff model, but also to less accurate results. On the other hand, integrated models are large and stiffer, but provide more accurate results. The choice, which modelling technique is best, certainly depends on the requirements of the system in regard.

24.2   Responsiveness

Responsiveness combines the two classical metrics *availability*, which is known from reliable computing, and *task completion probability*, which is commonly used in real-time systems. *Task responsiveness* was defined in Malek [329] as

$$\mathfrak{R}_i(t) = a_i \, p_i$$

where a_i is the availability of a task τ_i and p_i is the probability of completion in time (before the deadline). Therefore, responsiveness characterizes the ability of a system, to fulfill a task even in the presence of failures. Werner [510] gives an illustrative example of six depending tasks and computes responsiveness of several scheduling paradigms. It is shown that responsiveness varies significantly depending on the scheduling algorithm.

The concept of task responsiveness is related to the definition of *system responsiveness after execution of n tasks* [328]:

$$\mathfrak{R}(n) = \sum_{i=1}^{n} a_i \, c_i \, t_i$$

where a_i denotes availability of task i, c_i is the criticality of task i and t_i equals one iff task i has been completed in time (before the deadline). Task criticalities c_i are a weighting factors with

$$\sum_{i=1}^{n} c_i = 1$$

Please note that task responsiveness is defined in terms of time whereas system responsiveness is a function of the number of processed tasks. Nevertheless, both metrics are essential for the design of *fault tolerant real-time systems*.

25 Reliability vs. Security: A Subjective Overview

Felix C. Freiling[1] and Max Walter[2]

[1] University of Mannheim, Germany
[2] TU München, Germany

This chapter presents a preliminary overview of the research area on the border be-tween reliability and security (termed "relurity") together with extensive pointers to the literature.

25.1 Introduction

Although reliability and security are both necessary attributes of dependable systems (see Chapter 1), these properties have traditionally been treated separately in different research communities. However, there are strong similarities between the ways of mod-eling and handling uncertainty in these different areas of dependable systems. But there also seem to be fundamental tradeoffs that lead the different communities into different directions.

Today, we can observe a renaissance of research on the border between reliability, safety and fault-tolerance on the one hand and security on the other. However, the pre-cise relations of concepts and techniques are still very much unclear. In this chapter, we therefore cannot present a comprehensive and structured overview of this field, but merely sketch some preliminary insights into a structure of the area and together with some pointers to the literature which we feel important.

It seems that the existence of an *intelligent* and *strategic adversary* creates a signifi-cant difference between the areas of security and dependability. The coverage problem of Byzantine failures (see below) is only one manifestation of this fact. Another exam-ple is that the requirements of secure and dependable applications sound very similar, the techniques used to implement the requirements are however very different. Integrity requirements for example are common to systems in both areas. But while systems tol-erant to random hardware faults can use invertible functions like CRCs or Hamming codes for integrity checking, secure systems must revert to non-invertible hash func-tions and other cryptographic techniques.

Many of the topics have been discussed at the Dagstuhl seminar "From Security to Dependability" [80] which was held in September 2006 at Dagstuhl Castle, Germany. The structure of the area discussed below however is a preliminary sketch by the authors of this chapter.

25.2 Byzantine Failures, Security and Failure Independence

One of the largest areas in which dependability and security overlap are protocols that tolerate a certain number of arbitrary failures (commonly called Byzantine failures in

I. Eusgeld, F.C. Freiling, and R. Reussner (Eds.): Dependability Metrics, LNCS 4909, pp. 255–257, 2008.

the literature). Stemming from early work in the fault-tolerance field, arbitrary failures can also be regarded as malicious and targeted attacks. Therefore today, tolerance to Byzantine failures is now an accepted area of study in both fields of security and dependability (see for example Cachin et al. [78], Correia et al. [107], Kihlstrom et al. [275], Kubiatowicz [286], Malkhi [330], Yin et al. [518].

Rabin [405] studied the security aspects of replication strategies that are usually employed to boost reliability. He developed schemes based on secret sharing to add security features in such settings.

It has been argued however, that Byzantine failures should be applied in a security setting with care [181]. The main point for this is the fact that it is hard to quantify the coverage of the classical threshold assumption that at most t out of n processes can behave arbitrarily. In the dependability area where Byzantine faults model random hardware failures, failure independence can be justified and therefore assumption coverage can often be calculated. In the security area there has been work that lead to protocols which arguably can map their failure assumptions better to practical scenarios. The idea is to generalize the thresholds and specify which sets of processes can jointly fail and which ones can not. This allows to specify things like "either all Linux machines or all Windows machines fail but not both types together". The concepts developed were called *adversary structures* [163, 215], *core/survivor sets* [265] and *fail-prone systems* [331]. Warns et al. [503] proved that all these concepts have the same expressiveness and proposed an even further generalization to *directed dependent failures*. Quantification of coverage, however, is still very far out of reach. Problematic is also the complexity of the formalism since specifying all subsets of a set of processes causes a possibly exponential set of items which an algorithm must manage. These problems have been discussed by Kursawe and Freiling [290].

25.3   Secure Multiparty Computation

Secure multiparty computation (sometimes also called *secure function evaluation*) is a very general security problem. The setting is as follows: a set of n parties jointly wants to compute the result of an n-ary function F. Every party provides its own input to this function but the inputs should remain secret to the other parties, except for what can be derived from the result of F. The problem is easy to solve if you assume the existence of a trusted third party (TTP) which collects the inputs, computes F and distributes the result to everyone. However, the problem is very challenging if you assume that there is no TTP available and parties can misbehave arbitrarily, e.g., they can send wrong messages or fail to send messages at all. Still, the protocol must correctly and securely compute F as if a TTP were available. Secure multiparty computation can be regarded as a generalization of Byzantine agreement in the sense that Byzantine agreement can be formulated as secure multiparty computation and that confidentiality aspects (keeping inputs private) are usually of no concern in Byzantine agreement. So solutions to secure multiparty computation are in the classical sense Byzantine fault-tolerant, but achieve also confidentiality albeit at extra costs.

The problem was initially proposed by Yao [516], first solutions were presented by Goldreich et al. [187] and Chaum et al. [92]. For a long time, the area seemed closed.

However, after almost 15 years there was an increasing interest in the area again [50, 238, 324, 332, 527]. While most work focusses on efficient implementation of the basic cryptographic solutions (see MacKenzie et al. [324], Malkhi et al. [332], other authors gave novel solutions based on trusted hardware (see Benenson et al. [50], Iliev and Smith [238]) or trusted networks (see Correia et al. [108]).

Regarding the differences between reliability and security, especially work by Benenson et al. [50] seems noteworthy since it contains the reduction of secure multiparty computation, a security problem, to consensus, a problem usually investigated in the fault-tolerance area which is close to reliability. The reduction is a generalization of a result by Avoine et al. [27]. The general idea for the reduction is that trusted hardware (together with standard cryptographic tools) deals with the more security related "non-functional" requirements like confidentiality. All "functional" requirements are handled by the underlying fault-tolerant agreement abstraction. The security proofs however are not as rigorous as in many other areas of security. A first draft of a theoretical basis for such a security argument was given by Benenson et al. [51] (see also Cachin [77]).

25.4   Transfering Metrics from Dependability to Security

The similarity between dependability and security has been reported on a number of times [182, 216, 311, 345, 346, 347, 393, 422]. Consequently, attempts have been made to transfer concepts and metrics from one area to the other. It seems that Littlewood et al. [311] form a starting point for research in measuring operational security similar to reliability. Then there were a couple of large-scale European projects that had general dependability metrics as part of their focus: MAFTIA [76], funded 2000-2003, and DBench (see [267], funded 2001–2003.

Part of MAFTIA was a terminological discussion which equated concepts of reliability (like fault and failure) with security concepts (like attack) [485]. A similar survey with a much broader scope was published before by Rushby [421]. Work that related metrics from reliability to a security setting is Nicol et al. [375], Walter and Trinitis [499]. In these works, traditional modeling techniques for complex fault-tolerant systems like fault trees, Markov chains, or stochastic Petri nets were investigated for their applicability to security measurements. The main barriers which still exist in these areas is the quantification of basic events and the treatment of the manyfold inter-component dependencies which are inherent to secure systems.

In general it seems that security metrics can learn a lot from the area of software fault-tolerance, since most successful attacks are based on some form of software fault. Examples of this path of research are Voas et al. [489], Wang and Wang [502].

Appendix

26 Biographies of Contributors

Steffen Becker

Steffen Becker is a member of the research staff at the Chair for Software-Design and -Quality at the University of Karlsruhe since 2006. In his PhD thesis he concerned with combining model driven software development and prediction of the resulting Quality of Service properties of component based software systems. As part of his work he is working on a component model enabling the prediction of component based software systems. He gained practical experiences during his internship as software engineer in Johannesburg, ZA in 2000 as well as during consulting activities at the OFFIS in Oldenburg, Germany. He holds a diploma in business administration and computer science combined (Dipl.-Wirschaftsinformatik) from the Darmstadt University of Technology.

Zinaida Benenson

Zinaida Benenson is finishing her PhD at the University of Mannheim, Germany. Previously she was a PhD student at the RWTH Aachen University, Germany, and a guest researcher at the Uppsala University, Sweden. She is interested in security issues in distributed systems, especially focusing on pervasive computing and sensor networks.

Rainer Böhme

Rainer Böhme holds an M.A. degree in communication science, economics and computer science from Technische Universität Dresden. He is researcher and PhD candidate in the privacy and security group of Technische Universität Dresden. His particular interests include steganography and steganalysis, economics of information security as well as behavioural aspects of privacy and security.

Kenneth Chan

Kenneth Chan is a PhD student at King's College London under the supervision of Iman Poernomo at the Predictable Assembly Laboratory. His PhD research focuses on using model driven architecture to support the automated development of instrumentation for quality of service mananagement. He completed a BSc in Computer Science at King's College London in 2005.

Irene Eusgeld

Irene Eusgeld received a Diploma Degree in 1986, and a Doctor Engineer Degree in Reliability Engineering in 1993, both from a High School in St. Petersburg, Russia. She is a Senior Scientist of the Laboratory for Safety Analysis at the Swiss Federal Institute of Technology (ETH) Zurich. She formerly worked at the Department of Safety

Engineering at the University of Wuppertal and at the Department of Computing Science at the University of Hagen. From 2001 till 2006 she was a scientific assistant in the group "Dependability of Computing Systems" at the University of Duisburg-Essen. Her research interests include dependability of computing systems, fault tolerance of distributed systems, reliability and safety analyses of technical systems, system design optimization using genetic algorithm, performability and modeling of distributed systems.

Bernhard Fechner

Bernhard Fechner has an accident insurance education and holds a diploma degree in computer science. He worked several years as a consultant and was involved in the conception and realization of the first telematic and virtual computer architecture lab for the University of Hagen, Germany. Mr. Fechner is teaching/research assistant at the Chair of Parallel Computing and VLSI (Prof. Dr. J. Keller), where he is currently finishing his PhD thesis. His research interests include (fault-tolerant) microarchitectures, their realization (FPGA and standard-cell) and computer graphics. He is a member of the ACM, IEEE, GM and UEFI (adopter) and has (co-)authored over 17 peer-reviewed articles in conference proceedings and workshops.

Viktoria Firus

After her maternity leave, Viktoria Firus is finalising her PhD at the University of Karlsuhe, Germany on analytical models for software performance prediction. Previously she was a PhD student at the University or Oldenburg, Germany, and a guest researcher at Politecnico Milano, Italy. She published about 15 refereed papers in her field of competence, model-based software performance prediction.

Falk Fraikin

Falk Fraikin is a software quality assurance consultant for sd&m AG. He holds a combined diploma degree in business administration and computer science and a PhD degree in computer science from Darmstadt University of Technology. Before joining sd&m he was managing director of the IT Transfer Office of Darmstadt University of Technology conducting research projects for major international software companies. He is interested in software testing, software engineering and security engineering.

Felix C. Freiling

Felix C. Freiling is a full professor of computer science at University of Mannheim, Germany. He holds a diploma and a PhD degree in computer science from Darmstadt University of Technology. Before joining Mannheim, he was a postdoctoral student in the Distributed Programming Laboratory at the Swiss Federal Institute of Technology, Lausanne, Switzerland, and then an associate professor at RWTH Aachen University, Germany. His research in Switzerland was sponsored by a prestigious Emmy Noether Scholarship from the Deutsche Forschungsgemeinschaft. He is interested in the areas of systems safety and systems security and the intersection between both areas.

Jens Happe

Jens Happe is a PhD student at the Graduate School "TrustSoft" of the University of Oldenburg. He wrote his master thesis at the Monash University in Melbourne (Australia) in cooperation with the University of Oldenburg and received his German diploma from the latter. His main research topic is the influence of concurrency on extra-functional properties of component-based software systems. There, he focuses on performance prediction based on design documents.

Thorsten Holz

Thorsten Holz is a PhD student at the Laboratory for Dependable Distributed Systems at the University of Mannheim, Germany. He received his diploma degree in Computer Science from RWTH Aachen University in September 2005. His research interests include the practical aspects of secure systems, but he is also interested in more theoretical considerations of dependable systems. Currently, his work concentrates on bots/botnets, honeypots, and malware in particular.

Heiko Koziolek

Heiko Koziolek is a PhD student at the graduate school "Trustsoft" at the University of Oldenburg, Germany. "Trustsoft" aims at providing methods to create trustworthy and dependable software systems. Heiko's PhD research focusses on usage modelling and performance prediction for component-based software systems. Before joining "Trustsoft", he studied computer science at the University of Oldenburg and received his diploma degree in 2004.

Ulrich Kühn

Ulrich Kühn is a Senior Systems Engineer and Senior Researcher at Sirrix AG. He holds a degree in Mathematics and a doctorate in Computer Science, both from the University of Münster, Germany. Before joining Sirrix, he worked as a Senior Research Scientist at the Deutsche Telekom Laboratories of the Technical University Berlin. Prior to that, he was a Research Scientist and IT Architect at Dresdner Bank in Frankfurt. Jointly with a fellow researcher, he received the third of the German IT Security Awards in 2006 for his research on network security. His research interests include IT and communication security as well as cryptography.

Michael Kuperberg

Michael Kuperberg is a PhD student in the "Software Design and Quality" research group of Prof. Ralf H. Reussner at the University of Karlsruhe, Germany. His interests include component architectures and the influence of execution systems on component performance. Before joining the research group, he studied computer science at the University of Karlsruhe and at University of Massachusetts, Boston, MA, USA. He received his diploma degree in 2005.

Philipp Limbourg

Philipp Limbourg holds a diploma degree in computer science from Universit"at Dortmund. He is a research assistant at the information logistics chair at Universit"at Duisburg-Essen since 2004. His main research interests include the application of imprecise probabilities in reliability modelling and evolutionary optimization.

Stefan Lucks

Stefan Lucks is a full professor for media security at Bauhaus-University Weimar, Germany. He had studied Computer Science, receiving a Diploma at University of Dortmund and a PhD at Georg-August-University Göttingen. After his PhD he became a postdoctoral researcher and senior lecturer at University of Mannheim. His core fields of research are Cryptography and Communications Security. He is both searching for an improved understanding and formal handling of security issues, and actively participating in the development of secure systems.

Martin Mink

Martin Mink (Dipl.-Inform.) currently works as research assistant and PhD student at the dependable distributed systems group at Mannheim University. Prior he worked with the same group at RWTH Aachen University. He got his diploma at Darmstadt University of Technology in 2003 (supervised by Prof. Ralf Steinmetz). His research interest is information security, focussing on methods for teaching IT security.

Thomas Nowey

Thomas Nowey (Dipl.-Wirtsch.-Inf.) is a scientific assistant at the Department for Management of Information Security at the University of Regensburg. His main research interest is information security management (especially methodologies and economical evaluation of investments in it-security).

Iman Poernomo

Iman Poernomo works at King's College London, where he heads the Predictable Assembly Laboratory research group. His interests range over dependent type theory, algebraic specification, enterprise software development and model driven architecture. Together with John Crossley and Martin Wirsing, he is co-author of the book "Adapting Proofs-as-Programs". Prior to joining King's, he was Senior Research Scientist at the Distributed Systems Technology Centre (DSTC) and an IT Research Fellow at Monash University, where he also completed his PhD.

Ralf Reussner

Ralf Reussner is full professor of software engineering at the University of Karlsruhe and has the chair of software design and quality. As director at the IT Research center

Karlsruhe (FZI) he consults various business partners in the area of software quality, software architecture and component-based software. Before joining Karlsruhe, he was a Juniorprofessor at the University of Oldenburg and a Senior Research Scientist at DSTC Pty Ltd in Melbourne and member of the board of Business Information Systems Section of the OFFIS in Oldenburg. He is speaker of the Software Architecture Section of the German Computer Science Society (G.I.) and is co-publisher of the German Handbook on Software Architecture. He published over 60 refereed paper in the field of software architecture, software components and software performance and is organisers of various workshops and conferences in this field. He received his PhD in 2001 from the Computer Science Graduate School at the University of Karlsruhe.

Matthias Rohr

Matthias Rohr is a PhD student in the Research Training Group "TrustSoft" at the University of Oldenburg, Germany. He studied computer science at the Monash University, Melbourne, Australia and at the University of Oldenburg, Germany. At present, he writes a PhD thesis on runtime failure diagnosis of large distributed software systems. His research interests include fault localization, software reliability, and dynamic architectures.

Antonino Sabetta

Antonino Sabetta is a PhD candidate at the University of Rome "Tor Vergata", Italy. He received a Laurea degree cum laude in Computer Engineering from the same university. His main research topic is the application of model-driven approaches to the automated derivation of analysis models (especially for performance and reliability) starting from software design models of component-based systems. He is also interested in aspect-oriented modeling, dynamic software architecture and mobile systems.

Felix Salfner

Felix Salfner is a Ph.D. student at Humboldt University Berlin, Communication and Computer Architecture group. His main research interests are failure prediction, reliability modeling of systems with proactive fault handling and predictive technologies in general. He is part of the project "Failure Prediction in Critical Infrastructures" supported by Deutsche Forschungsgemeinschaft (DFG).

Max Walter

Max Walter holds a diploma degree and a PhD from Technische Universität München. He currently works there at the Chair of Computer Architecture and Computer Organisation (Prof. Dr. A. Bode) as a senior research and teaching assistant. His areas of interest include computer architecture, microprocessors, parallel computing, dependable computing and modelling fault-tolerant systems, as well as the history of computing. He is main author of the software-tool OpenSESAME (Simple but Extensive Structured Availability Modeling Environment) and the book "The Modeling World of Reliability/Safety-Engineering", published by LiLoLe-Verlag, Hagen.

Ute Wappler

Ute Wappler holds a diploma degree in Computer Science from the Technische Universität Dresden. Since August 2004 she works as a research and teaching assistant at the Technische Universität Dresden, Department of Computer Science (Systems Engineering Group). Her main research interest is dependability of computing systems, especially software implemented fault tolerance and dealing with transient hardware errors. As a student she worked as an assistant at the DFG-founded project COMQUAD were she participated in the implementation of a case tool for specifying component architectures with non-functional properties.

Steffen Weiss

Steffen Weiss is an external PhD candidate at the University of Erlangen-Nuremberg and works for DATEV eG in Nuremberg. In 2005, he finished his diploma in Informatics. His main research interest is security, especially security assessment of organizations. Currently, he is developing a method for security assessment that is objective and applicable in real-world organizations.

Lijun Zhang

Lijun Zhang is a PhD student at the Dependable Systems and Software Group (Prof. Dr.-Ing. Holger Hermanns) at the Saarland University, Germany. He received his diploma degree in 2004 at the same chair. His main research interests include: simulation reduction, formal verfication for probabilistic systems.

27 References

[1] Information Security Management. Code of Practice for Information Security Management (BS 7799-1). British Standard Institute (1999)

[2] Information Security Management. Specification for Information Security Management Systems (BS 7799-2). British Standard Institute (1999)

[3] IT Baseline protection manual. Bundesamt für Sicherheit in der Informationstechnik (2004)

[4] Common Criteria for Information Technology Security Evaluation. Common Criteria Project Sponsoring Organizations (1999)

[5] Qualifizierung/Zertifizierung nach IT-Grundschutz – Prüfschema für Auditoren. Bundesamt für Sicherheit in der Informationstechnik (2003)

[6] Quality Concepts and Terminology, part 1: Generic Terms and Definitions. Document ISO/TC 176/SC 1 N 93 (February 1992)

[7] Information technology - Security techniques - Code of practice for information security management (final draft) (Standard 17799). ISO/IEC (2005)

[8] ISO/IEC 27001:2005. Information technology - Security techniques - Information security management systems - Requirements (2005)

[9] The Third International Knowledge Discovery and Data Mining Tools Competition (1999),
http://kdd.ics.uci.edu/databases/kddcup99/kddcup99.html

[10] Microsoft Baseline Security Analyzer V2.0. Technical report, Microsoft Corporation (2005)

[11] Offshore Reliability Data Handbook (OREDA), 4th Edition (2002)

[12] Acquisti, A., Friedman, A., Telang, R.: Is There a Cost to Privacy Breaches? An Event Study. In: Workshop of Economics and Information Security (WEIS), Cambridge University Press, Cambridge (2006),
http://weis2006.econinfosec.org/docs/40.pdf

[13] Agrawal, A., Barlow, R.: A Survey of Network Reliability and Domination Theory. Operations Research 32(3), 478–492 (1984)

[14] Al-Ali, R., Hafid, A., Rana, O., Walker, D.: An approach for quality of service adaptation in service-oriented Grids. Concurrency and Computation: Practice and Experience 16(5), 401–412 (2004)

[15] Alberts, C.J., Dorofee, A.J.: Managing Information Security Risks: The OCTAVE^{TM} Approach. Addison-Wesley, New York (2002)

[16] Albrecht, A.J.: Measuring Application Development Productivity. In: IBM Application Development Symposium, Monterey, California, USA, pp. 83–92 (1979)

[17] Amasaki, S., Takagi, Y., Mizuno, O., Kikuno, T.: A Bayesian Belief Network for Assessing the Likelihood of Fault Content. In: ISSRE, pp. 215–226. IEEE Computer Society, Los Alamitos (2003)

[18] Anderson, D., McNeil, G.: Artificial Neural Networks Technology. Technical report, Rome Laboratory (August 1992)

[19] Anderson, R.J.: Why Information Security is Hard – An Economic Perspective (2001), http://www.cl.cam.ac.uk/rja14/econsec.html.

[20] Applied Computer Security Associates. In: Proceedings of the Workshop on Internet Security Systems Scoring and Ranking (May 2001), http://www.acsac.org/measurement/proceedings/wisssr1-proceedings.pdf

[21] Applied Computer Security Associates. In: Workshop on Information-Security-System Rating and Ranking Homepage (2001), http://www.acsac.org/measurement/

[22] Arbaugh, B.: Security: Technical, social, and legal challenges, pp. 109–111. IEEE Computer, Los Alamitos (2002)

[23] Arlat, J., Aguera, M., Amat, L., Crouzet, Y., Fabre, J.-C., Laprie, J.-C., Martins, E., Powell, D.: Fault injection for dependability validation, a methodology and some applications. IEEE Transactions on Software Engineering, 166–182 (1990)

[24] Civil Aviation Authority. CAP 670 Air Traffic Services, Safety Requirements. London (2001)

[25] Avižienis, A.: The Methodology of N-Version Programming. In: Software Fault Tolerance, section 2, pp. 23–46. John Wiley & Sons, Inc, Chichester (1995)

[26] Avižienis, A., Laprie, J.-C., Randell, B., Landwehr, C.: Basic Concepts and Taxonomy of Dependable and Secure Computing. IEEE Transactions on Dependable and Secure Computing 1(1), 11–33 (2004)

[27] Avoine, G., Gärtner, F., Guerraoui, R., Vukolic, M.: Gracefully Degrading Fair Exchange with Security Modules. In: Dal Cin, M., Kaâniche, M., Pataricza, A. (eds.) EDCC 2005. LNCS, vol. 3463, pp. 55–71. Springer, Heidelberg (2005)

[28] Axelsson, S.: The Base-Rate Fallacy and its Implications for the Difficulty of Intrusion Detection. In: Proceeding of ACM CCS 1999 (November 1999)

[29] Axelsson, S.: Intrusion Detection Systems: A Taxomomy and Survey. Technical Report No 99-15, Dept. of Computer Engineering, Chalmers University of Technology (March 2000)

[30] Aziz, A., Sanwal, K., Singhal, V., Brayton, R.: Model Checking Continuous Time Markov Chains. ACM Trans. Computational Logic 1, 162–170 (2000)

[31] Backes, M., Pfitzmann, B., Waidner, M.: A Composable Cryptographic Library with Nested Operations. In: Proceedings of the 10th ACM Conference on Computer and Communications Security, Washington, DC, USA, ACM Press, New York (2003)

[32] Baecher, P., Koetter, M., Holz, T., Dornseif, M., Freiling, F.C.: The nepenthes platform: An efficient approach to collect malware. In: Zamboni, D., Krügel, C. (eds.) RAID 2006. LNCS, vol. 4219, pp. 165–184. Springer, Heidelberg (2006)

[33] Baier, C., Haverkort, B., Hermanns, H., Katoen, J.P.: Model-Checking Algorithms for Continuous-Time Markov Chains. IEEE Trans. Software Eng. 29(6), 524–541 (2003)

[34] Bailey, M., Cooke, E., Jahanian, F., Nazario, J., Watson, D.: The Internet Motion Sensor: A Distributed Blackhole Monitoring System. In: NDSS 2005: Proceedings of the 12th Annual Network and Distributed System Security Symposium (2005)

[35] Baker, F.: The Basics of Item Response Theory. ERIC Clearinghouse on Assessment and Evaluation, University of Maryland, 2nd edn. (2001) ISBN 9781886047037, http://edres.org/irt/baker/

[36] Balas, E., Viecco, C.: Towards a third generation data capture architecture for honeynets. In: Proceeedings of the 6th IEEE Information Assurance Workshop, West Point, IEEE, Los Alamitos (2005)

[37] Balbo, G.: Stochastic Petri Nets: Accomplishments and Open Problems. In: International Computer Performance and Dependability Symposium, pp. 51–60 (1995)

[38] Balsamo, S., Di Marco, A., Inverardi, P., Simeoni, M.: Model-Based Performance Prediction in Software Development: A Survey. IEEE Transactions On Software Engineering 30(5), 295–310 (2004)

[39] Barton, J., Czeck, E., Segall, Z., Siewiorek, D.: Fault Injection Experiments Using FIAT. IEEE Transactions on Computers 39(4), 575–582 (1990)

[40] Basel Committee on Banking Supervision. International Convergence of Capital Measurement and Capital Standards. A Revised Framework (June 2004)

[41] Basili, V.R., Caldiera, G., Rombach, H.D.: The Goal Question Metric Approach. In: Encyclopedia of Software Engineering - 2 Volume Set, pp. 528–532 (1994)

[42] Basili, V.R., Weiss, D.M.: A Methodology for Collecting Valid Software Engineering Data. IEEE Transactions on Software Engineering 1, 728–738 (1984)

[43] Bause, F., Kritzinger, P.S.: Stochastic Petri Nets: An Introduction to the Theory, Vieweg-Verlag (1996), ISBN 3528155353

[44] Becker, S., Grunske, L., Mirandola, R., OverhagePerformance Prediction, S.: OverhagePerformance Prediction of Component-Based Systems: A Survey from an Engineering Perspective. In: Reussner, R., Stafford, J.A., Szyperski, C.A. (eds.) Architecting Systems with Trustworthy Components. LNCS, vol. 3938, Springer, Heidelberg (2006)

[45] Bellare, M., Rogaway, P.: Optimal Asymmetric Encryption. In: De Santis, A. (ed.) EUROCRYPT 1994. LNCS, vol. 950, pp. 92–111. Springer, Heidelberg (1995)

[46] Bellare, M., Rogaway, P.: The Security of Triple Encryption and a Framework for Code-Based Game-Playing Proofs. In: Vaudenay, S. (ed.) EUROCRYPT 2006. LNCS, vol. 4004, pp. 409–426. Springer, Heidelberg (2006)

[47] Bellare, M., Kilian, J., Rogaway, P.: The Security of the Cipher Block Chaining Message Authenticati on Code. Journal of Computer and System Sciences 61(3), 362–399 (2000)

[48] Bellare, M., Pietrzak, K., Rogaway, P.: Improved Security Analyses for CBC MACs. In: Shoup, V. (ed.) CRYPTO 2005. LNCS, vol. 3621, pp. 527–541. Springer, Heidelberg (2005)

[49] Benedini, E., Di Perna, I.: Italtel Reliability Prediction Handbook, Italtel (1993)

[50] Benenson, Z., Fort, M., Freiling, F., Kesdogan, D., Penso, L.D.: TrustedPals: Secure Multiparty Computation Implemented with Smartcards. In: Gollmann, D., Meier, J., Sabelfeld, A. (eds.) ESORICS 2006. LNCS, vol. 4189, pp. 306–314. Springer, Heidelberg (2006)

[51] Benenson, Z., Freiling, F.C., Holz, T., Kesdogan, D., Penso, L.D.: Safety, Liveness, and Information Flow: Dependability Revisited. In: Proceedings of the 4th ARCS International Workshop on Information Security Applications, Springer, Heidelberg (2006)

[52] Berger, J.O.: Statistical Decision Theory and Bayesian Analysis. Springer, New York (1985)

[53] Berinato, S.: Finally a Real Return on Security Spending. CIO Magazine (2002)

[54] Billiton, R., Allan, R.N.: Reliability Evaluation of Engineering Systems: Concepts and Techniques. Plenum Press, London (1992)

[55] Binroth, W., Coit, D., Denson, W., Hammer, K.M.: Development of reliability prediction models for electronic components in automotive applications. Electronic Reliability SP-573, 1–8 (1984)

[56] Birnbaum, Z.W.: On the importance of different components in a multicomponent system. In: Krishnaiah, P.R. (ed.) Multivariate Analysis-II, pp. 581–592. Academic Press, New York (1969)

[57] Birolini, A.: Quality and Reliability of Technical Systems. Springer, Berlin (1994)

[58] Birolini, A.: Reliability Engineering, Theory and Practice. Springer, Heidelberg (2004)

[59] Black, J., Rogaway, P., Shrimpton, T.: Black-box analysis of the blockcipher based hash-function construction from PGV. In: Yung [520], pp. 320–335.

[60] Blakley, B.: An Imprecise but Necessary Calculation. Secure Business Quarterly 1 (2001)

[61] Blaze, M., Diffie, W., Rivest, R., Schneier, B., Shimomura, T., Thompson, E., Wiener, M.: Minimal Key Lengths for Symmetric Ciphers to Provide Adequate Commercial Security. Technical report, Report of Ad Hoc Group of Cryptographers and Computer Scientists (1996), http://www.schneier.com/paper-keylength.html

[62] Bleichenbacher, D.: Chosen ciphertext attacks against protocols based on the RSA encryption standard PKCS #1. In: Krawczyk, H. (ed.) CRYPTO 1998. LNCS, vol. 1462, pp. 1–12. Springer, Heidelberg (1998)

[63] Bobbio, A.: System Modelling with Petri Nets. In: Colombo, A.G., et al. (ed.) Systems Reliability Assessment. Proceedings of the Ispra Course, 1988, Madrid, Spain, pp. 103–143. Kluwer, Dordrecht (1990)

[64] Bodin, L.D., Gordon, L.A., Loeb, M.P.: Evaluating Information Security Investments Using the Analytic Hierarchy Process. Communications of the ACM 48(2), 78–83 (2005)

[65] Böhme, R.: Vulnerability Markets – What is the Economic Value of a Zero-Day Exploit? In: 22C3: Private Investigations, Berlin, Germany (December 27–30, 2005), https://events.ccc.de/congress/2005/fahrplan/attachments/542-Boehme2005_22C3_VulnerabilityMarkets.pdf

[66] R. Böhme. Cyber-Insurance Revisited. In: Workshop on the Economics of Information Security (WEIS), Cambridge, MA (2005), http://infosecon.net/workshop/pdf/15.pdf

[67] Böhme, R.: A Comparison of Market Approaches to Software Vulnerability Disclosure. In: Müller, G. (ed.) ETRICS 2006. LNCS, vol. 3995, pp. 298–311. Springer, Heidelberg (2006)

[68] Börjesson, A., Loll, V., Kristensen, A.M.: Reliability Stress Screening of Components. In Nordtest project 1034-992, Swedish National Testing and Research Institure, Physics and Electronics, SP Report: 48 (1993)

[69] Bortz, J., Döring, N.: Forschungsmethoden und Evaluation für Human- und Sozialwissenschaftler, 3rd edn. Springer, Heidelberg (2002)

[70] Botella, P., Burgues, X., Franch, X., Huerta, M., Salazar, G.: Modeling Non-Functional Requirements. In: Applying Requirements Engineering, Catedral publicaciones (2002), ISBN 84-96086-06-02

[71] Bouissou, M., Martin, F., Ourghanlian, A.: Assessment of a Safety-Critical System Including Software: A Bayesian Belief Network for Evidence Sources. In: Free. Ann. Reliability and Maintainability Symp (1999)

[72] Brocklehurst, S., Littlewood, B.: Techniques for Prediction Analysis and Recalibration. In: Lyu, M.R. (ed.) Handbook of software reliability engineering, ch. 4. pp. 119–166. McGraw-Hill, New York (1996)

[73] Brocklehurst, S., Chan, P.Y., Littlewood, B., Snell, J.: Recalibrating Software Reliability Models. IEEE Transactions on Software Engineering 16(4), 98–5589 (1990)

[74] British Standards Institute (BSI). Environmental testing. Tests. Test J and guidance. Mould growth. BSI (1989)

[75] BT. Handbook of Reliability Data for Components Used in Telecommunications Systems. British Telecom (BT) (1993)

[76] Cachin, C., Camenisch, J., Dacier, M., Deswarte, Y., Dobson, J., Horne, D., Kursawe, K., Laprie, J.-C., Lebraud, J.-C., Long, D., McCutcheon, T., Müller, J., Petzold, F., Pfitzmann, B., Powell, D., Randell, B., Schunter, M., Shoup, V., Veríssimo, P., Trouessin, G., Stroud, R.J., Waidner, M., Welch, I.S.: Reference Model and Use Cases (August 2000); Deliverable D1 of the MAFTIA project In: [327]

[77] Cachin, C.: Modeling complexity in secure distributed computing. In Proceedings of the International Workshop on Future Directions in Distributed Computing (FuDiCo), Bertinoro, Italy (2002), http://www.zurich.ibm.com/security/publications/2002/cachin02.pdf

[78] Cachin, C., Kursawe, K., Shoup, V.: Random Oracles in Constantinople: Practical Asynchronous Byzantine Agreement Using Cryptography. In: Proceedings of the Symposium on Principles of Distributed Computing, Portland, Oregon, pp. 123–132 (2000)

[79] Cachin, C., Freiling, F.C., Hoepman, J.-H.: Dagstuhl Seminar Proceedings 06371: From Security to Dependability (September 2006), http://drops.dagstuhl.de/portals/index.php?semnr=06371

[80] Cachin, C., Freiling, F.C., Hoepman, J.-H.: 06371 Executive Summary – From Security to Dependability. In: Cachin, C., Freiling, F.C., Hoepman, J.-H. (eds.) From Security to Dependability, number 06371 in Dagstuhl Seminar Proceedings. Internationales Begegnungs- und Forschungszentrum fuer Informatik (IBFI), Schloss Dagstuhl, Germany (2007), [date of citation: 2007-01-01], http://drops.dagstuhl.de/opus/volltexte/2007/851

[81] CAIDA. CAIDA, the Cooperative Association for Internet Data Analysis. Internet (accessed, 2006), http://www.caida.org/

[82] Calzarossa, M., Serazzi, G.: Workload Characterization: A Survey. Proc. IEEE 81(8), 1136–1150 (1993), citeseer.ist.psu.edu/calzarossa93workload.html

[83] Campbell, K., Gordon, L.A., Loeb, M.P., Zhou, L.: The Economic Cost of Publicly Announced Information Security Breaches: Empirical Evidence from the Stock Market. Journal of Computer Security 11(3), 431–448 (2003)

[84] Canetti, R.: Universally Composable Security: A New Paradigm for Cryptographic Protocols. In: FOCS 2001: Proceedings of the 42nd IEEE symposium on Foundations of Computer Science, IEEE Computer Society Press, Washington (2001)

[85] Canetti, R., Goldreich, O., Halevi, S.: The random oracle methodology, revisited. J. ACM 51(4), 4–5411 (2004), http://doi.acm.org/10.1145/1008731.1008734

[86] Carreira, J., Silva, J.: Why do Some (weird) People Inject Faults? ACM SIGSOFT Software Engineering Notes 23(1), 42–43 (1998)

[87] Carreira, J., Madeira, H., Silva, J.G.: Xception: A Technique for the Experimental Evaluation of Dependability in Modern Computers. IEEE Transactions on Software Engineering 24 (1998)

[88] Cashell, B., Jackson, W.D., Jickling, M., Webel, B.: CRS Report for Congress: The Economic Impact of Cyber-Attacks. The Library of Congress (2004), http://www.pennyhill.com/telecommunications/rl32331.html

[89] Cavusoglu, H., Mishra, B., Raghunathan, S.: The Effect of Internet Security Breach Announcements on Market Value: Capital Market Reactions for Breached Firms and Internet Security Developers. International Journal of Electronic Commerce 9(1), 69–104 (2004)

[90] CCC. Homepage 23C3 Capture The Flag (2006), http://events.ccc.de/congress/2006/CTF

[91] Chang, Y.R., Amari, S.V., Kuo, S.Y.: Computing system failure frequencies and reliability importance measures using OBDD. IEEE Transactions on Computers 53, 54–68, 1 (2004)

[92] Chaum, D., Crepeau, C., Damgård, I.: Multiparty unconditionally secure protocols. In: Cole, R. (ed.) Proceedings of the 20th Annual ACM Symposium on the Theory of Computing, May 1988, ACM Press, Chicago (1988)

[93] Chen, F., Rosu, G.: Towards Monitoring-Oriented Programming: A Paradigm Combining Specification and Implementation. In: Proc. of 3rd International Workshop on Runtime Verification (RV 2003). Electronic Notes on Theoretical Computer Science, vol. 89(2), Elsevier Science, Amsterdam (2003)

[94] Chen, L., Avižienis, A.: N-Version Programming: A Fault-Tolerance Approach To Reliability Of Software Operation. In: Digest of Papers of the 8th International Symposium on Fault-Tolerant Computing (FTCS) (reprint in Proc. FTCS-25), pp. 3–9. IEEE, Los Alamitos (1978)

[95] Cheung, R.C.: A user-oriented software reliability model. In: Proceedings of the Second International Computer Software and Applications Conference, pp. 565–570. IEEE, Los Alamitos (1978)

[96] Cheung, R.C.: A User-Oriented Software Reliability Model. IEEE Trans. Software Engineering 6(2), 118–125 (1980)

[97] Chillarege, R., Biyani, S., Rosenthal, J.: Measurement of Failure Rate in Widely Distributed Software. In: FTCS 1995: Proceedings of the Twenty-Fifth International Symposium on Fault-Tolerant Computing, pp. 424–432. IEEE Computer Society Press, Los Alamitos (1995)

[98] Choi, H., Kulkarni, V.G., Trivedi, K.S.: Transient Analysis of Deterministic and Stochastic Petri Nets. In: Proceedings of the 14th International Conference on Application and Theory of Petri Nets, pp. 3–540. Springer, London (1993)

[99] Ciardo, G., Muppala, J.K., Trivedi, K.S.: Analyzing Concurrent and Fault-Tolerant Software Using Stochastic Reward Nets. Journal of Parallel and Distributed Computing 15(3), 255–269 (1992)

[100] Clark, D.K., Pradhan, J.A.: Fault Injection: A method for Validating Computer-System Dependability. IEEE Trans. on Computers, 47–56 (1995)

[101] Clusif Groupe de Travail ROSI. Retour sur investissement en sécurité des systémes d'information: Quelques clés pour argumenter (October 2004)

[102] Coit, D.W., Baheranwala, F.: Solution of stochastic multi-objective system reliability design problems using genetic algorithms. In: Kolowrocki, K. (ed.) European Conference on Safety and Reliability - ESREL 2005, Gdynia-Sopot-Gdansk, Poland, Balkema, vol. 1, pp. 391–398 (2005)

[103] Computer System Security and Privacy Advisory Board. Report of NIST CSSPAB workshop on security metrics. NIST, Gaithersburg, MD, USA (June 2000) (website offline, papers available via archive.org), http://csrc.nist.gov/csspab/june13-15/sec-metrics.html

[104] Cooke, E., Bailey, M., Mao, Z.M., Watson, D., Jahanian, F., McPherson, D.: Toward Understanding Distributed Blackhole Placement. In: WORM 2004: Proceedings of the 2004 ACM Workshop on Rapid Malcode, pp. 54–64. ACM Press, New York (2004)

[105] Cooke, R.M.: Experts in Uncertainty; Opinion and Subjective Probability in Science. Oxford University Press, Oxford (1991)

[106] Coolen, F.: On the use of imprecise probabilities in reliability. Quality and Reliability Engineering International 20, 193–202 (2004)

[107] Correia, M., Lung, L.C., Neves, N.F., Veríssimo, P.: Efficient Byzantine-Resilient Reliable Multicast on a Hybrid Failure Model. In: Proc. of the 21st Symposium on Reliable Distributed Systems, Suita, Japan (October 2002), http://www.navigators.di.fc.ul.pt/docs/abstracts/brm-srds02.html

[108] Correia, M., Veríssimo, P., Neves, N.F.: The Design of a COTS-Real-Time Distributed Security Kernel. In: Bondavalli, A., Thévenod-Fosse, P. (eds.) EDCC-4. LNCS, vol. 2485, pp. 234–252. Springer, Heidelberg (2002), http://link.springer.de/link/service/series/0558/bibs/2485/24850234.htm

[109] Cortellessa, V., Singh, H., Cukic, B.: Early reliability assessment of UML based software models. In: WOSP 2002: Proceedings of the 3rd international workshop on Software and performance, pp. 302–309. ACM Press, New York (2002), http://doi.acm.org/10.1145/584369.584415

[110] Crovella, M., Bestavros, A.: Self-Similarity in World-Wide Web Traffic: Evidence and Possible Causes. In: Proc. 1996 ACM SIGMETRICS Conf. on Measurement of Computer Systems, Philadelphia, Pennsylvania, pp. 160–169 (May 1996)

[111] Curnow, H.J., Wichmann, B.A.: A Synthetic Benchmark. The Computer Journal 19(1), 43–49 (1975)

[112] CYMRU. Team Cymru: The Darknet Project. (accessed, 2006), http://www.cymru.com/Darknet/

[113] Dawson, S., Jahanian, F., Mitton, T.: ORCHESTRA: A Fault Injection Environment for Distributed Systems. In: University of Michigan Technical Report CSE-TR-318-96, EECS Department (1996)

[114] Club de la securite des systemes d'information francais (publisher). Mehari (2000)

[115] de Silva e Souza, E., Gail, H.R.: Performability Analysis of Computer Systems: From Model Specification to Solution. Performance Evaluation 14(3-4), 157–196 (1992)

[116] Dempster, A.P.: Upper and lower probabilities induced by a multivalued mapping. Annals of Math. Statistics 38, 325–339 (1967)

[117] Denning, P.J., Buzen, J.P.: The Operational Analysis of Queueing Network Models. ACM Comput. Surv. 10(3), 225–261 (1978)

[118] Centre National D'Etudes des Telecommunications. In: Recueil De Donnes De Fiabilite Du Centre National D'Etudes des Telecommunications (CNET). CNET (2000)

[119] Digital Evolution. Wargames Digital Evolution (2007),
      http://wargames.dievo.org/ Closed down at the end of 2006.
[120] Dimov, A., Punnekkat, S.: On the Estimation of Software Reliability
      of Component-Based Dependable Distributed Systems. In: Reussner, R.,
      Mayer, J., Stafford, J.A., Overhage, S., Becker, S., Schroeder, P.J. (eds.)
      QoSA 2005 and SOQUA 2005. LNCS, vol. 3712, pp. 171–187. Springer,
      Heidelberg (2005)
[121] Dinda, P.A.: Online prediction of the running time of tasks. In: 10th IEEE
      International Symposium on High Performance Distributed Computing,
      pp. 383–394 (May 2001)
[122] Distributed Net Project (July 2005), http://www.distributed.net
[123] DoD. DoD-HDBK-344A (USAF), Environmental Stress Screening of
      Electronic Equipment. Department of Defense, Washington DC (1993)
[124] DoD. MIL-STD-1686C, Electrostatic Discharge Control Program for Pro-
      tection of Electrical and Electronic Parts, Assemblies and Equipment (Ex-
      cluding Electrically Initiated Explosive Devices). Department of Defense,
      Washington DC (1995)
[125] DoD. MIL-S-19500H Semiconductor Devices, General Specifications for.
      Department of Defense, Washington DC (1990)
[126] DoD. MIL-HDBK-2164 Environmental Stress Screening Process for Elec-
      tronic Equipment (EC). Department of Defense, Washington DC (1985)
[127] DoD. MIL-HDBK-217F Reliability Prediction of Electronic Equpment.
      Department of Defense, Washington DC (1990)
[128] DoD. MIL-HDBK-750D Test Method Standard for Semiconductor De-
      vices. Department of Defense, Washington DC (1995)
[129] DoD. MIL-STD-781D: Reliability Testing for Engineering Development,
      Qualification and Production. Department of Defense, Washington DC
      (1986)
[130] DoD. MIL-STD-810F Test Method Standard for Environmental Engi-
      neering Considerations and Laboratory Tests. Department of Defense,
      Washington DC (2000)
[131] DoD. MIL-STD-883F, Test Method Standard Microcircuits. Department
      of Defense, Washington DC (2004)
[132] Dodge, R., Ragsdale, D.J., Reynolds, C.: Organization and Training of
      a Cyber Security Team. In: Proceedings of the 2003 IEEE International
      Conference on Systems, Man & Cybernetics (2003)
[133] Dolev, D., Yao, A.C.: On the security of public key protocols. IEEE Trans.
      Inform. Theory 29(2), 198–208 (1983)
[134] Douglas, B.G., Koval, D.O., Bollen, M.H.J., et al.: IEEE Recommended
      Practice for the Design of Reliable Industrial and Commercial Power Sys-
      tems (The Gold Book), IEEE Std. 493-1997. IEEE, Los Alamitos (1998)
[135] Douglass, B.P.: Real-Time UML - Advantages in the UML for Real-Time
      Systems, 3rd edn. Addison-Wesley, Reading (2004)
[136] Downs, D.D., Haddad, R.: Penetration Testing - The Gold Standard
      for Security Rating and Ranking. In: proceedings of the Workshop on
      Information-Security-System Rating and Ranking held in Williamsburg,
      VA, pp. 21–23 (May 2001)

[137] Durães, J., Madeira, H.: Emulation of Software Faults by Educated Mutations at Machine-Code Level. In: IEEE Proceedings of 13th International Symposium on Software Reliability Engineering (ISSRE 2002), pp. 329–340. IEEE Computer Society Press, Los Alamitos (2002)

[138] Durães, J., Madeira, H.: Definition of Software Fault Emulation Operators: A Field Data Study. In: Proceedings of Dependable Systems and Networks (DSN 2003), San Francisco, CA, pp. 105–114. IEEE Computer Society Press, Los Alamitos (2003)

[139] Echtle, K., Silva, J.G.: Fehlerinjektion - ein Mittel zur Bewertung der Maßnahmen gegen Fehler in komplexen Rechensystemen. Informatik Spektrum 21(6), 328–336 (1998)

[140] Electronic Frontier Foundation. Cracking DES: Secrets of Encryption Research, Wiretap Politics and Chip Design. O'Reilly & Associates, Inc., Sebastopol, CA, USA (1998)

[141] Elegbede, C., Adjallah, K.: Availability allocation to repairable systems with genetic algorithms: a multi-objective formulation. Reliability Engineering and System Safety 82(3), 319–330 (2003)

[142] Elnaffar, S. Martin, P.: Characterizing Computer Systems' Workloads. Submitted to ACM Computing Surveys Journal (2002), citeseer.ist.psu.edu/elnaffar02characterizing.html; Elnaffar, S. Martin, P.: Characterizing Computer Systems' Workloads, Technical Report 2002-461, School of Computing, Queen's University, Canada, (December 2002)

[143] Emerson, E.A., Clarke, E.M.: Using Branching Time Temporal Logic to Synthesize Synchronization Skeletons. Science of Computer Programming 2, 241–266 (1982)

[144] Eskin, E., Arnold, A., Prerau, M., Portnoy, L., Stolfo, S.: A Geometric Framework for Unsupervised Anomaly Detection: Detecting Intrusions in Unlabeled Data. Kluwer Academic Publishers, Norwell (2002)

[145] Espinoza, H., Dubois, H., Gérard, S., Medina, J., Petriu, D.C., Woodside, M.: Annotating UML Models with Non-functional Properties for Quantitative Analysis. In: Bruel, J.-M. (ed.) MoDELS 2005. LNCS, vol. 3844, pp. 79–90. Springer, Heidelberg (2006)

[146] Ettredge, M., Richardson, V.J.: Assessing the Risk in E-Commerce. In: Sprague, H.R. (ed.) Proc. of the 35th Hawaii International Conference on System Sciences, IEEE Press, Los Alamitos (2002)

[147] Huh, E.-n., Welch, L.R., Shirazi, B., Tjaden, B.C., Cavanaugh, C.: Accommodating QoS Prediction in an Adaptive Resource Management Framework. In: IPDPS 2000: Proceedings of the 15 IPDPS 2000 Workshops on Parallel and Distributed Processing, pp. 792–799. Springer, London (2000)

[148] European Commission. The Bologna Process – Towards the European Higher Education Area (2007), http://ec.europa.eu/education/policies/educ/bologna/bologna_en.htmlx

[149] European Network of Excellence in Cryptology. ECRYPT Yearly Report on Algorithms and Keysizes (2006) (2007)

[150] Eusgeld, I., Müller-Clostermann, B.: Performability Modelling of High Available Systems: Framework and Examples, journal = Journal of Risk and Reliability (submitted, 2008)

[151] Everett, W.W.: An extended execution time software reliability model. In: Proceedings of the Third International Symposium on Software Reliability Engineering, pp. 4–13. IEEE, Los Alamitos (1992)

[152] Everett, W.W.: Software component reliability analysis. In: Proceedings of the Symposium on Application-Specific Systems and Software Engineering and Technology, pp. 204–211. IEEE, Los Alamitos (1999)

[153] Faisst, U., Prokein, O., Wegmann, N.: Ein Modell zur dynamischen Investitionsrechnung von IT-Sicherheitsmanahmen. Zeitschrift für Betriebswirtschaft 77(5), 511–538 (2007)

[154] Farr, W.: Software Reliability Modeling Survey. In: Lyu, M.R. (ed.) Handbook of software reliability engineering, ch. 3, pp. 71–117. McGraw-Hill, New York (1996)

[155] Fechner, B.: Fehlerinjektion für rekonfigurierbare Hardware. In: In Proc. Diskussionskreis Fehlertoleranz, Shaker-Verlag, pp. 43–51 (2005)

[156] Fechner, B.: Dynamic delay-fault injection for reconfigurable hardware. In: In Proc. 10th IEEE Workshop on Dependable Parallel, Distributed and Network-Centric Systems (2005)

[157] Fenton, N.E., Neil, M.: A Critique of Software Defect Prediction Models. IEEE Trans. Softw. Eng 25(5), 675–689 (1999), http://dx.doi.org/10.1109/32.815326

[158] Fenton, N.E., Neil, M.: Software metrics: successes, failures and new directions. The Journal of Systems and Software 47(2–3), 149–157 (1999), http://dx.doi.org/10.1016/S0164-1212

[159] Fenton, N.E., Ohlsson, N.: Quantitative Analysis of Faults and Failures in a Complex Software System. IEEE Trans. Softw. Eng 26(8), 797–814 (2000), http://dx.doi.org/10.1109/32.879815

[160] Ferson, S., Joslyn, C.A., Helton, J.C., Oberkampf, W.L., Sentz, K.: Summary from the epistemic uncertainty workshop: consensus amid diversity. Reliability Engineering and System Safety 85(1-3), 355–369 (2004)

[161] Finkelstein, M.: Simple Repairable Continuous State Systems of Continuous State Components. In: Mathematical Methods in Reliability (MMR) 2004, Santa Fe, USA (2004)

[162] Fischer, G.H., Molenaar, I.W.: Rasch models: foundations, recent developments and applications, 1st edn. Springer, Heidelberg (1995)

[163] Fitzi, M., Maurer, U.: Efficient Byzantine Agreement Secure Against General Adversaries. In: Kutten, S. (ed.) DISC 1998. LNCS, vol. 1499, Springer, Heidelberg (1998)

[164] International Organization for Standardization. ISO 26262: Road vehicles - Functional safety, Planned Standard (2006)

[165] Fortier, P.J., Michel, H.E.: Computer Systems Performance Evaluation and Prediction. Digital Press (2003), ISBN 0-55558-260-5

[166] Fox, D., Kaun, S.: Security Awareness-Kampagnen (2005), http://www.secorvo.de/publikationen/awareness-kampagnen-fox-kaun-2005.pdf

278   References

[167] DIN Deutsches Institut für Normung e.V. DIN EN 62061 Sicherheit
      von Maschinen - Funktionale Sicherheit sicherheitsbezogener elektrischer,
      elektronischer und programmierbarer elektronischer Steuerungssysteme.
      Beuth, Berlin (2006)
[168] DIN Deutsches Institut für Normung e.V. DIN EN 954-1 Sicherheit von
      Maschinen, sicherheitsbezogene Teile von Steuerungen - Teil 1: Allge-
      meine Gestaltungsleitsätze. Beuth, Berlin (2006)
[169] Fricks, R., Trivedi, K.S.: Importance Analysis with Markov Chains. In:
      Proceedings of the 2003 International Reliability and Maintainability
      Symposium (2003)
[170] Frølund, S., Koistinen, J.: QML: A Language for Quality of Service Spec-
      ification. Technical Report HPL-98-10, Hewlett Packard, Software Tech-
      nology Laboratory (February 1998),
      http://www.hpl.hp.com/techreports/98/HPL-98-10.html
[171] Fuchs, E.: An Evaluation of the Error Detection Mechanisms in MARS
      Using Software Implemented Fault Injection. In: Hlawiczka, A., Si-
      moncini, L., Silva, J.G.S. (eds.) EDCC-2. LNCS, vol. 1150, pp. 73–90.
      Springer, Heidelberg (1996)
[172] Fujisaki, E., Okamoto, T., Pointcheval, D., Stern, J.: RSA-OAEP is Se-
      cure under the RSA Assumption. In: Kilian [276], pp. 260–274
[173] Bundesamt für Sicherheit in der Informationstechnik. BSI-Standard 100-
      3. Risikoanalyse auf der Basis von IT-Grundschutz. Version 2.0, (2005)
[174] Fussell, J.B.: How to hand-calculate system reliability and safety charac-
      teristics. IEEE Trans. on Reliability R-24, 169–174 (1975)
[175] Abraham, J.A., Kanawati, G.A., Kanawati, N.A.: FERRARI: A Flexible
      Software- Based Fault and Error Injection System. IEEE Transactions on
      Computers 44, 248–260 (1995)
[176] Gaffney, J.E., Ulvila, J.W.: Evaluation of Intrusion Detectors: A Deci-
      sion Theory Approach. In: Proceeding of the 2001 IEEE Symposium on
      Security and Privacy (May 2001)
[177] Gal-Or, E., Ghose, A.: The Economic Incentives for Sharing Security
      Information. Information Systems Research 16(2), 186–208 (2005)
[178] Garg, A., Curtis, J., Halper, H.: Quantifying the Financial Impact of IT
      Security Breaches. Information Management & Computer Security 11(2),
      74–83 (2003)
[179] Garg, S., Telek, M., Puliafito, A., Trivedi, K.S.: Analysis of Software Re-
      juvenation using Markov Regenerative Stochastic Petri Net. In: Proceed-
      ings of the International Symposium on Software Reliability Engineering
      (ISSRE 1995) (October 1995)
[180] Garlan, D., Schmerl, B., Chang, J.: Using Gauges for Architecture-Based
      Monitoring and Adaptation. In: Working Conference on Complex and Dy-
      namic Systems Architecture, Brisbane, Australia, December 12-14, 2001.
      DSTC (2001)
[181] Gärtner, F.C.: Byzantine Failures and Security: Arbitrary is not (always)
      Random. In: GI Jahrestagung (Schwerpunkt "Sicherheit - Schutz und
      Zuverlässigkeit"), pp. 127–138 (2003)

[182] Gärtner, F.C., Buttyán, L., Kursawe, K.: Dependable Systems: Podsy Workshop Report - From Fault Tolerance to Security and Back. IEEE Distributed Systems Online 4(9) (2003), http://dsonline.computer.org/0309/f/gar_intro.htm

[183] Gellert, O., Dörges, T., Kossakowski, K.-P.: Ein Netzwerk von IDS-Sensoren für Angriffsstatistiken. In: Detection of Intrusions and Malware, and Vulnerability Assessment, DIMVA 2004, Dortmund, Germany, July 6-7, 2004. Proceedings, Lecture Notes in Informatics (2004)

[184] Giry, D.: Keylength.com Homepage (2006), http://www.keylength.com

[185] Gnedenko, B.W.: Theory of Probability. Chelsea, New York (1967)

[186] Gokhale, S.S., Lyu, M.R., Trivedi, K.S.: Reliability simulation of component-based software systems. In: Proceedings of the 9th International Symposium on Software Reliability Engineering, pp. 192–201. IEEE, Los Alamitos (1998)

[187] Goldreich, O., Micali, S., Wigderson, A.: How to play any mental game — a completeness theorem for protocols with honest majority. In: Proceedings of the 19th ACM Symposium on the Theory of Computing (STOC), pp. 218–229 (1987)

[188] Gordon, L.A., Loeb, M.P.: Return on Information Security Investments: Myths vs. Reality. Strategic Finance 84(5), 26–31 (2002)

[189] Gordon, L.A., Loeb, M.P.: The Economics of Information Security Investment. ACM Transactions on Information and System Security 5(4), 438–457 (2002)

[190] Gordon, L.A., Loeb, M.P.: Budgeting Process for Information Security Expenditures. Communications of the ACM 49(1), 121–125 (2006)

[191] Gordon, L.A., Loeb, M.P., Sohail, T.: A Framework for Using Insurance for Cyber-Risk Management. Communications of the ACM 46(3), 81–85 (2003)

[192] Goševa-Popstojanova, K., Trivedi, K.S.: Architecture-based approaches to software reliability prediction. Computers & Mathematics with Applications 46(7), 1023–1036 (2003)

[193] Gray, J.: Why do computers stop and what can be done about it? In: Proceedings of Symposium on Reliability in Distributed Software and Database Systems (SRDS-5), pp. 3–12. IEEE CS Press, Los Angeles (1986)

[194] Gray, J.: A census of tandem system availability between 1985 and 1990. IEEE Transactions on Reliability 39(4), 409–418 (1990)

[195] Grira, N., Crucianu, M., Boujemaa, N.: Unsupervised and semi-supervised clustering: a brief survey (July 2004)

[196] Groen, G.J., Jiang, S., Mosleh, A., Droguett, E.L.: Reliability data collection and analysis system. In: Proceedings of the 2004 Reliability and Maintainability Symposium (RAMS), Las Vegas, pp. 43–48 (2004)

[197] Grottke, M., Dussa-Zieger, K.: Prediction of Software Failures Based on Systematic Testing. In: Ninth European Conference on Software Testing Analysis and Review (EuroSTAR), Stockholm, Sweden (2001)

[198] Grunske, L., Luck, E.: Application of Behavior-Preserving Transformations to Improve Non-Functional Properties of an Architecture Specification. In: ACIS Fourth International Conference on Software Engineering, Artificial Intelligence, Networking and Parallel/Distributed Computing SNPD 2003, ACIS (2003)

[199] Grunske, L., Neumann, R.: Quality Improvement by Integrating Non-Functional Properties in Software Architecture Specification. In: 2nd Workshop on Evaluating and Architecting System dependabilitY EASY 2002 at ASPLOS-X, San Jose-California, October 3-6 2002 (2002)

[200] Grzebiela, T.: Insurability of Electronic Commerce Risks. In: Sprague, H.R. (ed.) Proc. of the 35th Hawaii International Conference on System Sciences, IEEE Press, Los Alamitos (2002)

[201] Gu, G., Fogla, P., Dagon, D., Lee, W., Skoric, B.: An Information-Theoretic Measure of Intrusion Detection Capability. Technical Report Technical Report GIT-CC-05-10, College of Computing, Georgia Tech (2005)

[202] Gunnetlo, O., Karlsson, J., Tonn, J.: Evaluation of Error Detection Schemes Using Fault Injection by Heavy-ion Radiation. In: Proc. 19th Annual IEEE Int'l. Symposium on Fault-Tolerant Computing, FTCS-19, pp. 340–347 (1989)

[203] Guo, L.: Software Quality and Reliability Prediction Using Dempster-Shafer Theory. PhD thesis, West Virginia University (2004)

[204] Hachman, M.: Security Metrics Consortium Formed. eWeek.com (February 2004),
http://www.eweek.com/print_article/0,3048,a=120180,00.asp

[205] Hack this page. Homepage Hack this page (2006),
http://www.hackthispage.tk/

[206] hack.lu. Homepage hack.lu Capture The Flag (2006),
http://www.hack.lu/index.php/CTF_Contest

[207] Hamlet, D., Mason, D., Woit, D.: Theory of Software Reliability Based on Components. In: Proceedings of the 23rd International Conference on Software Engineering, pp. 361–370. IEEE, Los Alamitos (2001)

[208] Han, S., Shin, K.G., Rosenberg, H.A.: DOCTOR: an integrated software fault injection environment for distributed real-time systems. In: Proc. of the 1995 IEEE International Computer Performance and Dependability Symposium, pp. 204–213. IEEE, Los Alamitos (1995)

[209] Hansche, S.: Designing a Security Awareness Program: Part I. Information Systems Security 9(6), 14–22 (2001)

[210] Havekort, B.R., Marie, R., Rubino, G., Trivedi, K.S.: Performabiliy Modelling. Wiley, Chichester (2001)

[211] Haverkort, B.R., Hermanns, H., Katoen, J.-P.: On the Use of Model Checking Techniques for Dependability Evaluation. In: SRDS, pp. 228–237 (2000)

[212] Haverkort, B.R., Marie, R., Rubino, G., Trivedi, K.S.: Performability Modelling: Techniques and Tools. Wiley, Chichester (2001)

[213] Helman, P., Liepins, G.: Statistical Foundations of Audit Trail Analysis for the Detection of Computer Misuse. IEEE Transactions on Software Engineering 19(9), 886–901 (1993)

[214] Debar, M.D.H., Wespi, A.: A Revised Taxonomy of Intrusion-Detection Systems. Annales des Télécommunications 55(7-8), 83–100 (2000)

[215] Hirt, M., Maurer, U.: Complete Characterisation of Adversaries Tolerable in Secure Multi-Party Computation (Extended Abstract). In: Proceedings of the Sixteenth Annual ACM Symposium on Principles of Distributed Computing, Santa Barbara, California, 21–24 August 1997, pp. 25–34 (1997)

[216] Hoepman, J.-H.: Security, Fault-Tolerance and their Verification for Ambient Systems. In: Gritzalis, D., di Vimercati, S.D.C., Samarati, P., Katsikas, S. (eds.) Security and Privacy in the Age of Uncertainty. IFIP TC11 18th Int. Conf. on Information Security (SEC2003), Athens, Greece, pp. 441–446. Kluwer Academic Publishers, Dordrecht (2003)

[217] Horn, P.: Autonomic Computing: IBM's perspective on the State of Information Technology (October 2001), http://www.research.ibm.com/autonomic/manifesto/autonomic_computing.pdf

[218] Hosford, J.E.: Measures of Dependability. Operations Research 8(1), 53–64 (1960)

[219] Hovav, A., D'Arcy, J.: The Impact of Denial-of-Service Attack Announcements on the Market Value of Firms. Risk Management and Insurance Review 6(2), 97–121 (2003)

[220] Hovav, A., D'Arcy, J.: The Impact of Virus Attack Announcements on the Market Value of Firms. Information Systems Security 13(2), 32–40 (2004)

[221] Howard, R.A.: Dynamic Probabilistic Systems. In: Semi-Markov and Decision Processes, vol. 2, Wiley, Chichester (1971)

[222] Hryniewicz, O.: Evaluation of reliability using shadowed sets and fuzzy lifetime data. In: Kolowrocki, K. (ed.) European Conference on Safety and Reliability, ESREL 2005, Gdynia-Sopot-Gdansk, Poland, Balkema, vol. 1, pp. 881–886 (2005)

[223] Hsueh, M.-C., Tsai, T.K., Iyer, R.K.: Fault Injection Techniques and Tools. IEEE Transactions on Computers 30(4), 75–82 (1997)

[224] Huang, Y., Kintala, C., Kolettis, N., Fulton, N.: Software Rejuvenation: Analysis, Module and Applications. In: Proceedings of IEEE Intl. Symposium on Fault Tolerant Computing, FTCS 25 (1995)

[225] Hudson, G.R.: Program Errors as a Birth and Death Process. Report SP-3011, System Development Corporation (1967)

[226] Internatinal Atomic Energy Agency (IAEA). Survey of Ranges of Component Reliability Data for Use in Probabilistic Safety Assessment. IAEA-TECDOC-508 (1989)

[227] Ibe, O.C., Choi, H., Trivedi, K.S.: Performance Evaluation of Client-Server Systems. IEEE Trans. Parallel Distrib. Syst 4(11), 1217–1229 (1993)

282   References

[228] IEC. Reliability stress screening. International Electrotechnical Commission (IEC) (1998)

[229] IEC. Electronic components - Reliability - Reference conditions for failure rates and stress models for conversion. International Electrotechnical Commission (IEC) (1996)

[230] IEC. IEC 62308. Reliability assessment methods. International Electrotechnical Commission (IEC), Geneva, Switzerland (2004)

[231] IEC. EC62380/TR 62380 - Ed. 1.0, Reliability data handbook - Universal model for reliability prediction of electronics components, PCBs and equipment. International Electrotechnical Commission (IEC) (2004)

[232] CENELEC / International Electrotechnical Commission (IEC). IEC 62278: Railway applications - The specification and demonstration of Reliability, Availability, Maintainability and Safety (RAMS). IEC, Geneva, Switzerland (2000)

[233] CENELEC / International Electrotechnical Commission (IEC). IEC 62279: Railway Applications, Software for Railway Control and Protection Systems. IEC, Geneva, Switzerland (2001)

[234] CENELEC / International Electrotechnical Commission (IEC). IEC 62280: Railway Applications, Safety Related Electronic Systems for Signalling. IEC, Geneva, Switzerland (2003)

[235] International Electrotechnical Commission (IEC). IEC 61508 Functional Safety of electrical/ electronic/ programmable electronic safety-related systems - Part 1 to Part 7. IEC, Geneva, Switzerland (2001)

[236] IEEE. IEEE Standard Test Access Port and Boundary-Scan Architecture (Revision of IEEE Std 1149.1-1990 and IEEE Std 1149.1b-1994). IEEE (2001)

[237] IEEE. Standard 1413: IEEE Standard Methodology for Reliability Prediction and Assessment for Electronic Systems and Equipment. IEEE, New York (1998)

[238] Iliev, A., Smith, S.: More Efficient Secure Function Evaluation Using Tiny Trusted Third Parties. Technical Report TR 2005-551, Dartmouth College, Computer Science, Hanover, NH (July 2005), ftp://ftp.cs.dartmouth.edu/TR/TR2005-551.pdf

[239] The SANS Institute. Distributed Intrusion Detection System (accessed, 2006), http://dshield.org/

[240] The SANS Institute. Internet Storm Center (accessed, 2006), http://isc.sans.org/

[241] Internet Security Systems (2006), http://www.iss.net

[242] ISO/IEC. ISO/IEC60068 Environmental Testing. General guidance and descriptions of environmental test methods for a range of conditions. ISO/IEC (1990)

[243] ISO9126-1. Software engineering - Product quality - Part 1: Quality model. ISO/IEC (June 2001)

[244] ISO9126-2. Software engineering - Product quality - Part 2: External Metrics. ISO/IEC (June 2001)

[245] ISO9126-3. Software engineering - Product quality - Part 3: Internal Metrics. ISO/IEC (June 2001)

[246] ISO/IEC 14598-1. ISO/IEC 14598-1: Information technology – Software product evaluation – Part 1: General overview. ISO/IEC (1999); Published standard

[247] Jackson, J.R.: Network for waiting lines. Operations Research 5, 518–521 (1957)

[248] Jain, A.K., Murty, M.N., Flynn, P.J.: Data clustering: a review. ACM Computing Surveys 31(3), 264–323 (1999),
citeseer.ist.psu.edu/jain99data.html

[249] Jain, R.: The Art of Computer Performance Analysis. John Wiley & Sons, Chichester (1991)

[250] Jaquith, A.: Security Metrics. Addison-Wesley, Reading (2007)

[251] A. Jaquith. MetricCon 1.0 (August 2006),
http://www.securitymetrics.org/content/
Wiki.jsp?page=Metricon1.0

[252] A. Jaquith. MetriCon 2.0 (August 2007), http://www.securitymetrics.
org/content/Wiki.jsp?page=Metricon2.0

[253] A. Jaquith. Securitymetrics.org Homepage (June 2006),
http://www.securitymetrics.org

[254] Jaulmes, É., Joux, A., Valette, F.: On the Security of Randomized CBC-MAC Beyond the Birthday Paradox Limit: A New Construction. In: Daemen, J., Rijmen, V. (eds.) FSE 2002. LNCS, vol. 2365, pp. 237–251. Springer, Heidelberg (2002)

[255] Jawad, F.A., Johnsen, E.: Performability: The vital evaluation method for degradable systems and its most commonly used modelling method, Markov Reward Modelling. Information Systems Engineering Journal 4 (1995)

[256] Jelinski, Z., Moranda, P.B.: Software Reliability Research. In: Freiberger, W. (ed.) Statistical Computer Performance Evaluation, pp. 465–484. Academic, New York (1972)

[257] Jenn, E., Arlat, J., Rimen, M., Ohlsson, J., Karlsson, J.: Fault injection into VHDL models: the MEFISTO tool. In: Digest of Papers of the 24th International Symposium on Fault-Tolerant Computing, pp. 66–75. IEEE, Los Alamitos (1994)

[258] Jensen, F.: Electronic Component Reliability. J. Wiley and Sons, Chichester (1995)

[259] Jensen, F.V.: Introduction to Bayesian Networks. Springer, Heidelberg (1996)

[260] Jezequel, J.-M., Defour, O., Plouzeau, N.: An MDA Approach to tame component based software development. In: de Boer, F.S., Bonsangue, M.M., Graf, S., de Roever, W.-P. (eds.) FMCO 2003. LNCS, vol. 3188, p. 260. Springer, Heidelberg (2004)

[261] Johnson, A.M., Malek, M.: Survey of Software Tools for Evaluating Reliability, Availability, and Serviceability. ACM 20, 227–269 (1988)

[262] Jonsson, Olovsson: A Quantitative Model of the Security Intrusion Process Based on Attacker Behavior. IEEETSE: IEEE Transactions on Software Engineering, 23 (1997)

[263] Jorstad, N.D., Smith Jr., L.T.: Cryptographic Algorithm Metrics. In: 20th National Information Systems Security Conference NISSC (October 1997), http://csrc.nist.gov/nissc/1997/proceedings/

[264] Junginger, M., van Balduin, A., Krcmar, H.: Operational Value at Risk und Management von IT-Risiken. WISU - Das Wirtschaftsstudium 3, 356–364 (2003)

[265] Junqueira, F.P., Marzullo, K.: Synchronous Consensus for Dependent Process Failures. In: Proceedings of the 23rd International Conference on Distributed Computing Systems (ICDCS 2003) (2003)

[266] Kanoun, K., Kaâniche, M., Laprie, J.-C.: Qualitative and Quantitative Reliability Assessment. IEEE Software 14(2), 740–7459 (1997)

[267] Kanoun, K., Madeira, H., Crouzet, Y., Cin, M.D., Moreira, F., García, J.-C.R. (eds.): DBench Dependability Benchmarks, LAAS-CNRS, France (2004), http://www.laas.fr/DBench/Final/DBench-complete-report.pdf

[268] Karunanithi, N., Whitley, D., Malaiya, Y.K.: Using Neural Networks in Reliability Prediction. IEEE Softw. 9(4), 53–59 (1992), http://dx.doi.org/10.1109/52.143107

[269] Karunanithi, N., Whitley, D., Malaiya, Y.K.: Prediction of Software Reliability Using Connectionist Models. IEEE Trans. Softw. Eng 18(7), 563–574 (1992), http://dx.doi.org/10.1109/32.148475

[270] Kelsey, J., Schneier, B., Wagner, D.: Key Schedule Cryptanalysis of IDEA, G-DES, GOST, Safer, and Triple-DES. In: Koblitz, N. (ed.) CRYPTO 1996. LNCS, vol. 1109, pp. 237–251. Springer, Heidelberg (1996)

[271] Kerlinger, F.N., Lee, H.B.: Foundations of behavioral research, 4th edn. Harcourt College Publ. (2000), ISBN 0155078976

[272] Kerscher, W.J., Booker, J.M., Meyer, M.A., Smith, R.E.: PREDICT: a case study, using fuzzy logic. In: Proceedings of the 2003 Reliability and Maintainability Symposium (RAMS), pp. 188–195 (2003)

[273] Kesan, J.P., Majuca, R.P., Yurcik, W.J.: The Economic Case for Cyberinsurance. In: Illinois Law and Economics Working Paper Series (2004), http://ssrn.com/abstract=577862

[274] Khoshgoftarr, M., Pandya, A.S., More, H.B.: A neural network approach for predicting software development faults. In: Proc. 3rd Int. Symp. on Software Reliability Engineering, pp. 83–89. IEEE Computer Society Press, Los Alamitos (1992)

[275] Kihlstrom, K.P., Moser, L.E., Melliar-Smith, P.M.: Byzantine fault detectors for solving consensus. The Computer Journal 46(1) (2003)

[276] Kilian, J. (ed.): CRYPTO 2001. LNCS, vol. 2139. Springer, Heidelberg (2001)

[277] Kim, J., Shin, K.G.: Performance Evaluation of Dependable Real-Time Communication with Elastic QoS. In: DSN 2001: Proceedings of the 2001 International Conference on Dependable Systems and Networks (formerly: FTCS, Washington, DC, USA, pp. 295–303. IEEE Computer Society Press, Los Alamitos (2001)

[278] Klir, G.J.: Generalized information theory: aims, results, and open problems. Reliability Engineering and System Safety 85(1-3), 21–38 (2004)

[279] Knight, J.C., Leveson, N.C.: An Experimental Evaluation of the Assumption of Independence in Multi-version Programming. Transactions on Software Engineering 12(1), 96–109 (1986)

[280] Knudsen, L.R., Kohno, T.: Analysis of RMAC. In: Johansson, T. (ed.) FSE 2003. LNCS, vol. 2887, pp. 182–191. Springer, Heidelberg (2003)

[281] Kochs, H.-D., Petersen, J.: A Framework for Dependability Evaluation of Mechatronic Units. In: Brinkschulte, U., Becker, J., Fey, D., Grosspietsch, K.-E., Hochberger, C., Maehle, E., Runkler, T. (eds.) ARCS 2004 Organic and Pervasive Computing, Lecture Notes in Informatics (LNI) Proceedings, pp. 92–105, Augsburg (2004) GI-Edition

[282] Koziolek, H., Firus, V.: Empirical Evaluation of Model-based Performance Predictions Methods in Software Development. In: Reussner, R., Mayer, J., Stafford, J.A., Overhage, S., Becker, S., Schroeder, P.J. (eds.) QoSA 2005. LNCS, vol. 3712, pp. 188–202. Springer, Heidelberg (2005)

[283] Krawczyk, H.: The order of encryption and authentication for protecting communications (Or: how secure is SSL). In: Kilian[276], pp. 310–331

[284] Krishnamurthy, S., Mathur, A.P.: On the estimation of reliability of a software system using reliabilities of its components. In: Proceedings of the Eighth International Symposium On Software Reliability Engineering, pp. 146–155. IEEE, Los Alamitos (1997)

[285] Kubat, P.: Assessing reliability of modular software. Operations Research Letters 8(1), 35–41 (1989)

[286] Kubiatowicz, J.: Extracting guarantees from chaos. Comm. ACM 46(2), 33–38 (2003)

[287] Kulturel-Konak, S., Smith, A., Coit, D.: Efficiently Solving the Redundancy Allocation Problem Using Tabu Search. IIE Transactions 35(6), 515–526 (2003)

[288] Kumar, V., Grama, A., Gupta, A., Karypis, G.: Introduction to Parallel Computing: Design and Analysis of Algorithms. Benjamin/Cummings, Redwood City (1994)

[289] Kuo, S.-K., Lu, S.-K., Yeh, F.-M.: Determining Terminal-Pair Reliability Based On Edge Expansion Diagrams Using OBDD. Transaction on Reliability 48(3) (1999)

[290] K. Kursawe, F.C. Freiling. Byzantine Fault Tolerance on General Hybrid Adversary Structures. Technical Report AIB-2005-09, RWTH Aachen (April 2005),
http://aib.informatik.rwth-aachen.de/2005/2005-09.ps.gz

286   References

[291] Lapa, C.M.F., Pereira, C.M.N.A., Frutuoso e Melo, P.F.: Surveillance test policy optimization through genetic algorithms using non-periodic intervention frequencies and considering seasonal constraints. Reliability Engineering and System Safety 81(1), 103–109 (2003)

[292] Laprie, J.C.: Dependability Evaluation of Software Systems in Operation. Transactions on Software Engineering 10(6), 701–714 (1984)

[293] Laprie, J.-C. (ed.): *Dependability: Basic concepts and Terminology.* Dependable Computing and Fault-Tolerant Systems, vol. 5. Springer, Heidelberg (1992)

[294] Laprie, J.-C., Arlat, J., Beounes, C., Kanoun, K.: Architectural Issues In Software Fault Tolerance. In: Lyu, M.R. (ed.) Software Fault Tolerance, pp. 47–80. John Wiley & Sons, Inc., New York (1995)

[295] Lazowska, E.D., Zahorjan, J., Graham, G.S., Sevcik, K.C.: Quantitative System Performance - Computer System Analysis Using Queueing Network Models. Prentice-Hall, Englewood Cliffs (1984)

[296] Ledoux, J.: Availability modeling of modular software. Transactions on Reliability 48(2), 159–168 (1999)

[297] Lenstra, A.K.: Key Lengths. In: Bidgoli, H. (ed.) Handbook of Information Security. Information Warfare, Social, Legal, and International Issues and Security Foundations, vol. 2, chp. 114, Wiley, Chichester (2006), http://cm.bell-labs.com/who/akl/key_lengths.pdf

[298] Lenstra, A.K., Verheul, E.R.: Selecting Cryptographic Key Sizes. Journal of Cryptology 14(4), 255–293 (2001)

[299] Leuschen, M.L., Walker, I.D., Cavallaro, J.R.: Robot Reliability Through Fuzzy Markov Models. In: Annual Reliability and Maintainability Symposium, Los Angeles (1998)

[300] Limbourg, P., Germann, D.: Reliability Assessment and Optimization under Uncertainty in the Dempster-Shafer Framework. In: 27th ESReDA Seminar, Glasgow, GB (2004)

[301] Lindemann, C., Ciardo, G., German, R., Hommel, G.: Performability modeling of an automated manufacturing system with deterministic and stochastic Petri nets. In: IEEE International Conference on Robotics and Automation (1993)

[302] Lippmann, R.P., Fried, D.J., Graf, I., Haines, J.W., Kendall, K.P., McClung, D., Weber, D., Webster, S.E., Wyschogrod, D., Cunningham, R.K., Zissman, M.A.: Evaluating Intrusion Detection Systems: The 1998 DARPA Off-line Intrusion Detection Evaluation. In: Proceeding of the 2000 DARPA Information Survivability Conference and Exposition (DISCEX 2000) (January 2000)

[303] Lippmann, R.P., Haines, J.W., Fried, D.J., Korba, J., Das, K.: The 1999 DARPA Off-line Intrusion Detection Evaluation. Technical report, MIT Lincoln Lab (2000)

[304] Liskov, M., Rivest, R., Wagner, D.: Tweakable Block Ciphers. In: Yung [520], pp. 31–46

[305] Littlewood, B.: A reliability model for systems with Markov structure. Journal of the Royal Statistical Society. Series C. Applied Statistics 24(2), 172–177 (1975)

[306] Littlewood, B.: How to measure software reliability, and how not to. In: ICSE 1978: Proceedings of the 3rd international conference on Software engineering, Piscataway, NJ, USA, pp. 37–45. IEEE Press, Los Alamitos (1978)

[307] Littlewood, B.: A Software Reliability Model for Modular Program Structure. IEEE Transactions on Reliability R-28, 241–246 (1979)

[308] Littlewood, B.: Dependability assessment of software-based systems: state of the art. In: ICSE 2005: Proceedings of the 27th international conference on Software engineering, pp. 6–7. ACM Press, New York (2005), http://doi.acm.org/10.1145/1062455.1062461

[309] Littlewood, B., Strigini, L.: Software reliability and dependability: a roadmap. In: Proceedings of the Conference on The Future of Software Engineering (ICSE 2000), pp. 1–58113. ACM Press, New York (2000), http://doi.acm.org/10.1145/336512.336551

[310] Littlewood, B., Verrall, J.L.: A Bayesian Reliability Growth Model for Computer Software. Royal Statistical Society - Series C 22(3), 332–346 (1973)

[311] Littlewood, B., Brocklehurst, S., Fenton, N.E., Mellor, P., Page, S., Wright, D., Dobson, J., McDermid, J., Gollmann, D.: Towards Operational Measures of Computer Security. Journal of Computer Security 2(2-3), 211–230 (1993)

[312] Liu, Z., Joseph, M.: Transformation of Programs for Fault-Tolerance. Formal Aspects of Computing 4(5), 442–469 (1992)

[313] Locher, C.: Methodologies for evaluating information security investments - What Basel II can change in the financial industry. In: ECIS (2005)

[314] Lovric, T.: Requirements for the Certification of Safety Critical Railway Systems Testing. In: Proceedings of the 1st International Conference on Software Testing, ICS Test, Bonn (2000)

[315] Lovric, T.: Fault Injection for Quantitative Safety Validation of Software Based Reactive Systems. In: Proceedings of COMPRAIL 2000, Computer Aided Design, Manufacture and Operation in the Railway and Other Mass Transit Systems, p. 135, Bonn (2000)

[316] Lovric, T.: Dependability Evaluation Methods: Classification. In: Fault Injection Techniques and Tools for VISI Reliability Evaluation, pp. 41–48. Kluver Academic Publisher, Bonn (2003)

[317] Lovric, T.: Safety-critical communication systems under scrutiny. In: risk.tech 2005, Risk Management in the Automotive Industry, Bonn, p. 135 (2005)

[318] Lovric, T.: Intolerable Risks for Safety-related Automotive Electronics. In: 26. Tagung Elektronik im Kfz, Dresden, p. 135 (2006); Haus der Technik e.V

[319] Lovriç, T.: Processor Fault Simulation with ProFI. In: Proc. of the European Simulation Symposium (ESS), pp. 353—357 (1995)

[320] Lu, C., Stankovic, J.A., Abdelzaher, T.F., Tao, G., Son, S.H., Marley, M.: Performance Specifications and Metrics for Adaptive Real-Time Systems. In: Real-Time Systems Symposium, 2000, pp. 13–23 (2000)

[321] Lucks, S.: Attacking Triple Encryption. In: Vaudenay, S. (ed.) FSE 1998. LNCS, vol. 1372, pp. 239–253. Springer, Heidelberg (1998)

[322] Lucks, S.: Ciphers Secure Against Related-Key Attacks. In: Roy, B., Meier, W. (eds.) FSE 2004. LNCS, vol. 3017, pp. 359–370. Springer, Heidelberg (2004)

[323] MacDonald, I.L., Zucchini, W.: *Hidden Markov and other models for discrete-valued time series*. Chapman and Hall, Boca Raton (1997)

[324] MacKenzie, P., Oprea, A., Reiter, M.K.: Automatic Generation of Two-Party Computations. In: SIGSAC: 10th ACM Conference on Computer and Communications Security, ACM SIGSAC (2003)

[325] MacKinlay, C.A.: Event Studies in Economics and Finance. Journal of Economic Literature 35(1), 13–39 (1997)

[326] Madeira, H., Rela, M., Moreira, F., Silva, J.G.: RIFLE: A General Purpose Pin-Level Fault Injector. In: Echtle, K., Powell, D.R., Hammer, D. (eds.) EDCC-1. LNCS, vol. 852, pp. 199–216. Springer, Heidelberg (1994)

[327] MAFTIA. Malicious-and Accidental-Fault Tolerance for Internet Applications (MAFTIA) (2003), http://www.maftia.org/deliverables/

[328] Malek, M.: Responsive Systems: A Challenge of the Nineties. Microprocessing & Microprogramming 30(1-5), 9–16 (1990)

[329] Malek, M.: Responsive Systems: A Marriage Between Real time and Fault Tolerance. In: Fault-Tolerant Computing Systems, pp. 1–17 (1991)

[330] Malkhi, D.: From Byzantine agreement to practical survivability. In: Proceedings of the Symposium on Reliable Distributed Systems Workshop on Self-Repairing and Self-Configurable Distributed Systems, pp. 374–379. IEEE Computer Society Press, Los Alamitos (2002); Invited Presentation

[331] Malkhi, D., Reiter, M.: Byzantine Quorum Systems. In: Proceedings of the 29th Annual ACM Symposium on the Theory of Computing (STOC 1997), pp. 569–578. Association for Computing Machinery, New York (1997)

[332] Malkhi, D., Nisan, N., Pinkas, B., Sella, Y.: Fairplay — A Secure Two-Party Computation System. In: Proceedings of the 13th USENIX Security Symposium. USENIX (August 2004), http://www.cs.huji.ac.il/~noam/fairplay.pdf

[333] Manger, J.: A Chosen Ciphertext Attack on RSA Optimal Asymmetric Encryption Padding (OAEP) as Standardized in PKCS #1 v2.0. In: Kilian [276], pp. 230–238

[334] Marsan, M.A., Chiola, G.: On Petri Nets with Deterministic and Exponentially Distributed Firing Times. In: Rozenberg, G. (ed.) APN 1987. LNCS, vol. 266, pp. 132–145. Springer, Heidelberg (1987)

[335] Marsan, M.A., Conte, G., Balbo, G.: A Class of Generalized Stochastic Petri Nets for the Performance Evaluation of Multiprocessor Systems. ACM Transactions on Computer Systems 2(1), 93–122 (1984)

[336] Marsan, M.A., Balbo, G., Bobbio, A., Chiola, G., Conte, G., Cumani, A.: The Effect of Execution Policies on the Semantics and Analysis of Stochastic Petri Nets. IEEE Trans. Softw. Eng 15(7), 832–846 (1989)

[337] Marseguerra, M., Zio, E., Podofillini, L., Coit, D.: Optimal Design of Reliable Network Systems in Presence of Uncertainty. IEEE Transactions on Reliability 54(2), 243–253 (2005)

[338] Martins, A., Jan, H., Eloff, P.: Information Security Culture. In: Security in the Information Society: Visions and Perspectives, IFIP TC11 17th International Conference on Information Security (SEC2002), May 2002, pp. 203–214 (2002)

[339] Martorell, S., Carlos, S., Sanchez, A.: Use of metrics with multiobjective GA. Application to the selection of an optimal maintenance strategy in the RCM context. In: Kolowrocki, K. (ed.) European Conference on Safety and Reliability - ESREL 2005, Gdynia-Sopot-Gdansk, Poland, Balkema, vol. 2, pp. 1357–1362 (2005)

[340] Masters, M.W.: Real-time computing cornerstones: a system engineer's view. In: WPDRTS 1995: Proceedings of the 3rd Workshop on Parallel and Distributed Real-Time Systems, Washington, DC, USA, p. 8. IEEE Computer Society Press, Los Alamitos (1995)

[341] Mathisen, J.: Measuring Information Security Awareness. Master's thesis, Royal Institute of Technology, Sweden (2004)

[342] Matsuura, K.: Security Tokens and Their Derivatives. Technical report, Centre for Communications Systems Research (CCSR), University of Cambridge, UK (2001)

[343] McHugh, J.: Testing Intrusion Detection Systems: A Critique of the 1998 and 1999 DARPA Off-line Intrusion Detection System Evaluation as Performed by Lincoln Laboratory. ACM Transactions on Information and System Security, 3(4) (November 2000)

[344] McHugh, J.: Quantitative Measures of Assurance: Prophecy, Process or Pipedream? In: Proceedings of the Workshop on Internet Security Systems Scoring and Ranking [20]

[345] Meadows, C.: The need for a failure model for security. In: Dependable Computing for Critical Applications (DCCA4), Springer, Heidelberg (1994)

[346] Meadows, C.: Applying the dependability paradigm to computer security. In: Proceedings of the 1995 New Security Paradigms Workshop, IEEE Computer Society Press, Los Alamitos (1996)

[347] Meadows, C., McLean, J.: Security and dependability: then and now, pp. 166–170. IEEE Computer Society Press, Los Alamitos (1999)

[348] Menasce, D.A., Almeida, V.A.F.: Capacity Planning for Web Services. Prentice-Hall, Englewood Cliffs (2002)

[349] Menasce, D.A., Almeida, V.A.F., Dowdy, L.W.: Performance by Design. Prentice-Hall, Englewood Cliffs (2004)

[350] Merilinna, J.: A Tool for Quality-Driven Architecture Model Transformation. PhD thesis, VTT Electronics, VTT Technical Research Centre of Finland, Vuorimiehentie 5, P.O.Box 2000, FI-02044 VTT, Finland (2005)

[351] Meyer, J.F.: Performability evaluation: where it is and what lies ahead. In: Proceedings of the International Symposium Computer Performance and Dependability, pp. 334–343. IEEE, Los Alamitos (1995)

[352] Meyer, J.F.: Performability: A Retrospective and Some Pointers to the Future. Performance Evaluation 14(3-4), 139–156 (1992)

[353] Meyer, M.A., Butterfield, K.B., Murray, W.S., Smith, R.E., Booker, J.M.: Guidelines for eliciting expert judgment as probabilities or fuzzy logic. In: Fuzzy logic and probability applications: bridging the gap. Society for Industrial and Applied Mathematics, pp. 105–123 (2002)

[354] Ministry of Defence. Defence Standard 00-40: Guidance for Writing NATO R&M Requirements Documents. In: Reliability and maintainability (R&M), vol. 4. Defence Procurement Agency (2003)

[355] Mitnick, K., Simon, W.: The Art of Deception. Controlling the Human Element of Security, Professional, Managerial & Chichester (2002)

[356] Mogul, J.: Network Behavior of a Busy Web Server and its Clients. Res. Rep. 95/5, DEC Western Research, Palo Alto, California (1995)

[357] Molloy, M.K.: On the Intergration of Delay and Throughput Measures in Distributed Processing Models. PhD thesis, University of California, Los Angeles (1981)

[358] Moore, D., Voelkeroffrey, G.M., Savage, S.: Inferring Internet Denial-of-Service Activity. In: Proceedings of the 10th USENIX Security Symposium (August 2001)

[359] Muppala, J.K., Ciardo, G., Trivedi, K.S.: Stochastic Reward Nets for Reliability Prediction. Communications in Reliability, Maintenability and Serviceability 1(2), 9–20 (1994)

[360] Musa, J.D.: Operational profiles in software-reliability engineering. *Software* 10(2), 14–32 (1993)

[361] Musa, J.D.: A Theory of Software Reliability and its Application. IEEE Transactions on Software Engineering SE-1(3), 312–327 (1975)

[362] Musa, J.D.: Software Reliability Engineering: More Reliable Software Faster And Cheaper. Authorhouse, Bloomington, Indiana, 2nd edn. (2004), ISBN 1-4184-9388-0

[363] Musa, J.D., Iannino, A., Okumoto, K.: Software Reliability: Measurement, Prediction, Application, 1st edn. McGraw-Hill, New York (1987)

[364] Nagappan, N., Williams, L., Vouk, M.A., Osborne, J.: Using In-Process Testing Metrics to Estimate Software Reliability: A Feasibility Study. In: Proceedings of IEEE International Symposium on Software Reliability Engineering, pp. 21–22 (2004)

[365] Nagappan, N.: Toward a Software Testing and Reliability Early Warning Metric Suite. In: ICSE, IEEE Computer Society, Los Alamitos (2004)

[366] Nagappan, N., Williams, L., Vouk, M., Osborne, J.: Early estimation of software quality using in-process testing metrics: a controlled case study. In: 3-WoSQ: Proceedings of the third workshop on Software quality, pp. 1–7. ACM Press, New York (2005),
http://doi.acm.org/10.1145/1083292.1083304

[367] National Bureau of Standards. Guideline for Automatic Data Processing Risk Analysis, FIPS PUB 65 (1979)

[368] National Bureau of Standards (NBS). Specification for the Data Encryption Standard. Federal Information Processing Standards Publication (FIPS PUB)46 (January 1977)

[369] National Institute of Standards and Technology. Draft recommendation for Block Cipher Modes of Operation: the RMAC authentication mode. NIST Special Publication 800-38b (2002)

[370] National Institute of Standards and Technology. Recommendation for Key Management. NIST Special Publication 800-57 (2005)

[371] Stéphane Natkin. Les reseaux de Petri stochastiques et leur application a l'evaluation des systemes informatiques. PhD thesis, Conservatoire National des Arts et Metier, Paris (1980)

[372] NESSIE. Final report of European project IST-1999-12324: New European Schemes for Signatures, Integrity, and Encryption (February 2004), https://www.cosic.esat.kuleuven.be/nessie/

[373] Nessus. Homepage (2006), http://www.nessus.org

[374] Next Generation Security Technologies. NGSEC's games (2007), http://quiz.ngsec.com/

[375] Nicol, D.M., Sanders, W.H., Trivedi, K.S.: From Dependability to Security. IEEE Transactions on Dependable and Secure Computing 1(1), 48–65, 1 (2004)

[376] Niggemann, H.: Die IT-Grundschutz-Methodik. Datenschutz und Datensicherheit 28(2), 98–101 (2004)

[377] NSWC. Handbook of Reliability Prediction Procedures for Mechanical Equipment (NSWC-98/LE1). Naval Surface Warfare Center (NSWC) (1998)

[378] Oberkampf, W.L., Helton, J.C., Joslyn, C.A., Wojtkiewicz, S.F., Ferson, S.: Challenge problems: uncertainty in system response given uncertain parameters. Reliability Engineering and System Safety 85(1-3), 11–19 (2004)

[379] OECD. OECD Guidelines for the Security of Information Systems and Networks: Towards a Culture of Security (2002), http://www.oecd.org/dataoecd/16/22/15582260.pdf

[380] Reliability Committee of Intellect in cooperation with Relex Software Corporation. Fault tree analysis. In *Reliability: A Practitioner's Guide*, Greensburg, PA : Relex Software Corporation, chp. 5, pp. 30–35 (2004); The guide has been jointly created by a subgroup of the Reliability Committee of Intellect in cooperation with Relex Software Corporation. Intellect is the trade as-sociation representing over 1000 UK-based organizations in the information technology, telecommunication and electronics industries.

[381] Department of Trade and Industry. Information Technology Security Evaluation Criteria (ITSEC). Version 1.2 (June 1991)

[382] U.S. Department of Transportation. NCSA TRAFFIC SAFETY FACTS 2004 - A Compilation of Motor Vehicle Crash Data from the Fatality Analysis Reporting System and the General Estimates System (2004)

[383] Object Management Group (OMG). UML Superstructure Specification, v2.0 (May 2004), http://www.omg.org/cgi-bin/apps/doc?formal/05-07-04.pdf

[384] Object Management Group (OMG). UML Profile for Modeling Quality of Service and Fault Tolerance Characteristics and Mechanisms (May 2005), http://www.omg.org/cgi-bin/doc?ptc/2005-05-02

[385] Object Management Group OMG. UML Profile for Schedulability, Performance and Time (2005), http://www.omg.org/cgi-bin/doc?formal/2005-01-02

[386] Ozment, A.: Bug Auctions: Vulnerability Markets Reconsidered. In: Workshop of Economics and Information Security (WEIS), Minneapolis, MN (2004), http://www.dtc.umn.edu/weis2004/ozment.pdf

[387] Pai, P.-F., Lin, K.-P.: Application of Hybrid Learning Neural Fuzzy Systems in Reliability Prediction. Quality and Reliability Engineering International (2005)

[388] Panzieri, F., Davoli, R.: Real Time Systems: A Tutorial. Technical report, University of Bologna (1993)

[389] Parhami, B.: From defects to failures: a view of dependable computing. Computer Architecture News 16(4), 157–168 (1988)

[390] Paxson, V.: Towards a Framework for Defining Internet Performance Metrics. In: Proceedings of INET (1996)

[391] Pearl, J.: Probabilistic reasoning in intelligent systems: networks of plausible inference. Morgan Kaufmann Publishers Inc., San Francisco (1988)

[392] Petri, F.A.: Entwicklung eines Security Assessment Tools. Master's thesis, Fachgebiet Sicherheit in der Informationstechnik, Fachbereich Informatik, Technische Universität Darmstadt (2004)

[393] Pfitzmann, A.: Why safety and security should and will merge. In: Heisel, M., Liggesmeyer, P., Wittmann, S. (eds.) SAFECOMP 2004. LNCS, vol. 3219, pp. 1–2. Springer, Heidelberg (2004)

[394] Pfitzmann, B., Schunter, M., Waidner, M.: Cryptographic Security of Reactive Systems. Electronic Notes in Theoretical Computer Science (ENTCS), 32 (2000), http://citeseer.ist.psu.edu/pfitzmann00cryptographic.html

[395] Pfleeger, C.P., Pfleeger, S.L.: Security in Computing. Prentice-Hall, New Jersey (2003)

[396] Pham, H.: Reliability Engineering. Springer, Heidelberg (2003)

[397] Philips. Internal Standard UAT-0387, Reliability Prediction Failure Rates. Philips (1988)

[398] Pimenidis, L.: Homepage C.I.P.H.E.R. Capture The Flag (2006), http://www.cipher-ctf.org

[399] Popper, K.: The logic of scientific discovery, Hutchinson (1968)

[400] Portokalidis, G., Slowinska, A., Bos, H.: Argos: an emulator for fingerprinting zero-day attacks for advertised honeypots with automatic signature generation. SIGOPS Oper. Syst. Rev. 40(4), 15–27 (2006)

[401] Pouget, F., Holz, T.: A Pointillist Approach for Comparing Honeypots. In: Julisch, K., Krügel, C. (eds.) DIMVA 2005. LNCS, vol. 3548, pp. 51–68. Springer, Heidelberg (2005)

[402] Provos, N.: A Virtual Honeypot Framework. In: Proceedings of 13th USENIX Security Symposium, pp. 1–14 (2004)

[403] Provos, N., Holz, T.: Virtual Honeypots: From Botnet Tracking to Intrusion Detection. Addison-Wesley, Professional (2007)

[404] Purser, S.A.: Improving the ROI of the security management process. IEEE Computers & Security 23, 542–546 (2004)

[405] Rabin, M.O.: Efficient dispersal of information for security, load balancing, and fault tolerance. Journal of the ACM 36(2), 335–348 (1989)

[406] RAC. Electronic Parts Reliability Data Book (EPRD). IIT Research Institute/ Reliability Analysis Center (RAC), 201 Mill Street, Rome, New York, 13440–6916 (1997)

[407] RAC. Nonelectronic Parts Reliability Data Book (NPRD). IIT Research Institute/ Reliability Analysis Center (RAC), 201 Mill Street, Rome, New York, 13440–6916 (1995)

[408] RAC. Electrostatic Discharge Susceptibility Data. SRC/ Reliability Analysis Center (RAC), New York (1995)

[409] Rader, J.: A look at measures of computer security from an insurance premium perspective. In: Proceedings of the Workshop on Internet Security Systems Scoring and Ranking [20]

[410] Rakowsky, U.K.: Some Notes on Probabilities and Non-Probabilistic Reliability Measures. In: Kolowrocki, K. (ed.) European Conference on Safety and Reliability, ESREL 2005, Gdynia-Sopot-Gdansk, Poland, Balkema, vol. 2, pp. 1645–1654 (2005)

[411] Ramamritham, K., Stankovic, J.A.: Scheduling algorithms and operating systems support for real-timesystems. In: Proceedings of the IEEE, vol. 82, pp. 55–67 (1994)

[412] Rauzy, A.: New algorithms for fault tree analysis. Reliability Engineering and System Safety 40(3), 203–211 (1993)

[413] Reussner, R.H.: Parametrisierte Verträge zur Protokolladaption bei Software-Komponenten, Logos Verlag, Berlin (2001)

[414] Reussner, R.H., Schmidt, H.W., Poernomo, I.: Reliability Prediction for Component-Based Software Architectures. Journal of Systems and Software – Special Issue of Software Architecture - Engineering Quality Attributes 66(3), 241–252 (2003)

[415] Riley, S.: Password Security: What Users Know and What They Actually Do (2006), http://psychology.wichita.edu/surl/usabilitynews/81/Passwords.htm

[416] Rivest, R.: Cryptography. In: van Leewen, J. (ed.) Handbook of Theoretical Computer Science, volume A: Algorithms and Complextiy, pp. 717–755. Elsevier and MIT Press (1990)

[417] Roscoe, A.W.: CSP and Determinism in Security Modelling. In: Proc. IEEE Symposium on Security and Privacy, pp. 114–127. IEEE Computer Society Press, Los Alamitos (1995)

[418] Ross, R., Katzke, S., Johnson, A., Swanson, M., Stoneburner, G., Rogers, G., Lee, A.: Recommended Security Controls for Federal Information Systems (Final public draft; NIST SP 800-53). NIST (2005)

[419] Ross, S.A., Westerfield, R.W., Jaffe, J.: Corporate Finance, 6th edn. McGraw-Hill, New York (2002)

[420] RTCA. DO-178B, Software Considerations in Air-borne Systems and Equipment Certification (1992)

[421] Rushby, J.: Critical System Properties: Survey and Taxonomy. Reliability Engineering and System Safety 43(2), 189–219 (1994)

[422] Saglietti, F.: Interaktion zwischen funktionaler Sicherheit und Datensicherheit. In: Dittmann, J. (ed.) Sicherheit – Schutz und Zuverlässigkeit (Proceedings SICHERHEIT 2006), Gesellschaft für Informatik, Number P-77 in Lecture Notes in Informatics, pp. 373–383 (February 2006)

[423] Sahner, R.A., Trivedi, K.S., Puliafito, A.: Performance and Reliability Analysis of Computer Systems: An Example-Based Approach Using the SHARPE Software Package. Kluwer Academic Publishers, Boston (1995)

[424] Salfner, F., Malek, M.: Proactive Fault Handling for System Availability Enhancement. In: IEEE Proceedings of the DPDNS Workshop in conjunction with IPDPS 2005, Denver (2005)

[425] Samson, J.R., Moreno, W., Falqez, F.: A technique for the automated validation of fault tolerant designs using laser fault injection (LFI). In: Digest of Papers of the 28th International Symposium on Fault-Tolerant Computing, IEEE, Los Alamitos (1998)

[426] Schechter, S.E.: Computer Security Strength & Risk: A Quantitative Approach. PhD thesis, Harvard University, Cambridge, MA (2004)

[427] Schepens, W.J., James, J.: Architecture of a Cyber Defense Competition. In: Proceedings of the 2003 IEEE International Conference on Systems, Man & Cybernetics (1998)

[428] Schieferdecker, I., Stepien, B., Rennoch, A.: PerfTTCN, a TTCN Language Extension for Performance Testing. Testing of Communicating Systems, 10

[429] Schlienger, T., Teufel, S.: Analyzing Information Security Culture: Increased Trust by an Appropriate Information Security Culture. In: DEXA Workshops, pp. 405–409 (2003)

[430] Schneeweiss, W.G.: Advanced Fault Tree Modeling. Journal of Universal Computer Science 5(10), 633–643 (1999)

[431] Schneidewind, N.F.: Analysis of Error Processes in Computer Software. In: Proceedings of the International Conference on Reliable Software, Los Angeles, pp. 337–346 (1975)

[432] Schneier, B.: Secrets and Lies: Digital Security in a Networked World. John Wiley and Sons, Inc., New York (2000)

[433] Schneier, B.: A Cyber UL. In: Crypto-Gram Newsletter. Counterpane Internet Security, Inc. (January 2001), http://www.counterpane.com

[434] Schneier, B.: Insurance and the future of network security. In: Crypto-Gram Newsletter (March 2001), http://www.schneier.com/crypto-gram-0103.html, Reprint of [435]

[435] Schneier, B.: Schneier on Security: The Insurance Takeover. Information Security Magazine (February 2001)

[436] Seliya, N., Khoshgoftaar, T.M., Zhong, S.: Analyzing Software Quality with Limited Fault-Proneness Defect Data. High Assurance Systems Engineering, pp. 89–98 (October 2005)

[437] Sentz, K., Ferson, S.: Combination of Evidence in Dempster-Shafer Theory. SAND REPORT (2002-0835) (2002)

[438] Sharma, P.K., Loyall, J.P., Heineman, G.T.: Component-Based Dynamic QoS Adaptations in Distributed Real-Time and Embedded Systems. In: Meersman, R., Tari, Z. (eds.) OTM 2004. LNCS, vol. 3291, pp. 1208–1224. Springer, Heidelberg (2004)

[439] Shinberg, D.A.: A Management Guide to Penetration Testing. SANS Institute (2003)

[440] Shooman, M.L.: Probabilistic Models for Software Reliability Prediction. In: Freiberger, W. (ed.) Statistical Computer Performance Evaluation, pp. 485–502. Academic, New York (1972)

[441] Shooman, M.L.: Structural models for software reliability prediction. In: Proceedings of the 2nd International Conference on Software Engineering, pp. 268–280. IEEE Computer Society Press, Los Alamitos (1976)

[442] Shoup, V.: OAEP Reconsidered. In: Kilian [276], pp. 239–259

[443] Shoup, V.: Sequences of games: a tool for taming complexity in security proofs. Manuscript (November 2004)

[444] Sieh, V., Tschaeche, O., Balbach, F.: Comparing Different Fault Models Using VERIFY. In: Proc. 6th Conference on Dependable Computing for Critical Applications (DCCA-6), Grainau, Deutschland, pp. 59–76 (1997)

[445] Siemens. Siemens Standard SN 29500, Reliability and Quality Specification Failure Rates of Components. Siemens (1999)

[446] Siemens. Siemens Norm SN 29500 Ausfallraten Bauelemente. Erwartungswerte. Allgemeines. München: Siemens AG (1999)

[447] Sigurdsson, J.H., Walls, L.A., Quigley, J.L.: Bayesian belief nets for managing expert judgement and modelling reliability. 14th advances in reliability technology symposium (ARTS) 17(3), 181–190 (2001)

[448] Silva, J.G., Madeira, H.: Experimental Dependability Evaluation. John Wiley & Sons, Inc., Chichester (2005)

[449] Silverman, R.D.: A Cost-Based Security Analysis of Symmetric and Asymmetric Key Lengths. RSA Labs Bulletin #13 (2001), http://www.rsasecurity.com/rsalabs/

[450] Skene, J., Lamanna, D.D., Emmerich, W.: Precise Service Level Agreements. In: 26th international conference on software engineering, London, United Kingdom, IEEE Computer Society Press, Los Alamitos (2004)

[451] Smith, C.U., Williams, L.G.: Performance Solutions: A Practical Guide To Creating Responsive, Scalable Software. Addison-Wesley, Reading (2002)

[452] Smith, R.M., Trivedi, K.S., Ramesh, A.V.: Performability analysis: Measures, an algorithm and a case study. IEEE Transactions on Computers C-37(4), 406–417 (1988)

[453] Solberg, A., Husa, K. E., Aagedal, J.O., Abrahamsen, E.: QoS-aware MDA. In: Electronic publication from Model Driven Architecture in the Specification, Implementation and Validation of Object-oriented Embedded Systems (SIVOES-MDA 2003) in conjunction with UML 2003 (2003)

[454] Song, D., Malan, R., Stone, R.: A Global Snapshot of Internet Worm Activity (2001),
http://research.arbor.net/downloads/
snapshot_worm_activity.pdf

[455] Sonnenreich, W., Albanese, J., Stout, B.: Return On Security Investment (ROSI) – A Practical Quantitative Model. Journal of Research and Practice in Information Technology 38(1), 45–56 (2006)

[456] Kevin, J., Hoo, S.: How Much Is Enough? A Risk-Management Approach To Computer Security. PhD thesis, Stanford University, CA (2000),
http://cisac.stanford.edu/publications/11900/

[457] Soundappan, P., Nikolaidis, E., Haftka, R.T., Grandhi, R., Canfield, R.: Comparison of evidence theory and Bayesian theory for uncertainty modeling. Reliability Engineering and System Safety 85(1-3), 295–311 (2004)

[458] SPEC. SPEC Benchmark Suite Release. SPEC Newsletter, 2(2), 3–4 (1990)

[459] Stevens, S.S.: On the Theory of Scales of Measurement. Science 103, 677–680 (1946)

[460] Stoneburner, G., Goguen, A., Feringa, A.: Risk Management Guide for Information Technology Systems (NIST SP 800-30). NIST (2002)

[461] Sutton, M., Nagle, F.: Emerging Economic Models for Vulnerability Research. In: Workshop on the Economics of Information Security (WEIS), Cambridge, UK (2006),
http://weis2006.econinfosec.org/docs/17.pdf

[462] Swanson, M., Bartol, N., Sabato, J., Hash, J., Graffo, L.: Security Metrics Guide for Information Technology Systems (NIST SP 800-55). NIST (2003)

[463] Swanson, M., Bartol, N., Sabato, J., Hash, J., Graffo, L.: Security Metrics Guide for Information Technology Systems. NIST Special Publication 800-55, National Institute of Standards and Technology (2003)

[464] Telang, R., Wattal, S.: Impact of Software Vulnerability Announcements on the Market Value of Software Vendors – an Empirical Investigation. In: Workshop on the Economics of Information Security (WEIS), Cambridge, MA (2005),
http://infosecon.net/workshop/pdf/telang_wattal.pdf

[465] Telcordia. Telcordia SR-332, Issue 1, Reliability Prediction Procedure for Electronic Equipment. Telcordia (2001)

[466] Nippon Telegraph and Telephone Corporation (NTTC). Standard Reliability Table for Semiconductor Devices. NTTC (1986)

[467] Tennenhouse, D.: Proactive computing. Communications of the ACM 43(5), 43–50 (2000)

[468] The OpenVAS Project. Homepage (2006), http://www.openvas.org

[469] Tian, L., Noore, A.: Software Reliability Prediction Using Recurrent Neural Network With Bayesian Regularization. Int. J. Neural Syst. 14(3), 165–174 (2004)

[470] Tichy, W.F.: Should Computer Scientists Experiment More? - 16 Excuses to Avoid Experimentation. IEEE Computer 31(5), 32–40 (1998)

[471] Tonon, F.: Using random set theory to propagate epistemic uncertainty through a mechanical system. Reliability Engineering and System Safety 85(1-3), 169–181 (2004)

[472] Trivedi, K.S.: Probability and Statistics with Reliability Queuing and Computer Science Applications, 2nd edn. John Wiley & Sons, Inc, Chichester (2001)

[473] Trivedi, K.S., Malhotra, M.: Reliability and Performability Techniques and Tools: A Survey. In: Proc. 7th ITG/GI Conference on Measurement, Modelling and Evaluation of Computer and Communication Systems, pp. 27–48. Springer, Heidelberg (1993)

[474] Turner, D., Entwisle, S., Friedrichs, O., Ahmad, D., Hanson, D., Fossi, M., Gordon, S., Szor, P., Chien, E., Cowings, D.: et al. Symantec Internet Security Threat Report, Trends for July 2004 - December 2004. Technical report, Symantec (2005)

[475] Uhlig, R.A., Mudge, T.N.: Trace-driven memory simulation: a survey. ACM Comput. Surv. 29(2), 128–170 (1997)

[476] Ulvila, J.W., Gaffney, J.E.: Evaluation of Intrusion Detection Systems. Journal of Research of the National Institute of Standards and Technology 108(6) (2003)

[477] UML. The User-mode Linux Kernel Home Page (accessed, 2006), http://user-mode-linux.sourceforge.net/

[478] UNCTAD. Information Economy Report 2005. United Nations Conference on Trade and Development, Geneva, Switzerland (2005)

[479] Utkin, L.V.: A new efficient algorithm for computing the imprecise reliability of monotone systems. Reliability Engineering and System Safety 83(3), 179–190 (2004)

[480] Valetto, G., Kaiser, G.: A case study in software adaptation. In: WOSS 2002: Proceedings of the first workshop on Self-healing systems, pp. 73–78. ACM Press, New York (2002), http://doi.acm.org/10.1145/582128.582142

[481] van Solingen, R., Berghout, E.: The Goal/Question/Metric Method. McGraw-Hill, New York (1999)

[482] Varian, H.R.: Managing Online Security Risks. New York Times (June 1, 2000), http://www.nytimes.com/library/financial/columns/060100econ-scene.html

[483] Varian, H.R.: Intermediate Microeconomics: A Modern Approach, W. W. Norton, 6th edn (2002)

[484] Velleman, P.F., Wilkinson, L.: Nominal, Ordinal, Interval, and Ratio Typologies are Misleading. The American Statistican 47(1), 65–72 (1993)

[485] Verissimo, P.: MAFTIA – Malicious and Accidental Fault Tolerance for Internet Applications. Talk held at TF-CSIRT Workshop, Lisbon, Portugal (September 2005)

[486] Vigna, G.: Homepage UCSB Capture The Flag (2006), http://www.cs.ucsb.edu/~vigna/CTF/

[487] Vigna, G.: Teaching Network Security Through Live Exercises. In: Irvine, C.E., Armstrong, H.L. (eds.) World Conference on Information Security Education. IFIP Conference Proceedings, vol. 253, pp. 3–18. Kluwer, Dordrecht (2003)

[488] VMware. Virtual Infrastructure Software (accessed, 2006), http://www.vmware.com/

[489] Voas, J., Ghosh, A., McGraw, G., Charron, F.: Defining an Adaptive Software Security Metric from a Dynamic Software Failure Tolerance Measure. In: Proc. of the 11th Annual Conference on Computer Assurance (COMPASS 1996) (1996)

[490] Voas, J.M., Miller, K.W.: Examining Fault-Tolerance Using Unlikely Inputs: Turning the Test Distribution Up-Side Down. In: 10th Annual Conference on Computer Assurance, pp. 3–11. IEEE, Los Alamitos (1993)

[491] Voas, J.M., Miller, K.W.: Using Fault Injection to Assess Software Engineering Standards. In: International Software Engineering Standards Symposium, pp. 139–145. IEEE, Los Alamitos (1995)

[492] Völker, J.: BS7799 — Von Best Practice zum Standard. Datenschutz und Datensicherheit 28(2), 102–108 (2004)

[493] Voydock, V.L., Kent, S.T.: Security Mechanisms in High-Level Network. ACM Computing Surveys 15(2), 135–171 (1983)

[494] Vrable, M., Ma, J., Chen, J., Moore, D., Vandekieft, E., Snoeren, A.C., Voelker, G.M., Savage, S.: Scalability, Fidelity, and Containment in the Potemkin Virtual Honeyfarm. SIGOPS Oper. Syst. Rev. 39(5), 148–162 (2005)

[495] Priore, M.G., Denson, W.: Automotive Electronic Reliability Predication. SAE Paper 870050. Society of Automotive Engineers (SAE), Inc. (1988)

[496] Walley, P.: Statistical Reasoning with Imprecise Probabilities. Chapman and Hall, London (1991)

[497] Wallnau, K.C.: A Technology for Predictable Assembly from Certifiable Components. Technical Report 3, Carnegie Mellon Software Engineering Institute (2003)

[498] Walter, M., Schneeweiss, W.: The modeling world of Reliability/Safety Engineering. LiLoLe Verlag (2005)

[499] Walter, M., Trinitis, C.: Quantifying the Security of Composed Systems. In: Wyrzykowski, R., Dongarra, J., Meyer, N., Waśniewski, J. (eds.) PPAM 2005. LNCS, vol. 3911, Springer, Heidelberg (2006)

[500] Wang, C., Wulf, W.A.: Towards a Framework for Security Measurement. In: Proc. of the National Information Systems Security Conference (NISSC 1997) (1997)

[501] Wang, G., Wang, C., Chen, A., Wang, H., Fung, C., Uczekaj, S., Chen, Y.-L., Guthmiller, W., Lee, J.: Service Level Management using QoS Monitoring, Diagnostics, and Adaptation for Networked Enterprise Systems. In: Ninth IEEE International EDOC Enterprise Computing, pp. 239–247. IEEE, Los Alamitos (2005)

[502] Wang, H., Wang, C.: Taxonomy of security considerations and software quality. Comm. ACM 46(6), 75–78 (2003)

[503] Warns, T., Freiling, F.C., Hasselbring, W.: Solving Consensus Using Structural Failure Models. In: Proceedings of the 25th Symposium on Reliable Distributed Systems (SRDS 2006), pp. 212–221. IEEE Computer Society Press, Los Alamitos (2006)

[504] H. Wei, D. Frinke, O. Carter, C. Ritter. Cost-Benefit Analysis for Network Intrusion Detection Systems. In: Proc. CSI 28th Annual Computer Security Conference, October 29-31, 2001, Washington, DC. (2001), http://www.csds.uidaho.edu/deb/costbenefit.pdf

[505] Weicker, R.P.: Dhrystone: a synthetic systems programming benchmark. Commun. ACM 27(10), 1013–1030 (1984), http://doi.acm.org/10.1145/358274.358283

[506] Weiss, S.: Metric for IT security in an organization. Master's thesis, Institut für Informatik 7 , Friedrich-Alexander-Universität Erlangen-Nurnberg (2005)

[507] Weiss, S., Weissmann, O., Dressler, F.: A Comprehensive and Comparative Metric for Information Security. In: Proceedings of IFIP International Conference on Telecommunication Systems, Modeling and Analysis (ICTSM 2005), pp. 1–10 (November 2005), http://www7.informatik.uni-erlangen.de/dressler/publications/ictsm2005b-abstract_en.html

[508] Welch, L.R., Shirazi, B.A.: A Dynamic Real-time Benchmark for Assessment of QoS and Resource Management Technology. In: RTAS 1999: Proceedings of the Fifth IEEE Real-Time Technology and Applications Symposium, Washington, DC, USA, IEEE Computer Society Press, Los Alamitos (1999)

[509] Wensley, J.H., Lamport, L., Goldberg, J., Green, M.W., Levitt, K.N., Melliar-Smith, P.M., Shostak, R.E., Weinstock, C.B.: SIFT: Design and Analysis of a Fault-Tolerant Computer for Aircraft Control. Proceedings of the IEEE 66(10), 1240–1255 (1978)

[510] Werner, M.: Responsivität - Ein konsensbasierter Ansatz. WBI, Magdeburg, Germany (2000) ISBN 3-89811-924-6

[511] Wiener, M.J.: Efficient DES key search. Manuscript (August 1993)

[512] Wilson, M., Hash, J.: Building an Information Technology Security Awareness and Training Program. NIST Special Publication 800-50, National Institute of Standards and Technology (2003)

[513] Wilson, M., de Zafra, D.E., Pitcher, S.I., Tressler, J.D., Ippolito, J.B.: Information Technology Security Training Requirements: A Role- and Performance-Based Model. NIST Special Publication 800-16, National Institute of Standards and Technology (1998)

[514] Xie, M., Wohlin, C.: An additive reliability model for the analysis of modular software failure data. In: Proceedings of the Sixth International Symposium on Software Reliability Engineering, pp. 188–194. IEEE, Los Alamitos (1995)

[515] Yang, C., Bryant, B.R., Burt, C.C., Raje, R.R., Olson, A.M., Auguston, M.: Formal Methods for Quality of Service Analysis in Component-based Distributed Computing. In: 7th World Conference on Integrated Design and Process Technology. Society for Design and Process Science SDPS (2003)

[516] Yao, A.C.: Protocols for Secure Computations (Extended Abstract). In: 23th Annual Symposium on Foundations of Computer Science (FOCS 1982), pp. 160–164. IEEE Computer Society Press, Los Alamitos (1982)

[517] Yegneswaran, V., Barford, P., Jha, S.: Global Intrusion Detection in the DOMINO Overlay System. In: NDSS 2004: Proceedings of the 11th Annual Network and Distributed System Security Symposium (2004)

[518] Yin, J., Martin, J.-P., Venkataramani, A., Alvisi, L., Dahlin, M.: Byzantine Fault-Tolerant Confidentiality. In: Proceedings of the International Workshop on Future Directions in Distributed Computing, pp. 12–15 (2002),
http://www.cs.utexas.edu/users/jpmartin/papers/BFTC-2.ps

[519] Yngström, L., Björck, F.: The Value and Assessment of Information Security Education and Training. In: Proceedings of the IFIP TC11 WG11.8 First World Conference on Information Security Education, June 17-19, 1999, Kista, Sweden, pp. 271–292 (1999)

[520] Yung, M. (ed.): CRYPTO 2002. LNCS, vol. 2442. Springer, Heidelberg (2002)

[521] Yurcik, W., Doss, D.: CyberInsurance: A Market Solution to the Internet Security Market Failure. In: Workshop on Economics and Information Security (WEIS), Berkeley, CA (2002),http://www.sims.berkeley.edu/
resources/affiliates/workshops/econsecurity/

[522] Zadeh, L.A.: Fuzzy sets as a basis for a theory of possibility. Fuzzy Sets Syst 1, 3–28 (1978)

[523] Zafiropoulos, E.P., Dialynas, E.N.: Reliability and cost optimization of electronic devices considering the component failure rate uncertainty. Reliability Engineering and System Safety 84(3), 271–284 (2004)

[524] Zeng, L., Benatallah, B., Ngu, A.H.H., Dumas, M., Kalagnanam, J., Chang, H.: QoS-Aware Middleware for Web Services Composition. IEEE Transactions On Software Engineering 30(5), 311–327 (2004)

[525] Zevin, S.: Standards for Security Categorization of Federal Information and Information Systems (FIPS PUB 199), Gaithersburg. National Institute of Standards and Technology (2003)

[526] Zhong, S., Khoshgoftaar, T.M., Seliya, N.: Unsupervised Learning for Expert-Based Software Quality Estimation. In: 8th IEEE International Symposium on High-Assurance Systems Engineering (HASE 2004), Tampa, FL, USA, March 25-26, 2004, pp. 149–155. IEEE Computer Society Press, Los Alamitos (2004)

[527] Zhou, L., Schneider, F.B., van Renesse, R.: COCA: A Secure Distributed On-line Certification Authority. ACM Transactions on Computer Systems 20(4), 329–368 (2002)

[528] Zimmermann, A., Freiheit, J., Hommel, G.: Discrete Time Stochastic Petri Nets for Modeling and Evaluation of Real Time Systems. In: International Parallel and Distributed Processing Symposium, pp. 1069–1074 (2001)

[529] Echtle, K., Eusgeld, I.: A Genetic Algorithm for Fault-Tolerant System Design. In: de Lemos, R., Weber, T.S., Camargo Jr., J.B. (eds.) LADC 2003. LNCS, vol. 2847, pp. 197–213. Springer, Heidelberg (2003)

Subject Index

Author Index

Lecture Notes in Computer Science

Sublibrary 2: Programming and Software Engineering

For information about Vols. 1– 4354
please contact your bookseller or Springer

Vol. 4735: G. Engels, B. Opdyke, D.C. Schmidt, F. Weil (Eds.), Model Driven Engineering Languages and Systems. XV, 698 pages. 2007.

Vol. 4716: B. Meyer, M. Joseph (Eds.), Software Engineering Approaches for Offshore and Outsourced Development. X, 201 pages. 2007.

Vol. 4709: F.S. de Boer, M.M. Bonsangue, S. Graf, W.-P. de Roever (Eds.), Formal Methods for Components and Objects. VIII, 297 pages. 2007.

Vol. 4680: F. Saglietti, N. Oster (Eds.), Computer Safety, Reliability, and Security. XV, 548 pages. 2007.

Vol. 4670: V. Dahl, I. Niemelä (Eds.), Logic Programming. XII, 470 pages. 2007.

Vol. 4652: D. Georgakopoulos, N. Ritter, B. Benatallah, C. Zirpins, G. Feuerlicht, M. Schoenherr, H.R. Motahari-Nezhad (Eds.), Service-Oriented Computing ICSOC 2006. XVI, 201 pages. 2007.

Vol. 4640: A. Rashid, M. Aksit (Eds.), Transactions on Aspect-Oriented Software Development IV. IX, 191 pages. 2007.

Vol. 4634: H. Riis Nielson, G. Filé (Eds.), Static Analysis. XI, 469 pages. 2007.

Vol. 4620: A. Rashid, M. Aksit (Eds.), Transactions on Aspect-Oriented Software Development III. IX, 201 pages. 2007.

Vol. 4615: R. de Lemos, C. Gacek, A. Romanovsky (Eds.), Architecting Dependable Systems IV. XIV, 435 pages. 2007.

Vol. 4610: B. Xiao, L.T. Yang, J. Ma, C. Muller-Schloer, Y. Hua (Eds.), Autonomic and Trusted Computing. XVIII, 571 pages. 2007.

Vol. 4609: E. Ernst (Ed.), ECOOP 2007 – Object-Oriented Programming. XIII, 625 pages. 2007.

Vol. 4608: H.W. Schmidt, I. Crnković, G.T. Heineman, J.A. Stafford (Eds.), Component-Based Software Engineering. XII, 283 pages. 2007.

Vol. 4591: J. Davies, J. Gibbons (Eds.), Integrated Formal Methods. IX, 660 pages. 2007.

Vol. 4589: J. Münch, P. Abrahamsson (Eds.), Product-Focused Software Process Improvement. XII, 414 pages. 2007.

Vol. 4574: J. Derrick, J. Vain (Eds.), Formal Techniques for Networked and Distributed Systems – FORTE 2007. XI, 375 pages. 2007.

Vol. 4556: C. Stephanidis (Ed.), Universal Access in Human-Computer Interaction, Part III. XXII, 1020 pages. 2007.

Vol. 4555: C. Stephanidis (Ed.), Universal Access in Human-Computer Interaction, Part II. XXII, 1066 pages. 2007.

Vol. 4554: C. Stephanidis (Ed.), Universal Acess in Human Computer Interaction, Part I. XXII, 1054 pages. 2007.

Vol. 4553: J.A. Jacko (Ed.), Human-Computer Interaction, Part IV. XXIV, 1225 pages. 2007.

Vol. 4552: J.A. Jacko (Ed.), Human-Computer Interaction, Part III. XXI, 1038 pages. 2007.

Vol. 4551: J.A. Jacko (Ed.), Human-Computer Interaction, Part II. XXIII, 1253 pages. 2007.

Vol. 4550: J.A. Jacko (Ed.), Human-Computer Interaction, Part I. XXIII, 1240 pages. 2007.

Vol. 4542: P. Sawyer, B. Paech, P. Heymans (Eds.), Requirements Engineering: Foundation for Software Quality. IX, 384 pages. 2007.

Vol. 4536: G. Concas, E. Damiani, M. Scotto, G. Succi (Eds.), Agile Processes in Software Engineering and Extreme Programming. XV, 276 pages. 2007.

Vol. 4530: D.H. Akehurst, R. Vogel, R.F. Paige (Eds.), Model Driven Architecture - Foundations and Applications. X, 219 pages. 2007.

Vol. 4523: Y.-H. Lee, H.-N. Kim, J. Kim, Y.W. Park, L.T. Yang, S.W. Kim (Eds.), Embedded Software and Systems. XIX, 829 pages. 2007.

Vol. 4498: N. Abdennahder, F. Kordon (Eds.), Reliable Software Technologies - Ada-Europe 2007. XII, 247 pages. 2007.

Vol. 4486: M. Bernardo, J. Hillston (Eds.), Formal Methods for Performance Evaluation. VII, 469 pages. 2007.

Vol. 4470: Q. Wang, D. Pfahl, D.M. Raffo (Eds.), Software Process Dynamics and Agility. XI, 346 pages. 2007.

Vol. 4468: M.M. Bonsangue, E.B. Johnsen (Eds.), Formal Methods for Open Object-Based Distributed Systems. X, 317 pages. 2007.

Vol. 4467: A.L. Murphy, J. Vitek (Eds.), Coordination Models and Languages. X, 325 pages. 2007.

Vol. 4454: Y. Gurevich, B. Meyer (Eds.), Tests and Proofs. IX, 217 pages. 2007.

Vol. 4444: T. Reps, M. Sagiv, J. Bauer (Eds.), Program Analysis and Compilation, Theory and Practice. X, 361 pages. 2007.

Vol. 4440: B. Liblit, Cooperative Bug Isolation. XV, 101 pages. 2007.

Vol. 4408: R. Choren, A. Garcia, H. Giese, H.-f. Leung, C. Lucena, A. Romanovsky (Eds.), Software Engineering for Multi-Agent Systems V. XII, 233 pages. 2007.

Vol. 4406: W. De Meuter (Ed.), Advances in Smalltalk. VII, 157 pages. 2007.

Vol. 4405: L. Padgham, F. Zambonelli (Eds.), Agent-Oriented Software Engineering VII. XII, 225 pages. 2007.

Vol. 4401: N. Guelfi, D. Buchs (Eds.), Rapid Integration of Software Engineering Techniques. IX, 177 pages. 2007.

Vol. 4385: K. Coninx, K. Luyten, K.A. Schneider (Eds.), Task Models and Diagrams for Users Interface Design. XI, 355 pages. 2007.

Vol. 4383: E. Bin, A. Ziv, S. Ur (Eds.), Hardware and Software, Verification and Testing. XII, 235 pages. 2007.

Vol. 4379: M. Südholt, C. Consel (Eds.), Object-Oriented Technology. VIII, 157 pages. 2007.

Vol. 4364: T. Kühne (Ed.), Models in Software Engineering. XI, 332 pages. 2007.

Vol. 4355: J. Julliand, O. Kouchnarenko (Eds.), B 2007: Formal Specification and Development in B. XIII, 293 pages. 2006.